CISTERCIAN STUDIES SERIES: NUMBER TWO HUNDRED SEVEN

Words to Live By
Journeys in Ancient and Modern Egyptian Monasticism

by
Tim Vivian

With the Assistance of
Apostolos N. Athanassakis
Maged S.A. Mikhail
and
Birger A. Pearson

Cistercian Publications
www.cistercianpublications.org

LITURGICAL PRESS
Collegeville, Minnesota
www.litpress.org

A Cistercian Publications title published by Liturgical Press
Cistercian Publications
Editorial Offices
161 Grosvenor Street
Athens, Ohio 54701
www.cistercianpublications.org

The work of Cistercian Publications is made possible in part
by support from Western Michigan University
to the Institute of Cistercian Studies.

Cistercian Publications expresses its gratitude to the following journals
for their permission to include essays first published in their pages.

American Benedictine Review 49.1 (March 1998) 3–32 and 50.3 (Sept 1999) 227–310.
   'The Monasteries of the Wadi al-Natrun: A Personal & Monastic Journey' and 'A Journey to the Interior: The Monasteries of Saint Antony and Saint Paul by the Red Sea'
Anglican Theological Review 80.3 (Summer 1998) 338–365.
   'The Good God, the Holy Power, and the Paraclete'
Bulletin of the Saint Shenouda and Archimandrite Coptic Society 4.3 (N.S.I.) (1998) 2–9, and 5 (1998–1999) 1–17.
   'Standing up to Leo' and 'Ama Sibylla of Saqqara: Prioress or Prophet?'
Cistercian Studies Quarterly 34.4 (1999) 425–454, and 39.5 (2004) 235–269.
   'The Ascetic Discourse of Stephen of Thebes'
   'Holy Men and Business'
Coptic Church Review 20.1 (Spring 1999) 2–30.
   'Humility and Resistance in Late Antique Egypt: The Life of Longinus'
Hallel 23:2 (1998) 86–107.
   Saint Paul of Tamma and the Life of the Cell
Journal of Early Christian Studies 7:4 (Winter 1999) 547–572.
   'Monks, Middle Egypt, and Metanoia: The Life of Apa Phib'
Saint Vladimir's Theological Quarterly 39:2 (1995).
   'Words to Live By: A Conversation that the Elders Had with One Another Concerning Thoughts'

© 2005 by Cistercian Publications, © 2008 by Order of Saint Benedict, Collegeville, Minnesota. All rights reserved. No part of this book may be reproduced in any form, by print, microfilm, microfiche, mechanical recording, photocopying, translation, or by any other means, known or yet unknown, for any purpose except brief quotations in reviews, without the previous written permission of Liturgical Press, Saint John's Abbey, P.O. Box 7500, Collegeville, Minnesota 56321-7500. Printed in the United States of America.

Library of Congress Cataloging-in-Publication Data

Vivian, Tim.
   Words to live by : journeys in ancient and modern Egyptian monasticism / by Tim Vivian ; with the assistance of Apostolos N. Athanassakis, Maged S.A. Mikhail, and Birger A. Pearson.
   p. cm. — (Cistercian studies series ; no. 207)
   Summary: "Personal accounts of journeys to present-day monasteries in Egypt and translations of ancient monastic texts"—Provided by publisher.
Includes bibliographical references and index.
   ISBN- 13:978-0-87907-657-3 (pbk. : alk. paper)
   ISBN- 10:0-87907-657-7 (pbk. : alk. paper)
   1. Monastic and religious life—History—Early church, ca. 30–600—Sources. 2. Monastic and religious life—Egypt—History—Sources. 3. Vivian, Tim—Travel. 4. Egypt—Description and travel. 5. Monastic and religious life—Egypt. I. Athanassakis, Apostolos N. II. Mikhail, Maged S.A. III. Pearson, Birger Albert. IV. Title. V. Series.

BR190.V58 2005
271'.009'015—dc22

2005019611

To Joyce

Four Funerals and a Wedding

(Plus One)

It's just incredible. It just does not explain. Or perhaps that's it: they don't explain and we are not supposed to know. We have a few old mouth-to-mouth tales; we exhume from old trunks and boxes and drawers letters without salutation or signature, in which men and women who once lived and breathed are now merely initials or nicknames out of some incomprehensible affection which sounds to us like Sanskrit or Choctaw; we see dimly people, the people in whose living blood and seed we ourselves lay dormant and waiting, in this shadowy attenuation of time possessing now heroic proportions.

— William Faulkner, *Absalom! Absalom!*

And so, brothers, if we love our life, let us imitate those who pleased God, and let us walk in their footsteps, for they have found the good path.

— Abba Isaiah, *Asceticon*, Logos 30.5G (= Syriac Logos VI)

Remember the words of the old men and you will find help in them and you will be saved.

— Abba Poemen, The Ethiopic *Collectio Monastica*

Table of Contents

Foreword   xi

Preface   xv

Glossary   xxi

Introduction   xxix

PROLOGUE   1

  1. Words to Live By   3

Part One: Journeys

  2. The Monasteries of the Wadi al-Natrun, Egypt:
A Monastic and Personal Journey   25

  3. A Journey to the Interior:
The Monasteries of Saint Antony and
Saint Paul by the Red Sea   59

Part Two: Translations

  4. The Good God, the Holy Power, and the Paraclete:
Ad filios Dei (To the Sons of God) by Saint Macarius
the Great   101

5. Saint Paul of Tamma and the Life of the Cell　139
　　I. *The Life of Paul of Tamma*　154
　　II. Four Short Works　165
　　III. *On the Cell*　178

6. Monks, Middle Egypt, and Metanoia:
　　The Life of Phib　203

7. Humility and Resistance in Late Antique Egypt:
　　The Life of Longinus　237

8. *The Ascetic Discourse* of Stephen of Thebes　283

9. Holy Men and Businessmen:
　　Monks as Intercessors in Fourth-Century Egypt　323

APPENDIX

Ama Sibylla of Saqqara:
Prioress or Prophet? Monastic, or Mythological Being?　377

Bibliography　395

Index　417

Foreword

AT THE TURNING OF THE MILLENNIUM, I was living in Los Angeles, a desert masked as oasis, concentric circles of suburban Shangri-la surrounding the core, the heart, the inner city ravaged by the reign of Reaganomics. L.A.—capital of celluloid and the catalytic converter, where inhabitants imbibe technology, rage at immigrants, and proclaim their town a new Jerusalem. I drive on freeways every day, and try not to lookie-loo my way into becoming a pillar of salt. L.A. is nothing if not the present writ large, the propleptic and chaotic future of a nation seen through brown skies.

I work in Inglewood, a much-maligned city. In truth, this is an ordinary place: the schizophrenic, homeless woman and alcoholic, homeless man somewhere on the grounds; the teenager smoking crack outside the office last week; the people who come each Friday for food; the children who come every afternoon for sanctuary, tutoring, and play; the youth who come once a week to learn 'alternatives to violence', the primary ones being faith, hope, and love. Our church here is a 'multicultural community of celebration, transformation, and compassion'—so we like to say, so we hope. Part African-American, part Hispanic, part Anglo, part Nigerian, part West Indian, part Asian. We are nothing if not a vision of a hopeful future, diverse peoples struggling to climb over linguistic and cultural barriers, pushing against the invisible powers that divide us, that seek by dividing us to conquer us in an endless, meaningless quest to subdue each other.

I live in L.A.; I work in this church. So what do coptic desert-dwellers of the first millenium have to do with the present and the future of this desert city, so far removed from their barbarians and temptations? We seem closer to the mythology of Star Wars than to the theology of desert monks.

At first glimpse, the christian faith of their time and place seems strange to us, but which version, or variety, of the christian faith would seem more strange to Jesus? We have our own, so familiar, so 'normal', so 'modern' idiosyncrasies and idolatries, massaged and amputated distortions of the christian faith. Then, as now, we find misogyny. Then, as now, we see or hear of miraculous healings but, unlike the healers and charlatans of today, Longinus fled from fame as if it were a ravenous lion anxious to tear him limb from limb, flesh from spirit. If our age is amazed by their physical and spiritual rigor, theirs would be aghast by our intricate layering of self-indulgence. Now, unlike then, many Christians are sent out by their churches to become apostles of success. Now, unlike then, scripture is used, not as a wise companion, but as a weapon to strangle the spirit and oppress the other. Now, unlike then, the church endorses and exalts economic exploitation, and succumbs to the seduction of guns and violence. It inverts the beatitudes, blessing the rich and cursing the poor; it flattens the parabola in each parable and flushes the Sermon on the Mount as the irrelevant ravings of Jesus on a sunstroked day. The authority of the wise in the desert was relational, the fruit of listening and living; today's religious authoritarianism is rigid, oppressing those already oppressed.

In today's evolved, advanced society—so far from their primitive caves—corporate executives, basketball coaches, and talk-show hosts have been ordained our zen masters, gurus, and sages. The wisdom of the desert cell is based, not on financial success, a winning record, or high ratings, but on its relationship to Scripture and human experience. Desert sayings and stories are often simple, often direct, sometimes seemingly obvious or trivial: 'Do not associate with someone who *blabs*', said Stephen of Thebes. Reading it, I laughed out loud, wondering about the greek or coptic word for 'blab'. Then I reflected on the spirituality of blabbing, of someone whose mind and heart and spirit are disjointed, heading in every direction—and no direction—at once. Why choose a trusted companion who will dissemble your single-mindedness?

The sayings and stories of the desert are, as Tim Vivian says, an extension of Scripture, as we are—fellow travelers no farther along, just another branch of the same vine in another field. Reading desert writings is like reading Scripture: on one occasion you see nothing; on another you unveil depth, a pearl, a treasure. You go back to the same saying, the identical story, and your eyes are opened or the wind has blown the sand away, and you discover something that had been there all along. The stories and sayings wash over you like holy water and, whether you know it or not, some of your hard spiritual edges have worn away.

It was said that people gathered around Apa Apollo 'like bees collecting honey in their mouths' as they heard words of life. This is why people came from the cities to the desert, why they came from all Judea to John the Baptist at the Jordan, why they came to anchorites in the Middle Ages, why they look everywhere today— to find wisdom, truth, 'words to live by', the word of God spoken in their own vernacular, in their own time, in response to their own experience. In this book, people from one corner of the world speak words of wisdom to people in another corner who, as people of the city have always done, fancy their corner the center, their era a 'new age'.

Evelyn Underhill said that spiritual explorers—contemplatives, monks, mystics—used maps made by their faith community, then wrote in greater detail so that others could traverse the way through clouds and dark nights toward God. This has always been the gift of the desert to the city, of their desert to our city. In this book, Tim Vivian is our guide to egyptian monasticism, to its physical and spiritual topography. He has made a map for us by which to find the mapmakers of the spirit, past and present, so that we can find our way to God in our time. His voice sings with their wisdom: 'Solitude is not isolation, but quiet; not distance, but nearness: to oneself, to God—and then, its fruit, to others. . . . [It] *is* life without—or with a minimum of—distractions, things that pull us away from God; solitude allows us to live devoted to God'.

But the desert gives more than personal guidance; it also offers social perspective. Its 'protest against the city' was not against civilization or urbanization, much less against community, but again what we see today—against the pursuit of everything, people systematically deprived of a serious identity, power kept in the hands of an elected aristocracy while the hands of the powerless are virtually cut off at the wrist. The desert Christians walked away from the consumerism, greed, injustice, and violence that are today's daily norms. Rather, they taught how to live honestly with oneself, gracefully in community, and charitably with strangers, anchored by a deep knowledge of self and God.

What I, in Los Angeles, today, experience in these writings are people reaching out from their desert to redeem mine. If I can listen to what they have to say, maybe I can live in the world in a different way and, to some tiny extent, see the world—like an icon covered with dust and neglect—restored to its original nature, as each person is restored by taking up the work of restoration.

There is a legend about the tomb of five ancient monastic saints that 'unceasingly poured forth oil for healing so that it covered the slab on top of the tomb'. The quantity of healing oil is astounding, literally overwhelming the power of death; and pilgrims, hearing of this phenomenon, came long distances to be healed. So the word of those who have died pour forth for the healing of the nations, and we—as faithful people of every age—can touch and be healed by the wisdom of these saints, and find our lives, our desert, our cities, and our time reshaped and transformed by the wisdom and mercy of God.

Gary Commins

Inglewood, California

Preface

THIS BOOK IS INTENDED both for scholars and for non-scholars, for those who study the Early Church professionally and for those who study it spiritually. The texts of each chapter are meant for both groups of readers, while the footnotes, though not exclusively for scholars, often point to scholarly material for those who are interested. In collecting already published articles for *Journeying into God: Seven Early Monastic Lives* (Minneapolis: Fortress, 1996), I decided to eliminate most scholarly references in an attempt to make the book more accessible to a non-scholarly audience. In this volume I have changed strategies: I have retained all the scholarly material in the footnotes while striving to make the text completely accessible to general readers. Readers will have to judge whether the resulting hybrid bears good fruit.

I have intended each chapter to stand on its own while at the same time gathering them together for a group portrait, where the monastic saints portrayed in each chapter grow more familiar in relation with one another. Therefore, at the risk of redundancy, in the notes to each chapter I have repeated full bibliographical references as well as explanatory notes and definitions of words. Although each chapter is independent, the two chapters in 'Part I: Journeys' can serve as introductions to both the history of monasticism in Egypt, ancient and modern, and its different types.

Books are not written alone. I am grateful to the following persons for reading portions of the manuscript during its gestation: Apostolos Athanassakis, Elizabeth Bolman, Charles Cummings, OCSO, James E. Griffiss, William Harmless, SJ, Bruce Jones, Terrence Kardong, OSB, Maged Mikhail, Jeffrey Russell, and the anonymous readers who juried the articles for various journals. My thanks to Gary Commins for reading through the finished manuscript and for writing the foreword, and my deeper thanks for our many years of friendship. I wish to thank Graham Gould, Tito Orlandi, Mark Sheridan, Hany Takla, and Terry Wilfong for their correspondence on particular questions. I also thank the following for their expertise in and help with various languages: Apostolos Athanassakis (Greek), Jennifer Hevelone-Harper (Syriac), Maged Mikhail (Arabic), Birger Pearson (Coptic), and Jeffrey Russell (Latin). Birger Pearson and I together translated 'On the Cell' by Paul of Tamma, and Apostolos Athanassakis and I co-translated the *Ascetic Discourse* by Stephen of Thebes. Jennifer Hevelone-Harper, Maged Mikhail, and Jeffrey Russell provided translated materials that I have incorporated into my efforts. I wish to thank Maged Mikhail who unfailingly and without complaint got me bibliographical material from UCLA. My thanks to the staff at the Document Delivery Department at the library at California State University Bakersfield for obtaining over a hundred books and articles for me: Lorna Frost, Gina Bahr, Janet Gonzales, Roberto Samidin, and Maria Valdovinos. Keith Granger and Andreas Markloff gave me valuable computer assistance. I wish to express my deep thanks to William Harmless, SJ for his electronic correspondence and for his constant support and encouragement. I finished the manuscript for this volume while on a working retreat at the Monastery of Our Lady of New Clairvaux; I wish to thank Fr Thomas X. Davis, OCSO and the entire community for their warm hospitality. Finally, my deepest thanks to my family: Miriam, Meredith, John, and David.

All of the translations in Part II, except for parts of chapter nine, are, as far as I know, the first in English. The chapters in this book previously appeared, in different form, in the following journals, to whose editors grateful acknowledgement is made for permission to reprint:

1. 'Words to Live By: "A Conversation that the Elders Had with One Another Concerning Thoughts (ΠΕΡΙ ΛΟΓΙΣΜΩΝ)"', *Saint Vladimir's Theological Quarterly* 39:2 (1995).

2. 'The Monasteries of the Wadi Natrun, Egypt: A Personal and Monastic Journey', *American Benedictine Review* 49:1 (March 1998) 3–32.

3. 'A Journey to the Interior: The Monasteries of Saint Antony and Saint Paul by the Red Sea', *American Benedictine Review* 50.3 (September 1999) 277–310.

4. 'The Good God, the Holy Power, and the Paraclete: "To the Sons of God" (Ad filios Dei) by Saint Macarius the Great', *Anglican Theological Review* 80.3 (Summer 1998) 338–365.

5. 'Saint Paul of Tamma: Four Works Concerning Monastic Spirituality', *Coptic Church Review* 18:4 (Winter 1997) 105–116, and 'Saint Paul of Tamma: *On the Monastic Cell (De cella)*' (with Birger A. Pearson), *Hallel* 23:2 (1998) 86–107.

6. 'Monks, Middle Egypt, and Metanoia: The Life of Phib', *Journal of Early Christian Studies* 7.4 (Winter 1999) 547–572.

7. 'Standing Up to Leo: Chapters 29–37 of the *Life of Longinus* and Opposition to Chalcedon in Late Antique Egypt', *Bulletin of the Saint Shenouda the Archimandrite Coptic Society* 4.3 (N.S. 1) (1998) 2–9, and 'Humility and Resistance in Late Antique Egypt: *The Life of Longinus*', *Coptic Church Review* 20.1 (Spring 1999) 2–30.

8. 'The *Ascetic Teaching* of Stephen of Thebes', *Cistercian Studies Quarterly* 34.4 (1999) 425–454.

9. 'Holy Men and Businessmen: Monks as Intercessors in Fourth-Century Egypt' *Cistercian Studies Quarterly* 39.3 (2004) 235–269.

Appendix: 'Ama Sibylla of Saqqara: Prioress or Prophet, Monastic or Mythological Being?' *Bulletin of the Saint Shenouda the Archimandrite Coptic Society* 5 (1998–1999) 1–17.

Quotations from Scripture usually follow the Revised Standard Version or the New Revised Standard Version, adapted to fit the ancient texts.

Since these chapters appeared as journal articles and since I collected them for inclusion here, a number of books have appeared on ancient and modern Coptic Egypt. For the most part I have not incorporated them in the present volume but wish to list some of them here for interested readers:

> Massimo Capuani, *Christian Egypt: Coptic Art and Monuments Through Two Millenia* (Collegeville, Minnesota: The Liturgical Press, 2002).

> Vincent Desprez, OSB, *Le monachisme primitif: Des origines jusqu'au concile d'Éphèse*, Spiritualité Orientale 72 (Bégrolles-en-Mauge: Abbaye de Bellefontaine, 1998).

> Nelly van Doorn-Harder and Kari Vogt, eds., *Between Desert and City: The Coptic Orthodox Church Today* (Oslo: Novus forlag, 1997).

Jeremy Driscoll, OSB, trans., *Evagrius Ponticus: Ad Monachos*, Ancient Christian Writers 59 (New York/Mahwah, New Jersey: The Newman Press/Paulist Press: 2003).

Gawdat Gabra, ed., *Be Thou There: The Holy Family's Journey in Egypt*, A National Egyptian Heritage Revival Book (Cairo – New York: The American University in Cairo Press, 2001).

Gawdat Gabra, with Tim Vivian, *Coptic Monasteries: Egypt's Monastic Art and Architecture* (Cairo – New York: The American University in Cairo Press, 2002).

James E. Goehring, *Ascetics, Society, and the Desert: Studies in Early Egyptian Monasticism*, Studies in Antiquity and Christianity 6 (Harrisburg, Pennsylvania: Trinity Press International, 1999).

Mark Gruber, OSB, *Journey Back to Eden: My Life and Times among the Desert Fathers* (Maryknoll, New York: Orbis Books, 2002).

S. S. Hasan, *Christians versus Muslims in Modern Egypt: The Century-Long Struggle for Coptic Equality* (Oxford – New York: Oxford University Press, 2003).

Jill Kamil, *Christianity in the Land of the Pharaohs: The Coptic Orthodox Church* (London – New York: Routledge, 2002).

Rebecca Krawiec, *Shenoute and the Women of the White Monastery: Egyptian Monasticism in Late Antiquity* (Oxford – New York: Oxford University Press, 2002).

Matthew the Poor, *Orthodox Prayer Life: The Interior Way* (Crestwood, New York: Saint Vladimir's Seminary Press, 2003).

Michael W. McClellan, *Monasticism in Egypt: Images and Words of the Desert Fathers* (Cairo: American University in Cairo Press, 1998).

Otto F.A. Meinardus, *Two Thousand Years of Coptic Christianity* (Cairo – New York: American University in Cairo Press, 1999).

Stelios Ramfos, translated by Norman Russell, *Like a Pelican in the Wilderness: Reflections on the Sayings of the Desert Fathers* (Brookline, Massachusetts: Holy Cross Orthodox Press, 2000).

Ashraf and Bernadette Sadek, *L'Incarnation de la Lumière: Le renouveau iconographique copte à travers l'oeuvre d'Isaac Fanous*, Le Monde Copte 29–31.

John H. Watson, *Among the Copts* (Brighton: Sussex Academic Press, 2000).

Claudia Yvonne Wiens, *Coptic Life in Egypt* (Cairo–New York: The American University in Cairo Press, 2003).

Tim Vivian

Ash Wednesday, 2004

Glossary

All dates are CE (AD).
Terms followed by an asterisk have entries in the Glossary.

Abba: 'Father', a title of respect, taken from Aramaic, given to older or respected monks.
Abouna: Literally 'our father' in Arabic, a title (from *abba**) given to monks.
Abu Salih: The traditional attribution given to the author of a thirteenth-century chronicle, the Arabic *History of the Churches and Monasteries of Egypt*.
Alexandria: The great seaport city on the northern coast of Egypt, founded by Alexander the Great and long the capital of Egypt.
Ammonas (4th c.): A disciple of Saint Antony* who wrote letters on the monastic life.
Anachorêsis (Greek): Withdrawal from society, usually to the desert.
Amoun (4th c.): A monk who founded monasticism in Nitria* about 330.
Anchoritic Monasticism: A type of monasticism where monks lived alone; from the Greek word *anachorein*, 'to withdraw'.
Anthropomorphites: Monks, mostly Copts* apparently, who tended to follow the Bible literally and give human (anthropomorphic) attributes to God; opposed by Palladius*, Cassian*, and the origenist* monks.
Antony the Great, Saint (251–356): The 'father' of monasticism who embraced the monastic life about 269 and withdrew as an anchorite* to the desert about 285.

Apollo (4th–5th c.): A coptic monk whose monastic activity centered around Hermopolis Magna in the Thebaid (see the map); especially associated with monasteries at Bawit and Saqqara (see map).

Apophthegmata: See **Sayings of the Desert Fathers**.

Arianism: A christological view, declared heretical by Athanasius* and the Council of Nicea, propagated by Arius, an alexandrian priest; in seeking to uphold the unity of God Arianism held that the Son was somehow inferior to the Father.

Ascêsis (Greek): Literally 'practice' or 'training', the discipline by which monks sought to live lives in God; the root of 'asceticism' and 'ascetic'.

Athanasius the Great, Saint (296–373): Archbishop of Alexandria* and great supporter of monasticism who wrote the *Life of Antony** about 357.

Baramus: Deir el-Baramus, the Monastery of the Romans, one of four ancient monasteries of the Wadi al-Natrun* still flourishing today.

Basil, Saint (330–379): Bishop and monastic leader from Cappadocia (in modern Turkey) who founded cenobitic* communities and wrote monastic 'rules' (guidelines, really).

Bawit: A famous early monastic site; see the map.

Bishoi (or Bishoy): The Monastery of Saint Bishoi, Deir Anba Bishoi, one of the four ancient monasteries of the Wadi al-Natrun* still active today.

Cassian, John, Saint (360–435): A monk, probably from Scythia, who traveled to the Holy Land and Egypt and, drawing on his experiences, later wrote the *Institutes* and *Conferences.*

Cave of Saint Antony: SW of Saint Antony's*, 300 meters (1000 feet) above the monastery, the traditional site of Antony's cave mentioned in the *Life of Antony.*

Cell: The dwelling place of a monk, often consisting of two rooms: an anteroom for work and a back room for prayer and sleep.

Cenobitic Monasticism: A type of monasticism formed around communal, cloistered life. The word comes from two Greek words meaning 'common life'.

Chalcedon (451): The fourth ecumenical council, called by the emperor Marcian, that formulated the 'two nature' Christology that led to the split between the Imperial, Greek-Latin Church and the Coptic* Church of Egypt.

Church of Saint Antony: The 'old church' at the Monastery of Saint Antony* which houses the thirteenth-century wall paintings.

Colzim, Mount: Antony's 'inner mountain', the present day Monastery of Saint Antony*, to which he moved in 313.

Constantine († 337): Roman emperor who inaugurated the 'peace of the Church' in 313 making Christianity legal. He favored Christianity and called the Council of Nicea in 325.

Coptic: The word, derived via Arabic from Greek *aigyptos*, 'Egypt', denoting the ancient and modern egyptian people and their Church, language, art, and culture.

Deir Anba Bishoi: See **Bishoi.**

Deir Anba Bula: See **Saint Paul's.**

Deir Anba Maqar: See **Saint Macarius'.**

Deir el-Baramus: See **Baramus.**

Deir el-Souriani: See **Syrian Monastery.**

Didymus the Blind (313–398): A follower of Origen who wrote a treatise on the Holy Spirit.

Enaton: A well-known monastery at the ninth milestone from Alexandria*. See the map.

Ephraem, Saint (308–373): A syrian monk and writer who came to the Wadi al-Natrun* in the second half of the fourth century.

Evagrius of Pontus († 399): A monk from Asia Minor who came to Nitria* and Kellia* late in the fourth century and wrote a number of treatises on monastic spirituality.

Fanous, Abouna: A monk from Saint Paul's* considered a modern coptic* saint.

Gebel al-Galala: The two mountain ranges that lie north and south of Saint Antony's*.

Gnosis (Greek): 'Knowledge'. An important term in the New Testament, in gnostic writings, and in the *Letters* of Antony*.

Great Persecution: The final persecution of Christians from 306–311; started by the emperor Diocletian.

Gregory of Nyssa, Saint (330–395): Bishop and theological and spiritual writer from Cappadocia (in modern Turkey).

Hêgoumenos (Greek): The superior or head of a monastery.

Hesychia (Greek): Peace, quiet, stillness.
Historia Monachorum *(Historia monachorum in Aegypto)*: An account written at the end of the fourth century of a journey by a group of pilgrims to various monasteries in Middle and Lower Egypt*.
Isaac, Abouna: A monk of Saint Antony's who left the worldly life of New York to live as a monk at Saint Antony's*.
Isaiah of Scetis, Saint (4th c.): A respected monk of Scetis* who wrote or handed down a number of *Logoi* or *Discourses*.
John the Little, Saint (339–409): Famous monk of Scetis* and namesake of an ancient monastery in the Wadi al-Natrun*.
Keep *(Qasr)*: A fortified tower containing supplies at a monastery, usually dating to the fifth or sixth century; the monks could retreat there during an attack.
Kellia: The Cells, about ten–twelve miles south of Nitria*, founded by Amoun* and Antony*.
Kom: literally 'mound'. In archaeological terms, a mound of dirt and debris under which lie ancient remains.
Laura (Lavra): a semi-anchoritic* community.
Lazarus: Father Lazarus, originally from Australia, lives as a solitary in a hermitage in the mountain range above Saint Antony's.
Lent: The period of prayer, fasting, and penitence leading up to Easter. Coptic Lent is known as 'The Great Lent' and lasts fifty days.
Life of Antony: The first monastic Life, written about 357 by Saint Athanasius the Great*.
Life of the Desert Fathers: See Historia Monachorum.
Logismoi (Greek): Thoughts, usually bad thoughts that distract the monk from focusing on God.
Lower Egypt: Northern Egypt ('lower' because the Nile flows from the south into this region), the area roughly from modern Cairo to Alexandria.
Lycia: A mountainous country in SW Asia Minor.
Macarius the Great, Saint (300–390): Founder of monasticism in Scetis* about 330.
Martyrion (Greek): A church or shrine dedicated to a martyr.
Mazices: Berber invaders who devastated Scetis* several times in the fifth century.

Maximous, Abouna: A priest of Saint Antony's* who serves as the liaison between the monastery and outside visitors and scholars.

Menas, Saint: A famous martyr whose sanctuary, not far from Enaton* and Alexandria, was one of the most famous in antiquity; also called Abu Mina.

Melitianism: A rigorist schismatic group in fourth-century Egypt, started by Melitius, that opposed the lenient views toward apostates held by the alexandrian* hierarchy.

Monastêrion (plural: *monastêria*): A word designating first a monastic cell, then a monastic community, and finally a monastery.

Moses the Black († 434): Famous monk of Scetis*, an Ethiopian who was martyred by invaders.

Nome: Geographical and political districts in ancient and roman Egypt.

Onnophrius, Saint (4th c.?): Famous coptic* hermit and desert dweller.

Origen († 254): Great theologian and biblical commentator whose writings laid the groundwork for christian monasticism and mysticism; he greatly influenced a number of monastic writers including Evagrius*.

Origenist Monks: Those monks, including Evagrius*, the Tall Brothers*, Cassian*, and Palladius*, followers of Origen* who read the Bible figuratively and allegorically.

Pachomius, Saint (290–346): Founder of cenobitic* or communal monascticism in Upper Egypt about 320.

Palladius (365–425): A monk (and later bishop) who travelled to Egypt at the end of the fourth century and later wrote the *Lausiac History*, an important eyewitness account of early monasticism.

Paraclete (Greek): 'Comforter'. Another name for the Holy Spirit whom Jesus sends to his disciples (see Jn 14:25) .

Patristics: The study of the Church Fathers (hence the name, from Latin *pater*) and Mothers.

Pispir, Mount: Antony's* 'outer mountain' (Deir el-Maimoun), about seventy-five kilometers south of Memphis on the east bank of the Nile; he moved there about 285.

Pneumatomachoi: 'Fighters against the Spirit' (so dubbed by their opponents) who believed that the Holy Spirit was inferior to the Father and Son.

Politeia (Greek): Way of life; citizenship.

Pseudo-Macarius: The name given to the author of the *Fifty Spiritual Homilies* attributed in antiquity to Saint Macarius the Great.*

Rufinus (345–410): Latin monk and translator of many monastic works from Greek to Latin.

Qasr: See **Keep**.

Saint Antony's: The Monastery of Saint Antony by the Red Sea, founded at the site traditionally associated with Saint Antony's* last monastic dwelling place. See map.

Saint Macarius': Deir Anba Maqar, one of the four ancient monasteries in the Wadi al-Natrun* still flourishing today.

Saint Paul's: Deir Anba Bula, the monastery twenty kilometers southeast of Saint Antony's, dedicated to Saint Paul of Thebes, 'the first hermit', whom Antony (according to Jerome) met in the desert. See map.

Saqqara: A famous monastic site, the monastery of Apa Jeremias; see map.

Sayings of the Desert Fathers *(Apophthegmata):* Sayings and stories mostly by and about the early desert monks. The origins of the Sayings, edited and written down in the sixth century, perhaps in Palestine, probably lie in Scetis*.

Scetis: From Coptic *shi hêt*, 'to weigh the heart', the ancient name for the Wadi al-Natrun*, the famous monastic community about forty miles south of Nitria* founded by Saint Macarius* about 330.

Semi-anchoritic Monasticism: A type of monasticism where the monks lived alone in scattered cells (a laura* or lavra) but came together on Saturday and Sunday for communal worship and meals.

Shenouda III, Pope: The present patriarch of the Coptic* Orthodox Church; he takes his name from Saint Shenoute the Great*.

Shenoute, Saint († 450): Great coptic* monastic leader, founder of the Red and White Monasteries near Sohag in Upper Egypt. See map.

Socrates (380–450): Church historian who wrote an *Ecclesiastical History*.

Sulpicius Severus (360–420): Latin monk from Gaul (France) who apparently visited Saint Antony's* and Saint Paul's* before 400 and mentioned them in his *First Dialogue*.

Synaxary (Synaxarion): A short account of a saint or feast appointed to be read during a liturgical service or the book that contains these accounts.

Syrian Monastery: Deir el-Souriani, one of the four ancient monasteries still active in the Wadi al-Natrun*.

Tabbennisi: The site of Pachomius'* first monastic community in Upper* Egypt.

Tall Brothers: Four origenist* monks, with Ammonius as their leader, who fled Egypt for Constantinople after the condemnation of Origenism in 399.

Thebaid: The upper part of the Nile valley, named after its chief city, Thebes; an important area of early monasticism. See map.

Theophilus († 412): Patriarch of Alexandria. In 399 he first condemned the Anthropomorphites*, but then reversed himself and condemned the origenist monks* and drove their leaders out of Egypt.

Tome of Leo: The letter from Leo I, Pope of Rome, which defined the 'two nature' Christology accepted by the Council of Chalcedon*.

Toou: Coptic* word meaning both 'mountain' and 'desert'.

Upper Egypt: Southern Egypt (from which direction the Nile flows).

Wadi al-Natrun (Scetis*): A wadi, or valley, twenty-twenty-five miles long, forty miles northwest of Cairo, with four flourishing monasteries today.

Wadi Arabah: The arid wadi, or valley, in which the monastery of Saint Antony* is situated.

Wisdom Literature: The Old Testament books of Psalms, Proverbs, Ecclesiastes, Song of Songs, Sirach, and the Wisdom of Solomon and such Greco-Roman works as *The Sentences of Sextus* and *The Teachings of Silvanus*.

Yustus: Bishop and abbot of Saint Antony's*.

Introduction

WAR! HUH! WHAT IS IT GOOD FOR? Absolutely nothing! Say it again!' Those words from a Vietnam War-era song are as true now as they were then. Most North Americans believe that we are now engaged in perpetual war against evil enemies. But making the enemy 'other' is an illusion, denial. Perhaps peace was the twentieth century's greatest illusion. Or its greatest fear. Our domestic violence, if nothing else, should demonstrate to us that there is no peace. Children with guns pick off other children in schoolyard cafeterias and playgrounds and the evening news adds up the daily body count. And we adults act even more violently. Perhaps we should all crouch about with flak jackets, shouting 'Incoming!' That would at least acknowledge the reality of our situation: that we are our own worst enemies.

Warfare, it may surprise most of us (it did me) to learn, is one of the chief themes of early christian monasticism; it is, therefore, one of the main themes of the pieces collected in this book. And, in crazy and paradoxical contradiction to the song quoted above, monastic war *is* good for something. Actually, for a lot. In the world of early monasticism, it is not 'Jesus saves' but 'War saves'. Or, more accurately, both save. Together. This warfare, we might be relieved to know, is spiritual, waged within the human heart and soul (though plenty of monks, ancient and modern, have died at the hands of warring marauders). But if we read these monks attentively, our relief will be short-lived, because for them the spiritual world is more real than the temporal, more real, more holy and more deadly. That fact alone makes these monks worth reading still today: they remind us that evil is very real. It is not only all around us, but within us, a clear and present danger. We have met the enemy and he is us. The missiles we (still) aim target not only foreign enemies but ourselves and others; and in targeting ourselves and others, we target God.

These monks also understand a corollary truth: that the spiritual life, life in God, is hard work. The Christian is a warrior and an athlete. Those metaphors are not original with them; they come from Saint Paul and, antecedent to him, from Greco-Roman ethics and philosophy. Yet the monks took those metaphors and with them built dwellings in the desert and inhabited them, then they built churches, then monasteries, then they created writings. Then those monasteries and writings, and the monks themselves, returned these metaphors to the Church as flesh and bone and brick and mortar. They lived a long time ago, these monks. Their buildings are now mostly obliterated or forgotten. But their descendants, both fleshly and architectural, still inhabit the desert places of Egypt; more importantly, they still bear witness from and to the heart of Christianity.

What can spiritual warfare and the rigors of the godly life (how antiquated the phrase sounds!) have to do with CNN, cyberspace, suburbia, and the global economy? Either everything or nothing. It is all or nothing, because the monastic world is biblical; if it falls, the Bible falls. The monks did not imitate the biblical figures; they *became* them. They *are* (not *were*) Abraham embarking on his long journey into God; they *are* (not *were*) Moses and the people of Israel fleeing Egypt into the desert in order to reach the Promised Land, only to confront in the wilderness their self-made, thus golden, idols; they *are* (not *were*) Christ bearing his cross to heaven. The early monks believed with all their hearts that they were 'Abraham's offspring, heirs according to the promise' (Gal 3:29). That is why, despite the warfare, the lives they lived and the writings they left are hopeful, optimistic, joyful, full of promise. This is why they are ultimately worth reading. The monks are fully aware that the kingdom of God is obtainable, palpable even, and that, like Paul, they are straining ahead to find it, to arrive at the place where they will meet God face to face.

That such meetings are still possible is the premise revealed by the title and structure of this book: monasticism is not ruins and antique writings; it is a way of life, a gospel way of life. Monasticism is not only ancient, but also modern. The ancient monks, who looked to Abraham as their spiritual father, fulfilled God's promise to Abraham by spiritually fathering generations of offspring. Their monastic children in turn have taken christian monasticism to every part of the world, where it survives today. In many places, such as Egypt and Africa, monasticism is thriving. So the children of Abraham live in ancient and modern juxtaposition, sometimes in tension, sometimes in symbiosis. In this book I have attempted to describe journeys in both ancient and modern worlds because I believe that ultimately both worlds are one, and that world is Christ.

All reconstructions, ancient or modern, are imagined (*not* imaginary) and partial, in both senses that the latter word conveys. Reconstructing early monasticism is like looking at my seven-year old son's team soccer picture. Someone looking from outside at that photograph would see one boy among many posed in their sunlit uniforms on green, suburban fields, never supposing or even imagining what only his mother and father know, the struggles that lay behind the picture and the practices: the fits of temper, uncaged anger, and slammed doors that usually, mercifully, go unphotographed. Team pictures cannot capture the demons that direct their dank ministrations at our children.

The chapters in this book, then, are partial; perhaps they hide as much as they reveal. The ancient world was very different from our own, and any explorer can hope to experience it only partially. My travels to modern monasteries were made as an outsider, both denominationally and linguistically. Nevertheless, my hope is that these chapters, though partial, will lead the reader beyond the tourist's and scholar's snapshots to the persons themselves, the ancient and modern monks who manifest Christ to the world. These chapters are also partisan because I believe that monastic spirituality saves. It does not claim to be the only way to God. Nor does it suggest that we should all be cloistered and celibate. But monasticism, I believe, does offer the fullest, most complete, form of christian spirituality. It teaches quiet withdrawal (from the world's mad frenzies and trappings), peace, prayer and work as a loving couple (not, as for most of us, divorced from each other), hospitality, simplicity, care for others, real community, and, finally, union with God.

The nine chapters of this book are set in Egypt. To paraphrase Henry David Thoreau, I would not write about Egypt so much if I knew any place better. My hope is that egyptian monasticism will be or become familiar enough that the reader will see in these chapters both his or her own journey and monasticism in general. After a Prologue, 'Words to Live By', Part I, 'Journeys', consists of two narratives of trips I made to monasteries in Egypt: in 1996 to the Wadi al-Natrun between Cairo and Alexandria; and in 1998 to the monasteries of Saint Antony and Saint Paul by the Red Sea. It is my hope that, in addition to being interesting travelogues, these two essays will provide an historical introduction to the second major part of the volume. Part II, 'Translations', offers translations of seven early monastic literary texts, along with some documentary texts (Chapter Nine), and provides introductions that give settings to those texts and suggest the spirituality that lies behind and informs them. Because each of the chapters in Part II offers an extensive introduction, I will not duplicate those efforts here.

The texts in this volume come from the fourth, fifth, and sixth centuries or else, if written later, they attempt to describe events from those centuries. The fourth century may well have been the golden age of christian monasticism, but the following two centuries, despite the grumblings we sometimes hear in the sources, were by no means centuries of bronze or lead; if they were silver and not gold, it was nevertheless a wonderfully brilliant silver, well worth keeping, and keeping in use. It is my hope that these translations and this volume can take such precious metal, tarnished partially by time and partially by inattention, burnish it, and make it new. Perhaps that sheen can even act as a mirror in which we see ourselves, not darkly, but as we really are.

Prologue:
Words to Live By

1

Words to Live By:

A Conversation that the Elders Had with One Another Concerning Thoughts

Introduction

GIVE ME A WORD, FATHER'. From the time of Saint Antony —at least—younger monks would ask older monks, *abbas* or *ammas* ('fathers' or 'mothers'), for a saving word, for advice, for wise counsel on how to live.[1] Many of the answers given by the abbas were remembered and eventually written down, becoming, in some cases, a kind of christian midrash, a commentary on Scripture and on its continuing relevance and importance; in other cases, what the abba says does not directly allude to Scripture but becomes a second canon. 'The words of elders and of Scripture', as Douglas Burton-Christie has observed, 'constituted a double tradition of authority for those living in the desert'.[2] This double tradition, like good root stock, forms the secure foundation for the *apophthegmata*, or sayings, of the early desert monks; the sayings, like roses, or branches filled with grapes, rise from that stock. One such branch, fruit from the desert, is *A Conversation that the Elders Had with One Another Concerning Thoughts*.

In 1957 J.-C. Guy published this previously unedited and untranslated collection of thirty-one apophthegms which he termed 'le petit *Dialogue* monastique anonyme'.[3] Photius (810–895), patriarch of Constantinople and indefatigable bibliographer, apparently knew of this work, but *Concerning Thoughts* is not uniformly found in the medieval manuscripts of the *Apophthegmata*, or *Sayings of the Desert Fathers*, that had their origins in early desert monasticism.[4]

The *Apophthegmata* fall into two main groupings: (1) the Alphabetical Collection, sayings gathered under the names of well-known monks, called the *Apophthegmata Patrum* or *Paterikon*,[5] and (2) the Systematic Collection, known in the West as the *Verba Seniorum*, which is arranged topically.[6] There is also a combined grouping, the

Alphabetico-Anonymous or Anonymous Collection, some four hundred additional sayings handed down in antiquity without attribution.[7] The *Conversation Concerning Thoughts* translated below belongs to a different category: it is missing from several systematic collections and is not found in the alphabetico-anonymous collections; furthermore, it exists in several codices that are ignorant of both the systematic and the alphabetico-anonymous collections.[8] *Concerning Thoughts*, as Guy sees it, is like several other small collections of early monastic sayings that form appendices to the systematic collections but that also have an 'existence independent of these collections'.[9] The *Conversation on Thoughts* was apparently popular among medieval monks, and exists in a number of manuscripts.[10] This is not surprising: it is a wise, down to earth, sensible, and humane work.

From its earliest days, monasticism has had masters and disciples, those experienced in the tradition and those who have come to the desert to learn. Antony attached himself to an elder, as did Pachomius. For us to enter the world of the *Conversation Concerning Thoughts*, we must imagine two monks, or a group of monks, sitting together in quiet conversation. The title of this work suggests that it is a conversation between 'elders', but rather than think of a dialogue between two 'old men' *(gerontes)*, or experienced monks of whatever age, we would do better to understand 'elders' here as meaning 'the men of old', 'the monks of old'. The questions put forth clearly show that a disciple or novice is asking counsel of a monastic elder.[11] Although this piece was undoubtedly not the result of a single session between an abba and his disciple, it certainly comes out of the abba-disciple tradition. *Concerning Thoughts* is a collection of sayings, edited anonymously, that follows a question-answer format.[12] The subject of the conversation is thoughts, *logismoi*: how to deal with bad or evil thoughts, and how to cultivate good ones.[13]

In a lecture for the novices at the Abbey of Gethsemani in Kentucky, a monk of our own day, Thomas Merton, humorously defined logismoi:

> Logismoi are thoughts; we usually mean 'useless thoughts' or 'bad thoughts', or something like that. I remember—this occasionally happens here, it doesn't

happen to me 'cause I don't hear confessions in parishes, but priests who hear confessions in parishes—kids will come up and say, 'I had thoughts'.

—'Well that's not a sin. Glad you had thoughts; you've got a mind'.

—'No, but I had *thoughts*'. (Merton and the novices laugh.)

So, but the desert fathers are a little bit like that, see: logismoi are thoughts, but they're the kind of, any thought that you don't want, that you didn't ought to have.[14]

Merton's definition is accurate—at least with regard to *A Conversation Concerning Thoughts*. Thoughts were (and are) of paramount importance for monastics because monks are, at least theoretically, less concerned with *things*, 'the things of this world': cars, fashionable clothing, mortgage payments, appearances. As Evagrius of Pontus, the first systematic theologian of the monastic life, pointed out: 'With lay persons the demons fight rather by means of present things. . . . But with monks, [the demons fight] mostly by means of thoughts; for in the wilderness they have no things'.[15] Today, perhaps, we see that the line dividing monk and layperson is not so great: the Gospel asks all of us to be detached from worldly things. Jesus' instructions are specific and unambiguous: 'Give up everything'. 'Take nothing with you'. 'Consider the lilies of the field'. That's the first step.

The next step is even more difficult, and more necessary. Freed from things, the monk strives to be 'freed from thought' so that 'the knowledge of God might dwell in him' (Saying 1). As Andrew Louth has put it, 'the *logismoi* we encounter in the writings of the Desert Fathers are thought to be caused by demons . . . trains of thought, strings of considerations, that invaded the heart, occluded it, divided it, and destroyed any chance of a single-hearted devotion to, search for, God'.[16] The monk is safest when he is in his cell (2), but the Devil tries to lure the monk out of his cell with thoughts (3). Thoughts lead to sexual fantasies (26, 27), fornication (24), slander and backbiting (12, 25), distraction in prayer (14), and distraction while working (17). Thoughts, then, must be mastered if the monk is to live in solitude (23). We need to remember, though, that solitude is not an end, but a means; the means toward fellowship and, ultimately, to union with God. Solitude is not isolation, but contemplative quiet *(hesychia)*; not distance from, but nearness to—to oneself, to God, and then, as its fruit, to others. (Compassion comes when we are no longer preoccupied with things or ourselves; see below.) Solitude is life without—or with a minimum of—distractions: things pull us away from God; solitude allows us to live devoted to God. Solitude can, and should, be part of every christian life.

The early monastic understanding of thoughts probably seems at first a dour (though accurate!) assessment of human consciousness: thoughts can lead us into a variety of temptations.[17] The monk does initially seem like the kid in the confessional: 'Father, forgive me, for I had *thoughts*'. But *A Conversation Concerning Thoughts* is more lively and more hopeful—and more nuanced—than a cursory glance might indicate. It is lively because it is alive with metaphor, rich with the earthy analogies both of Jesus and the village: the monk is a dove (2) and the Devil an enchanter (3). In typical monastic imagery, the monk must do battle (4) and is an athlete in competition (23); a fire-throwing catapult moves beyond the typical and makes vivid the danger of speech (4). Fishermen and craftsmen, boats and waves, seeds and branches are all metaphorically enlisted in teaching the young monk.

A Conversation Concerning Thoughts is hopeful because it stresses moderation over severe austerity, the community over narcissistic individualism. Holiness, these sayings stress, is both sensible and concerned with others. False piety is drawn-in and withdrawn; *Concerning Thoughts* will have no truck with that. It is here that our text is most midrashic. The Bible could be, and was, and is, often used to foster a narrow, constricted view of human beings and their worlds—heaven as well as earth; instead of being a gift of the Holy Spirit, a wise friend, Scripture can become a rulebook. In Saying 6 the interlocutor asks, 'Is it good to possess two tunics?' Clearly in the background is Jesus' command: it is *not* good to possess two tunics (Mt 10:10; Lk 9:3). But the abba sensibly says that we need clothing; more important is moral purity.

In Saying 19 when the questioner asks, 'Can a person sin because of an idea?' he may have in mind Mt 5:28, where Jesus says, 'But I say to you that everyone who looks at a woman with lust has already committed adultery with her in his heart'. The abba insists, though, that ideas *in themselves* are not sinful; 'any sin not brought to completion is not a sin'.[18] In the same way, when the abba is asked about nocturnal fantasies, he replies that 'temptation that comes while we're asleep is ineffectual' (27). Saying 7 seems to summarize the abba's outlook: Do what is required; don't strive unnecessarily. We need to remember, though, that what was *required* of the monks was a great deal; but fanaticism leads to ruin.

This moderate attitude combines, interestingly, with hardheaded realism: the Devil is a very real and very threatening presence;[19] slander and backbiting are enemies of community;[20] distractions are common, and the spiritual life is rife with seductions. The greatest seduction for someone seeking holiness, in fact, may be self-absorption. The abba will not allow that. In three of the sayings, the monk asks questions about individual piety and personal holiness: 'I want to be a witness for God' (13), 'How can a person love God?' (28), and 'How can a person know that his prayer is acceptable to God?' (31). In each case the abba tells the monk that his first concern is not for himself but for his neighbor: you are a witness for God if you bear with your neighbor (13), you love God by helping a brother in difficulty (28), and your prayer is acceptable before God if you do not wrong your neighbor. 'But if someone wrongs his neighbor in any way whatsoever, either physically or spiritually, his prayer is an abomination and is unacceptable' (31). Handiwork, the monk's chief occupation in prayer, is good because it allows monks to give to the poor (17). No solipsism here, no hoarding of the spiritual self. Humility is the chief virtue, humility not as a debasing but as a realistic—and non-competitive—understanding of the self, humility that allows you to put your neighbor before yourself (30).

This is not likely to be a popular spirituality for the twenty-first century West—but then it probably never has been popular. Yet if we take the spirituality of these monks seriously, we take Jesus seriously. J.-C. Guy has commented that the number of manuscripts of *Concerning Thoughts* reveals the interest that the medieval monks had in this early monastic work and that this is 'sufficient reason for it to remain ours also'.[21] No, that's not enough. *A Conversation Concerning Thoughts* should hold our interest because it is, in the main, true.[22] It has in it much—not all—of the truth of the Gospel; its monks are trying to be, as Joan Chittister has put it, 'Gospel persons';[23] prayerful, reflective, quiet ('above all the virtues God has chosen silence'),[24] compassionate, giving. In an age (and a Church?) of consumerism and misguided individualism, these are virtues worthy of our emulation, virtues worth the attention of pastors, preachers, spiritual directors, everyone. The words here are still words to live by.[25]

Concerning Thoughts

1. *Question:* How should the monk live in his cell?

Answer: He should keep away from human knowledge so that when he is freed from thought the knowledge of God might dwell in him.

2. *Question:* What does the monk try to do?

Answer: The monk is a dove: when it's time for a dove to fly it spreads its wings and flies, but if it remains outside its nest too long it is set upon by wild birds and loses its dignity and beauty. It's the same with a monk: there comes a time at the public assembly[26] for him to 'give wing' to his thoughts, but if he remains outside his cell too long he is set upon by the demons and his thoughts are darkened.

3. *Question:* With what kind of thought does the Devil lure the monk out of his cell?

Answer: The Devil is an enchanter. With enticing words the enchanter lures the wild beast out of its lair and, catching it, drags it into the streets of the city where he releases it to people's laughter, and when later it grows old in his captivity he consigns it to the flames or tosses it into the sea. It is the same with a monk: his way of life suffers when, drawn outside by his thoughts, he abandons his cell.

4. *Question:* If the brother leaves his cell in order to do some ministry and a woman meets him on the road, how can he flee this battle with fornication?

Answer: The battle he can *not* flee, but the act he *can* flee if he keeps silent when he meets her. For just as the fire-throwing catapult, by igniting sulfur, hurls forth fire, in the same way a man's speech with a woman also ignites and causes sin.[27]

5. *Question:* With what kind of thought does fornication enter into a person?

Answer: Not one, not two, not five, nor ten paths are enough for fornication, for all thoughts that come from the Devil have fornication hidden within.[28]

6. *Question:* Is it good to possess two tunics? [Mt 10:10, Lk 9:3]

Answer: To possess two tunics and not to possess evil that stains[29] the whole body is a good thing, for the soul has no need of evil, but the body needs clothing. Since we have the things we need and they are sufficient, we are satisfied with them [Prv 30:8 (LXX) and 1 Tm 6:8].

7. *Question:* How should we perform the service of singing the psalms, and what are the proper limits of fasting?

Answer: Do nothing more than what is required of you; for many wish to excel, and a little later are unable to achieve their goal.

8. *Question:* If a brother urges me to drink a cup of wine in his cell, is it good to leave?

Answer: Flee wine-drinking and you will be saved like a deer from the net, for many on account of this need have fallen victim to thoughts.

9. *Question:* Why can't I live with the brothers?

Answer: Because you do not fear God. If you would remember what is written, that in Sodom Lot was saved because he passed judgement on no one [Gn 19] . . . and you would throw yourself in the middle of wild beasts to live![30]

10. *Question:* If a brother causes me offense, do you want me to ask his forgiveness?

Answer: Ask his forgiveness and cut him off from you, for we have Abba Arsenius who says, 'Have love for everyone, but live apart from everyone'.[31]

11. *Question:* What does it mean for a person to bring the eucharistic thank-offering into the church?

Answer: This act is treasure laid before God, and that which you set down here you will in turn receive above.

12. *Question:* What is the sin of slander?

Answer: The sin of slander most assuredly will not allow a person to come before God, for it is written: 'The person who secretly slanders his neighbor, this one have I driven out' [Ps 100:5 (LXX)].[32]

13. *Question:* I want to be a witness for God.

Answer: If someone bears with his neighbor during a fit of temper, it is equal to the furnace at the time of the three youths [Dan 3].[33]

14. *Question:* Why is it that when I stand in prayer I'm preoccupied with thoughts?

Answer: Because the Devil, from the beginning refusing to worship the God of all, was hurled from heaven and became an outcast from the kingdom of God, and therefore he distracts us from our prayer and wants to make us just like him.

15. *Question:* When thoughts suggest to me the pleasures of food, how is it they prevent me from fasting?

Answer: Because the Devil also tripped up Adam on account of food [Gn 3];[34] therefore, he also does the same thing to us.

16. *Question:* Why does fornication trouble us[35] so much?

Answer: Because the Devil knows that fornication alienates us from the Holy Spirit. Hear, then, what the Lord says: 'My spirit shall not abide in these mortals, for they are flesh' [Gn 6:3 (LXX)].[36]

17. *Question:* How does the Devil distract me so easily and preoccupy me so I neglect my handiwork?

Answer: Because Satan knows that our handiwork allows us to offer alms to the poor. Wishing therefore to keep us away from our almsgiving, he distracts us and preoccupies us so we neglect our handiwork.

18. *Question:* How can a person keep away from the plots of the demons?

Answer: A fish cannot stop a fisherman from casting his hook into the sea, but if the fish is aware of the hook's evil he can avoid it and be saved, leaving the fisherman empty handed. It's the same for a person.

19. *Question:* Can a person sin because of an idea?

Answer: Waves will never injure rock; in the same way an unsuccessful assault will never harm a person, for it is written that any sin not brought to completion is not a sin.[37]

20. *Question:* What does the Scripture mean: 'If someone has faith like a mustard seed'? [Mt 17:20]

Answer: A farmer plows the earth and sows seed, and when the seed finds free space in the earth it puts forth roots and produces branches above ground so that the birds of the air make their nests in them [Mt 13:32]. In the same way, if a person purifies his heart and receives the word of God and it resides there, it produces good thoughts so that the commandments of God reside in him.

21. *Question:* Is it good to live in the desert?

Answer: When the sons of Israel put an end to the distractions of Egypt and lived in tents, it was at that time made known to them how they ought to fear God. Indeed, boats driven about by storm in the middle of the sea accomplish nothing; but when they come to harbor, then they engage in business. In the same way, if a person is not steadfast in one place he will never receive the knowledge of truth.[38] Indeed, above all the virtues God has chosen silence,³⁹ for it is written, 'Upon whom shall I look except upon the humble and quiet⁴⁰ and him who trembles at my words?'" [Is 66:2 (LXX)]⁴¹

22. *Question:* Is it good to mediate a dispute between brothers?

Answer: Flee such things, for it is written, 'stopping his ears from hearing bloody judgements and shutting his eyes from looking on evil' [Is 33:15 (LXX)].⁴²

23. *Question:* How can a person live in solitude?

Answer: If the athlete does not practice with other athletes he can not learn how to be victorious and so be able to compete alone with his opponent. It is the same with the monk: if he is not first trained with brothers and learns to master his thoughts, he cannot live in solitude and do battle with thoughts.⁴³

24. *Question:* If it's necessary to come into contact with women, how ought we to meet with them?

Answer: This 'necessity' is the Devil's doing, for the Devil has numerous 'necessary' pretexts. But if some need requires you to come into contact with a woman, do not allow her to say anything more than necessary. And you, if you just say a few words, finish your meeting and quickly dismiss her. If you loiter with her, know that her stench⁴⁴ will debase your thoughts.⁴⁵

25. *Question:* With what kind of thought can a person put an end to backbiting?⁴⁶

Answer: Just as the person who allows fire to be placed on his chest is injured, so also the person who agrees to meet with people will never entirely get away from backbiting.⁴⁷

26. *Question:* Are nocturnal fantasies the Devil's doing?

Answer: Just as the Devil preoccupies us during the day with distracting thoughts that prevent us from devoting ourselves to prayer, so too at night he excites our thoughts with fantasies, hindering the purity of our sleep.⁴⁸

27. *Question:* What shall a person do with regard to the temptation that comes upon him to deride the flesh during sleep?

Answer: If someone finds his adversary asleep and strikes him, the one who does the striking cannot deride the one whom he has struck as though he had defeated him (for there is no victory for him but rather condemnation). In the same way, temptation that comes while we're asleep is ineffectual.[49]

28. *Question:* How can a person receive the gift[50] of loving God?

Answer: When someone sees his brother in difficulty and cries out to God to help him, then he receives knowledge how one ought to love God.[51]

29. *Question:* What sort of virtues or commandments does a person need to possess in order to be saved?

Answer: There are four virtues prescribed for us:[52] fasting, and prayer, and handiwork, and bodily chastity. When Satan overcame these virtues, he drove Adam out of paradise [Gn 3:23]. Deceiving Adam and dishonoring him by means of food, Satan drove him into hiding and away from the face of God so he would never ask God's forgiveness[53] and have his sin forgiven. When Adam had been driven out from paradise, on account of his idleness the Devil was intending to condemn him for another sin, expecting to gain possession of Adam on account of the despair he felt for himself. But the loving and merciful Lord, knowing the wickedness of the Devil, gave work to Adam, saying, 'Work the earth from which you were taken' [Gn 3:23], so that Adam, in his care for his work, might drive away the evil devices of the Devil. The Devil, therefore, works against fasting, against prayer, against handiwork, for handiwork cuts off at the knees the Devil's many evil devices. And he also opposes virtuous chastity. But if someone is deemed worthy of the labor of these four virtues, then he will gain mastery of all other virtues.

30. *Question:* What does a person do to receive the gift of these virtues?

Answer: If someone wishes to learn a skill, he abandons all anxious thoughts and humbles himself, and through his humility receives the gift of the skill. It is the same with a monk: if he does not exclude all human anxieties and humble himself before everyone, not reckoning 'I'm better than this fellow', or 'I'm this one's equal', he will never possess virtue in its entirety. But if he humbles himself and considers all his deeds to be insignificant, then when the virtues establish his way of life they are automatically at hand, for it says, 'while you are still speaking, he will say, "Here I am"' [Is 58:9 (LXX)].[54]

31. *Question:* How can a person know that his prayer is acceptable to God? [1 Pt 2:5]

Answer: When a person makes sure that he does not wrong his neighbor in any way whatsoever, then he can be sure that his prayer is acceptable to God. But if someone harms his neighbor in any way whatsoever, either physically or spiritually, his prayer is an abomination and is unacceptable. For the wailing of the one who is being wronged will never allow this person's prayer to come before the face of God. And if indeed he does not quickly reconcile with his neighbor, he will certainly not go unpunished his whole life by his own sins, for it is written that 'whatever you bind on earth will be bound in heaven' [Mt 18:18].[55]

NOTES

[1] For examples see Alphabetical Apophthegmata Antony 19; Arsenius 9; Eupreprius 7; Macarius 23, 28 & 41; Moses 6; Poemen 69; Sisoës 35; Serapion 2; N 91 & 387; Felix 1. On this genre, see the classic article of Jean-Claude Guy, 'Remarques sur le texte des *Apophthegmata Patrum*', *Recherches de science religieuse* 43 (1955) 252–258; also Graham E. Gould, 'A Note on the *Apophthegmata Patrum*', *Journal of Theological Studies* n.s. 37 (1986) 133–138; Benedicta Ward, 'Traditions of Spiritual Guidance: Spiritual Direction in the Desert Fathers', *The Way* 24 (1984) 61–70, reprinted in *Signs and Wonders* (London: Variorum Reprints, 1993).

[2] Douglas Burton-Christie, *The Word in the Desert: Scripture and the Quest for Holiness in Early Christian Monasticism* (Oxford: Oxford University Press, 1993) 110.

[3] J.-C. Guy, 'Un Dialogue monastique inédit: ΠΕΡΙ ΛΟΓΙΣΜΩΝ, *Revue d'ascétique et de mystique* 33 (1957) 171–188.

[4] On the origins of the desert apophthegmata, see Burton-Christie, 76–81.

[5] For an english translation, see Benedicta Ward, trans., *The Sayings of the Desert Fathers: The Alphabetical Collection* (Kalamazoo: Cistercian Publications, 1975; rev. ed., 1984).

⁶ A first volume of the Systematic Collection was published by Sources chrétiennes: Jean-Claude Guy, ed., *Les Apophtegmes des Pères: Collection systématique* (Paris: Cerf, 1993); the second will apparently not appear. Chiara Faraggiana is preparing a complete edition, of which Apostolos N. Athanassakis and I are preparing an english translation. The latin edition appears in Heribert Rosweyde, ed., *Vitæ patrum, sive, Historiæ eremiticæ libri decem auctoribus suis et nitori pristino restituti ac notationibus illustrati* (Paris 1849, 1879). For an english translation of Rosweyde's text, see Owen Chadwick, trans., *Western Asceticism*, The Library of Christian Classics, 12 (Philadelphia: The Westminster Press-London: SCM Press, 1958) 33–189. For a translation in French, see Lucien Regnault, *Les Chemins de Dieu au désert: Collection systematique des Apophtegmes des Pères* (Solesmes: Éditions de Solesmes, 1992).

⁷ For a partial english translation, based on the text published by F. Nau, see Columba Stewart, trans., *The World of the Desert Fathers* (Oxford: SLG Press, 1986), and Benedicta Ward, trans., *The Wisdom of the Desert Fathers: Apophthegmata Patrum from the Anonymous Series* (Oxford: SLG Press, 1975) [Both available in the US from Cistercian Publications]. For a concise discussion of the various collections, see Burton-Christie, 85–88, and for a complete bibliography of the sayings see Burton-Christie, 305–306.

⁸ Guy, 171–173. Ten of the sayings do occur elsewhere in virtually the same form. See N 506 (which reproduces #s 25, 26, 23, and 24 of the present collection), N 507 (#s 21, 30), N 508 (#31), N 623 (#22) N 624 (#23), N 627 (#9), and N 636 (#28) in Lucien Regnault, trans., *Les Sentences des Pères du desert: serie des anonymes* (Solesmes: Bellefontaine, 1985), 183–184, 268, and 276. Regnault's cross-references are incorrect for N 506 and 507.

⁹ Guy, 173. The other collections he adduces are *The Account (or Narrative) of the Twelve Anchorites*, the twelve chapters of the *De virtutibus* of Abba Moses, and the *Sententiae* of Hesychius.

¹⁰ For a discussion of the manuscripts see Guy, 173–176.

¹¹ This is corroborated by the ten *apophthegmata* from *Concerning Thoughts* found in the collection translated by Regnault; of these ten, nine explicitly refer to an elder being questioned by a disciple: four have the formula 'Un ancien fut interrogé. . . . Il repondit' (N 623–624, 636), while four begin 'Le (Et le) frère dit. . . . L'ancien repondit' (N 506), and two begin 'Un frère demanda (encore) a un ancien. . . . Et l'ancien lui repondit' (N 507). Only one (N 508) retains the format of *Concerning Thoughts*: 'Demande. . . . Réponse'.

¹² This was the format later used by Saint Basil the Great in his (misnamed) 'Rules', which are not Rules but rather responses to questions.

¹³ Of the thirty-one apophthegms, though, eight or nine are concerned with more general issues of monastic life: possessions (Saying 6), psalmody and fasting (7), wine-drinking (8), judging others in community (9), forgiving others (10), bringing the eucharistic thank-offering (11), slander (12), faith (20), and mediating disputes (22).

¹⁴ Thomas Merton, 'Prayer and Self-Growth' (Credence Cassettes; Kansas City: The National Catholic Reporter Publishing Co., n.d.), side two; my transcription. By contrast, compare the definition of Evagrius of Pontus, which Thomas Spidlik characterizes as 'too complicated', in Spidlik, *The Spirituality of the Christian East: A Systematic Handbook* (Kalamazoo: Cistercian Publications, 1986) 239.

¹⁵ Evagrius Ponticus, *Praktikos* 48 [CS 4:29]; in Spidlik, 237 (modified). For Spidlik's definition of *logismoi* in early desert spirituality, and especially in evagrian thought, see 237–242.

¹⁶ Andrew Louth, *The Wilderness of God* (Nashville, Tennessee: Abingdon, 1991) 56.

¹⁷ Though Evagrius primarily emphasized the negative aspects of thoughts, he did recognize that there could be good *logismoi* prompted by nature, deliberate choice, or by an angel; see Elizabeth A. Clark, *The Origenist Controversy: The Cultural Construction of an Early Christian Debate* (Princeton: Princeton University Press, 1992) 77; and Gabriel Bunge, *Akêdia: Die geistliche Lehre des Evagrios Pontikos von Überdruss* (Cologne: Luther Verlag, 1983) 33.

¹⁸ Guy adduces an analogous saying wise in its understanding: 'For the person who does not have evil and good thoughts is like the land of Sodom and Gomorrah inasmuch as it is salty and bears neither fruit nor plants. But good earth brings forth wheat and tares'. See n. 37 below.

¹⁹ On the Devil's role in thoughts, see Spidlik, 240–241.

²⁰ On the importance of this theme for the early monks, see Tim Vivian and Apostolos N. Athanassakis, trans., *The Life of Saint George of Choziba and the Miracles of the Most Holy Mother of God at Choziba* (San Francisco: Catholic Scholars Press, 1994) 23–24, 67–71, and 73–89.

²¹ Guy, 176.

²² The work does, unfortunately, cast a cold eye on women; see especially Saying 24.

²³ Joan Chittister, *Wisdom Distilled from the Daily: Living the Rule of Saint Benedict Today* (San Francisco: Harper-San Francisco, 1990) 17.

²⁴ Saying 21.

²⁵ Two good modern discussions on 'thoughts' are Columba Stewart, 'Radical Honesty about the Self: The Practice of the Desert Fathers', *Sobornost* 12 (1990) 25–39; and Mary Margaret Funk, *Thoughts Matter: The Practice of the Spiritual Life* (New York: Continuum, 1998), which treats the writings of John Cassian.

²⁶ Gk *sunaxis*; see Tim Vivian, 'Eucharist and Synaxis: The Celebration of Community', *St. Vladimir's Theological Quarterly* 37:1 (1993) 73–78; rpt in Vivian, trans., *Paphnutius: Histories of the Monks of Upper Egypt and the Life of Onnophrius*, CS 140 (rev. ed.; Kalamazoo: Cistercian Publications, 2000) 26–30.

²⁷ In the *Life of Onnophrius*, the monk Timothy tells Paphnutius about how words with a woman led to such a sin: 'When we had become accustomed to talk freely, we ate bread together. The affair continued to grow until finally we gave birth to death and brought forth wickedness' (Jas 1:15); see Vivian, trans., *Paphnutius*, CS 140:148-149.

²⁸ In the *Life of Antony* 6, the Devil tells Antony: 'I am the friend of fornication. I am the one who possesses its traps and desires, waging war against the young. They call me "the spirit of fornication". How many wanted to live wisely, and I deceived them! How many were quietly patient, and I deceived them by casting into them daily preoccupations! I am the one whom the prophet accuses on account of those who have fallen: "They have been led astray by a spirit of fornication". I am the one who led them astray. On account of me they fell'. See Tim Vivian, *Journeying into God: Seven Early Monastic Lives* (Minneapolis: Fortress, 1996) 16–17.

[29] Gk *spiloun*; see Jas 3:6 ('The tongue . . . stains [*spilousa*] the whole body') and Jude 23 ('save others by snatching them out of the fire . . . hating even the tunic defiled [*espilomenon*] by their bodies').

[30] Saying 9 is found at N 627 in Regnault's collection (p. 269).

[31] See Alphabetical Apophthegmata Arsenius 13: 'Abba Mark said to Abba Arsenius, "Why do you avoid us?" The old man said to him, "God knows that I love you, but I cannot live with God and with men"'. Ward, trans., *The Sayings of the Desert Fathers* 11.

[32] See also Saying 25 below. Slander and backbiting were real problems in monastic communities; an anonymous apophthegm says that through slander the monks 'drag one another to hell'. See Ward, trans., *The Wisdom of the Desert Fathers* 33 (#106).

[33] See Dn 3. An anonymous apophthegm says, 'The monk's cell is like the furnace of Babylon where the three children found the Son of God'. See Ward, *Wisdom* 24 (#74 [N 206]). F. Nau, in a series of articles published in *Revue de l'orient chrétien* 12–18 (1907–1913), published the anonymous sayings; I have put his numbering in brackets.

[34] See Saying 29 below.

[35] Literally 'trouble a person *(anthrôpon)*'; immediately below 'mortals' translates *anthrôpois*.

[36] The quotation from Genesis however, lacks "forever" after "mortals."

[37] Guy notes, p. 185, n. 7: 'A quotation whose origin I have not been able to identify. It can be found in a similar form, but without being given as a quotation, in an apophthegm that gives it thus: An old man said, Any evil not completed is not evil; and any righteous action not completed is not a righteous action. For the person who does not have evil and good thoughts is like the land of Sodom and Gomorrah inasmuch as it is salty and bears neither fruit nor plants. But good earth brings forth wheat and tares'. As Douglas Burton-Christie has observed (*The Word in the Desert* 109), 'the words of the elders were often seen as carrying the same weight of authority as those of Scripture'. An anonymous apophthegm puts the matter differently but comes to the same conclusion: 'A brother asked one of the Fathers if one is defiled by having evil thoughts. There was a discussion on the subject, and some said, "Yes, one is defiled", and others, "No, or else—poor men that we are—we could not be saved; what counts is not to carry them out corporally"'. A 'very experienced old man' concurs. See Ward, *Wisdom* 28 (#84 [N 216]). As Elizabeth Clark has summarized, *The Origenist Controversy*, 83, 'The issue, then [for Evagrius]—as in Stoic epistemology and ethics—is one of consent: although we do not have the power to eradicate "unclean thoughts" completely, we can withold our assent to them'. See 83, n. 304 for the sources on Evagrius.

[38] An anonymous apophthegm uses the following metaphor for monastic stability: 'Just as a tree cannot bring forth fruit if it is always being transplanted, so the monk who is always going from one place to another is not able to bring forth virtue'. Ward, *Wisdom* 24 (#72 [N 204]).

[39] Gk *hesychian*.

[40] Gk *hesychion*, which can also mean 'solitary' or 'eremitical'.

[41] Saying 21 occurs as part of N 507 in Regnault's collection (p. 183).

[42] Saying 22 occurs, in very nearly the same form, as N 623 in Regnault's collection (p. 268).

[43] Saying 23 is virtually the same as N 624 in Regnault's collection (p. 268), and is included, in the same form, as part of N 506 (p. 183).

[44] Gk *dusodia*, a harsh term meaning 'stench, foulness, or filthiness', associated with demonic possession in *Life of Antony* 63 and with heresy in the *Life of Pachomius*. *Dusodia* is clearly being contrasted here with *euodia*, 'fragrance', which is what would attract the monk. But this fragrance, the elder is saying, is a deception of the Devil; it is in actuality stench. See B. Caseau, *Euodia: The Use and Meaning of Fragrances in the Ancient World and their Christianization (100–900)* (Ann Arbor: University of Michigan Press, 1994), and Susan Ashbrook Harvey, 'On Holy Stench: When the Odor of Sanctity Sickens', *Studia Patristica* 35, ed. M. F. Wiles and E. J. Yarnold (Leuven: Peeters, 2001) 90–101.

[45] Saying 24 is included in N 506 of Regnault's collection (p. 183).

[46] Gk *katalalias*, which was translated as 'slander' in Saying 12 above.

[47] Saying 25 is included in N 506 in Regnault's collection (p. 183).

[48] Saying 26 occurs as part of N 506 in Regnault's collection (p. 183).

[49] A concise answer to a sometimes vexing problem. See Tim Vivian '"Everything Made by God is Good": A Letter concerning Sexuality from Saint Athanasius to the Monk Amoun', *Église et Théologie* 24 (1993) 75–108.

[50] Gk *charisma*.

[51] Saying 28 occurs as N 636 in Regnault's collection (p. 276).

[52] Literally, 'for man'.

[53] Or 'worship before God'.

[54] Saying 30 is included in N 507 in Regnault's collection (p. 184), without, however, the final clause including the quotation from Isaiah.

[55] See Alphabetical Apophthegmata Antony 9. Saying 31 is found as N 508 in Regnault's collection (p. 194), without, however, the last sentence including the quotation from Matthew.

Part One

Journeys

In memoriam
Bastiaan Van Elderen

2

The Monasteries of the Wadi al-Natrun, Egypt: A Monastic and Personal Journey

IN JANUARY AND FEBRUARY 1996 I had the great good fortune of joining the team of american archeologists, faculty, and students who went to the Wadi al-Natrun, Egypt.[1] We were there to excavate the Monastery of Saint John the Little and to study at first-hand coptic monasticism and Church history.[2] Since I am a patristics scholar and have been writing about early monasticism since my graduation from seminary in 1988, for me this trip was a personal monastic journey: an exciting chance to experience in the desert what I had learned from books, an opportunity to participate in the history and spirituality of egyptian monasticism. In this chapter I combine historical research, on-site reporting, and personal reflection to suggest the historical importance and spiritual relevance of coptic monasticism for those of us in the West.

I. BACKGROUND:
A BRIEF HISTORY OF MONASTICISM IN THE WADI AL-NATRUN

Widespread monasticism in lower (northern) Egypt in the fourth century may have had its origins, oddly enough, in two unconsummated marriages. Around 313, shortly after Constantine had brought an end to state persecution of Christians and ushered in 'the peace of the Church', a young Christian named Amoun, living in the Nile delta, was forced by his uncle to marry. On his wedding night, however, he persuaded his new wife that they ought to live together, not as husband and wife, but as brother and sister, devoting themselves to the Lord. She agreed, and they lived this way for eighteen years before he was called to the solitary life of a monk. Around 330, he left his home and 'went to the inner mountain of Nitria', forty miles south of Alexandria and west of the delta, 'built himself two rounded cells and lived another twenty-two years in the desert'.[3] Attracted to his way of life, disciples soon joined Amoun, and monasticism began to flourish in Nitria. Within ten years, Nitria had become too crowded for Amoun, so he and Saint Antony together founded Kellia, the Cells, about 10-12 miles south of Nitria.[4] Later monastic tradition remembered Amoun of Nitria with such reverence that Antony 'saw his soul borne up to heaven by angels'.[5]

A shotgun 'wedding', tradition says, brought Saint Macarius the Great to the desert of Scetis (Wadi al-Natrun), forty miles south of Nitria, about the same time as Amoun was establishing desert monasticism to the north. In one of the most delightful stories from the *Apophthegmata (Sayings of the Desert Fathers)*, Macarius offers an autobiographical sketch of his early monastic life: Already a monk, he fled to an unnamed village in order to avoid ordination. A young girl in the village became pregnant and, when she was asked 'who was to blame', identified 'the anchorite'—Macarius—as the father. Then, Macarius narrates,

they came to seize me, led me to the village and hung
pots black with soot and various other things round
my neck and led me through the village in all directions, beating me and saying, 'This monk has defiled our
virgin, catch him, catch him', and they beat me almost
to death.

The girl's parents insist that Macarius 'keep' her, which he does:
'Going to my cell, I gave [my servant] all the baskets I had, saying,
"Sell them, and give my wife something to eat"'. When the time
comes for Macarius' 'wife' to deliver, she is unable to give birth until
finally she confesses that she has lied and that Macarius is not the
father. When the villagers hear this they repent, and they want to
come to Macarius 'and do penance'. But, as Macarius concludes
the story, 'when I heard this, for fear people would disturb me,
I got up and fled here to Scetis'.[6]

Both these stories are inherently plausible. The action of Amoun
and his wife, vowing themselves to virginity, would not have been
unfamiliar in the early fourth century. Macarius flees ordination, a
not uncommon act of monastic protest. The story of Macarius'
'wife' seems to acknowledge that such false accusations were not
unknown in the villages of Egypt.[7] Both stories, in fact, are very
human and very monastic: they show persons caught up in the
world who wish to flee worldly ways for the silence and solitude
of the desert.

The monastic historian Palladius says that when Amoun went
to Nitria, 'there were no monasteries there as yet', which may be
true, though both the phrase and the idea are similar to sentiments expressed about Saint Antony in the *Life of Antony*.[8] One of
the purposes of the *Life of Antony*, in fact, was to make Antony the
'father' of egyptian monasticism; yet even so, the *Life* acknowledges
that before Antony there were monks and 'monasteries'—not
monasteries in the later and modern sense, but rather cells, or
small groups of monastics living together (see *Life* 3–4). With regard
to Nitria and Scetis, the same may have been true of Amoun and
Macarius: isolated solitaries may have already been living in the
desert west of the Nile delta, but Amoun and Macarius were
remembered as the founders of an enduring monasticism in these
areas.

By 330 Egypt was becoming recognizably monastic. Antony had been a monk for some forty-five years and around 313 had moved to his interior mountain by the Red Sea. Around 320 Pachomius founded the first community of his *koinonia* at Tabennisi in Upper (southern) Egypt. In 328 Athanasius became bishop of Alexandria, and by 330 was visiting the monks in the Thebaid; thus by 330 the alliance between the episcopate of Alexandria and the monks of Egypt was already being formed.[9] It is an alliance that continues to this day. The present leader of the Coptic Orthodox Church, His Holiness Pope Shenouda III, is a monk and takes his papal name from one of the most famous monks of Egypt, Saint Shenoute the Great (385–465). The pope spends part of each week in Cairo and Alexandria and part at the patriarchal compound at the monastery of Saint Bishoi, one of four active monasteries in the Wadi al-Natrun.

The Wadi al-Natrun, then, has been the site of continuous monastic life for over sixteen hundred years. Its ancient name, Scetis, comes from the Coptic *shi hêt*, 'to weigh the heart', a most appropriate name for a place long dedicated to silence, prayer, and contemplation.[10] The Wadi itself is a well-watered strip of oases about twenty to twenty-five miles long that runs in a northwesterly direction. Its southeast end is about forty miles northwest of Cairo,[11] making it neighbor to one of the largest cities in the world. Writing some thirty years ago, Derwas Chitty described Nitria as

> the gateway of the Egyptian desert. Scetis is its citadel, with a stark abased remoteness (three of its surviving monasteries are set below sea-level) that even a motor-road from Alexandria to Cairo passing within sight along the low scarp to the north cannot really destroy.[12]

The Wadi is not as remote now as when Chitty wrote: you can travel there by car from Cairo in one and a half to two hours, and freeway signs in Arabic and English point the way to the monasteries. Modern irrigation has made the desert alongside the road green; the freeway has become a kind of asphalt Nile. Green fields, speeding cars and trucks—and billboards, those ubiquitous signs of the modern—all conspire to take away remoteness.

And yet the Wadi al-Natrun is nearly as far off the beaten path today as it was in antiquity, though for different reasons. The author of the *Historia Monachorum* reports that in 394 his group of spiritual tourists traveled down the Nile to Nitria but did not go to Scetis because the desert route was too dangerous.[13] Modern tourists skip the Wadi al-Natrun, not because of danger, but because they are more interested in King Tut than in coptic monasteries.[14] As in the fourth century, however, there are still pilgrims. On Fridays through Sundays, especially before Lent, busloads of Copts—men, women, and numerous children—come to visit the monasteries, considered some of the holiest sites of the Coptic Church. These latter-day pilgrims, thousands of them, connect the present to the past and the past to the present; their presence and devotion provide convincing and powerful testimony to the continuing vital heritage of monasticism in Egypt.[15]

At the Syrian Monastery, just a short walk west of the monastery of Saint Bishoi, stands Saint Ephraem's tree. According to coptic tradition, when Saint Ephraem (308–373) came to the Wadi al-Natrun from Syria, he planted his staff in the ground; because of God's grace, it budded and grew into a tamarind tree, which, sixteen hundred years later, still graces the courtyard of the monastery.[16] That tree both symbolizes and actualizes the deep roots of monasticism in the Coptic Church: growing out of the desert sand, its green branches represent God's nurturing care for the monks over the centuries through straitened circumstances. At the Syrian Monastery, a room has been built around Saint Ephraem's tree. Once housing a printing press, it now houses the monastery's museum, and every afternoon the monks meet under the tree to say vespers.[17]

To the monks, Ephraem's tree, with its roots literally in the fourth century, is a living reminder—as are their liturgy, monastic offices, and ancient buildings—of the history of monasticism in the Wadi al-Natrun. To the monks, that history probably appears more linear and continuous than it does to the western historian or the archeologist or other non-monastic looking on. To an outsider the history of monasticism in the Wadi al-Natrun seems above all precarious—and tenacious, like a tree in desert soil.[18] Monasticism's survival here, as one monk has said about the revival of the monastery of Saint Macarius, is impossible according to the will of man, possible only by the grace of God.

By the end of the fourth century, a mere fifty years after Amoun and Macarius had gone out into the desert, Nitria is said to have had as many as three – five thousand monks.[19] More important than numbers is the spiritual tradition the monks bequeathed, a tradition that was profoundly to affect all of Christendom. The early fruits of this tradition can best be seen in *The Sayings of the Desert Fathers*, which probably had their origins in Scetis.[20] Originally written in Greek and translated into Latin, Coptic, and Syriac, then Armenian, Georgian, Arabic, Ethiopic, and Old Slavonic, the *Sayings* deeply influenced both eastern and western spirituality.

As auspicious as were the beginnings of monastic life in Nitria, Kellia, and Scetis, the first full flowering of monasticism lasted only a hundred years before two disasters shook the three settlements. The very vitality of the tradition created internal tensions that by the end of the fourth century began to fracture monasticism, making it a house divided against itself. Shortly afterwards external forces attacked. The internal destruction came at the very end of the fourth century because of theological conflicts over Anthropomorphism and Origenism; the external devastation came shortly afterwards at the hands of barbarian raiders at the beginning of the fifth century.

Apparently there had long been tensions between the educated greek-speaking monks and their simpler coptic brethren. The Greeks (with Evagrius of Pontus as their spiritual leader) tended to follow the thinking of the great exegete and theologian Origen of Alexandria († 254) and read much of the Bible figuratively and allegorically. The Copts tended to be more literal in reading Scripture.[21] Theophilus, bishop of Alexandria, in his Easter Letter of 399 condemned the more literal interpretation, censuring it for what came to be called anthropomorphism, an understanding of God as having human speech, emotions, and parts. Many of the monks of Nitria and Kellia applauded this decision, but according to John Cassian it 'was received with such great bitterness by nearly all the various sorts of monks who were living throughout the province of Egypt'.[22] At Scetis only one of the four congregations would allow the letter to be read. One old monk, on hearing the condemnation of anthropomorphism, reportedly cried out, 'Woe is me, wretch that I am! They have taken my God from me, and I have no one to lay hold of, nor do I know whom I should adore or address'.[23]

The Church historian Socrates reports that as a result of Theophilus' Easter Letter, the monks 'left their monasteries and came to Alexandria, where they raised a tumult against the bishop, accusing him of impiety and threatening to put him to death'.[24] As a result, Theophilus did an abrupt about-face and condemned Origenism. Some three hundred monks, including four learned and famous monks known as the Tall Brothers, then fled Nitria for Palestine and Constantinople, where they embroiled the beleagured bishop, John Chrysostom, in further conflicts.[25] How many returned is unknown.[26]

Nitria, Kellia, and Scetis, though damaged, would have survived such turmoil (especially Scetis, which was less affected by the origenist exodus),[27] but just a few years later, in 407 or 408, the Mazices, berber invaders from the western desert, devastated Scetis.[28] Three years later, in 410, the year of Alaric's sack of Rome, invaders struck again. In one of the more poignant exclamations in Church history, one monk reportedly cried out, 'The world has lost Rome; the monks Scetis'. A third sack occurred in 434. Each time the monks returned and rebuilt, at least to some extent, and, by the beginning of the fifth century, they started to add fortifications. But Scetis had lost many of its most eminent monks: Moses the Black and seven companions were slain;[29] John the Little and Bishoi, founders of two monasteries in Scetis, fled and soon died in exile.[30] Destruction and rebuilding recurred over and over again at the monasteries down through their later history.[31] After the muslim conquest of Egypt in 641, persecution *de jure* and usually, though not always, *de facto* replaced outright destruction, and the fortunes of the four surviving monasteries of the Wadi al-Natrun have ebbed and flowed until their current revitalization.[32]

II. FOREGROUND: MONASTERIES ANCIENT AND MODERN[33]

Today there are again four flourishing monasteries in the Wadi al-Natrun: Deir Anbâ Bishoi (the Monastery of Saint Bishoi), Deir al-Barâmûs (Baramus; from the Coptic *Pa Romeos*, 'the [Monastery] of the Romans'), Deir el-Souriani (the Monastery of the Holy Virgin and Saint John Kame; the Syrian Monastery), and Deir Abû Maqâr (the Monastery of Saint Macarius).[34] Of these four monasteries, three—Bishoi, Baramus, and Macarius—go back to the fourth century, but not in their present form and location. The Syrian Monastery, the result of a schism at Bishoi, dates to the sixth century or later.[35] Each preserves traditions connecting it to the beginnings of monasticism in the Wadi al-Natrun.

Saint Macarius may have first settled at the western end of the Wadi, near Baramus, and later moved near the monastery that now bears his name.[36] When John Cassian visited Scetis at the end of the fourth century, there were four *ecclesiae* or 'congregations':[37] Saint Macarius, the Monastery of the Romans, Saint Bishoi, and the Monastery of Saint John the Little, which was apparently abandoned in the fifteenth century.[38] In the middle of the fourth century, Athanasius proclaimed, a bit hyperbolically and proleptically, that the desert was becoming a city.[39] What he intended by that metaphor, it seems, was to picture the large, the unprecedented, number of people who were populating the desert.[40] But it is not an image a monk would have readily used; the monks were leaving their towns and cities! And, significantly, the coptic version of the *Life of Antony* drops the metaphor.[41] This tension still characterizes modern coptic monasticism. In one sense, the monasteries of the Wadi al-Natrun *are* cities. The majority of the monks are highly educated and trained in many of the arts and trades of the modern city.[42] At the same time, the monasteries are cities hidden behind high walls, and the casual bypasser would not know there are cities within. Originally erected to keep out invaders, the walls now symbolize a determined resistance to invasions against the spirit. The city is not far away. To get to the Wadi al-Natrun, you have to pass through Cairo. After you experience the noise, pollution, and crush of this megalopolis, you immediately see that the desert monasteries are not cities at all! Seen from this perspective, they preserve the ancient monastic protest against the city.

Yet a modern Athanasius would be firmly justified in his enthusiasm for the revival of monasticism in Egypt. Thirty or forty years ago, coptic monasticism was in serious decline, with falling numbers, an aging population, and decrepit buildings. In 1960, nine major monasteries numbered two hundred monks; in 1986, that number had risen to six hundred, a three-fold increase.[43] In addition, in Upper Egypt two new monasteries have been officially recognized by the Church, and 'formerly abandoned monasteries . . . have been repeopled with monks'.[44] In the last twenty-five years, all the monasteries of the Wadi al-Natrun have undertaken large-scale building projects (often made difficult by the government), including large, new dormitories for the increased number of monks.

More importantly, largely through the leadership of Pope Shenouda III, the monasteries have built new retreat centers and implemented evangelical programs.[45] With the increased numbers of monks, a renewed spirit, and—not unimportant—improved roadways linking the monasteries with cities and towns, the monasteries have gone from a position of mere survival to one of active participation in the Coptic Church as a whole: 'the desert monasteries are woven into the fabric of the parish churches of the cities, towns, and villages'.[46]

What are the reasons for this renaissance? Many westerners offer economic explanations for the increased number of monastic vocations—the worsening economy in Egypt and the rise of muslim fundamentalism. Since all new monastic applicants must have college degrees, however, these are individuals with good prospects for jobs and the things good jobs can buy. Yet they exchange these worldly goods for celibacy, poverty, and labor.[47] One very important factor in the revival of monasticism is the intimate relationship in Egypt between monasticism and the parish. Monastic saints and ideals are spoken of in all aspects of the Church's teaching; whatever the topic, a monastic reference will inevitably be made. The monastic fathers are mentioned, prominently, in every liturgy; the long office is dominated by monks. In the Coptic Church, encountering a monk is commonplace; he is as near as the next sermon, the next liturgy, or the next book that a friend recommends. The revival of coptic monasticism is part of an overall revival of the Coptic Church; at the same time, however, the revival must be seen as the germination of a seed ever latent within the Coptic Church.[48] The Coptic Church, like the celtic irish Church of Saint Patrick, is ascetic and monastic.

If you stand on the roof of the retreat center adjoining Saint Bishoi, where our group stayed, and look in each direction, you can see in a series of snapshots, as it were, the external features of this monastic renaissance. All around is desert: 'On every Egyptian [the desert] continually imposes its presence. It is at his doorway, at the end of his field, his view, his life'.[49] But in the midst of desolation is the monastic garden.[50] In the distance to the west, toward the sunset, is the Syrian Monastery. In the foreground, the small 'city' of Saint Bishoi spreads out before you. To the west is its imposing cathedral. To the northwest is the monastery proper, with its high walls, towers, domes, and palm trees. South of—and therefore outside—the main monastery lie the agricultural and industrial areas, complete with automotive garage; toward dusk each day you can watch the tractors returning from the fields. Further south is the patriarchal compound where the pope lives. To its west is a large new building of cells as imposing as a hotel. To the north and south of our retreat center are orchards: olive, tangerine, apricot, grapefruit, and grape. In the west and south you can see small retreat cells for the monks, some in an orchard, others just beyond it in the desert. In the distance to the southeast, barely perceptible, is a marker for the abandoned monastery of Saint John the Little. When you take the road south past the modern monastery to the ancient monastery of Saint John, you see more hermits' cells out in the desert, just off the roadway; each has a little wall, and some have trees and a garden (see below for a description of a visit with a hermit). I saw one hermitage with solar heating panels on the roof.[51]

As striking as all this is, it is the Monastery of Saint Macarius that most impressively captures the remarkable revival of the monasteries of the Wadi al-Natrun. I told the students at our dig that I could think of no monastic parallel of physical and spiritual renaissance since Cluny at its height and the cistercian renewal of the late eleventh and twelfth centuries.[52] In 1969, Saint Macarius had five 'old and sick' monks, as our guide, Fr Philemmon, told us; today it has one hundred twenty, and seven hundred agricultural and industrial workers on 12,500 square meters of land. Macarius reportedly supplies the five-star hotels of Alexandria and Cairo with their produce, and the monks have brought in pedigreed cattle from Germany; Baramus will soon have the largest olive press in Egypt.

But these are recent developments. In the late '60s 'all the historical buildings' at Saint Macarius 'were close to collapse and ruin', and had to be restored and rebuilt.[53] Today at Macarius there are new churches, cells for the monks, guest quarters, an infirmary,[54] refectory, library, printing offices, farm buildings, and dormitories for industrial and agricultural workers. Fr Philemmon told us that now that he is too old for physical labor, his work is to translate, mostly from English into Arabic. He proudly showed us the library which, in addition to housing ancient manuscripts in Coptic and Arabic, has extensive holdings of western books, including the Patrologia Graeca and Sources chrétiennes series; the monastery also subscribes to several foreign-language journals. In fact, the library symbolizes, and has contributed to, the spiritual and monastic revival in Egypt. Almost all of the best spiritual writing in Egypt today is by monastics, including numerous books and pamphlets by the pope.[55]

What most impresses the visitor about all this new building is how well it harmonizes with the ancient structures. The new buildings are not merely nostalgic and slavish imitations of the old—they are clearly modern. A new bell tower at Macarius shows the monks' practical genius: it doubles as a water tank! The buildings typify monastic humility: they do not impose themselves; rather, they blend together the new and the old: tradition at its best. The ancient archway at Saint Macarius, now reinforced and restored, exemplifies the valuing and preservation of tradition made new. When you enter the monastery and cross the courtyard down the steps toward the three main churches of the monastery, you step down under an ancient arch, the northern entrance to the monastery before the ninth century, and into a corridor canopied by trees. The original arch is made of fired red brick, the same plentiful and inexpensive brick you see today at the entrance to the Syrian Monastery and in the ruined walls of the Monastery of Saint John the Little. As Fr Matta el-Meskeen describes it:

> This arch was discovered while removing layers of the enclosure wall whose construction and heightening around the church began in the fourteenth century. Other outer layers had been added in modern times to reinforce the dilapidated walls, and it took us six months to tighten up the ruined arch with a reinforced concrete layer from top to bottom, and to support its flanks with concrete pedestals, beams, and stone blocks—so as to keep it in balance after uncovering it on all sides and removing the masonry which had been built within the archway.

> Archaeologists and architects are amazed that this arch stood fast, not surrendering to our tampering—despite its ruinous state, and that we have been able to anchor it as tightly as we have: this was a feat of construction made possible only through prayers for Divine assistance.[56]

The arch at Saint Macarius literally represents the old embedded in the new; the great genius of modern coptic monasticism is its synthetic theological and practical imagination. How many of us would patiently labor six months to keep an old brick arch alive while we built a new entryway over and around it! For the Copts, these bricks are not just bricks—they are spiritual reminders of their past, and the foundation of their present and future. At Macarius, a small museum displays a row of fine marble columns taken from the ancient church during restoration work. Fr Matta illustrates the synthetic understanding of the monks by entitling the final chapter in his little book on the monastery 'The Architectural and Spiritual Revival since 1969'.[57] Architecture and spirituality inform one another just as the bricks of the old archway help create the new.[58]

The place of the monastic cell, that most basic architectural element of monasticism, in the modern monasteries of the Wadi al-Natrun perfectly illustrates this understanding. Each of the monasteries in the Wadi has large new dormitories for the monks' cells, but they have been built with a very clear eye on the past and a solid understanding of the contemplative life:

> In the design of the cell we have kept in mind the principle of seclusion, which is a characteristic of Coptic monasticism. It is arranged in such a way that the monk may stay alone for many days with no need at all to leave the cell. It is provided with sufficient windows to admit fresh air, sunshine, and light, has a bathroom connected with a main sewage system, a separate kitchen, a small room—'a closet'—with a wooden floor on which a monk may sleep with no danger to his health, no matter how thin he may be, and a room for study and keeping vigil with a desk and wall cupboards. In

order to ensure the necessary quietness, care was taken that each cell should be completely separate from the neighbouring cells, having a spacious veranda on one side and a staircase leading to the upper floors on the other. The roofs have been made thick, giving almost double the usual amount of sound insulation, and most of the furniture used is fixed to avoid noise.[59]

    This description, with a few strategic changes, could belong in a brochure for a five-star hotel room in Alexandria—except for one thing: the monk's cell is designed for prayer. The cell follows a very ancient monastic pattern, allowing for two rooms (the addition of a kitchen does modify the ancient pattern). At the Syrian Monastery, the new cells for the monks—in a spacious and æsthetically-pleasing two-storey building west of the church—face, across a garden, several restored cells dating back to the seventh century that now make up part of the monastery's museum. These ancient cells do not have the 'fresh air, sunshine, and light' of the modern ones but, like the modern cells, they do have two rooms: an anteroom for work, and an inner chamber for prayer and sleep. The monastery has kept these ancient cells—in use until about thirty years ago—as they were centuries ago. The anteroom has the monk's work implements: palm fronds for weaving baskets, tools, and a leather apron. The back room has a simple mat on the floor and niches in the walls to hold icons, candles, and books. Much has changed in coptic monasticism in thirteen hundred years, but the most basic element has not: the cell is the center of monastic life, and it, like the life, was and is designed for quiet and prayer.

    For the ancient monks, the desert was a cell, so they lived in a cell within a cell,[60] quiet within contemplative quiet. As I mentioned earlier, monasticism in the Wadi al-Natrun was originally anchoritic or semi-anchoritic; each monk lived alone in a cell, often within proximity of other monks in their cells, and not in large cenobia or monasteries as developed later and exist today. Today, a coptic monk may move to a hermitage after living a long time in the cenobium; one monk at Saint Bishoi was preparing to become an anchorite after eight years of living in community. Two members of our group were granted permission to visit a solitary. One of them reported:

From the first five minutes with the hermit it was obvious that I was in the presence of a monk. Not a bearded man wearing a black garment, but a *monk*. There was a gentle grace about him that is very difficult to explain. He was at peace. He was 'other worldly' in the best possible sense. He was a living Saying of the Fathers. As we continued to question him, we asked him about 'the attacks or dangers a hermit encounters'. We were thinking of snakes and scorpions; the hermit, however, talked not of snakes and scorpions but of the attacks of the Devil, both mental and physical, and of apparitions. Then he realized what he was saying, and quickly, even abruptly, changed the course of our conversation: the monks understand that these temptations are not to be shared with the general public. It's one thing for a monk of a monastery to tell how Saint Antony was tempted, but it is quite another for the one who has been tempted in the same way as Antony to share his story with anyone other than his father confessor.

For the length of those few short sentences, when the hermit was talking about the attacks of the Devil, I felt as if I were back in the fourth century, where demonic warfare was understood to be real—not a mental battle between virtue and vice, but a true battle in which blows are exchanged. . . . Was the hermit speaking of himself? I believe that he certainly was. He was not speaking like a military historian, but like a soldier. . . . Is he crazy? No. The man sitting before me was definitely sane. Is he lying? No, for the man before me was one in whom there is no guile.[61]

The hermit, though alone, is still very much part of the monastic and ecclesiastical community. Monasteries, like houses, have individual and communal space. The cell is the personal center of a coptic monastery, while the church (or churches) provides the communal center. And always located close to the church is the ancient keep *(qasr)*, or tower, the monastery's self-contained fortress in times of invasion. The juxtaposition of the church and the keep is striking. Both provide sanctuary: the church, a communal sanctuary of spiritual calm, prayer, and worship; the keep, sanctuary for the community in time of danger. The keep is a powerful reminder of the precariousness of monasticism—and Christianity—in Egypt.

Before you enter a church—or a mosque—in Egypt, you take off your shoes, because you are about to step on holy ground. When you enter a monastic church, you smell the incense as you feel the coolness of the air and as your eyes adjust to the darkened interior. What struck me most about the monastery churches was how *palpable* everything is: icons are to be touched because they embody the holy (the worshiper touches the icon, then kisses his or her fingers). So too are reliquaries (each church conspicuously contains relics) and even the door which screens off the sanctuary where the priests celebrate the Holy Eucharist from the rest of the church. In one church, a newly discovered ancient wall painting has been placed in the church where, shielded by plexiglass, it can still be 'touched' by the faithful. In the Church of the Virgin at the Syrian Monastery, a team from France, while cleaning and restoring the painting of the Ascension above the entrance to Saint Bishoi's hermitage in 1991, discovered beneath it a brilliantly-colored ninth-century wall painting of the Annunciation. This painting was somehow taken down and placed in a corner of the church near the apse, where it is protected by a wooden grille, inside of which visitors can see slips of paper dropped in by the faithful with petitions for the Mother of God.

Coptic spirituality is not abstract. Just as it is physical, it is also intensely symbolic and mythological (I am using 'myth', not in the secular sense of a falsehood, but rather in the sense of a sustaining and foundational religious story). At the Syrian Monastery, our guide lovingly explained the rich symbolism of the sanctuary door and of the ostrich eggs that hang, suspended from the ceiling in long bronze holders, just above worshippers' heads. The sanctuary screen, known as the 'Door of Symbols' (there are two doors, really), dates to the tenth century. It consists of six leaves, three on each side; 'each leaf has seven panels of ebony magnificently inlaid with ivory'.[62] The seven leaves from top to bottom illustrate the seven epochs of the christian era. The door also contains numerous crosses and other symbols, including the swastika which, our guide said, expresses the spread of heresies. A cross encircled by a crescent symbolizes the appearance of Islam.[63] The ostrich egg symbolizes both the human person and the soul. The ostrich lays the egg and buries it in the sand; like the ostrich, God watches the human being, whom God has placed in the world, for signs that he or she is ready to hatch, or to go to heaven. The person 'hatches' when the soul has developed and is ready to shed its shell, the body, when it is ready to die to this life. The egg may also represent the world, which God watches for indications that it is ready for atonement.

'Symbol' is not an adequate term for these stories; they are beliefs, they are actualities. Perhaps 'lived symbol' can approach their real meaning. For example, the monks believe that their monasteries are in the shape of an ark and represent Noah's salvific craft; they are, then, both metaphorically and eschatalogically, riding out the storms of a drowning world on the way to salvation.[64] Each monastery is steeped in myth, with stories of its eponymous founder or founders. Saint Ephraem's tree, mentioned earlier, offers a good example,[65] and there are many others. When Christ one time passed by the cell of Saint Bishoi, the saint washed his Master's feet. Another time, Saint Bishoi carried an old man whom the monks found alongside the road and whom other monks had passed by; the old man was Christ.[66] The Mother of God visited Saint John Kame.[67] The western visitor, university-trained and saturated with secular culture, has an instinctive desire, even if he or she is a Christian, to separate 'fact' and 'myth' (in its pejorative sense), but Otto Meinardus, probably the westerner best informed about coptic monasticism, offers this salutary reminder:

> Historical writings describe events which others remember and project upon paper. Therefore, it is always difficult to distinguish later between projected memory and projected imagination, realizing that imagination is one of the creative aspects of our mind. I do not claim to be the judge to determine where actual history ends and imagination commences. This every reader will have to do for him- or herself.[68]

Tradition and history blend together in the story of the keep at the Syrian Monastery, unfortunately closed during our visit.

According to tradition, the keep was built in the fifth century by Emperor Zeno (450–491), whose daughter, Saint Hilaria, lived as a monk at Scetis under the name Hilarion.[69] Scholars regard the story of Hilaria as apocryphal, but the story fits the current understanding of when keeps came into existence.[70] Early monasticism in the Wadi al-Natrun was anchoritic (solitary) or semi-anchoritic (an abba and his disciples). After the destructions of the early fifth century, the monks gradually became more cloistered or cenobitic, not out of any monastic theory, but by necessity. Keeps apparently appeared in the fifth century, and thick, high defensive walls in the ninth century.[71] Perhaps history, legend, myth, and tradition are not the easily compartmentalized catagories we in the West think they are.[72] A poet may have greater insight into these stories than the historian. As Kathleen Norris has recently commented in *The Cloister Walk*:

> To appreciate the relevance of [hagiographical stories] for our own time, we need to ask not whether or not the saint existed but why it might have been necessary to invent her; we need not get hung up on determining to what extent her story has been embellished by hagiographers but rather ask why the stories were so popular in the early church, and also what we have lost in dismissing them.[73]

The keep at each monastery in the Wadi al-Natrun is 'one of the oldest monuments in the monastery, and the most imposing'.[74] All the keeps have undergone extensive recent restoration; when we visited Baramus, we got a guided tour of the keep and saw the restoration in progress; the ancient wooden door had big wooden nails in it just like the ancient ones we were finding in the ruins at the monastery of Saint John the Little. The keep is a self-contained monastery, contracted to a defensible space. At the Syrian Monastery the keep is 13 x 14 meters, and 18 meters high.[75] At Saint Macarius, the keep

> has a ground floor and two upper floors, and is separated from the stairs leading to it by the narrow drawbridge which could be raised after the monks had taken refuge in it. The ground floor consists of spacious

vaulted rooms which were used for storage. At the northern extremity is a wall from which the monks could draw water during a raid. The first storey consists of two parts: the eastern section forms the Chapel of the Holy Virgin Mary, which has three altars; . . . in the western portion there are rooms used in late periods for pressing wine and olive oil. [The keep at Saint Bishoi also has a bakery; undoubtedly, they all did.] A trapdoor in the floor of this southern room led to an oubliette for manuscripts.

The second storey at Saint Macarius contains churches dedicated to Saint Michael, guardian of keeps, Saint Paul the Hermit, and Saint Antony (with a fine, but faded, icon of these saints), and a church dedicated to 'the Pilgrims or Wanderers (al-Suwah) who were staunch defenders of the faith in times of tribulation and persecution'. The roof of the keep served as a watchtower,

where a sharp-eyed monk . . . watched day and night and, in cases of threatening danger, rang the alarm. In the early centuries, this was a huge slab of hard wood, beaten with a hammer to resound throughout the desert, for originally the function of the alarm was to call the solitaries living in distant places, or to warn them against danger.[76]

At Saint Macarius, a wooden drawbridge, about thirty feet high, connects the keep with an entry tower. In times of danger, as when the monasteries were threatened by marauding tribes of Berbers from the desert, the bridge could be quickly withdrawn behind the monks as they fled into the keep. What is impressive about the monks who built these keeps and fortress-like monasteries is that they did not forget their obligations to others; in protecting themselves, they did not lose sight of monastic—gospel—hospitality. Each monastery has a *matama*, or 'feeding place', a hole from which the gatekeeper could look out when someone below at the entrance to the monastery rang a bell. Without opening the gate, the gatekeeper could lower bread to those asking for it, often non-christian Bedouins.[77]

The dangers facing the monks now have apparently changed. The monasteries no longer face 'barbarian' invasions; 'today', Father Philemmon at Saint Macarius told us, 'the Berbers are in the heart'. This insight deepens as one reflects on the history of monasticism in Lower Egypt: Saint Antony and the early monks confronted both the demons of the desert and the demons of the human heart. And the monks know just how destructive marauders can be. Father Philemmon's metaphor has a history, and that history is bloody: the Wadi al-Natrun was devastated, almost wiped out, in the fifth century by invaders from the desert; Abba Moses and seven companions chose not to flee and were murdered.[78] Since the muslim conquest, the monks, like the Coptic Church, have been sporadically persecuted. In Egypt, however, you wonder if the dangers facing the monks are only interior and spiritual: the Copts are still a persecuted minority, and there are, sadly, still martyrs in the Coptic Church.[79] An abandoned mosque less than a hundred yards from the front entrance to Bishoi bears eloquent witness to modern attempts at intimidation and acts of violence by muslim extremists are on the rise.[80] Not long ago, Anwar Sadat, the late president of Egypt, subjected Pope Shenouda to house arrest at the monastery of Saint Bishoi and had the monastery surrounded by tanks and soldiers.[81] Recently, muslim fundamentalists attempted to assassinate Bishop Samuel, one of the most respected bishops in the Coptic Church. The images should startle us: assassins shooting at bishops, tanks beseiging monasteries. Egypt is a country where the religion of each citizen is stamped on his or her identification card, and where Copts make up less than ten percent of the population[82] and are systematically excluded from many professions. We in the West need to remember that if these monastery keeps are now symbolic, it is a heavy-hearted symbolism.[83]

The purpose of the monastic life, whether the monks are oppressed or living in peace, is to enable Christians to live a life of prayer in union with God; that goal, and the way of life needed to accomplish it, has not changed in sixteen hundred years. The booklet that the Syrian Monastery provides for visitors summarizes very simply the requirements of the monastic way of life by including a list entitled 'How Monks Live': every monk occupies a private cell with two rooms; monks usually eat alone in their cells;[84] monks 'enjoy periods of hermitage' in cells in the orchard or out in the desert; each monk has his daily work; the monks meet together twice a day for prayer: at dawn, followed by the Mass, and at sunset.[85] As Abba Poemen of Scetis summarized it sixteen hundred years ago:

> A brother asked Abba Poemen, 'How should I live in the cell?' He said to him, 'Living in your cell clearly means manual work, eating only once a day,[86] silence, meditation; but really making progress in the cell means to experience contempt for yourself wherever you go,[87] not to neglect the hours of prayer and to pray secretly. If you happen to have time without manual work, take up prayer and do it without disquiet. The perfection of these things is to live in good company and be free from bad'.[88]

III. A Monastic Journey

My journey to the Wadi al-Natrun was the momentary culmination of a longer, increasingly monastic, personal journey. Most journeys, even if carefully mapped out beforehand, rarely turn out exactly as planned. In my experience, this is especially true of spiritual journeys—in fact, our spiritual journeys *never* proceed exactly as we think they're going to. I managed to get a Ph.D. in patristics and graduate from seminary without taking any interest in monasticism. Truth be told, I realized in seminary that I had come to study for Holy Orders without really knowing much about spirituality or having much sense of my own spiritual direction. I was fortunate that others could discern something of a direction! In what turned out to be a gift from God, the best course I had in seminary was one for which my school would not give credit: an informal class in the practice of the classic forms of christian meditation, taught by a husband and wife team of fellow seminarians. We met weekly, seminarians and spouses, in the basement of the school's guest hall: we prayed, meditated, and began learning to enter that silence where God meets us most fully.

That 'course' must have planted seeds of contemplation, but when I graduated from seminary in 1988 the seeds were still patiently waiting in the earth. As seminary drew to a close, neither my wife nor I had been able to find a full-time university teaching position (I was not looking for parish ministry), so I applied for, and received, a two-year post-doctorate fellowship at Yale Divinity School. The terms of the fellowship required each fellow to have a research project, so I dutifully concocted one. It promptly fell through when I discovered that another scholar was already working on it. I impatiently looked for a topic and in the meantime began reading E. A. Wallis Budge's *Coptic Texts* in order to keep up the Coptic I had learned in graduate school. One day I came across the story of Abba Pambo, a coptic monk who journeys across the desert in search of both himself and God. That story was a revelation. In typical academic fashion, I first saw Abba Pambo and early monasticism as a research topic, but soon I realized that these ancient monastic stories were speaking to heart and soul, and I began searching them out and hungrily devouring them.[89]

As the seeds planted in seminary began to take root and put forth new growth, other seeds long in the ground also burst forth. Before I went to seminary, my parish priest had taught a course on *New Seeds of Contemplation* by Thomas Merton; now I eagerly sought out and read everything I could by Merton (and I still do). And I realized that monastic spirituality spoke more deeply and truthfully to me than anything else, secular or sacred. My translation of Abba Pambo turned out to be my first monastic publication, and I dedicated my first book of monastic studies to Merton. Willy-nilly, at least on my part, God was making me—a secular priest, married, with a one-year old child—a monastic-in-spirit.[90]

So, eight years later (with three children now), it was with great excitement that I anticipated going to Egypt for the first time. Not only was I going to study and teach early monasticism, not only was I going to participate in an archeological dig of an ancient monastic site, but I was going to live at a coptic monastery and for six weeks participate in the monastic way of life! But our journeys rarely turn out as we plan. Our group did in fact stay 'at' the monastery of Saint Bishoi, but we were in a retreat compound outside the monastery proper. Not only were we locked out of the monastery, but we were also locked *in* our compound—it was often only with great difficulty and the honking of the car horn that we could get out to go to the dig, much less entertain thoughts of regularly going to the monastery for worship. In addition, the only monastic service open to us was the morning office at 6 AM, which, for most of us, after the rigors of working at the site each day, was too early. Even if we had ventured forth early in the morning, it wasn't clear that we could have gotten out of the compound.

So my dreams of living the monastic life, however briefly, were dashed. What happened with our group of faculty and students, however, surprised me and, I think, all of us: our way of life became increasingly, recognizably monastic. This came as a shock to me because, except for one Orthodox Copt and four Episcopalians, the students and faculty in our dorm were all from Protestant, mostly conservative and evangelical, backgrounds. I discovered very early on in the course I was teaching on 'Early Egyptian Monasticism' that the students, most of them undergraduates from small christian colleges, did not have much knowledge or awareness of monasticism. In fact, there was open and honest hostility to the monastic way of life: Aren't monks, by going off to the desert, denying God's gifts of family and society? Isn't asceticism a denial of God's good creation? Isn't monastic spirituality selfish?

But two things happened. First, since the students were all Christians, and since I wasn't teaching at my state university, I decided to abandon a strictly academic approach and instead emphasize monastic spirituality and its continuing value. After our second meeting, on *The Lives of the Desert Fathers*, several students told me that they very much appreciated the connection I was making between early monastic spirituality and the modern world. For our third meeting, on *The Sayings of the Desert Fathers*, I told the students that, instead of meeting in our classroom, we would gather together in the dormitory chapel. I asked them to read as many of the sayings as they could, but to read them prayerfully, seeking wisdom, not knowledge. Instead of having a lecture and discussion, we sat in a circle in front of the apse, with a large modern icon of Christ offering benediction; we took turns reading our favorite sayings aloud, with periods of silence and discussion following. We had taken the *apophthegmata* out of the lecture hall and scholarly journals and returned them, quite literally, to their original setting: the word in the desert. We were saying that these words were more than objects of study; they still could make a difference in the way we live.

This much was intentional. What happened next was not. Because of the wear and tear from our work on the dig, because of the normal stresses and strains that come when a group of people live together, and because of the abusive behavior of one leader, tensions and conflicts were straining, even overwhelming, our community. The students called a meeting to discuss the problems, and we decided to hold nightly prayer meetings to help keep us focused. When I first arrived, the students, who had come several weeks earlier, were already having weekly Bible study on Sunday with one of the faculty; a number of us decided it would be good also to have a weekly Eucharist, which we had on Saturday nights in the chapel. Now we were also praying together daily as a group. One student then suggested that at dinner, instead of having our usual conversations and chit chat, we have silence and listen to reading from a spiritual book. Appropriately, we began with a book by Matthew the Poor, the abbot of Saint Macarius.[91] This nascent monastic impulse then emboldened me to suggest that after evening prayer we observe the Great Silence until morning. This was not a big hit! From nine to eleven each night was the time when many of the students let off steam by getting loud and silly. But one of the students suggested that things be toned down at night for those of us who wanted to be in silence, and we all agreed on that—a dormitory full of college students out in the egyptian desert, with some of them observing the Great Silence!

So our little group, studying monasticism, living just outside a coptic monastery and digging in the ruins of an ancient monastic settlement, was taking on the shape of a rag-tag monastic community, with manual labor, study, and prayer. The bells at the monastery called the monks to prayer at a quarter to 6; at 6:30 most of us were, however reluctantly, waking up. From 7–1 we were at the site or working in the lab; after lunch at 2, people had time for pottery or lab work or study; class was often held at 6; dinner, with its spiritual reading, was around 8; then came evening prayer, and afterwards, until bed time, there was time (at least theoretically!) for study or quiet. The week was anchored with weekly Bible study and Eucharist.

The students' views of monasticism had changed; monasticism had changed the lives of some of them. One student has since joined the Coptic Orthodox Church. As one student wrote in her reflection paper on early monasticism:

> Before I had ever been introduced to Coptic Christianity, my knowledge of monasticism was limited to what I had learned from Disney's depiction of the medieval Friar Tuck in the animated movie *Robin Hood*, and to the Kellogg company's 'Rice Krispies' commercial of the monk catching nasty looks from his brothers because his cereal was disturbing the monastic silence . . . One of the most meaningful things that I learned about monks is that they are human. . . . Our *abuna* [father] and friend Nofer spoke with us sincerely and almost tearfully our last night at Deir Anba Bishoi. He shared very honestly with us how difficult the life of the monk is, and asked us to pray for him and all the monks of Egypt, that they would not lose hope or strength to continue their sometimes lonely fight. I could have simply read the *Sayings* and believed that monks struggle with the same sins as any other human being. But although listening to Abuna Nofer was much more painful, I thank God for our friendship with him, and for just such an emotional and meaningful lesson from a present day father. . . . To have studied this literature, to have learned about the namesakes of the extant monasteries of Egypt, then to visit those monasteries, to have contact with the spiritual sons of the first desert fathers, to have conducted an archeological excavation at the monastery founded by one of the fathers we read about, to walk into its excavated church, and sit down in the cell of some long dead monk, are experiences that no language created by God can be suffered to even begin to describe. To remember such an opportunity, what now seems like such an ethereal experience, is itself a treasure, a gift from a gracious God.[92]

My trip to Egypt had begun with excitement (teaching, the dig, sightseeing) and trepidation (the fear of diarrhea and assassins).

Then came disappointment (not participating actively in the regimen of the monastery). The excitement (and trepidation) continued, but the disappointment turned into sustained thanksgiving, wonder, and admiration: for the first time in my eight-year monastic journey, I was connecting what I had learned from books with what I could study in the field and hold in my hands; for only the second time in my academic career, I was teaching the subject I care about most, and I saw the spirituality of the early desert fathers connect with my young students. Visiting the coptic monasteries of the Wadi al-Natrun showed me the many strengths and beauties of ongoing monastic tradition. I marvelled at the monastic renaissance taking place in Egypt, and I could only admire these monks and lay Christians who devote themselves to Christ in the face of persistent adversity.

I can close the description of my journey to the Wadi al-Natrun with no better words than these from Psalm 107, appointed for the Last Sunday in Epiphany; words we read in our desert dormitory chapel at saturday-night Eucharist. These words still speak of God's living—and surprising—presence in the desert, which means every desert:

> He turns a desert into pools of water,
>   a parched land into springs of water.
> And there he lets the hungry live,
>   and they establish a town to live in;
> they sow fields, and plant vineyards,
>   and get a fruitful yield.
> By his blessing they multiply greatly,
>   and he does not let their cattle decrease.
>
> Psalm 107: 35-38, NRSV

NOTES

[1] See the Glossary, pages xxi–xxvii, for definitions of names and terms. The archeological dig was sponsored by the Scriptorium Insitute for Christian Antiquities, then in Grand Haven, Michigan; the academic portion was part of the Scriptorium's Semester in Egypt Program. Although the academic program was eliminated and the dig was cancelled for 1997–1998, the latter resumed in 1999 and there are hopes for continuing it.

[2] John Kolobos, or John the Little, is also known as John the Short and John the Dwarf. For a discussion of his life and the founding of the monastery bearing his name, see H. G. Evelyn White, *The Monasteries of the Wâdi 'n Natrûn*, pt. 2, *The History of the Monasteries of Nitria and of Scetis* (New York, 1926–33; repr., New York: Arno, 1973) 106–111. For sayings attributed to him, see *The Sayings of the Desert Fathers: The Alphabetical Collection*, trans. Benedicta Ward (Kalamazoo: Cistercian, rev. ed., 1984) 85–96, 109. There is a coptic *Life* by the seventh-century bishop, Zacharias of Sakha; see Maged S. Mikhail and Tim Vivian, 'Life of Saint John the Little', *Coptic Church Review* 18: 1 & 2 (Spring/Summer, 1997) 3–64. For the most recent study, with full bibliography, see Lucien Regnault, 'John Colobos, Saint', *The Coptic Encyclopedia*, ed. Aziz S. Atiya (New York: Macmillan, 1991) vol. 5, 1359–61; see also Regnault, 'Le vrai visage d'un père du désert ou abba Jean Colobos a travers ses apophtegmes', in E. Lucchesi and H. D. Saffrey, eds., *Mémorial André-Jean Festugière: Antiquité païenne et. chrétienne* (Geneva: Patrick Cramer, 1984) 225–234. Because the archeological team plans to publish a report of the excavation, I will not go into details about the dig here.

[3] Palladius, *Lausiac History* 8; *Palladius: The Lausiac History*, trans. Robert T. Meyer (New York: Newman Press, 1964) 41–43. The version in *Historia Monachorum* 22 differs: Amoun left 'a few days' after his wedding night, and his wife 'exhorted all her servants to adopt the celibate life, and indeed converted her house into a monastery'. See *The Lives of the Desert Fathers: The Historia Monachorum in Aegypto*, trans. Norman Russell, CS 34 (Kalamazoo: Cistercian, 1980) 111. The Church historian Socrates, in his *Ecclesiastical History* 4.23, has yet a different version: both Amoun and his wife moved to Nitria, where they lived together for a short time in a hut with an oratory. See also Derwas J. Chitty, *The Desert a City* (Crestwood, NY: St. Vladimir's, n.d.) 11, and Evelyn White, 45–50; Evelyn White believes, 47, that Amoun came to Nitria in 315. For sayings attributed to Amoun, see Ward, trans., 31–32.

[4] See Chitty, 29. Kellia has been so far the best excavated early monastic site in Egypt. For a recent presentation, with a bibliography of earlier publications, see *Les Kellia: Ermitages coptes en Basse-Égypte* (Geneva: Musée d'art et histoire, 1989); for a good popular presentation, see *Dossiers histoire et archéologie* 133 (Decembre 1988). There is no good full account in English.

[5] *Historia Monachorum* 22; Russell, CS 34:112. See also *Life of Antony* 60.

[6] *Apophthegmata* Macarius the Great 1; Ward, CS 59:124-125. See Evelyn White, 62–63. There is a considerably longer version of this story in the *Life of Macarius of Scetis;* see Tim Vivian, *Saint Macarius the Spiritbearer* (Crestwood, New York: St. Vladimir's, 2004).

[7] Chitty, 11–13, and Evelyn White, 45–50, 62–63, accept both stories.

[8] *Life of Antony* 3. See *Lausiac History* 8; Meyer, trans., 43.

[9] An icon of Saint Athanasius in a chapel dedicated to him at the monastery of Saint Antony by the Red Sea depicts the great bishop with monastic headdress; see Nabil Selim Atalla, *Coptic Art*, volume 1, *Wall-paintings* (Cairo: Lehnert & Landrock, n.d.), 89, and now, for a much better photograph, Elizabeth S. Bolman, ed., *Monastic Visions: The Wall Paintings at the Monastery of Saint Antony by the Red Sea* (New Haven: Yale University Press, 2002). David Brakke has written extensively on Athanasius and monasticism; see his *Athanasius and the Politics of Asceticism* (Oxford: Clarendon, 1995).

A Monastic and Personal Journey   51

[10] 'Shiêt, the place where hearts and thought are weighed with true discernment'. Zacharie, 'Vie de Jean Colobos', ed. E. Amélineau, *Annales du Musée Guimet* 25 (Paris, 1894) 316–410, 326; Mikhail and Vivian, 21.

[11] Otto F. A. Meinardus, *Monks and Monasteries of the Egyptian Desert* (Cairo: American University in Cairo Press, rev. ed., 1992) 50.

[12] Chitty, 13.

[13] On the dangers of desert travel, see for example Alphabetical Apophthegmata John Colobos 17; Ward, trans., 89: 'One day when Abba John was going up to Scetis with some other brothers, their guide lost his way for it was night-time. So the brothers said to Abba John, "What shall we do, abba, in order not to die wandering about, for the brother has lost the way?"'

[14] Most westerners know little or nothing about the Coptic Church and its ancient history and traditions, much less anything about muslim Egypt; Egypt remains the land of the pharoahs. For example, an ad in a recent edition of *Archaeology* (March/April 1996), 27, offers this tour: 'Travel from Cairo to Aswan and Luxor visiting many world famous sites including: the Great Pyramids and the Sphinx at Giza, the Temples of Luxor and Karnak, the painted tombs in the Valley of the Kings, the Valley of the Queens, and the golden treasures of Tutankhamen'.

[15] The most recent history of the Coptic Church is that of Theodore Hall Partrick, *Traditional Egyptian Christianity: A History of the Coptic Orthodox Church* (Greensboro, NC: Fisher Hall Press, 1996). See also Otto F.A. Meinardus, *Two Thousand Years of Coptic Christianity* (Cairo: The American University in Cairo Press, 1999) and John Watson, *Among the Copts* (Portland, OR.: Sussex Academic Press, 2000).

[16] For the story of the stick planted in desert sand that grows into a tree for John the Little, see *Apophthegmata* John Colobos 1 (Ward, trans., 85–86), and Evelyn White's discussion, 108. Evelyn White suggests, 108 n. 9, that this latter story in fact was 'the model' for the story of Saint Ephraem's tree. John's tree, 'the tree of obedience', could still be 'seen' in 1921 growing on top of the wall of the abandoned monastery of John the Little; for a photograph, see Evelyn White, *History*, plate VA, following p. 497.

[17] See Meinardus, *Monks and Monasteries of the Egyptian Desert*, 106.

[18] The definitive early history is still that of Evelyn White, *History*. See also Chitty, 11-13, 29-35, and J.-C. Guy, 'Le centre monastique de Scété dans la litterature du Ve siècle', *Orientalia Christiana Periodica* 30 (1964) 129–147. For the history of each existing monastery from its origins to the present, see Meinardus, *Monks and Monasteries of the Egyptian Deserts*.

[19] Rufinus, *Ecclesiastical History* 2.3, reports 3,000 around the year 373, while Palladius (*Lausiac History* 7; Meyer, trans., 40), about twenty years later, speaks of 5,000 at Nitria and 600 at Kellia.

[20] See Douglas Burton-Christie, *The Word in the Desert: Scripture and the Quest for Holiness in Early Christian Monasticism* (New York & Oxford: Oxford UP, 1993) 77.

[21] One should not push this dichotomy too far. As the *Letters* of Antony the Great show, Copts could be sophisticated followers of Origen. Antony was not, presumably, the simple illiterate depicted in the *Life of Antony*.

[22] Cassian, *Conferences* 10.2.2; *John Cassian: The Conferences*, trans. Boniface Ramsey (New York: Paulist, 1997) 371. Cassian, a follower of Evagrius of Pontus, an Origenist, was disdainful of 'the absurd heresy of the Anthropomorphites'.

[23] Cassian, *Conferences* 10.3.4-5; Ramsey, trans., 373. Serapion, one notes, is an egyptian name, not greek.

[24] Socrates, *Ecclesiastical History* 6.7.

[25] The brothers were Ammonius, Dioscorus, Eusebius, and Euthymius. On these brothers, see Evelyn White, 136–144, and the 'Index of Persons', 482; for a recent summary of the events in Egypt (disparaging Theophilus, 'the Egyptian Pharoah') and an account of the brothers' flight to Constantinople and the embroilment over them between Chrysostom and Epiphanius, see J.N.D. Kelly, *Golden Mouth: The Story of John Chrysostom* (Ithaca, NY: Cornell, 1995) 191–210.

[26] See Chitty, 58, and for a detailed study, Evelyn White, *History*, 125–144; the latter, however, 127, too readily accepts as primary later anti-Origenist material in the Pachomian corpus. For this early stage of the controversy over Origen and Origenism, see Elizabeth A. Clark, *The Origenist Controversy: The Cultural Construction of an Early Christian Debate* (Princeton: Princeton UP, 1992) 43–84.

[27] Evelyn White, 133–134, estimates, though without saying where he derives his figures, that Anthropomorphists 'appeared' to outnumber Origenists at Scetis by three to one, with the 'disproportion' less at Nitria and Kellia.

[28] See Evelyn White, *History*, 151–161.

[29] See Alphabetical Apophthegmata Moses 10; Ward, trans, 140.

[30] Evelyn White, *History*, 157–159.

[31] For the monastery of Saint Macarius as an example, see Father Matta el-Meskeen, *Coptic Monasticism and the Monastery of St. Macarius: A Short History* (Cairo: St. Macarius, 1984) 36–39.

[32] On the later histories of the monasteries in the fifth to seventh centuries, see Evelyn White, *History*, and Meinardus, *Monks and Monasteries*.

[33] I will not discuss the historical and traditional origins of each monastery here. See Evelyn White, *History*, 95–115, and Meinardus, *Monks and Monasteries*, in the chapter on each monastery. For descriptions of the modern monasteries, see Meinardus, and O.H.E. KHS-Burmester, *A Guide to the Monasteries of the Wadi 'N-Natrun* (Cairo: Société d'archéologie copte, 1954). Burmester's little book, like the first edition of Meinardus' *Monks and Monasteries of the Egyptian Deserts* (1961), was written before the present renaissance of monasticism in the Wadi al-Natrun and thus provides an excellent opportunity for the interested reader to make comparisons. Burmester's volume also has thirty-two black and white photographs that provide numerous striking contrasts with the present-day monasteries. An excellent book on modern Egyptian monasticism, with wonderful color photographs, is Alain and Evelyne Chevillat, *Moines du désert d'Égypte* (Lyon: Terre du Ciel, 1990). Mark Gruber has published very insightful work on modern coptic monasticism. See his two articles, 'Coping with God: Coptic Monasticism in Egyptian Culture' and 'The Monastery as the Nexus of Coptic Cosmology', in Nelly van Doorn-Harder and Kari Vogt, eds., *Between Desert and City: The Coptic Orthodox Church Today* (Oslo: Novus forlag, 1997), and his book, *Journey Back to Eden: My Life and Times among the Desert Fathers* (Maryknoll, New York: Orbis Books, 2002). On coptic monastic liturgy, see Robert Taft, 'Praise in the Desert: The Coptic Monastic Office Yesterday and Today', *Worship* 56 (1982) 513–529.

[34] In this article I have not treated the topic of nuns in the Coptic Church, not because it is not an important subject, but because I did not have the opportunity to visit any monasteries of women or talk with any nuns. On the subject of

ancient women ascetics in Egypt, see Susanna Elm, 'Virgins of God': The Making of Asceticism in Late Antiquity (Oxford: Clarendon, 1994) esp. 227–372; on modern female monastics, see Pieternella Van Doorn-Harder, Contemporary Coptic Nuns (Columbia, SC: University of South Carolina Press, 1995).

[35] The Syrian Monastery probably dates to the eighth century (see Evelyn White, 309–321), or the sixth century (see Gawdat Gabra with Tim Vivian, Coptic Monasteries: Egypt's Monastic Art and Architecture [Cairo-New York: American University in Cairo Press, 2002] 35–63).

[36] See Evelyn White, 102, 104–106.

[37] Conferences 10.2.

[38] See Chitty, 35, and Evelyn White, 95–124, supplemented by Meinardus. See also Hany N. Takla, 'The Library of the Monastery of St. John the Little: A Colophon from a Vatican-preserved Coptic Manuscript', Saint Shenouda the Archimandrite Society Newsletter 3.1 (<http://www.stshenouda.com/newsltr/nl3_1.htm>). A bohairic-arabic manuscript, Vatican Copt. 21, a complete codex of the Liturgy of Saint Cyril dated to 1059 AM (1343 AD) comes from this monastery's library. It is mentioned among six coptic manuscripts inventoried in MS. Vat. Lat. 7136, from the papacy of Pope Julius II, 1503–1513. The last mention that the monastery was inhabited was in 1493.

[39] Life of Antony 14.

[40] Some cities, like Oxyrhynchus, may in fact have become virtually monastic. That is, at least, what the Historia Monachorum 5 reports; Russell, trans., 67.

[41] See Tim Vivian, trans., 'Life of Antony by St. Athanasius of Alexandria', Coptic Church Review 15.1 & 2 (Spring and Summer 1994) 17, and Vivian and Apostolos N. Athanassakis, The Life of Antony, CS 202 (Kalamazoo: Cistercian Publications, 2003).

[42] Since the accession of Pope Shenouda III no one is accepted as a novice unless he has a college degree. When I became sick with dysentery during my stay in the Wadi al-Natrun, I was taken good care of by Fr. Nofer, who had been trained as a pharmacist and whom I had met in our compound as he supervised the work in the orchard, and Fr. Isidorus, a medical doctor, with whom I had long sickbed discussions about Anglicanism and ecumenism.

[43] The numbers have apparently continued to increase, though I do not have current figures.

[44] Meinardus, Monks and Monasteries, x.

[45] On the revitalization of eremitic monasticism in Egypt under Abd al-Masih al-Habashi (the Ethiopian) and Abouna Mina el-Baramousi, later to become Pope Kyrillos, the immediate predecessor of Pope Shenouda, see John Watson, 'Abba Kyrillos: Patriarch and Solitary', Coptic Church Review 17: 1 & 2 (Spring & Summer 1996) 7–48, esp. 10–11, and the notes there for further references.

[46] Meinardus, x. For the recent renaissance of the Coptic Church in general, see Partrick, chapter eleven, whose 'principal focus' is the 'ongoing revival in the Coptic Church since 1959'. For earlier accounts, see Otto F.A. Meinardus, 'Recent Developments in Egyptian Monasticism', Oriens Christianus 49 (1965) 79–89, and Meinardus, 'Zur monastischen Erneuerung in der koptischen Kirche', Oriens Christianus 61 (1977) 59–70.

[47] See the account of Abouna Isaac in chapter three of this volume. See also the insightful account of modern coptic pilgrimage to monasteries by Elizabeth Oram in Elizabeth S. Bolman. ed., Monastic Visions: The Wall Paintings at the Monastery of St. Antony at the Red Sea (New Haven: Yale University Press: 2002) 203–213.

⁴⁸ I wish to thank Maged S.A. Mikhail for his thoughts on this question, many of which I have silently quoted or paraphrased.

⁴⁹ Lucien Regnault, *La vie quotidienne des Pères du Désert en Égypte au IVe siècle* (Paris: Hachette, 1992) 15.

⁵⁰ For the theme that the monks recreated the garden of paradise, see Helen Waddell, Beasts and Saints (London: Darton, Longman and Todd, 1995 [1934]), and Vivian, *Journeying into God*, 166–187.

⁵¹ For a stark contrast with all this new building, see Evelyn White, *History*, plate VB, following p. 497. The photograph of Bishoi and the Syrian Monastery reproduced there, taken, presumably, in the 1920s, shows absolutely nothing but sand outside the monastery walls.

⁵² For a recent report of a westerner's visit to Saint Macarius and a deep appreciation of the monastery's spiritual gifts, see Alan Jones, *Soul Making: The Desert Way of Spirituality* (San Francisco: Harper & Row, 1985) 12–16, and the entire book for Jones' fascinating integration of modern psychology and desert spirituality.

⁵³ Fr. Matta, 73. As Burmester observed, 34, the number of monks and the church shrank together: 'since the number of the monks became greatly reduced, those who remained either did not wish to maintain the original dimensions of the church, since it was too large for them, or were unable to provide the necessary material for restoration, and in consequence, those parts which needed repair were allowed to fall into ruin'.

⁵⁴ As Fr. Matta reports, 76, 'We hope that when the infirmary is completely fitted out with modern medical equipment and has an ambulance, it will be able to serve the victims of the many road accidents that occur on the nearby Cairo-Alexandria desert highway'.

⁵⁵ The pope and Fr. Matta el-Meskeen, to name just two of the more important writers, have together written about a hundred books.

⁵⁶ Fr. Matta, 50–51.

⁵⁷ Fr. Matta, 61–83.

⁵⁸ Fr. Matta's final chapter includes not only a discussion of architecture, but also the printing press, farm buildings, generator and fuel station, housing for the agricultural workers, the monastery's land, and agricultural activity and livestock production. In other words, everything has its spiritual place in the design of the monastery, which is a microcosm of God's creation.

⁵⁹ Fr. Matta, 62.

⁶⁰ I owe this striking image to Susan Power Bratton, in her fascinating interdisciplinary essay, 'The Original Desert Solitaire: Early Christian Monasticism and Wilderness', *Environmental Ethics* 10.1 (Spring 1988) 31–53.

⁶¹ I wish to thank Maged Mikhail for these reflections.

⁶² Deir el-Souriani, 'The Monastery of the Holy Virgin and St. John Kame' (visitor's booklet) 7.

⁶³ Deir el-Souriani, 8. A photograph of the doors may be see in Burmester, plate XIV.

⁶⁴ A poster available in the monastery gift shops shows the ark of the Church riding out the tempest. The animals of Noah's ark have been replaced by photographs of all the coptic bishops.

⁶⁵ On the story, see Evelyn White, 114–115.

⁶⁶ 'The Monastery of Saint Bishoy' (visitor's booklet), 6: 'We are told that Saint Bishoy carried Our Lord, Who met him as an old man on his way, and that it is

for this reason that his body remains uncorrupted to this day. He is also said to have washed the feet of the Lord, Who visited him as a poor stranger'.

[67] These stories are often depicted on icons, and were told to us by the monks. Meinardus, *Monks and Monasteries*, relates them on 105 and 121. What strikes a western historian is the mixture of history, tradition, legend, and myth: both our monastic guides and the monastery guidebooks were really quite accurate (according to western historical standards) on the dates and historical circumstances of figures like Bishoi and Macarius.

[68] Meinardus, *Monks and Monasteries*, xi. Lucien Regnault, *La vie quotidienne*, 35, sensibly reminds us that 'a legendary tradition' has made the founders of Baramus 'the sons of the emperor Valentinian, Maximus and Domitian, but it is better to respect the mystery in the apophthegmata that surrounds the luminous figures of these two young anchorites predestined to die prematurely after having passed only three years in the desert'.

[69] Fr. Matta, 58, says that the keep at Saint Macarius was built by Zeno in 482.

[70] See Chitty, 147; Regnault, 38 ('a tissue of improbabilities'); and Evelyn White, 224–227, who notes, 'It is clear that the story of Hilaria *as a whole* is a pious legend and no more. . . . But the benefactions bestowed upon Scetis by Zeno cannot be similarly dismissed'.

[71] C. C. Walters, *Monastic Archaeology in Egypt* (Warminster: Aris & Phillips, 1974) 11–12, 86.

[72] Regnault, 38, concludes his discussion of Hilaria thus: 'When one visits in our day a monastery of the Wadi al-Natrun, the guide never fails to recall—gravely or with a smile—the origins of the keeps that exist still in the four monasteries'.

[73] Kathleen Norris, *The Cloister Walk* (New York: Riverhead Books, 1996) 195. For a sobering reminder of spirituality at the interstices of history and hagiography (a *point vierge*, as Thomas Merton says), see Norris, 186–205.

[74] Fr. Matta, 58. For archeological descriptions of the keeps at the monasteries of the Wadi al-Natrun, see Walters, 87–90, written before the recent restorations.

[75] Deir el-Souriani, 6. The keep at Saint Bishoi is '22 meters in length, 22 meters in breadth, and 15 meters in height'; 'The Monastery of Saint Bishoy' (vistor's booklet), 18.

[76] Fr. Matta, 59–60.

[77] We saw the same arrangement at the Greek Orthodox monastery of Saint Catherine in Sinai.

[78] See Alphabetical Apophthegmata Moses 10 (Ward, trans., 140) and Evelyn White, 156–157.

[79] A reality not much reported in the West. See Rodolph Yanney, 'A New Martyr: Father Ruais Fakher', *Coptic Church Review* 14.4 (Winter 1993) 109–12. In the Middle East, persecution is an equal opportunity thug. Archimandrite Boniface, a Uniate monk, reports, 'I remember that during my stay at St. Catherine's Monastery on Mt. Sinai, the Israeli occupants caused much trouble and constantly harassed the monks. One day the local commander threatened the ekonomos of the Monastery, saying they would "liquidate" them all. The ekonomos answered, "Wait a moment, and first come with me; I'll show you something". Reluctantly, the commander followed him, and he showed him the charnel-house, especially pointing out a group of skeletons, saying, "These here are the monks killed by the Bedouins (he gave the date, but I forgot) . . . we are not afraid of undergoing the

same lot at the hands of you guys'". See Archimandrite Boniface [Luykx], *Eastern Monasticism and the Future of the Church* (Redwood Valley, CA: Holy Transfiguration Monastery; Stamford, Conn: Basileos Press, 1993) 119, n. 48.

[80] Among many examples, see recently John Daniszewski, 'Mideast Enmities Outlast Muslims' Month to Purify', *Los Angeles Times*, February 22, 1996, A9. After our group's departure in March of 1996, a number of Greek tourists (mistaken for Israelis) were murdered outside a posh suburban Cairo hotel.

[81] See Rodolph Yanney, 'Preface', *Coptic Church Review* 17: 1 & 2 (Spring & Summer 1996): 4: 'On September 2, 1981, President Sadat of Egypt deposed Pope Shenouda III and exiled him to the desert monastery of St. Bishoi, replacing him with a five-bishop committee. He put eight coptic bishops, 24 priests and more than 100 laymen and women in prison. He also ordered the closure of two Coptic newspapers and three welfare societies'. Sadat was assassinated on October 6, 1981 (ironically, another victim that day on the parade grounds was Bishop Samuel, an eminent Copt), but the troops remained around Bishoi for some time, and the pope's house arrest lasted until January, 1985. See also Kenneth Cragg, *The Arab Christian: A History in the Middle East* (Louisville, KY: Westminster/John Knox, 1991) 191 and 201 n. 36.

[82] John Watson, 'Abba Kyrillos', 5, estimates that there are 8 million Copts out of a population in excess of 55 million. Other estimates range from 3–5 million; see Watson, 5 n. 1, who points out that there has not been a census of the number of Copts in Egypt. In the late 1970s, Robert Brenton Betts suggested that Copts numbered 'between 3 and 3 1/2 millions, or roughly 10% of the total population'. See Betts, *Christians in the Arab East: A Political Study* (London: SPCK, 1979) 50, 58–66; the quotation is on. p. 61. Due to a rising muslim birthrate and the emigration of large numbers of Copts, this percentage is steadily declining and may now be as low as 6%; see Maurice Martin, 'The Renewal in Context', in van Doorn-Harder and Vogt, eds., *Between Desert and City*, 15, and 20 n. 1.

[83] As John Watson, an anglican clergyman, has observed ('Abba Kyrillos', 31), 'The Copts identify themselves as a suffering community. They may not have experienced state-controlled and state-directed persecution like the Russian or Ethiopian churches but they have borne centuries of deadly, daily discrimination'. See Hany N. Takla, 'Martyrs and Martyrdom in the Coptic Church', *Bulletin of Saint Shenouda the Archimandrite Coptic Society* 1 (1983–84) 1–229.

[84] According to Fr. Matta, 63, the monks at Macarius, 'trying to draw water' from the 'early springs' of Church tradition, are changing this tradition; they have built a new refectory 'which gathers the monks together daily according to the model of the Last Supper on Holy Thursday'.

[85] Deir el-Souriani, 20.

[86] For a spirited modern defense of fasting, see Adalbert de Vogüé, *To Love Fasting: The Monastic Experience* (Petersham, Mass., Saint Bede's, 1989).

[87] This understanding will strike many moderns as unduly harsh (as it did some of the students in my early monasticism class), but Thomas Merton says that the goal of the monastic life is to lose the false, ego-driven, self; I understand 'contempt' here to mean contempt for this false self that makes itself a god at the expense of God and neighbor. But Merton, speaking from his experience as novice master, goes on to point out that the problem for modern monks is that they first must have a self to lose!

[88] Alphabetical Apophthegmata Poemen 168; Ward, trans., 190, slightly altered.

[89] For some of these monastic stories, see Vivian, *Journeying into God*.
[90] For an excellent recent appreciation of monastic spirituality by a married layperson, see Norris, *The Cloister Walk*.
[91] Matthew the Poor, *Community of Love* (Crestwood, New York: St. Vladimir's Seminary Press, 1984). 'Matthew the Poor' translates Matta el-Meskeen, whom we have met above.
[92] I wish to thank Reagan Wicks (now Mikhail) for these observations from her paper 'Reflections on Monasticism'.

3

A Journey to the Interior:
The Monasteries of Saint Antony and Saint Paul by the Red Sea

JOURNEYING TO THE INTERIOR is both physical fact and spiritual reality, especially in Egypt, where the physical interior is clearly marked and life-threatening. The attacks of the demons in the *Life of Antony* demonstrate that the spiritual interior can also be dangerous. For millennia Egyptians have lived and died alongside the Nile: where the great River and its tributaries flow, the country is green and well-watered. Then there is a narrow strip, mostly arid, a border zone that divides the habitable region from what lies beyond; next is the desert, hundreds and hundreds of miles where there is virtually no water and very little vegetation. Except for the inhabitants of sparsely populated oases and a few nomadic Bedouin, no one lives here now or lived here in ancient times.

In the third and fourth centuries, however, a few hearty followers of Christ crossed over the border and journeyed to the interior, seeking to confront God, the Devil, and themselves in ways they considered not practical or possible within the cultivated regions. Such persons, like Saint Onnophrius (Abu Nofer), naked with his long beard serving as clothing, were immortalized in Egypt in both story and painting and became heroes of the monastic endeavor.[1] Onnophrius' fame even crossed the Mediterranean, making him an important figure in both Italy and Spain (San Onofrio).[2] 'The Story of Abba Pambo', about an otherwise unknown figure, has Pambo journey further and further into the interior. To the first two anchorites he meets in the desert he poses the question 'Is there anyone beyond you?' The Coptic for 'beyond' also suggests 'within', 'to the interior'. When he finds that the answer is yes, he journeys further into the desert until an old man tells him there is nothing beyond him 'except darkness and the punishments that sinners are enduring. Sit down here, my brother, and this hour you shall see mighty wonders'. And indeed, he is given vision of God. Pambo, paradoxically, has found the center, the answer to all his questioning, in the middle of nowhere.[3]

The most famous of all these spiritual desert explorers is Saint Antony the Great (251–356), one of the most important figures of ancient Christianity. Late in the third century, around 270, Antony had a conversion experience. He heard Christ calling him to the ascetic life (*Life of Antony* 2). After spending some time as an ascetic near his home village, Antony began a series of withdrawals to the interior. At first he lived in a tomb 'that lay at a distance' from his village (*Life* 8.1), fighting the Devil and his minions. Then, in 285, he journeyed to 'the outer mountain', Mount Pispir (Deir el-Maimoun), about seventy-five kilometers south of Memphis on the east bank of the Nile; here he continued his asceticism and attracted numerous disciples. Twenty-eight years later, in 313, Antony journeyed into full desert, stopping finally at Mount Colzim, 'the inner mountain'.[4]

In Egypt, the Nile is the center of geography. Away from it is desert; beyond that is the 'further' or 'remoter' desert.[5] Therefore, although the Nile is in the center of the country, to move away from it is to journey not to the exterior, as we would think, but to the interior, to the desert. The early monks saw this interior wilderness as both geographical and spiritual reality; there they confronted the aridity of the earth and of the heart. But in this desert the monk, as new Adam and Eve, also found paradise regained.[6] In this interior Antony found a water source and a cave and cultivated a garden (*Life* 49-50). Here he would spend the rest of his life. Fame, and disciples, followed him, however, and he journeyed back and forth between Colzim and Pispir to minister to the crowds calling on him. Shortly after Antony's death, a monastic community was founded honoring his memory and the sanctity that he had given to the mountain. This early foundation would eventually become Deir Anba Antunius, the Monastery of Saint Antony, a community that flourishes today deep in the interior of the egyptian desert.[7]

Thousands of coptic pilgrims, the lineal and spiritual children of Antony's late antique Egypt, come to Deir Anba Antunius each year, most to visit the famous cave of Saint Antony, and yet the monastery, despite Antony's renown, is relatively unknown in the West.[8] That may soon change. Saint Antony's is the home of a series of remarkable wall paintings that date to 1232–1233 and have no fully extant parallel in the monasteries of Egypt. For centuries westerners have known of these paintings, and scholars and travelers have studied and written about them over the years, but they have seen through a glass darkly: nearly eight centuries of dirt and smoke had colored the paintings black and made them almost invisible. Now they have been cleaned and restored. The Antiquities Development Project (ADP) of the American Research Center in Egypt, funded by USAID, undertook the cleaning and restoration by a team of italian conservators, a task that was completed in 1999. As part of the endeavor, a book on Saint Antony, the monastery, and the wall paintings, was prepared by an international team of scholars, led by Elizabeth S. Bolman.[9] To my great delight, I was asked to participate in the project, so two years after my visit to the monasteries of the Wadi al-Natrun, I spent the week of March 29–April 5, 1998,[10] in the company of Dr Bolman (Betsy), at the monasteries of Saint Antony and Saint Paul by the Red Sea. Like Pambo, Onnophrius, and Antony, I was able, however briefly and incompletely, to make my own journey to the interior.

LEAVING THE WORLD

We left Cairo the afternoon of the 29th and traveled east on Highway 44 for one hundred eighteen kilometers, turning south short of Suez. The traditional route, taken by earlier travelers who have left accounts of their journey (see below), was to take the highway south from Cairo to Beni Suef, then turn east (see the map). The coastal route, however, seems to be preferred now. Near Suez, we traveled another one hundred six kilometers south until we reached the lighthouse at Zafarana, where we turned west at a military checkpoint onto Highway 54 for forty-five kilometers. This highway cuts through the Wadi Arabah that lies between the northern and southern Galala mountain ranges. About half an hour later we came to a marker (a set of benches under a roof) with the sign *Deir Anba Antonius*, written in Arabic and English, hanging above the entrance; it was very much like those used by ranchers in the western United States to identify their property. We turned southwest towards the monastery, now seventeen kilometers distant, and in ten to fifteen minutes reached Saint Antony's.

In 1884, the Jesuit priest Michel Jullien made the journey to Saint Antony's and nearby Saint Paul's under very different circumstances—by camel caravan.[11] We had a very comfortable trip by automobile, the chief annoyance (for me) being the music that the driver loudly played–assuming, I suppose, that since we were Americans we would of course enjoy Whitney Houston and Michael Jackson. About two hours into our trip he asked if arabic music was OK. Yes! we hastened to reply. The music was very pleasant and, for whatever reason, he now turned down the volume. Along the Red Sea, with its waters of aqua and blue and green and with enormous tankers lumbering down the Gulf, we passed both army posts and new resorts springing up like mushrooms in the desert sand. Because of terrorist threats, soldiers, police and tourist police are ubiquitous in Egypt. The resorts, with their hopeful names, Marlin Beach, Laguna Beach, and Esperanza, made me think for a minute that I was in Southern California or Florida. The building boom, after the recent massacre at Luxor and the subsequent exodus of tourists, had temporarily busted, however: construction looked like it had come to a stop, and the palm trees planted optimistically at the entrances to the resorts appeared to be dead or dying.

Our trip took about three and a half hours. In 1884 Jullien, by contrast, travelled by train for three hours from Cairo to Beni Suef; from there, he said, 'you take camels in order to cross the desert. It takes from four to ten days of travel'.[12] His descriptions of his journey are both picturesque and, at times, appealing; in the section entitled 'Night in the Desert', he offers this account:

> Silence takes over, true silence of the desert. One hears no more than the muffled noise of beans being ground beneath the teeth of the camels. Soon even the noise ceases, and there is complete death. No cry from a bird of prey or a jackal; no buzzing of mosquitoes; the wind itself is silent, finding nothing to hit against.[13]

Remembering Jullien's description, I reflected that after Cairo's clamor and all-night honking of horns, not to mention Michael Jackson, such silence would indeed be very welcome.

At dusk, we saw the gates of the monastery to the west. These turned out to be the gates in the new, outer, perimeter of Saint Antony's, an expanse four or five times the size of the older walls. Saint Antony's is like a medieval european city outgrowing its old walls or a modern desert suburb, annexing land to the north and west for building projects. To each side of the new gate are large modern wall paintings of Saint Antony and the Mother of God. After the driver talked a moment with the gatekeeper, a young Copt, we drove on through, heading west into the enormous compound, down a paved drive bordered on both sides by recently-planted olive trees.

In a minute we were at the old gate, which faces north. The sign, in black paint on white-plastered walls, announces in Arabic and English the Monastery of Saint Antony. Beyond the walls we could see the lighted spires of a church and palm trees. To the north of the old compound is a row of new dormitories for workers and guests; these buildings also contain the gift store and a canteen. To the west are industrial buildings and a building housing the monastery generator, whose loud hum would be a constant companion during the week. We got out of the car under a crescent moon and were greeted by our guide, Abouna[14] (Father) Isaac. To the right of the entrance I saw an ancient hand-operated lift, as I had previously seen at the monasteries of the Wadi al-Natrun; it was in use, we were later told, until the 1950s. Until that time the gate was always kept closed against both spiritual and physical marauders; the only way into the monastery was by way of the lift. Abouna Isaac would later tell me that the gate used to be opened only twice a year, to let in the camels with the monastery's grain supply. Agnes Smith Lewis, an american traveller who visited Saint Antony's in 1905 and wrote a delightful, if condescending, travelogue of her journey, reports that at the time of her visit there was 'a small opening in the wall', a doorway through which visitors entered,

> then through a ponderous gate (unlocked by two clumsy wooden keys), which had been donated to the monastery fifty years earlier by the coptic pope Cyril IV, who had been a monk of Saint Antony's. Lewis reports that the gate was opened only once a year, but that an exception was made in their honor, 'for the monks still cling to their ancient mode of entrance by a windlass and a rope.[15]

Just twenty years earlier, Père Jullien had made his way into the monastery via that same 'ancient mode of entrance'. He is blunt: 'Do not look for the gate; there is none. You will find in the wall only a semi-cylindrical niche three and a half meters long and eight to nine meters high and overhead an opening of the same width trimmed with wainscoting half way up and forming a balcony'. He goes on to give a picturesque description of how his company entered the monastery:

> In 1616 Father Sicard was hoisted up on a large basket; for us it was less easy. The large rope that hung in the

> middle of the niche was divided at its end into two
> parts, each ending with a strong metal hook. Place your
> face against the rope, put the two ends under your
> armpits, and buckle the two hooks together behind
> your back. Grip in your hands the two ends in front of
> your chest. Now you're set. When the signal is given,
> they rapidly hoist you up eight and a half meters until
> you're above the trap-door, where a monk takes you
> into his arms in order to haul you onto the floorboard.
> If you're lucky, as you've been twisting around during
> your ascent you haven't banged your shoulders against
> the rocky wall.[16]

I thought of poor Père Jullien as I stood before the gate. Picking up my bag (the airline had shipped my other one to Rome, where it vacationed for a week), I walked with Betsy and our guide and driver into the monastery. In the partially-lit darkness, the spires of a church rose upward with lighted crosses at the summit of each; to the left foreground were a dozen palm trees rustling in the wind; behind us the sun cast just enough light to show the outline of mountains high at the monastery's back. We were here.

> *Interlude, March 29: Bishop Yustus*
>
> Bishop Yustus, the monastery's abbot; a serious face behind dark-framed glasses, yet with a ready smile. Wearing a crucifix as a large pectoral cross, extremely rare in ancient coptic art, and unusual still today, a vivid reminder of Lent.

THE MONASTERY PAST AND PRESENT

The origins of the Monastery of Saint Antony (Deir Anba Antunius) lie not in history or tradition but in silence, both the eremitical silence of Antony himself and the silence of our historical sources.[17] Saint Antony's apparently produced no histories, chronicles, or lives of saints with which a historian might chart its course through the centuries. Very little is known, therefore, about the monastic community that grew up in the second half of the fourth century near the site of Antony's 'inner mountain'. Numerous monasteries were founded near a famous anchorite's dwelling, and Saint Antony's was undoubtedly one of them.[18] According to local monastic tradition, the first construction of the monastery took place in 315. While at present this date is impossible to verify, it suggests that the first community and buildings came into being near the site of the saint's water source and, possibly, the site of the present-day Old Church.

'Abu Salih', the thirteenth-century chronicler, reports that Saint Antony's was built during the reign of Emperor Julian (the Apostate) (355–361).[19] Rufinus, a latin monk and translator of many monastic works from Greek into Latin, apparently visited the area around 375.[20] Sulpicius Severus, a gallic monk and hagiographer, says that he visited 'two monasteries of the blessed Antony, which are today occupied by his disciples', as well as stopping at the site of Paul the hermit.[21] Since Sulpicius' *First Dialogue* can be dated to the year 400, this suggests that a second antonian community developed between Antony's death and the end of the fourth century; perhaps Sulpicius was referring to monastic communities at Pispir and Colzim, Antony's outer and inner 'mountains' (in Coptic, *toou* can mean both 'mountain' and 'monastery').[22] Rufinus and Sulpicius, in these earliest known reports concerning Antony's 'monasteries' demonstrate the renown that Antony had in the latin West already during the fourth century.

Since the area around and under Deir Anba Antunius has never undergone systematic excavation, it is not possible to give an archeological history of the monastery, although parallel developments elsewhere provide a plausible picture. The first community at Saint Antony's—and we should think of monastic 'communities' rather than anything like monastic complexes of today—was undoubtedly a *laura*, a monastic community consisting of scattered cells or *monastêria*, 'small, low houses', where the monks lived separately, as did their brethren at Kellia and other fourth-century monastic communities.[23] The 'monastery' most likely included a well and a church, with a refectory being added later. This community was undoubtedly semi-anchoritic, like those at Kellia and Scetis in their early years, rather than cenobitic like the communities of Pachomius and Shenoute;[24] the monks lived in individual cells, separate from each other, and they gathered together on Saturday and Sunday (as the two hermits at the monastery still do) for a communal meal and worship. Thus they combined, in the felicitous phrasing of Antoine Guillaumont, 'la vie solitaire et la vie solidaire' (solitary life and communal life).[25] Organization was minimal: an abba or 'father' was the leader and there was no formal Rule.[26] As with other semi-anchoritic communities in Egypt, however, a centripetal tendency gradually brought the monks together behind great walls, primarily for reasons of safety and security, in more of a cenobitic community, as one sees today in the monasteries of Egypt.[27]

This evolution usually had two stages: first, a keep (*qasr* in Arabic) or tower of refuge was built, to which the monks could flee from marauders. The monasteries of Scetis (Wadi al-Natrun) were devastated many times in the fifth century, and it appears that keeps were built there in the mid-fifth century.[28] Later, in the ninth century, the central monastic area was fortified with a high wall.[29] Saint Antony's, however, may have been fortified as early as the sixth century, possibly because of its remoteness and susceptibility to raiders.[30] Even after the 'enclosing' of the monastery, it is probable that some monks continued their semi-anchoritic lives outside the walls.[31]

Saint Antony's is a very large monastery; at least in circumference it is one of the largest in Egypt (Saint Macarius' in the Wadi al-Natrun must rival it in size). Its walls have been expanded in the eighteenth, nineteenth, and twentieth centuries, enormously increasing its dimensions. A photograph, taken about 1930, of the Monastery of Saint Bishoi in the Wadi al-Natrun also provides a good idea of the appearance of Saint Antony's seventy years ago: outside the monastery walls there is only the vast expanse of sand, whereas today at Bishoi this same area encompasses gardens, orchards, dormitories for guests, and agricultural and industrial buildings.[32] At Saint Antony's (with fewer irrigated areas), the only difference is that a new wall encompasses the entire complex. Otto Meinardus reported in 1992 that the 'walls enclose an area of eighteen *feddans* [about nineteen acres], of which ten belong to the garden', but this calculation must not include the area inscribed by the new walls, which probably quadruples the monastery's size.[33]

Saint Antony's has six churches, the newest being the Church of Saint Antony and Saint Paul, whose spires rise over the monastery wall. It is the first building the visitor sees upon walking through the old gate. The swaying palm trees and garden and grape arbor to the left offer a very picturesque scene: 'from the walls one looks down into the monastery which looks like a typical Egyptian village with mud brick houses, narrow streets, numerous churches, gardens, palm trees, and water channels'.[34] Piles of rubble and building material seem to be everywhere. At first this gives the monastery a disordered feel, but these actually indicate the monastery's vitality; construction and repair are taking place throughout: new cells, the new museum, the keep, several of the churches. This physical growth accurately symbolizes the phenomenal growth in egyptian monasticism in the past forty years, not just at Saint Antony's, but throughout the country. In 1936 Saint Antony's had ten priests and fifteen lay brothers, a number that held steady over the next quarter century. In 1960, the monastery had twenty-four monks. In 1986, by contrast, the number had grown to sixty-nine,[35] and is holding steady today,[36] partly because monks from Saint Antony's have left on assignment to teach and work in egyptian parishes and to found new monasteries in Australia and the United States.[37]

This continuing rapid expansion (three novices were consecrated as monks during our visit) has undoubtedly not been without some cost. Saint Antony's has changed enormously in the past forty years. Obviously some of this is good: the increased numbers indicate a new dynamism and spiritual force. Monasticism in Egypt is growing, both spiritually and physically, not just holding on, as is often the case elsewhere. Thousands of pilgrims seek out the monastery each year. When the wall paintings are cleaned and restored, there will probably be a significant influx of tourists, bussed in from the new Red Sea resorts. These visitors, unfortunately, will also bring increased noise and disturbance. They raise an important question: Is the role of the monk to pray in quiet or to be a tour guide?

A chance conversation that Betsy and I had with Abouna Maximous one day crystallized this dilemma. As the articulate, English-speaking liaison for Bishop Yustus, Father Maximous spends much of his time dealing with the outsiders who are rapidly bringing change to Saint Antony's. We ran into Father Maximous as we were strolling about one afternoon taking pictures. When the conversation turned to some of the features of the monastery, Maximous turned wistful, his voice tinged with regret: 'The elevator'—what I have called the 'lift'—'was used until the '50s. Until then you could enter the monastery only by way of the elevator. There was no gate. At that time one visitor wanted to come through the wall; he was so respected and so important that they knocked a hole in the wall. Later they put in a gate'. As we have already seen, this account of the origin of the gate may not be historically accurate, but it is symbolically factual: visitors are changing the monastery, Father Maximous believes, and not always for the better.[38]

'Back then', Abouna Maximous continued, 'the bell used to ring to announce visitors; it was very rare. One almost never heard the bell ring'. Sixty years ago, one traveller recorded his impressions of such an event: the silence 'is broken only by the explosive clanging of the bell which, swaying at the end of its long rope, announces one's arrival with almost indecent suddenness and vigour'.[39] Père Jullien reported that at the time of his visit in 1884 his party were the first visitors to the monastery in four years; by 1936 the number of visitors had increased to fifty a year.[40] 'Now we have too many visitors to ring the bell', Father Maximous lamented; 'it would ring all the time. It was paradise here then. Only monks; no workers, no visitors. It was quiet. Now all has changed'.[41]

Most of us tend to romanticize 'the good old days'; perhaps it is even easier to sentimentalize the past in a monastery, where dizzying change is not supposed to occur. But the sense of loss in Abouna Maximous' voice was real, and painful. I don't believe it is inaccurate to say that for a thousand years daily life at Saint Antony's changed very little: it was a life of prayer and work, with few outside distractions. Now the lift and the old mills used for grinding olives and grain are merely part of the tour given to visitors. Cars drive in through the old gate and wheat is trucked in from Cairo. There are, thank goodness, still no outside telephones at Saint Antony's (though there is an intercom telephone system), but the monastery has offices in Cairo, and Father Maximous himself often drives to the capital.[42] When he took us to Saint Paul's Monastery (see below), he talked there with a monk, just returned from surgery in the United States, who had visited much of the eastern seaboard. On the one hand, Father Maximous craves isolation; on the other, jet travel allows for medical care and the founding of far-flung monastic dependencies. The monks will increasingly confront rapid social and technological changes. They are not alone; Thomas Merton voiced many of Maximous' complaints and concerns in the '60s at Gethsemani. If the monastery has changed more in the past forty years than in the previous thousand, the wall paintings themselves will bring about even more change—and already have. Perhaps it is not surprising that some monastic bishops have been wary of outside financial help. That is one way of dealing with change. The monks at Saint Antony's will have to decide if it is the best way.

Interlude, March 30: Martyrs

Jet-lagged, two AM, the wind whistling about the dormitory, a door or window left open banging open and shut, open and shut. Lying in bed in monastery darkness thinking of the cistercian brothers and fathers of Atlas, Algeria, their throats slit, murdered by islamic extremists, thinking it could happen here, right now, the forces of real darkness pouring through the unguarded gates in dead rage trying to murder the little bit of light there is in the world. Watch, holy fathers and martyrs of Atlas, over those of a different communion but same faith gathered together in this desert community, under the shadow of these rocks.[43]

ABOUNA ISAAC

I asked Abouna Isaac, who speaks good English, if I could talk with him about his life at the monastery. He hesitated: 'It's not easy to speak about your inner life, but OK, I'll be happy to talk with you'. We met one evening before dinner in the refectory in the guest building where the conservators were staying. We sat at the table and talked over tea.

'Tell me about your life here, Father'.

Pause. 'Shall I go get my book of prayers? I have one in English in my room, but all I have with me (patting his cassock pocket) is one in Arabic.[44]

'Our life, of course, is built on prayer. About every three hours we pray, either together or individually. Each office opens with prayers and Psalm 50; the opening prayers are designed for the time of day of each particular office.

'Now we start our prayers at four in the morning because it is Lent. But usually we pray at the first hour, about six or seven. Of course, this office varies during the year, depending when the sun rises.[45] This is the office of resurrection. We say the opening prayers and then the prayers and psalms and gospel passage for the morning, then we conclude with prayer.[46] Next we pray at the third hour, about nine. This is the office that commemorates Christ's betrayal and also the gifts of the Holy Spirit. In the same way, the sixth hour marks Christ's crucifixion and the ninth hour his death. The eleventh hour is also called the Sunset Prayer. It's the time when Jesus was taken from the cross and prepared for burial. It's my favorite. I like to stand, walk, and pray when I say the offices, so I go where I can see the sunset.[47] At this time we say the *Kyrie* forty-one times. Do you know why forty-one? [No]. Thirty-nine for the lashes, once for the crown of thorns, and once for the spear in Jesus' side. Then comes the Prayer of the Veil, which is for monks only; it focuses on Judgement. Finally, the midnight prayers, which remember Jesus in the garden of Gethsemane. We say the midnight prayers together, unless you have a special dispensation. Because it's Lent, we're saying them now from 4 to 6 in the morning. All these prayers have something working in them; if you say them, God will then work in you. After that we go to our work. I help with financial matters or I assist Abouna Maximous; I do whatever needs doing'.

'Could you tell me about yourself?'

'Yeah, sure'.

'How long have you been a monk?'

'I was ordained in 1987. I came to the monastery in 1985 as a novice. I had gone to school in Cairo, majoring in Business Administration. I was born in Cairo. I have two brothers and two sisters in Australia. We had talked about all being together, in the same country, so in 1993 I went with two others to found a monastery in Australia, Saint Antony's in Melbourne. Now there is another monastery in Sydney. I've been back here for two and a half years.

'My family traveled a lot when I was a kid, so when I got older I wanted to live somewhere else, in Europe or America. So I went to New York. I was there for five years, from when I was twenty-four to twenty-nine. I worked for Republic National Bank of New York. I was in the Big Apple. Americans would look at me now here, out in the desert, and ask, "Why aren't you making big bucks in America?" It's difficult to talk about one's personal relationship with God. I don't talk about it much, but I'll tell you; I don't know why.

'It was my dream since I was young to go to Europe. When I was nineteen I went to London for three years. I returned to Cairo just before the death of my father. I thought a really exciting place to go would be America. I finished my last year at the university, and went to the States.

'I was very fortunate. I had a really good income. My boss was a Jew born in Egypt; he had to leave Egypt at sixteen. He took a shine to me, and was always looking to advance me, help me move up. But I still had a very big question in my life. I had a good position, but what came after that? Every night after work I would go to the top of the World Trade Center. I could see all of New York from up there. All my life I had dreamed of going to Europe or America. Now I was in America, the best country in the world. Now what? I used to sit there at night. Can you imagine—all of New York at your feet! If this is the best, where do I go from here? Why am I not happy? Is everything here everlasting? No, my mother and my father had died. Is there another life? God is life. I'd look up. "Please let me know you", I'd say.

'There was a cemetery in front of the World Trade Center. I'd look down at it and think, "As much as a person goes up, no matter how high we go, we have to come down, and we'll be buried there".

'Was I going to church? Not much. But then I started going to church. In New Jersey. I kept asking and searching. Then an answer came. This part I can't talk about. Sorry. Three years and a half of asking, little by little I got an answer. God did not abandon me. I started to read: the Bible, saints' lives, the monastic life. The more I get close to God, the more I need to know more. I really feel good when I pray, go to church, and confess to a priest.

'Yeah, I believe there is a time when the whole world is disturbing you and you really want to be with the One you love with all your heart. I did not hesitate. There was a holiday. I told my boss I was going to Egypt. Everyone asked, "Are you going to get married?" "Yes", I told them. (I meant that I was going to marry Christ, the bridegroom.) My boss was happy for me. He got me a present, increased my salary, and gave me a promotion. He told me he would throw a big party for me when I got back. I never went back. I left a letter, explaining to him why I was going to the monastery'.

'Why did you choose Saint Antony's?'

'Because I had read about him. I went to Bishoi to see the pope and asked him if I could go to Saint Antony's, and he said yes. I now have a relationship with God. I'm looking forward to meeting him.'

Interlude, March 31: Tuesday Afternoon

A silver-bearded monk in the afternoon sun beating the dust out of brightly-colored persian carpets. A wizened nut-brown man riding a small donkey up a back street. A generator running all day at the western perimeter, up close sounding like an idling big-rig, from far away like distant traffic on a freeway. Young copt boys kicking up dust as they walk, joking and laughing. A boy driving an empty donkey cart with two boys running at his side. The wind rustling the palm trees with a single black crow hovering overhead, then flying behind the domes of the new church and away from view. The sky a startling blue overhead, in the distance cairo-hazy with dust. A donkey braying while pigeons rise and circle over the dovecote.

An ancient stone capital (sixth century?) sitting on a patio with the shaft and wheels of a mill no longer used. Six monks, bearded and clothed in black, emerging from a doorway and walking together down the main street, talking and laughing, going in and out of sun and shadow.

Three small round loaves of bread, dried out and brittle, on a stone bench, looking like broken sand dollars washed ashore on a California beach. Two yellow crosses, one on top of a portal, the other the apex of a church steeple, the only two objects of that color in sight. Afternoon shadows moving up the wall of the ancient keep. A cat meowing. Hammering. Arabic voices.

The Wall Paintings and the Conservators

The church of Saint Antony's was closed to the public while I was there, so it was a great privilege to be inside. Scaffolding was everywhere—put together, I noticed, without nails; how old was that tradition?–some of it ten and fifteen feet high. I felt like Pinocchio looking up at the ribbing of Monstro, the giant whale that swallowed him.

The wall paintings in the Old Church at Saint Antony's are unique in coptic art in being unusually complete. These paintings, which run the full length of the church of Saint Antony, depict equestrian martyrs (popular in coptic devotion, they guard church entrances), monastic saints, Old Testament patriarchs, archbishops of Alexandria, the archangels Michael and Gabriel, the four living creatures of the Apocalypse, Cherubim, Mary the Mother of God, and Christ himself, risen and enthroned. No painted churches from before the islamic conquest of 641 AD survive in Egypt. Several monastery churches, including Saint Paul's, have surviving paintings from later centuries, but none approaches the completeness of the painted program at the Monastery of Saint Antony. Remarkably, this is also one of a small number of coptic painted programs that include a dated inscription. The inscription states that the paintings were finished in AM 949 (1232–1233 AD).[48] Few coptic paintings can be accurately dated, and the secure date for these paintings will allow art historians to provide better dates for other coptic wall paintings. In their newly cleaned state, the paintings at Saint Antony's are striking and powerful, painted in brilliant colors.

The restoration work at Saint Antony's is also contributing to our understanding of the monastery's history. Up to this time, the Old Church had been dated to the early thirteenth century, but it is clear now that the church itself can be dated at least four hundred years earlier than previously thought, and probably more. Just as importantly, a thorough study of the paintings and the church will reveal a good deal about the worship and devotional practice of the monks of the monasteries and the many pilgrims who have come to Saint Antony's over the centuries. The paintings in the nave begin about five feet from the floor, leaving the lowest zone of the church without paintings. For centuries, pilgrims, monks, and crusaders have been inscribing prayers, their names, and, in some cases, heraldic insignia, on these walls. Around the nave at least three layers of inscribed plaster exist below the paintings. The graffitti on these layers provide direct textual evidence of those who came to the church over the years. These scratchings and writings offer a unique and precious document of the devotional practices of people who usually leave no personal traces in the historical record. They will provide unusual evidence of the ways people used paintings, for example whether they addressed their prayers to the saint depicted above the wall where they were writing, and what kinds of things they were asking for.[49]

These paintings, when cleaned and restored and opened to the public, will take their place as one of the great monuments of ancient christian art.

We had hurried to the church the night we arrived to look quickly at the paintings, like children on Christmas or Easter morning. It was as Betsy was giving me a guided tour of the paintings the day after we arrived, that, to my delight, I recognized painted on the walls the figures of saints whose works I had translated: Athanasius, Peter of Alexandria, Antony, John the Little (the only extant painting of him), Pisentius. Here they were, gazing serenely down at me.

On the southwest wall of the sanctuary is a painting of Abraham, Isaac, and Jacob, each holding to his breast one of the saved in paradise. To their right is a recently-uncovered figure seated in flames. He is holding up the index finger of his right hand in supplication while he touches the index finger of his other hand to his lips. The inscription above him is fragmentary, while below him is written ⲁⲙⲏⲛ *(amen).*

'I haven't been able to figure out who this is', Betsy told me. This figure on the right has just been discovered with cleaning; earlier scholars didn't know he was here. But who is he?'

I looked at the figure. *Amen?* Why would you put 'Amen' below him? 'Wait a minute', I said. 'There's the top of another letter there. It's got to be † *(ti).* It spells ⲁⲙⲏⲛ[†] *(amenti)*—hell! That's Lazarus over there', I exclaimed, 'in the bosom of Abraham, and this guy in hell is the rich guy! You know—the story in Luke [16:19-31] about the poor man Lazarus and how he's ignored by this rich guy? Lazarus dies and goes to heaven, while the rich guy (*Dives* in Latin) goes to hell. He looks across the chasm separating him and Lazarus and sees Lazarus in the bosom of Abraham. And he says to Lazarus, "Please give me a drop of water so I can quench my thirst in these flames!".

'I translated a homily that's got this story! By Peter of Alexandria, *On Riches*. That's him there! Wow!'[50]

'I'm glad you're here!' Betsy exclaimed.

So was I.

Later I was able to recall the rich man's name in coptic tradition, Nineve. I wondered if the indecipherable writing above his picture on the wall included his name. And, if so, the scholar in me wondered, 'This raises the intriguing question: Did they have a copy of the homily by Peter here, or is this part of oral tradition?'

Perhaps the most unexpected delight of my trip to Egypt (other than the fact that I didn't get gravely ill with dysentery, like the previous time) was the time I spent with the five italian conservators who were working on the paintings. Every day I was with them for several hours in the church, watching their meticulous and painstaking work. Each day Betsy and I also had the great pleasure of having lunch and dinner with them. Adriano, Luigi, Alberto, Emiliano, Gianlucca: their faces are as vivid to my mind's eye now as are the beautiful wall paintings on which they were working. Adriano and Luigi are the 'old men', in their forties; Alberto, Emiliano, and Gianlucca are youngsters, in their twenties, with twenty-year-old characteristics: earrings, surfer haircuts, a love of junk food, delight in american action films. In a way, the paintings at Saint Antony's should be honored to have these conservators working on them; they've worked on some of the most famous works of art in Italy, among them Bernini's *Saint Teresa in Ecstasy*.

Their work day extends from 8:30 to 12:30, until lunch and siesta, then work again from 2:30 to 7:30. They work hard, squatting, standing, kneeling, sitting for hours while they carefully remove the dirt and grime of centuries, clean the paintings, then restore damaged portions where they can. 'Adriano', Betsy exclaimed one day, 'has the hands of a surgeon!' That's as good a description as one can give of their work, except to add (and I'm sure Betsy would agree) that he, along with the others, has the heart and soul of an artist (each evening he would sit at the dining table working on architectual plans for renovating his home and garden in Italy).

As we watched him in admiration in the church one day, he was deftly flicking away a more recent layer of plaster, revealing several inscriptions. 'I am on a mission', he said, 'to looka for the inscriptions.' These read *nishti* and *makarios,* and allowed us to identify two saints on the north wall of the nave as Makarios the Great *(nishti)* and Makarios of Alexandria, fourth-century monastic leaders at Scetis (Wadi al-Natrun) and Kellia, respectively. We were like children discovering a new toy at Christmas, excitedly exclaiming over our new gifts, these names.

> *Interlude: The Picasso Mary*
>
> Adriano is up on the scaffolding, patiently working on the painting of Mary and Child that adorns the northeast wall of the nave. He has worked in such a way as to leave Mary bifurcated: half of her is dark and grimy, half brilliantly clean. Over the centuries well-intentioned hands have overpainted her and her son, and they did not always get the lines right. So now, half cleaned, she is akilter, the right side of her face slightly higher than the left. 'She looks like a Picasso', I comment to Betsy.

All the conservators speak English, Adriano and Alberto quite well. The previous year had been very hard for them at the monastery. Far from home, without good accommodations or the food they were used to, they had, by the time I arrived, a brand new building put up just for them, and had brought one of their helpers from the church, a sweet young Copt by the name of Ramses, into the kitchen, and had taught him to cook *al dente.* So twice a day we feasted on egitto-italiano cuisine: pastas, zuppa, prosciutto, parmesan, olive oil. It was hardly ascetic! Even more delightful, however, was the conversation—a gabble of Italian and English and Arabic at each meal. Each Saturday they would stop work at five and drive with Abouna Maximous to one of the Red Sea resorts for a one-day holiday, coming back Sunday evening. Betsy and I laughed as they prepared to leave on Saturday: young

Emiliano, the baby of the group, was decked out as if he were about to hit the night spots of Rome.

The world owes a debt to these five *Italiani*. The wall paintings are wonderful works of art, but without the conservators, they would remain blackened ghosts. I'll never forget these conservators, or stop thanking them.

Interlude, April 1: Bishop Samuel

Bishop Samuel al-Syriany, bishop of Shibeen al-Qanatar, himself a scholar and avid supporter of monastic scholarship and archeology, sitting in one of the flimsy wicker chairs in the nave of the church one afternoon with Bishop Yustus, his walking stick in one hand, his other hand holding his pectoral cross, talking with Betsy about her proposed visit to his monastery to study the wall paintings there, saying, when she expresses doubts about her being let in during Lent, 'If they give you any trouble, I'll get my gun!', guffawing, clearly enjoying his joke. 'My gun, I'll go get my gun!'

Bishop Samuel saying he used to be thin but now that he is a bishop all he does is eat and sleep, laughing merrily at his own wit (we laugh with him), squeezing the hand of Bishop Yustus, the equivalent of an american 'high-five', as if he were saying, 'wasn't that a good one?'

Bishop Samuel saying with a great laugh how being a bishop makes you old: 'five years as a bishop equals fifty years as a monk!'

FATHER LAZARUS THE SOLITARY

When Abouna Isaac told me that Saint Antony's had a hermit living on the mountain, he immediately got my attention; Otto Meinardus had reported in 1960 that there were no longer any hermits at Saint Antony's.[51]

'There's a hermit here?'

'Oh, yeeaahh' (with a prounounced New York accent), 'there are two, in fact'.

I asked if we could go see him, with Father Isaac acting as translator.

'Oh, that won't be necessary', he said. 'He's from Australia. His name is Father Lazarus'.

'Does he mind having visitors?' I asked.

'Not at all. A woman from Australia went up to visit him recently. In fact, he told me to send up any English-speakers to see him'.

We eagerly left the monastery after breakfast, heading west, then north, toward the mountain range, having only vague directions for getting there. 'Don't worry', Isaac had said. 'There's a gully to the left that you follow. You can't miss it'. We did. We passed by it and started climbing a new cement staircase leading towards the cave of Saint Antony. Then we spotted a trail to the left winding up into the mountain. 'It *is* to the left', I pointed out hopefully. Betsy agreed. So off we went. 'Think of it as an adventure', she added. 'If we don't find him, we'll have had a nice hike. After being cooped up all the time in the church, it's good to get out'. She was right; it was good. Soon, to our delight, we picked up along the trail a series of markers, little piles of rock indicating the way east and north into the hills.

After about half an hour of steady walking and climbing in the cool sunny morning, we rounded a bend. Straight up into the mountain went the trail. Towards the top was what looked like a small shack. A tiny black figure had just come out. I waved my arms. The figure waved back.

'Are you Christians?' he quickly demanded as we arrived. Surprised, a bit taken aback, we nodded and said yes. 'Good. I'm happy to have visitors, but they have to be Christians. I don't want to waste my time with people who aren't Christians'.

Seated on a rock ledge, the sun warming our backs and glasses of cool water in our hands, we sat facing Father Lazarus, whose back was to the sweep of valley below.

'I'm just feeding the sparrows now, but you've chased them off. I put bread crumbs out for them. There used to be lots more, but I went away for two weeks to see my spiritual father in the Wadi al-Natrun and when I came back only two were left. The others had given up and gone away, but those two stayed. They're tough'.

We saw one of the sparrows safely at a distance. Father Lazarus looked.

'She's timid and won't come near. But he, he's a rascal. Audacious'.

He smiled. After we chatted a few minutes, explaining to him why we were at Saint Antony's, in response to a question from me about his vocation, he began speaking.

'I was in a Serbian Orthodox monastery in Australia, but I longed for solitude. When the war was going on in the Balkans, it seemed we spent all our time caring for refugees from Europe. It was good work, important work, necessary, but it wasn't what I had come to the monastery for. I became Coptic Orthodox and joined a monastery in Australia.

'I came here and was sent to Saint Bishoi's in the Wadi Natrun. Do you know it? I asked the pope if I could go to Saint Antony's. The pope is a very intelligent man. He understands things. He scowled and said, "You stay here". So I stayed. He's the pope. But I kept asking, and he would look at me; sometimes he'd be angry with me, but sometimes he would smile. "We'll see", he said. So I waited, and kept asking.

'One day there was a great celebration at Saint Macarius' in the Wadi Natrun. Thousands of people were there. As people were waiting for His Holiness' blessing, I went up to him, right in front of everyone; I prostrated myself and received his blessing. "Can I go to Saint Antony's?" He looked at me, very stern. The pope's assistant spends Holy Week each year at Saint Paul's. He's from that monastery. Have you been there? So the pope turned to him and said, "When you go to Saint Paul's, take this one with you and leave him at Saint Antony's".

'So I came here and asked Bishop Yustus if I could be a hermit. He looked at me. "Wait", he said. So I waited. One day I went up to the cave of Saint Antony for the first time. I was alone. I prostrated myself before the icon of Antony. I felt Antony's presence in the cave. I don't know how to describe it to you; he was just there. As I lay on the ground, I heard a voice say *"mai nshêre"*. I didn't know Coptic, so I asked the monks what it meant, and they said "loving the children". They said it meant that Antony was telling me to live on the mountain.

'The next time I went to the cave, it was with the priest (I'm not a priest) and some others to celebrate Mass. During the service, I looked at the holy bread that had just been blessed and light was emanating from it, streams of light. I looked at the wine, and it had become gold. I knew that Antony was telling me by these signs that I should be with him on the mountain. So I asked Bishop Yustus again, and he said "Wait".

'There's another hermit living on this mountain. He lives just over there [pointing southeast]; you can't see his hermitage from here. One day, when he was at the monastery for his weekly visit, I was talking with him and he told me about the cave that Abouna Moses had lived in. He was from Ethiopia, Abouna Moses was. He came here a couple years ago to spend the fifty days of Great Lent in a cave on Antony's mountain.[52] Before Easter he went back to Ethiopia.

'So I came up to see his cave. Right there, behind you. I'll show you in a minute. I started coming up here to pray when I could. The monastery is a good place, but it's no place for a monk. Too crowded. Too busy. After a while I asked for five copt boys to help me carry water and plaster and brick up here, to fix up the entrance to the cave a little, build this wall here. They said OK, so we did it. A little later I asked the master mason if he would come up here with some boys and help me build a hermitage. This was a big request. The mason was surprised, but he did it. He came up here, and in two hours we had built onto the front of the cave and added the kitchen here. In just two hours! You can see what a nice job we did!

'So I asked Bishop Yustus if I could become a solitary. Not a hermit. A hermit is someone who never sees anyone. A solitary is someone who lives alone, but still occasionally sees people. Each week I go down to the monastery on Saturday to participate in the liturgy. Saturday night I help bake the holy bread for Sunday. After Mass on Sunday and lunch, I come back here with water and supplies. It's Lent now, so I only go down each fortnight. Bishop Yustus looked at me, kind of scowling. "I've built a hermitage", I said. "Yes, I know", he replied. "Saint Antony told me to let you become a hermit". Bishop Yustus didn't tell me whether Saint Antony had spoken to him or whether he just felt it in his heart. But he knew that Saint Antony wanted me to be a solitary.

'So I came up here to live in the cave. It wasn't like it is now. There was no door, barely a roof. Abouna Moses had just used palm fronds or planks or something for a cover. The first night I was here, I was outside. I heard talking from within the cave, so I went inside. There was some language I couldn't understand.

Maybe it was Ethiopic. But I realized it was Father Moses telling me to stay. He had left his cross in the cave. I picked it up, and it was warm. I really can't describe it. It was like—what's the word?—an electrostatic shock. (I speak so seldom that I forget how!) That's it. Static electricity. There was a charge coming from the cross. And it was warm in the cave when it shouldn't have been. The monks ask me, "Abouna Lazarus, don't you get cold?" and I say, "No, never. It's always warm inside". Father Moses keeps the place warm for me.

'So I came here to stay. Here there is only me and God. The cenobitic monastery is like a school, where the teacher beats you if you don't learn your lessons. At the monastery, if you don't go to Mass, the Bishop calls you on the phone and says, "Where are you?" (He laughs, and we with him.) Here I am responsible to God.[53] Here there is peace. I am at peace'.

The monologue above is an accurate *précis* of what Father Lazarus said to us over the course of half an hour or so. We said very little. I didn't have a tape recorder. I did have a notebook, but as soon as he started speaking I knew it would be inappropriate to use it, not out of politeness, but because I knew his words were on fire and I would only smother the flames by trying to contain them. So he spoke and we listened, rapt.[54]

After talking, Father Lazarus gave us a tour. The cave, hollowed out of the rock face, serves as his sleeping quarters and place of prayer. To the right is his kitchen, which he took great pleasure in showing us. In the small glassed-in cabinets I noticed four or five jars of jam. 'Here is where I fix my meals. This is my table, where I eat and where I do my sewing', he said, indicating a low table with a spread covered by a glass pane, as in a restaurant, with his sewing on top. 'I'm very happy with the glass. The cloth was always getting dirty, but now with the glass, I just wipe the top off, and the cloth never gets dirty.'

'Here are my supplies', he indicated to his right: powdered milk, bread, vegetables, coffee, honey. 'I love coffee; I've never been able to give it up. I don't use sugar, but I have honey; I'm like Winnie the Pooh'.

'I used to have a mouse here, "Abouna Far", I called him, which means "Father Mouse". He used to be such a nuisance. He'd get into everything, chew holes in all my bags and eat up all my food!

"Abouna Far", I said, "we need to find another place for you to live". So when we built the WC—the brothers told me I had to have a WC; I couldn't just go in the mountains, although the sun would dry it up—I told Abouna Far to go live in the WC, and he did. He lives down there now, and we're both very happy with the arrangement!'

Next he showed us his cell, the cave. 'This is a holy place', he said. 'Please take off your shoes. Betsy, I'm afraid you can't come inside, but please, look in. The cave is like a womb. My cell *is* a womb. I am very devoted to Mary. She is our Mother, no?'

The front part of the cave, with an altar, or perhaps just a shelf, against the wall, has icons of Christ, Saint Mary, and Saint Antony, including a copy of the great early icon of Christ from Saint Catherine's Monastery in the Sinai. The back part, divided with a curtain, is for sleeping. 'Here are my books. I have Bible commentaries and other books, but all I need is the Bible and the lives and sayings of the desert fathers. Everything else is unnecessary.'[55]

Father Lazarus and I stood in the antechamber. He began the Lord's Prayer, and I joined in, then we said the Creed together. Afterwards he prayed, then anointed my forehead and wrists with holy oil and blessed me. Going outside, he did the same with Betsy.

Then he showed us the three additional places of prayer that he has built. To the north of his cave is a ledge with two stools where he recites morning and evening prayer. He has chosen this spot because from here he is able to see the entire valley floor and watch the movements of the setting sun.

'During the year the sun moves from there to there', he said, pointing to two places on the horizon. From here I can watch the sun set every night. During the winter, when there are clouds, I'm treated to the most glorious sunsets I've ever seen anywhere.

'From here I can also watch the moon. She is very important to me. I call her my Lady. Except for the time each month when she is away, she gives me light at night. When the monks come up the trail to Saint Antony's cave to say Mass at midnight, I come here at eleven o'clock. See that bend in the trail going up to Antony's cave? I wait for a lighted signal from the climbing monks. One signal says they will go on to the cave; another tells me that Mass that night will be at the church of Saint Paul the Simple, the disciple of Antony. They celebrate it in the small church if there are too many people to fit in the cave. As soon as I see the sign, I turn and head up the mountain to join them'.

Back towards the cave, there is an enclosed space he has built out of mud brick and plaster, modeled on sheep pens in Tasmania, where he comes from. 'Sit down', he tells me. 'It blocks the wind, doesn't it? Oh, the wind up here on this mountain is so strong a lot of the time that I can hardly leave my cell. Sir Blow-Me-Down, I call him. He barely lets you stand. But inside there he can't touch me, and it's nice and warm, so when ol' Sir Blow-Me-Down is acting up, I go in there to pray. You got a good day for your visit. Very little wind. The other day it was howling like crazy'.

Then he took us up some steps on the roof to his cell. 'I had them make the roof flat. That way I can come up here to pray'. We sat and looked out over the valley. 'I say the Jesus Prayer up here, in Greek. I was a monk on Mount Athos before I came here, so I say it in Greek. It's better in Greek. Do you know the prayer?'

'Yes', I replied.[56]

'You have to say it with your breath, like this (showing us). "Kyrie" goes much better with the breath than "Lord". It's hard to breathe in on "Lord". You place your head on your breast and look to your heart. You roll yourself into a ball, like this. People ask, "Why don't you pray like the Buddhists, sitting with your palms open?" but we say the ball, the circle, is the symbol of perfection'.

I told Father Lazarus that the monks at Kellia fifteen hundred years ago had prayed the Jesus prayer.[57]

'I didn't know that; I'm so glad to hear that. It is the best prayer'.

I also told him that the Jesus Prayer and centering prayer were popular in America, taught by the Benedictines and Cistercians.

'I'm very happy to hear that', he replied.

'These places of prayer', he said, 'show me the importance of the union of prayer and place. It's so important that your prayer be part of where you are and that where you are be part of your prayer'.

Father Lazarus walked us halfway down the mountain.

'Just step where I step, and you'll be fine. There used to be no trail here, but I've built one. After I test the rocks for three years, to make sure they're firm, I'll plaster them so the trail is secure'.

We said our goodbyes. We turned to go back down the mountain to the monastery; he slowly made his way back up. After we had left him, I said to Betsy, 'I don't think we'll ever forget that'.

'No', she said, 'I won't'.

'We've just seen Saint Antony', I said. 'Or as close as we're going to get at the end of the twentieth century. And the amazing thing is, he's not a relic. He's bearing all the tradition of fifteen hundred years of prayer and union with God; yet he's a modern man, too'.

What Antoine Guillaumont said about the ancient monks of Kellia perfectly describes Father Lazarus, too: 'The monks went there to leave their monastic houses and the excessive socializing of Nitria in order to live in solitude'.[58]

Further down the hill, we turned back and waved, but Father Lazarus had his back to us, making his way up the mountain. Betsy took a picture of him, a small black figure against the enormous backdrop of rock, with the immense, infinite, blue sky opening out above him.

Interlude, April 2: La Luna

Taking my nightly walk around the perimeter, looking up at the waxing moon, naming her, in honor of both Father Lazarus and the italian conservators, 'la luna di lazaro', which sounds a lot better than 'lazarus' moon'.

THE MONASTERY OF SAINT PAUL; ABOUNA FANOUS

The Monastery of Saint Paul (Deir Anbâ Bûlâ) is twenty kilometers southeast of Saint Antony's.[59] The latter lies on the northern slope of the South Galala range, while the former lies on the southern side of the same mountain chain. Père Jullien made the journey by camel in nine hours in 1884.[60] Our escort and driver, Abouna Maximous, walked the twenty kilometers the previous year with a party of foreign visitors, camping overnight in the desert and enjoying it immensely. They walked from 8 AM to 5 PM one day and from 7:30 to 7 the next. Less hardy, we took the longer but easier route and drove the eighty-nine kilometers, east to Zafarana and south towards Ras Gharib, before turning west for the final twelve kilometers to Saint Paul's. Abouna Maximous turned on the air conditioning and played a tape of gregorian chant.

Saint Paul's is much smaller than Saint Antony's, with many fewer monks. The reason is simple: water—or the lack thereof. The spring at Saint Antony's—Antony's well—provides the monastery with a hundred cubic meters of water a day; the spring at Saint Paul's, by contrast, produces only five. As a result, there is only one garden at the monastery and it is small. Saint Paul's has four churches, one of which, named after the monastery's eponymous saint, is erected over the cave that tradition assigns to Saint Paul. As at Saint Antony's, there is a keep, an old mill and lift, an old refectory (recently remodeled), a guest house, old and new cells, but all on a smaller scale.

We had come to Saint Paul's partly just to see it and primarily for Betsy to see the wall paintings in the old church; they have not been cleaned and restored and are badly faded.[61] 'The Church of Saint Paul or the Cave Church is the spiritual centre of the monastery,' Meinardus wrote. 'The sanctuary was originally built into the rock-cave, where St. Paul used to live. It is here where the bodily remains of Anbâ Bûlâ [Paul] are preserved'.[62] You go down stairs to enter the church, and the walls and dome as you enter are painted with equestrian saints who boldly guard the entrance to the church. We were able to watch the last half hour of Mass, look at the paintings in the church and photograph them. Then we were given a short tour by Abouna Maximous, the highlight of which came unexpectedly, both for him and for us.

As we were sitting in the anteroom of a building, sipping hot tea, Abouna Maximous was visiting with some monks of the monastery. Suddenly he became very excited when one of the monks whispered something to him. He got up and went into a room to our left whose doors had been closed. After a few minutes, he returned, clearly pleased. 'Today I am very happy', he said, as he bade us get up and ushered us into the room. Seated at the side of the room was an elderly *abouna* having an audience with a small group of lay people. He seemed short and a bit round, held a monastic staff, and had a kind, almost mischievous face. At first I thought he might be blind, but then I realized that his eyes were unusual. Maximous nudged me forward before the old man. I knelt. He placed his hands on my head, prayed over me, then anointed my forehead and wrists. He did the same for Betsy. After we left the room, Father Maximous kept telling us how happy he was, what a wonderful day it was for him, to have seen and been blessed by Abouna Fanous.

After we had left the monastery, in the car on the way home, Father Maximous told us his story.[63]

'Abouna Fanous (his name comes from Stephanos) came to Saint Paul's when he was very young, maybe fifteen or sixteen, back in the '40s probably. After a few years, there were almost no monks left, maybe he and one other monk left at the monastery.[64] It was a very strong life, very hard. Abouna Fanous spent most of his time at the little mountain inside the new nineteenth-century extension, breaking stones with a little hammer. Nobody cared. They thought he was crazy. Only later, after the monastery had been revived, did they understand. When they were renovating the monastery, they used the stones he had broken for building material for the new buildings.

'Nobody knows who he is until now. He is not famous. The bishop of the monastery didn't even know about him. But then people started to come to seek the blessing of Father Fanous. The bishop got angry at this; he was jealous maybe that they were seeking the blessing of Father Fanous instead of his own. Father Fanous does very strange things: he gives the impression that he has eaten before the Mass; he comes to Mass with crumbs of bread in his beard. This shocks people. So the bishop exiled him to the monastery's farm in the Fayum. When they prepare the car to take Father Fanous to the Fayum, he doesn't complain. The bishop says "Give Father Fanous' room to someone else"; he thinks Father Fanous will never return. When the monks open his room—it was a very old cell, and no one had entered—they found nothing, just walls. Just walls. They were very surprised.

'When he went to the farm, all the people go there, big busses. He was living on the second floor of a building. The bishop did not like what the people were doing, so he closed the second floor with wood, completely. It was like living in a prison, but Father Fanous doesn't complain: he's very happy. I went to the farm once with the Dutch ambassador. The ambassador left after spending one hour with Father Fanous. He said, "He's not a normal man; there is something in his eyes".

'After the bishop left, Father Fanous returned to his old cell. He looks like he is not a normal man. You could say "abnormal", but no, he is a holy man. When they killed [President Anwar] Sadat at noon, he was sitting with the youth at the gate that morning; he told them, "Today they will kill Sadat". He does many miracles. All the people are trying to see him, but they can't because he stays in his cell. He is a very holy man. I am so glad I got his blessing. He is the saint of this century, the only one left from last century; he is living the old fathers' life, a very holy man.

'A priest from our church was celebrating Mass at Saint Antony's, and he saw Father Fanous in the church. He wanted to greet Father Fanous after the Mass, but when it was over Father Fanous was not there. He had not come to Saint Antony's in body; he had come in spirit.

'He tries to protect his holiness, keeping it secret. He does strange things to make people think he's mad. One time he wrapped his fingers and hands in cloth so people would think he's mad. But they said "He is doing this because light is coming from his fingers". But it wasn't. He was just trying to tell the people that he is a man, not a holy man'.

> *Interlude, April 3: Saints*
>
> Saint Mark the ascetic, fourteenth century, who has had numerous miracles happen in his name since he went to his rest on July 15, 1386, his relics reposing in the northern part of the nave of the church named after him, built on the site of his cell.
>
> Bishop Yousab el Abah, went to his rest on January 24, 1826, his body, still intact, lies in the church of the apostles.
>
> Father Yustus el Antony, keeping silent most of the time, known for his humility, often found kneeling in prayer in front of the church throughout the night, having memorized all the psalms by heart, his prayers a source of healing for many, going to his rest on December 17, 1976.[65]

THE CAVE OF SAINT ANTONY

The cave of Saint Antony, a site of pilgrimage for thousands of Copts, lies southwest of the monastery in the Gebel al-Galala, three hundred meters (a thousand feet) above the monastery. Betsy and I headed out at 9:30, after breakfast and some picture-taking in the church, on a bright sunny day. Once again, as with our trip to see Father Lazarus, we were fortunate with regard to the wind: old Sir Blow-Me-Down was not stirring. Later, during our climb, we found it difficult to imagine climbing the mountain in a *Khahmseen;* a wind of forty-fifty miles an hour could peel you off the cliff face like a rock chip and hurl you below. As we headed out I thought about the wind that had come up suddenly the other day in the afternoon. It was hard to even *walk* in such a wind, much less climb.

We walked west out of the monastery, not out of a gate, as I had expected, but at a point where the monastery wall just sort of peters out. Maybe the builders of the wall didn't expect enemies from the west, I thought. We walked past some new industrial buildings made of plastered mud brick, then by some new monastic cells, apparently uninhabited as yet. Recently plastered and shining white in the morning light, they contrasted starkly with the old wall behind them, weathered and browned by sand, sun, and wind.

We followed the dirt road turning south. After a few minutes' hike we came upon a great stone relief chiseled in the rock face, as Egyptians millennia ago had carved images of their gods and pharaohs. But this image was that of Saint Antony. The chiseling is professional, very clean and precise. After about fifteen minutes we saw to the east, marked by three oil drums, the dry creek-bed that leads to the trail to Father Lazarus' hermitage. Just a few feet straight ahead the climb to the cave begins. From here it is a steady climb upwards, not exhausting or hazardous, just a slow steady climb up into the mountain. In 1884, the Jesuit Jullien commented that little piles of rock marked the way for the pilgrim,[66] as they today mark the trail to Father Lazarus'. The rock markers are gone now; in their place is a new wide cement staircase with guardrails. There are even newly-built rest stops, every fifty meters or so, that look like they will someday have covers to block the sun. Now the markers are left by the pilgrims, who use bricks to form small crosses on the ground to commemorate their coming.

More than halfway up we came upon a new barrel-vaulted church, two years old, set on a flat stretch of rock to the east, a church dedicated not to Saint Antony but to his disciple Paul the

Simple. A hundred years ago, Jullien's guide stopped him before a big rock within a small enclosure of dried brick and told him these were the ruins of Saint Paul's cell. He told the Jesuit this story:

> When the holy patriarch [Antony] found those who were ill or possessed whom he was unable to heal, he sent them to his disciple, convinced that Paul the Simple had received a more abundant grace in these matters. See this large rock weighing more than one hundred pounds: one day Paul placed it on his head, saying to God that he would not remove it until he had obtained healing for a possessed person who had been brought to him.[67]

Jullien, who had a condescending, if not dismissive, view of the 'schismatic' Copts, says he didn't know how much credence to give to 'this tradition of the monks'. One wonders if he was as skeptical of the traditions of his own Church.

Just before reaching Saint Paul's, we came upon a group of five or six Copts—all young boys except their supervisor—working on the trail, running a portable generator that gave them electricity to weld the guardrails. Now the trail steepened, and we were climbing right up against rock face. Jullien had uttered no complaints, but both of us, mildly acrophobic, were very glad for the cement steps and guardrails! Now we were high above the Wadi Arabah, which must have been a sea floor eons ago, stretching far away to the north. We could now just barely see the far western end of the monastery, the rest being hidden by mountains.

After a few more minutes of slow climbing, hugging the cliff face, we came up onto a ledge, and saw the mouth of the cave twenty feet to the west, in the south wall of the mountain. To our right, on a ledge below the cave and looking north to the Wadi, was a striking sight: dozens of wooden crosses planted by pilgrims, some still straight, others aslant, leaning crazily in all directions. 'That's a pretty good climb down there to leave those crosses', Betsy said. We looked at the crosses. It was very moving. I imagined the pilgrims carrying their crosses up the trail, like Christ. 'That's how Golgotha must have looked', I replied.

The entrance to the cave is unassuming. Unfortunately, you know you're at a pilgrimage site because of all the litter, even within the cave. A large picture of Saint Antony announces the entrance, along with dark black lettering in Arabic saying 'Please Take Off Your Shoes'. We removed our shoes, as one does before entering all churches in Egypt, and went inside. A long, narrow tunnel greeted us, less than six feet high (I had to bend over), and no more than a foot or two wide (I had to turn my shoulders sideways to move). 'It smells like dirty socks', I muttered as I moved inside. I think I was a bit disappointed. I suppose on reflection that I could try to say something pompously theological on the incarnational nature of sweaty feet. That thought makes me laugh, and we did find the smell funny. And that's OK. Copt pilgrims travel packed on busses without air conditioning for three or four hours from Cairo to get to Saint Antony's; then they hike for an hour straight uphill in the hot sun to get here. It's no wonder the cave smells like dirty socks. The shrine *should* smell like a gym! And the odor *does* in fact remind us of the very incarnational efforts and prayers of thousands of pilgrims.

The tunnel is about ten or twelve meters long. At its end, the cave turns down and to the right and, now beyond the light from the entrance, it is nearly pitch black. As we peered down into the darkness that seemed to go on forever, Betsy lamented the fact that she had forgotten her flashlight. We waited for our eyes to adjust as we debated whether to drop down into the dark hole or turn around and head back. Finally, I took a step forward—and found that there was an immediate ledge just a foot or two below, and then, to my left, another few feet down, the grotto itself. As Jullien observed, the cave was evidently carved out by water running over the white limestone of the mountain.[68] The grotto is seven meters long, running from west to east, two meters high at its entrance, and three meters at its greatest height. The floor, like a church, is covered with carpets. There is an altar, icons of Antony and Mary, and a small locked closet to store communion vessels. We sat down, happy to be here, and were silent.

I didn't hear Saint Antony speaking to me in Coptic as Father Lazarus had, but then I didn't expect to. Only someone with Father Lazarus' burning desire and vocation can be vouchsafed such an experience. We were more like tourists, but I feel we were honest ones: we respected the site, and honored its founder and shared the faith of those who come to see him. The next day, at dinner in the refectory, to our great surprise and delight, in came Father Lazarus, on his fortnightly visit to the monastery, to have dinner with us. We eagerly told him we had gone to the cave. His eyes grew large and shone as he said, 'Yes, yes', over and over to our narration. I told him that touching icons and kissing one's fingers afterwards is not part of my Church's tradition, but that I had touched the icon of Antony at the cave and kissed my fingers in benediction. He was very pleased.

Interlude, April 4: Death, Life, and the Ringing of Bells

The feast of Saint Macarius the Great, Vespers, three novices dressed in white gowns and white skullcaps. All the monks of the monastery gathered in the small church in the garden, circumambulating the altar three times, following the bishop who walks behind a novice carrying a flowered icon of Saint Macarius, censing it, cymbals and triangles singing, the monks chanting in unison.

Now coming out of the sanctuary through portals in the wooden sanctuary screen, chanting and censing and circumambulating the front of the nave over and over, Lazarus and Isaac among them, clouds of incense billowing, the chant rising and falling in waves.

Lay people coming forward to touch the icon of Saint Macarius, bringing their fingers to their lips.

Later that night, at midnight, the monks of the monastery praying the liturgy of the dead, the novices lying on the ground with winding sheets placed over them, and afterwards rising to receive new, monastic, names.

The bells ringing out at midnight, then again at four, on and on, for fifteen minutes ringing in celebration for these three young men, now clothed in monastic black, their death day, their birth day, their baptism, two weeks before Easter their Easter.

Returning

Today is Palm Sunday[69] in the Western Churches; for the Orthodox it's still one week away. For millions of Western Christians, today commemorates the day that Jesus entered the gates of Jerusalem to take on the Principalities and Powers. You could say that Jesus lost, but Christ won.

The Principalities and Powers have not gone away. They are still out there, beyond the gates, barbarians ever at the gate. I say 'outside' because for one brief week here, without newspaper or radio or television, I haven't felt those Powers breathing down my neck or pounding within my rib cage, holding my heart prisoner. Except for some homesickness, I have been at peace within these monastery walls. When Father Lazarus speaks of peace, I think I have some small idea of what he means.

I know that that feeling is dangerously close to being sentimental and self-deceiving—and self-serving. I'm sure that if I spoke Arabic and lived permanently here within these gates, I would see plenty of sinful behavior, my own included. But for one week, at least, I have had a vacation from the Devil. The monastic desert tradition insists that the demons of this world do not shrink back at the sight of monastery gates (which we might see symbolically as the spiritual gates of the human heart and soul); rather, they see them as provocation, as insult. Someone is actually trying to live a holy life! How dare he! How dare she!

Yet I believe there are saints here, behind these walls. Three of them lie in churches, still very much alive to the faithful. Long rows of saints painted in glorious color on the walls of the Church of Saint Antony bless with their eyes and living countenance anyone who looks upon them. Anyone. I'm sure there are also saints dressed in black walking around here. Barriers of language and culture and tradition have prevented me from seeing them whole. But even a partial view, I realize, is valuable.

Going out through these gates is like entering Jerusalem, once again facing the Principalities and Powers that lie in wait. In seven days Christ will re-enter the gates here to remind the monks yet again that evil and malevolence do not crouch outside looking in, like terrorists with machine guns hiding in the hills; they live inside, like false friends, forcing their way into every nook and cranny of every stone and human heart.

But Christ showed the way, both coming and going. To me, leaving this place, that is our hope, our only hope, whichever side of whatever gate we live on. Holy Week. Hallelujah! Lord, in Egypt you are leading me in the desert from mountain top to mountain top. Amen.

NOTES

[1] For his story, see the *Life of Onnophrius* translated Tim Vivian in *Histories of the Monks of Upper Egypt and the Life of Onnophrius* (rev. ed., Kalamazoo: Cistercian, 2000) 143–166. A wall painting at the Monastery of Saint Jeremias at Saqqara depicts him with other monastic worthies. See J.E. Quibell, *Excavations at Saqqara (1906–1907)* (Cairo: IFAO, 1908) volume 2, Plate XLIV, with a description on p. 64; Nabil Selim Atalla, *Coptic Art: Wall Paintings* (Cairo: Lehnert and Landrock, n.d.) 15; Paul van Moorsel and Mathilde Huijbers, 'Repertory of the preserved wallpaintings from the monastery of Apa Jeremiah at Saqqara', *Acta ad archaeologiam et artium historiam pertinentia*, ed. Hjalmar Torp, et al. (Rome: Bretschneider, 1981) 9:131-135 and Plates IV–V; Marguerite Rassart-Debergh and Jacques Debergh, 'A propos de trois peintures de Saqqara', *Acta*, ed. Torp, et al., 9.187-201. An icon of Saint Nofeir may now be seen on the web at <http://pharos.bu.edu/cn/pictures/Icon. StTaklaAndNofeir.jpg>.

[2] See J. M. Sauget, 'Onofrio', *Bibliotheca sanctorum* 9 (1967) 1187–1197, and C.A. Williams, *Oriental Affinities of the Legend of the Hairy Anchorite* (2 vols; Urbana: University of Illinois, 1925–1926). His name survives in the name of the actor Vincent D'Onofrio and in the name of the California town San Onofre.

[3] For the story, see Tim Vivian, *Journeying into God: Seven Early Monastic Lives* (Minneapolis: Fortress, 1996) 25–36.

[4] The *Life of Antony* refers to both the 'outer' *(exō)* mountain, Pispir (54.6, 61.1, 63.1, and 91.1), where there was a community of disciples, and to the 'inner' *(esō, endon)* mountain, Colzim (51.1, 91.1), where he lived, which becomes just 'the mountain' (55.1, 60.1). Both occur in 91.1: as his life drew to a close, Antony wanted to thwart attempts to mummify his body and so 'shared his plans with the monks on the outer mountain [ἐν τῷ ἔξω ὄρει] and then hastened away. So he went to the inner mountain [τὸ ἔνδον ὄρος] and remained there, as was his custom'. Numerical references to the *Life* are to the Greek text edited by G.J.M. Bartelink, *Vie D'Antoine*, Sources chrétiennes 400 (Paris: Cerf, 1994) 123–377.

[5] See *Historia Monachorum* 1.44-45; translated Norman Russell, *The Lives of the Desert Fathers* (Kalamazoo: Cistercian Publications, 1981) 59. For a discussion of mountain and desert in early Egyptian monasticism, see Vivian, *Paphnutius*, 18–26.

[6] See Vivian, *Journeying into God*, 166–187.

[7] For more on Antony, see Vincent Desprez, 'Saint Antony and the Beginnings of Anchoritism', *American Benedictine Review* 43 (1992) 61–81 and 141–172.

[8] As recently as 1952, Jean Doresse could describe Saint Antony's and Saint Paul's, the sister monastery nearby, as 'forgotten'. See his 'Deux monastères coptes oubliés', *La Revue des Arts* 2 (1952) 3–14.

[9] The project is supervised by Michael Jones, head of the ADP. See Elizabeth S. Bolman, ed., *Monastic Visions: The Wall Paintings at the Monastery of Saint Antony by the Red Sea* (New Haven: Yale University Press, 2002).

[10] See Chapter Two, above.

[11] See Michel Jullien, 'Voyage dans le désert de la Basse-Thébaïde aux couvents de Saint-Antoine et de Saint-Paul', *Les Missions Catholiques* 16 (1884) 188–273.

[12] Jullien, 189 (my translation).

[13] Jullien, 203 (again, the translation is mine).

[14] The term *Abouna* literally means 'our father' (the 'Our Father' used in the Lord's Prayer is said in accordance with the more accurate arabic pronunciation of "Abana"). Among Copts, it has become customary to call monks by that title. 'Brother' is also used, but more often than not, especially if one is not familiar with the monk, one tries to err on the side of rank and address him as 'father'; 'father' is also seen as a term of endearment, respect, or spiritual fatherhood. Then too, at this time, in contrast to the pachomian norm, most monks are ordained priest at some point after taking the habit. So even if one guesses that the monk is not a priest, most likely he is or is on his way to becoming one.

[15] Agnes Smith Lewis, 'Hidden Egypt: The First Visit by Women to the Coptic Monasteries of Egypt and Nitria with an Account of the Condition and Reasons for the Decadence of an Ancient Church', *The Century Illustrated Monthly Magazine* 68 (1904) 745–758, at 749.

[16] Jullien, 224.

[17] For a discussion of Saint Antony and the history of the monastery, see Tim Vivian, 'Saint Antony and the Monastery of Saint Antony', in Bolman, ed., *Monastic Visions*. See also Otto Meinardus, *Monks and Monasteries of the Egyptian Desert*, rev. ed. (Cairo: The American University in Cairo Press, 1989) 5–6. For a brief history of early monasticism in Egypt, see Chapter Two above.

[18] For examples, see C. C. Walters, *Monastic Archaeology in Egypt* (Warminster: Aris & Phillips, 1974) 7.

[19] Abu Salih does not enhance his credibility, however, by adding that the monastery was built when 'Sapor, son of Artaxerxes', ruled (241–272). B.T.A. Evetts, ed. and trans., *The Churches and Monasteries of Egypt and Some Neighbouring Countries, Attributed to Abû Sâlih, the Armenian* (Oxford: Clarendon, 1895) 161. It seems probable now that this work should be attributed in the main to Abu al-Makarim, who was writing around 1170. The work has several layers and possibly redactors, one of whom may have been Abu Salih, and seems to have been composed from 1170 to 1208 (or 1220). See Johannes den Heijer, 'The Composition of the *History of the Churches and Monasteries of Egypt*: Some Preliminary Remarks', in David W. Johnson, ed., *Acts of the Fifth International Congress of Coptic Studies* (Rome: C.I.M., 1993) 2: 209–229. See 210–211 for a discussion of Evetts' volume and the full arabic edition of Anba Samuel.

[20] Cuthbert Butler, ed., *The Historia Lausiaca of Palladius* (Cambridge: The University Press, 1898–1904; rpt. Hildesheim: Olms, 1967) 1:223.

[21] See Sulpicius, *Dialogue* 1.17; Bernard M. Peebles, trans., in Gerald G. Walsh, et al., *Niceta of Remesiana: Writings, Sulpicius Severus: Writings*. . . . (Washington, D.C.: Catholic University of America Press, 1970) 184.

²² See Butler, 1:231-232 and 232 n. 2.
²³ Peter Grossmann, 'Dayr Anba Antuniyus', *The Coptic Encyclopedia*, ed. Aziz S. Atiya (New York: Macmillan, 1991) 3:724.
²⁴ Pachomius (c. 290–346) founded a cenobitic monastic community at Tabennisi in the Thebaid about 320. His 'Koinonia' eventually consisted of nine monasteries for men and two for women. See *Pachomian Koinonia*, 3 volumes, translated Armand Veilleux (Kalamazoo: Cistercian Publications, 1980–1982). Shenoute the Great († c. 450) founded the White and Red Monasteries in Upper Egypt and served as their archimandrite or leader.
²⁵ Antoine Guillaumont, 'Histoire des moines aux Kellia', *Orientalia Lovaniensia Periodica* 8 (1977) 187–203, at 194.
²⁶ The 'Rule' of Saint Antony is later. See H. G. Evelyn White, *The Monasteries of the Wâdi 'n Natrûn* (3 vols.; New York, 1926–33; rpt, New York: Arno, 1973) 2:16.
²⁷ Walters, 7.
²⁸ See Walters, 11–12, 86. See Chapter Two.
²⁹ Around 870, Patriarch Shenoudah had Deir Anba Maqar (Saint Macarius) surrounded by a high wall; see Evelyn White, 3:9.
³⁰ See Walters, 11–12. The dating, he says, is 'somewhat conjectural'. The booklet published at the monastery dates the keep to 537.
³¹ The excavators at Kellia have dated the abandonment of the outer cells and the concomitant retreat inside protective walls to the second half of the fifth century; however, at the end of the fifth century or beginning of the sixth, some monks remained in their isolated cells, fleeing inside the walls in danger. See Guillaumont, 200 and 202. Peter Grossmann reports that the monastery retained its original anchoritic structure as late as 1672.
³² See Evelyn White, volume 2, plate VB, following p. 497.
³³ Meinardus, 30.
³⁴ Meinardus, 31.
³⁵ For 1936, see H. Romilly Fedden, 'A Study of the Monastery of Saint Antony in the Eastern Desert', *Bulletin of the Faculty of Arts of the University of Egypt* 5.1 (1937) 1–60, 51. See also Meinardus, x.
³⁶ For coptic monks the proper term is 'consecration' rather than 'ordination'. In Arabic *siyama* (< *sama*) is sometimes used, which can mean either 'ordination' or 'consecration'. A distinction is usually made with the qualifier 'of the priests' or 'of the monks'. But another term, *takris*, which is more precise and means 'consecration, dedication', is also used specifically for monks, and is the one found printed in the book containing the actual rite. 'Brother' is the normal way of addressing the novices who are not yet consecrated.
³⁷ Monks from Saint Antony's also go to the Monastery of Saint Antony in Jerusalem; see Otto F. A. Meinardus, *The Copts in Jerusalem* (Cairo: Commission on Oecumenical Affairs of the See of Alexandria, 1960) 65.
³⁸ An illustration in Jullien's account of 1884, 211, shows a gate to the left of the lift, exactly where the gate is today, though it does appear to be blocked up.
³⁹ Fedden, 51.
⁴⁰ Jullien, 214; Fedden, 51.
⁴¹ Meinardus, 26, says that 'until the beginning of the twentieth century, the only contact that the monastery had with the outside world was the monthly camel caravan that supplied the desert monks with food and necessities from the dependency of Bûsh in the Nile valley'.

[42] On a return visit to the Wadi al-Natrun in 1999, I was struck by the number of monks who had cell phones!

[43] See Bernardo Olivera, *How Far to Follow? The Martyrs of Atlas* (Petersham, MA: Saint Bede's Press, 1997; reissued, Kalamazoo, Cistercian Publications, 2001).

[44] The english prayer book Abouna Isaac uses, the *Agpia* (or *Agbeya*): *The Prayer Book of the Seven Canonical Hours* (Sydney: C.O.P.T., rev.ed., 1997), may be ordered from C.O.P.T., P.O. Box B63, Bexley, N.S.W. 2207, Sydney, Australia. It is also available in the United States from Mr Wagdi Guirguis, 804 Eaton Drive, Pasadena, CA, 91107. There is another translation by Father M. Wahba, *The Agbeya: The Coptic Book of Hours* (San Francisco/Cairo, 1994).

[45] This way of reckoning the times of prayer by starting at sunrise, the first hour, is very ancient and may be found in the fourth-century monastic sources.

[46] Abouna Isaac told me that the monks pray the entire psalter each day.

[47] Several mornings I was out at dawn and I saw monks walking with their prayer books and praying.

[48] AM The date may be found in an inscription to the right of the painting of Saint Mercurios in the Khurus; see René-Georges Coquin and Pierre-Henry Laferriere, 'Les inscriptions pariétales de l'ancienne église du monastère de S. Antoine, dans le désert oriental', *Bulletin de l'Institut Français d'Archéologie Orientale de Caire* 78 (1978) 267–321 and Plates XXXVII–XCII; 304; see also Bolman, ed., *Monastic Visions*. The Coptic Church uses a calendar beginning in 284 AD which marks the beginning of the reign of Emperor Diocletian, the leader who instigated the Great Persecution, the last systematic oppression of Christians under roman rule. Thus 284 AD is 1 AM. Founded on the martyrs, the Coptic Church dates itself from their sacrifice. (AM = *Anno Martyrorum*).

[49] Most of the description is drawn from Elizabeth S. Bolman, 'Monastic Visions: The Wall Paintings at the Monastery of Saint Antony by the Red Sea. Prospectus for a Book on the Wall Paintings at the Monastery of Saint Antony by the Red Sea'. I wish to thank Dr Bolman for this material. See now Bolman, *Monastic Visions*.

[50] For the story, see Birger Pearson and Tim Vivian, *Two Coptic Homilies Attributed to Saint Peter of Alexandria* (Rome: C.I.M., 1993) 49–53 (Sahidic text), 72–74 (Bohairic), 104–108 (translation into English).

[51] Meinardus, *Monks and Monasteries of the Egyptian Deserts*, 1st ed. (Cairo: The American University at Cairo Press, 1961) 32. In the mid-1950s there was 'a young hermit', Abouna Buqtur (Victor), who, though living within the monastery walls, was living in a 'cave' scooped out of the rocky mountainside in imitation of Saint Antony; see Meinardus, *Monks and Monasteries* (1st ed.), 72–75.

[52] In the Coptic Church, Lent lasts around fifty days.

[53] Or, as an irish monk has wittily put it, 'A hermit is, as such, able to pull his own leg only'. Hugh McCaffery, "Saint Benedict," *Hallel* 24.1 (1999) 5–10, at 6.

[54] For a report by Maged Mikhail of his visit with a hermit in the Wadi al-Natrun, see Chapter Two.

[55] Later that week Father Lazarus asked me to send him copies of other collections of the Apophthegmata; when I did so, I wrapped them in Winnie-the-Pooh wrapping paper.

[56] The full prayer, which may be shortened, is 'Lord Jesus Christ, Son of God, have mercy on me, a sinner'.

[57] See Antoine Guillaumont, 'Histoire des moines aux Kellia', *Orientalia Lovaniensia Periodica* 8 (1977) 187–203, at 203. On the modern use of the Jesus

Prayer, see Kari Vogt, 'The Coptic Practice of the Jesus Prayer: A Tradition Revived', in Nelly van Doorn-Harder and Kari Vogt, edd., *Between Desert and City: The Coptic Orthodox Church Today* (Oslo: Novus forlag, 1997) 113–120.

[58] Guillaumont, 189.

[59] See now William Lyster, *The Monastery of Saint Paul* (Cairo: The American Research Center in Egypt Press, 2000).

[60] Jullien, 238.

[61] Meinardus comments, interestingly [*Monks and Monasteries* (1st ed.), 111], that in 1960 the paintings in the church of Saint Paul were in better condition (though of inferior artistic quality) than those of Saint Antony's.

[62] Meinardus, 111.

[63] I had a notebook in the car and took down Abouna Maximous' words as accurately as I could, so this faithfully represents his English.

[64] Meinardus, *Monks and Monasteries* (1st ed.), 114, says that there were twenty-two monks in 1960.

[65] See Meinardus' account, written while Yustus was still alive and had long been considered a saint by his fellow monks, *Monks and Monasteries* (1st ed.), 75–76.

[66] Jullien, 237.

[67] Jullien, 237.

[68] Jullien, 237.

[69] The Sunday before Easter.

Part Two

Translations

The Good God, the Holy Power, and the Paraclete:

'To the Sons of God'
(Ad Filios Dei)
by
Saint Macarius the Great

Introduction

SAINT MACARIUS THE GREAT

MACARIUS THE GREAT, also called Macarius the Egyptian (to distinguish him from Macarius of Alexandria) is one of the most venerated saints of the Coptic Church (his name, which means 'blessed', is 'Makarios' in Greek, in Arabic 'Maqar'). He was born around the year 300 in Jijber (present-day Shabshîr), a village in the southwest portion of the Nile delta. He was, therefore, a child during the Great Persecution of 306–311 and a teenager when Constantine promulgated the Edict of Toleration in 313.[1] As a young man he was a camel driver; as part of his job as a gatherer of natron, he may have visited the Wadi al-Natrun, his future monastic home.[2] Still a young man, he became a village ascetic or anchorite, like Saint Antony and others before him.[3]

About 330 Macarius went to the Wadi al-Natrun (Scetis), southwest of the Nile delta, about the same time as Amoun was founding a monastic settlement just to the north in Nitria during 'the finest epoch of Egyptian monasticism'.[4] The ancient sources differ on the reason for his *anachoresis* (withdrawal); the most lively and amusing story is an autobiographical report in the *Apophthegmata* or *Sayings* of the desert fathers and mothers in which Macarius flees the world after being falsely accused of getting a village girl pregnant.[5]

Settling eventually near the site of the present-day monastery named in his honor, Deir Anba Maqar, Macarius at first lived alone: 'When Abba Macarius dwelt in the great desert, he was the only one living as an anchorite, but lower down there was another desert where several brothers dwelt'.[6] Soon, however he began to attract disciples and a small community formed around him. By 340 a growing monastic settlement was solidly in place in Scetis; a mere sixteen years later, Abba Sisoës would leave Scetis for remoter regions, complaining that it was now too crowded.[7] Little more is known for sure of either Macarius or his community at this time. Macarius apparently was made a priest ten years after coming to the Wadi al-Natrun.[8] During the Arian persecution in 374 he was deported to an island in the delta, returned some time later to Scetis, and died about 390.[9] As with other monastic saints, his body underwent numerous adventures and movings about, coming to rest finally at Deir Anba Maqar, where it is venerated today.[10]

Macarius' life, as was often the case, too, soon became the stuff of legend.[11] In coptic tradition, legend and history are difficult, if not impossible, to untangle; they grow together like cucumber vines embracing tomato plants in a summer garden: each bears fruit, and is sustaining, but it is difficult to separate them without damaging both plants. In coptic tradition, Macarius was later hailed as 'the first shoot of this vine . . . that is Shiêt [Scetis]'.[12] In this case ancient greek and latin sources provide corroborating evidence that it was Macarius who founded and established monasticism in Scetis.[13] His importance, therefore, can scarcely be overstated: Scetis, along with Nitria and Kellia to the north, was to early christian monasticism in the greco-roman world (and not just in Egypt) what Cluny and Cîteaux were to the high Middle Ages in Europe. But Macarius' importance only begins there. The monasteries of Kellia and Nitria are long vanished, covered by the desert sand, but the monasteries of the Wadi al-Natrun are alive and flourishing (see Chapter Two above). Without them, it is very doubtful whether Christianity in Egypt, a minority religion in a Muslim land, would have survived to the present. In addition, the present-day monastery of Saint Macarius in the Wadi al-Natrun is leading a remarkable revival of monasticism in Egypt that affects the entire Coptic Church.[14]

Macarius came to preside, in a loose manner, over the monks of Scetis. These monks were semi-anchoritic; that is, they lived alone or in small groups in scattered cells, and came together as a larger community usually only on Saturday and Sunday, when they celebrated the Eucharist together and participated in a communal meal. We should not impose later structures, either architectural or monastic, on these monks. The monastic enclosure with its high defensive walls would not become the rule until the ninth century, and the rules and regulations of medieval, benedictine, monasticism, much less the rules of modern orders, were unknown to them. The best way to understand these early monks is not historically, but spiritually, through their thought and practices; the *Sayings* of the desert fathers and mothers offer the best access to their world.[15]

At their best, the early monks simplified the spiritual life to work and prayer, and they erected no boundaries between these two, seeing them as integral parts of life in God.[16] In the same way, they numbered their spiritual precepts as two or three, and not in the thousands: 'Do no evil to anyone, and do not judge anyone. Observe this and you will be saved', offered Macarius.[17] Macarius taught that prayer did not require 'long discourses; it is enough to stretch out one's hands and say, "Lord, as you will, and as you know, have mercy". And if the conflict grows fiercer say, "Lord, help!"'[18] The monk was to become 'a dead man'. When a brother asked Macarius how to be saved, he was told to go to the cemetery and insult the dead; when the brother reported that he had done as he was told, Macarius then told him to go praise the dead. When the monk returned again, Macarius asked him, 'Did they answer you?' The monk said no and Macarius drove home his point:

> You know how you insulted them and they did not reply, and how you praised them and they did not speak; so you too, if you wish to be saved, must do the same and become a dead man. Like the dead, take no account of either the scorn of men or their praises, and you can be saved.[19]

Such advice might seem quaint to us today, unrealistic, but it is unrealistic in precisely the way that the Sermon on the Mount is 'unrealistic'—that is, it challenges us so profoundly that our usual defense is to dismiss it. In the same way, Macarius' actions are impossible to emulate, just as Jesus' are impossible. But Macarius, like Jesus, was known for his wonderworking: 'The Egyptian had acquired such a reputation that he always had a disciple with him to receive "clients" on account of the number of those who came to be healed by him'.[20] One day Macarius discovered a man plundering his goods, 'so he came up to the thief as if he was a stranger and he helped him to load the animal. He saw him off in great peace of soul'.[21] Strange? Yes. But less strange, perhaps, than someone today watching, with fear and trembling, as the stock market plummets five hundred points one day and rockets up three hundred the next, and calling such a life 'normal'.

It is worth noting that Macarius assists his thieves while quoting Scripture: 'We have brought nothing into this world, and we cannot take anything out of the world' (1 Tim 6:7). As a baptist preacher once told me, 'The hearse don't have no U-Haul followin' behind it'. Macarius, it seems, tried to live (or die) this understanding each day.[22] Such detachment, ancient monasticism shows again and again, can lead to real peace. One time when Macarius visited Antony, the two stayed up all night praying and plaiting rope. In the morning, the rope that Macarius was making trailed all the way out the window and down into the cave. Antony admired its length and exclaimed, 'Great power comes from these hands!'[23] Macarius, and the other monks of the desert, still have the power to offer us insight about being human:

Another time a demon approached Abba Macarius with a knife and wanted to cut his foot. But because of Macarius' humility he could not do so, and the demon said to him, 'All that you have, we have also; you are distinguished from us only by humility; by that you get the better of us'.[24]

DEFINING THE NATURE OF THE HOLY SPIRIT

Before we turn to the work *Ad filios Dei*, the monastic milieu, and its understanding of the Holy Spirit, it will be useful to give a brief summary of fourth-century thought on the Spirit, especially as articulated by the alexandrian writers Origen (who belongs to the third century and whose influence was immense), Athanasius, Didymus the Blind, and Basil (who, though Cappadocian, was greatly influenced by the alexandrian tradition).[25] These writers provide a background for *Ad filios Dei* and at the same time underscore how its concerns are very different from their own. From a theological perspective, the middle fifty years of the fourth century, the years of Macarius' monastic activity, could be called 'the decades of the Holy Spirit'. It was during this period that the Church struggled to define the nature of the third person of the Trinity, from the scant mention of the Spirit in the Creed of Nicaea ('And [we believe] in the Holy Spirit') in 325, to the decree of Emperor Theodosius in 381 that the Father, Son, and Holy Spirit 'are of one majesty and virtue, of the same glory, and of one splendor' and the canonization of this view later that year by the Council of Constantinople.[26] Between 325 and 381, Athanasius, Didymus, and Basil all wrote important works that helped the Church come to its understanding of the Spirit.

Origen, the spiritual and intellectual godfather of early egyptian monasticism, did not write a treatise specifically on the Holy Spirit. His concerns with regard to the Spirit were not, on the whole, those of a systematic theologian, but were instead pastoral and soteriological.[27] Therefore he has more in common with *Ad filios Dei* than do Didymus, Athanasius, and Basil, whose writings are more systematically theological and polemical. For Origen, the chief activity of the Holy Spirit is to promote holiness among those who believe in Christ; the Spirit operates through Christ and turns believers towards God.[28] One obtains salvation through the entire Trinity: 'it is impossible to become partaker of the Father or the Son without the Holy Spirit'.[29] For Origen, no egalitarian, the gifts of the Spirit are not promiscuously given:

> In those persons alone do I think that the operation of the Holy Spirit takes place who are already turning to a better life, and walking along the way which leads to Jesus Christ, i.e., who are engaged in the performance of good actions, and who abide in God.[30]

This belief, as we will see below, will again be found in *Ad filios Dei* and in the monastic tradition in general.

Athanasius, bishop of Alexandria, was the great champion of orthodox—that is, non-melitian[31] and non-arian—monasticism, and even sought refuge among the monks during exile from his see city.[32] As one would expect, however, from the person who coined the term 'Ariomaniacs', Athanasius, when he wrote on the

Holy Spirit, was not writing as a spiritual director offering advice to his monastic disciple, as Macarius is in *Ad filios Dei*; he was waging all-out war against the Arians and arian fellow-travellers. It was not until the 360s that the bishop of Alexandria offered a detailed theology of the Holy Spirit, and this developed within a polemical context. An arianizing group, the Tropici, accepted Christ as divine, but refused to accept the divinity of the Spirit (Athanasius dubbed them 'Pneumatomachoi', 'enemies of the Spirit').[33] In response, a synod at Alexandria held in 362, with Athanasius presiding, declared that the Holy Spirit has the same substance and divinity as the other two persons of the Trinity.[34] Responding to a letter from Bishop Serapion of Thmuis (who had been a disciple of Antony), Athanasius declared that the Holy Spirit is a divine person.[35]

Athanasius spent much of his theological and episcopal life championing the divinity of Christ. It should not be surprising therefore that he was concerned not so much with the activities of the third person of the Trinity as with the Spirit's relationship with the other persons within the Godhead. The divinity of the Holy Spirit, he insisted, is bound up with the divinity of the Son; 'it is from our knowledge of the Son that we must derive our knowledge of the Spirit'.[36] If the Son is divine, the Holy Spirit is divine; if the Holy Spirit were a creature, he could not be part of the Trinity.[37] The Son, in fact, sends the Spirit; the Spirit is the energy and gift of the Son: 'when we are quickened by the Spirit, Christ himself is said to live in us'.[38] Athanasius' trinitarian concerns are foreign to *Ad filios Dei*, which does not even mention Christ in connection with the Spirit. The chief interest of the writer of *Ad filios Dei* is not the *nature* of the Spirit but its *workings*, the way it guides and instructs.

The same intellectual-practical divide that separates *Ad filios Dei* from the works of Athanasius on the Spirit also differentiates it from the writings of Didymus and Basil. Both alexandrian theologians wrote on the Spirit in polemical contexts. Didymus wrote *On the Holy Spirit* sometime before 381 against the Pneumatomachoi. In his work he asserts that the Spirit is not created, and is a divine person, one in essence with the Father and the Son.[39] Around 376, responding to the 'shipwreck of the faith' caused by the arian crisis, Basil wrote his great treatise *On the Holy Spirit* (a letter to Amphilochius). There he defends the equality and divinity of the Spirit against Eunomius, a radical Arian.[40] 'The Holy Spirit partakes of the fullness of divinity', Basil affirmed.[41] Although Basil does show some interest in the way the Spirit works in people's lives, he, like Didymus and Athanasius, devotes the vast majority of his treatise to detailed theological explication.[42]

When compared with the writings of Origen, Athanasius, Didymus, and Basil, *Ad filios Dei* may seem to be a poor cousin, unlettered and simple. One might sniff disdainfully and say that it's not proper theology at all. But if we remember the monastic definition, attributed to Evagrius of Pontus (who *was* learned), that the theologian is one who prays, then we come closer to the spirit of *Ad filios Dei*. Unlike Athanasius, Didymus, and Basil, Macarius has absolutely no interest in defining the nature of the Spirit; his concern is with the ups and downs of the spiritual life, with the Devil, temptation, the workings of the Spirit, and, ultimately, the triumph of the soul over the forces of evil on its journey to God. *Ad filios Dei* is realistic about the trials and tribulations of the spiritual life, but in the end it offers this hope: 'if the heart turns about and holds fast to the commandments of the Spirit, it knows that it continuously abides with God' (par. 16).

AD FILIOS DEI

Numerous writings that are attributed to Macarius have survived in Greek, Coptic, Latin, Syriac, and Armenian, including the famous *Fifty Spiritual Homilies* (discussed below), which are of syrian, not egyptian, provenance, and thus are commonly spoken of as belonging to 'Pseudo-Macarius'.[43] Of all these works, the only one thought to have 'some chance of being authentic'[44] is the letter translated below.[45] Extant in Greek, Latin, Coptic, and Syriac, it is known from its latin title *Ad filios Dei*, 'To the Sons of God'.[46]

'Authenticity', a term often unnecessarily contentious among scholars, needs careful definition when the subject is early monasticism. In the narrow sense, 'authentic' in the context of the present study would normally mean that *Ad filios Dei* is a work that we can, with some probability, certify as having come from Saint Macarius. Authenticity, however, can be many-sided. Even if *Ad filios Dei* is not macarian, it may still authentically represent the thought and spirituality of early monasticism. In other words, attribution, though important, does not resolve the question of a work's meaning and value. Therefore, since certainty is impossible here, and since tradition has attributed *Ad filios Dei* to Macarius of Egypt, I will refer to him as the author. The search for the origins of *Ad filios Dei* is valuable, not because we must figure out who its author is or is not, but because of what we may learn from the very foreignness of early christian monasticism and its spirituality —or spiritualities—and the uncompromising challenge that it continues to offer to the faithful. In this case, the journey has more value than the destination.

We do not have any indisputably 'authentic' works by Macarius. Since Macarius lived his whole life in Egypt, it seems best first to see if we can locate *Ad filios Dei* in that country in the fourth century. This, however, will not be easy: *Ad filios Dei* is an unusual work, especially within the world of early *egyptian* monastic literature.[47] First, the letter is Spirit-centered, which right away sets it apart from most early monastic literature in Egypt. The alphabetical collection of the *Apophthegmata*, for example, contains hundreds of sayings attributed to the fathers and mothers of the fourth and fifth centuries, and yet the Holy Spirit is mentioned only a handful of times.[48] *Ad filios Dei* also uses three signature terms, terms essential to its message, that are rare or nonexistent in most other monastic literature of the time in Egypt: 'the good God',[49] 'the Paraclete', and 'the power' (or 'holy power').[50]

These three terms define both the structure and spirituality of this work attributed to Saint Macarius. *Ad filios Dei* is a letter of instruction to an ascetic on how to live the spiritual life. In the first eight paragraphs, the good God, 'through his mercy and compassion' (par. 2), watches over the ascetic and helps him contend against the Devil by means of ascetic discipline and practice. (This ascetic, interestingly, is never identified as a monk; he is *anthrōpos*, any person.)[51] So far, this is prototypically egyptian. In paragraph 9, however, halfway through the letter, a change takes place: when the ascetic's 'heart grows weary and faint-hearted', God sends to him 'holy power' and strengthens him. With the help of this power, God continues his ministrations in paragraphs 10–12, but then in paragraph 13, it is the power who 'begins to reveal heavenly things' and appears to be acting on its own. Who, or what, is this 'holy power'?

Saint Macarius the Great

In paragraph 11 this mysterious power appears to be the Paraclete, 'the Holy Spirit', whom, Jesus said, 'the Father will send in my name', and who 'will teach you everything, and remind you of all that I have said to you' (Jn 14:25).[52] In John's Gospel, Jesus explicitly identifies the Paraclete with the Holy Spirit. In *Ad filios Dei*, the Paraclete first seems to be another name for the 'power' as it takes over God's care of the ascetic. In paragraphs 15–17, the power becomes fully interchangable with the Holy Spirit.[53] Thus, in *Ad filios Dei* God (the Father) begins the ministry, but halfway through the text, gives way to the power / Paraclete / Holy Spirit, who acts in his stead. By the end of the letter (par. 17), as a result, it is not the commandments of God but 'the commandments of the Spirit' that Macarius says the ascetic must keep and live by. The Holy Spirit is not a central presence, at least explicitly, in the *Sayings* and *Lives* of the desert fathers and mothers, the writings that have traditionally been seen as most representative of early egyptian monasticism. The Spirit is, however, vitally important to the spirituality of the *Virtues of Saint Macarius*, a neglected text from the desert.[54] If *Ad filios Dei* does not seem typical of egyptian monasticism, we may do better first to look for its provenance elsewhere before we return to Egypt. Since the *Fifty Spiritual Homilies* attributed to Macarius are syrian in origin, perhaps Syria, another birthplace of christian monasticism, is the place to search for clues concerning the origins of *Ad filios Dei*. After Syria we will return to Egypt, to the letters of Antony and Ammonas and, finally, to part of the macarian corpus, the *Virtues of Saint Macarius*.

THE *FIFTY SPIRITUAL HOMILIES* AND *THE GREAT LETTER*

If the literature of early egyptian monasticism is not especially Spirit-centered, it is safe to say that the *Fifty Spiritual Homilies* and *The Great Letter* attributed to Macarius are.

> A Christian cannot reach what Macarius calls 'true prayer' . . . without the power of the Holy Spirit. The Spirit alone can teach the Christian that prayer in which the mysteries of God are taught directly to the

soul. The soul then knows the sweetness, the spiritual experience, the joy, and the various forms of ecstasy.[55]

The soul is illumined with the glory of the light from Christ's face and 'is perfectly made a participator of the Holy Spirit'; indeed, the soul 'is inhabited by the Holy Spirit'.[56] Being renewed by the Holy Spirit makes one 'fit for the heavenly kingdom'.[57] In language very reminiscent of the last paragraph of *Ad filios Dei*, the author of the *Spiritual Homilies* insists that

> unless we will now receive the heavenly love of the Spirit through ardent petition and asking by faith and prayer and a turning away from the world, and unless our nature will be joined to love, which is the Lord, and we are sanctified from the corrupting power of evil by means of that love of the Spirit, and unless we will persevere to the end unshaken, walking with diligence according to all of his commands, we will be unable to obtain the heavenly kingdom.[58]

Despite these similarities, however, the spirituality of *Ad filios Dei* is very different from that of the *Fifty Spiritual Homilies*. The author of the *Homilies* does not use the phrases 'the good God' or 'the holy power', and appears to refer to the Paraclete only once (Homily 18.10). The *Homilies* also place much more emphasis on sin and on Christ.[59] Conversely, *Ad filios Dei* makes no mention of baptism in the Spirit, so important in the *Homilies*. More importantly, it lacks the Spirit-mysticism that indwells the *Homilies*:

> Finally, when a person reaches the perfection of the Spirit, completely purified of all passions and united to and interpenetrated by the Paraclete Spirit in an ineffable communion, and is deemed worthy to become spirit in a mutual penetration with the Spirit, then it becomes all light, all eye, all spirit, all joy, all repose, all happiness, all love, all compassion, all goodness and kindness.[60]

Ad filios Dei and the *Fifty Spiritual Homilies* resemble one another in the emphasis they put upon the activity of the Spirit, but in the end they seem too different to be by the same author. Given this, it is best to resume the search for the origins of Ad filios Dei in Egypt, this time among monastic literature that, until recently at least, has been less well known. Once again, it is the Holy Spirit who is central to the quest, this time conjoined with that quintessential greek—and alexandrian—virtue: gnôsis, knowledge.

THE LETTERS OF SAINT ANTONY

Gnôsis and its cognates occur five times in Ad filios Dei.[61] The first sentence, in fact, proclaims that one of the main themes of the letter is self-knowledge (epignôsis) accompanied, importantly, by a turning to God:

> When a person turns to what is good and abstains from evil and devotes himself to learning about himself (epignôsin heautou) and regrets the things he has done in times of careless indifference and seeks God with his whole soul, then the good God makes him sorrowful for what he has done.

This emphasis on self-understanding and knowledge links Ad filios Dei directly with the heart of egyptian monastic spirituality. Abba Palamon tells Pachomius at the beginning of the latter's 'novitiate' that 'we will be ready, in so far as our weakness allows, to labor with you until you get to know yourself'.[62] Self-knowledge is central also to the letters attributed to Saint Antony, the 'father' of christian monasticism: 'Probably the most striking feature of the letters of Antony is their emphasis on knowledge, gnosis'; Antony 'invites and implores the reader to discover and understand himself. The chief criterion is experience'.[63] The Letters of Saint Antony have long been undervalued by scholars because their learning and philosophic background is indebted to Plato and Origen, and scholars assumed that these letters could not come out of the 'illiterate' monastic tradition of Egypt. Thanks in large part to the recent work of Samuel Rubenson, however, Antony's Letters now have a much more important place in our understanding of the world of early egyptian monasticism.[64] Although Rubenson's

'School of St Antony' has yet to be proven,[65] there can be no doubt that *Ad filios Dei* and Antony's letters share presuppositions, concerns, and even language. Indeed, they may come from the same monastic environment.

For Macarius, the spiritual life is conflict, struggle, and war against evil, Satan, and the self. This metaphorical reality—for the monks it was never 'mere' metaphor—may be found in the writings of the apostle Paul, Saint Antony, the monks of the desert and, from them, John Cassian in the West. But if this life is indeed struggle, 'the good and compassionate God' is ever present and ready with help: he freely sends his 'holy power', the Paraclete, the Holy Spirit.[66] Those of us in the West, heirs of Augustine and Luther and their ideas of prevenient grace, may be surprised to read that monastic spirituality requires that we first turn to God before God offers help. *Ad filios Dei* makes this explicit in its first sentence, and whoever authored the descriptive title of the letter in Greek perfectly understood the import of the letter: 'if he patiently endures the painful things that happen to him, little by little the grace of God will come upon him'.[67]

This understanding of grace as cooperating with human will (and vice versa) may be found in the controversial thirteenth of Cassian's *Conferences*, which conference, 'almost certainly, is responsible for the fact that Cassian hardly enjoys the title of Saint in the West, despite his vast influence'.[68] 'When [God] notices good will making an appearance in us,' Cassian wrote, 'he at once enlightens and encourages it and spurs it on to salvation, giving increase to what he himself planted and saw arise from our own efforts'.[69] Cassian visited Egypt at the end of the fourth century. The *Conferences*, although written some twenty-five years later, purport to represent the spirituality of early monastic Egypt and, for the most part, probably do. The *Life of Antony*, which became both a handbook and model for monasticism in the East and the West, vividly enacts the monastic understanding of grace represented by Macarius and Cassian. Early in the *Life*, Antony is tormented and assaulted by demons. And yet,

> the Lord did not forget Antony's struggle at that time, but became a support for him. Looking up, Antony saw that the roof appeared to be opening and a beam of

light descending toward him. Suddenly the demons vanished and the pain in his body immediately ceased and his dwelling was once again whole. Antony perceived the Lord's help, and when he took a deep breath and realized that he had been relieved from his suffering, he entreated the vision that had appeared to him, 'Where are you? Why did you not appear from the beginning so you could stop my sufferings?' And a voice came to him: 'Antony, I was here, but I waited to see your struggle. And now, since you persevered and were not defeated, I will be a helper to you always and I will make you famous everywhere.'[70]

Perseverance is extremely important in monastic spirituality and is necessary to gain God's help. For both the author of *Ad filios Dei* and the Antony of the letters, it is the Holy Spirit who works this cooperation between grace and human effort:

> If the soul endures and obeys what the Spirit has taught it about repentance, then the Creator has mercy on the weariness of its repentance through the labours of the body, such as prolonged fasts, vigils, much study of the Word of God and many prayers, as well as the renunciation of the world and human things, humility, and contrition. And if it endures in all this, then God the merciful sees its patience in the temptations and has mercy and helps it.[71]

This passage from Antony's first letter perfectly summarizes the spirituality of *Ad filios Dei*. As Rubenson has observed: 'Thus the Spirit is seen on the one hand as the initiator and guide to a life of virtue, and on the other as the gift granted to him who lives such a life. The Spirit summons man to repentance, but as a "holy power" it cannot enter a man unless he prepares himself'.[72] Antony's letters and *Ad filios Dei* share the spiritual terminology of the Holy Spirit as a 'power'; more importantly, both share the theological presupposition that divine help requires human effort.

The cooperation between God the Father and the Spirit links *Ad filios Dei* with the letters of Antony, especially the first letter, and distinguishes these writings from most other early monastic literature in Egypt. Yet, as we have seen, syrian monasticism emphasized the work of the Spirit. Of Antony's letters, only the first—the one with the closest correspondence with *Ad filios Dei*—is preserved in Syriac, with 'no trace of any translation of the other letters into Syriac'.[73] Thus it is possible that *Ad filios Dei* was written in Syria by someone who had knowledge of Antony's letter, perhaps in its syriac form.[74] Whether he was Egyptian or Syrian, the writer of *Ad filios Dei* firmly believed that God is 'good and compassionate'; and Antony speaks in similar terms: God is 'God the merciful'[75] and it is God 'in his benevolence' who acts on our behalf.[76] In Antony's letters God does not explicitly send the Spirit, but it is clear that the Spirit acts on God's behalf. First, as in *Ad filios Dei*, Antony writes that we must reach out to God, preparing ourselves through renunciation and ascetic discipline: 'Unless each one of you hates all earthly possessions,[77] and renounces them and all their workings with all his heart and stretches out the hand of his heart to heaven and to the Father of all, he cannot be saved'.[78] Then the Spirit comes: 'But I believe that those who have entered[79] with all their heart, and have prepared themselves to endure all the trials of the enemy until they prevail, are first called by the Spirit, who alleviates everything for them so that the work of repentance becomes sweet for them'.[80]

Both Antony and Macarius held that, if the believer perseveres through fasting and vigils and prayers, the Spirit will help him control every aspect of his life (understood in the letters of both writers by the use of the pauline image of 'the members' of the body). It is here that the most striking parallels occur between *Ad filios Dei* and Antony's first letter. For Macarius, after the believer 'acknowledges God and renders honor to God with great humility and contriteness of heart' (par. 13),

> then the Paraclete places laws in the pure heart of the soul and of the other members, and great humility of soul, and [instructs the person] to place himself beneath everyone and all of creation, and not to be concerned about the failings of others, and to see with the eyes what is right, and [instructs the person about]

guarding the tongue, and healing the feet to walk straight and the hands for working righteousness, worshiping with prayers, and bodily mortifications and vigils (14).

For Antony, the Spirit acts through 'many fasts and vigils, through the exertion and the exercises of the body, cutting off all the fruits of the flesh'. In this 'the Spirit of repentance is his guide, testing him through them, so that the enmity does not bring him back again. Then the guiding Spirit begins to open the eyes of the soul, to show it the way of repentance that it, too, may be purified'.[81] The Spirit 'leads each member of the body back to its original condition': thus, as in Macarius' letter, the Spirit 'sets a rule for the eyes that they may see rightly and purely', 'teaches the tongue its own purity, since its affliction is great', and also helps control 'the movements of the hand . . . now made firm by the Spirit and destined to move towards purity by prayers and acts of mercy'.[82] These powerful reflections on the working of the Spirit by monastic writers in Egypt and Syria become even more striking when we recall that their learned contemporaries, the bishops at the first ecumenical councils, were having a difficult time formulating much at all about the Spirit![83]

Both *Ad filios Dei* and Antony's letters are Spirit-centered and emphasize self-knowledge and renunciation, but they are different from one another. Macarius' letter does not emphasize repentance to the degree that Antony's letters (and the writings of Pseudo-Macarius) do, although in paragraph 16 *Ad filios* does say that if 'the heart turns about and holds fast to the commandments of the Spirit, it knows that it continuously abides with God'. More importantly, *Ad filios Dei* shows no knowledge of the platonist and origenist idea of 'the myth of the return', the return to our original being and goodness, that is so strong in Antony's letters and *Life*. Despite these differences, however, the abiding, even overwhelming, presence of the Spirit unites the writings. In both *Ad filios Dei* and Antony's *Letters*, the Spirit is a 'holy power' that supports, guides, and fills the believer. As Antony says in one letter, 'you should not regard your progress and entry into the service of God as your own work; rather a divine power supports you always'.[84]

The Letters of Ammonas

'Holy power', absent in the *Apophthegmata*, points both to the Bible and to Antony's disciple Ammonas, whose letters are another underappreciated source within early egyptian monastic literature, and the phrase therefore points back to Egypt. The 'quest for the historical Macarius' of *Ad filios Dei* thus ends in Egypt. This spiritual letter has affinities both with syrian monasticism (the *Fifty Spiritual Homilies* and possibly a syriac version of Antony's first letter) and with egyptian monasticism (the letters of Antony and Ammonas). The latter, however, seems to have the stronger claim. More important than its author, as I have suggested, is its milieu: rather than belonging to anything as specific as a 'school of Saint Antony', *Ad filios Dei* has spiritually tough roots deep in the desert soil of early egyptian monasticism. It seems reasonable to suggest that this letter comes from the same monastic environment as the letters of Antony and Ammonas, and that it also shares ideas with the *Life of Antony*. More important than even the milieu of *Ad filios Dei* is its spirituality, the way of life it so strongly recommended to the monks of the desert. The chief terms of *Ad filios Dei*—the good God, the holy power, and the Paraclete—come from the Bible, and there can be no doubt that Macarius believed he was recommending a way of life that was profoundly biblical, one that, if lived, would enable the believer to enjoy the power of the Spirit and the spiritual fruits of that power.

In the New Testament, power is both separate from (though intimately connected with) the Holy Spirit and identified with it. In Acts 10:38 Jesus, Peter says, was anointed 'with the Holy Spirit *and (kai)* with power'; in 1 Thessalonians 1:5, Paul speaks of *both* power *and (kai . . . kai)* the Holy Spirit. In Lk 4:14, Jesus is 'filled with the power *of* the Spirit" *(tou pneumatos),* and in Ephesians 3:16 Paul hopes that his readers will be filled 'with power *through [dia]* the Spirit'. In *Ad filios Dei* God first sends 'holy power' (9,11), then the power acts on its own (13); the power then becomes the Paraclete (14)—and there it is not clear whether the Spirit and the power are separate entities or synonymous (15). Finally, the power gives way (at least in name) to the Spirit.[85]

The letters of Ammonas, with their concern for righteousness and the resulting gifts of power and the Holy Spirit, come out of the same monastic and ascetic understanding as Origen, Antony, Athanasius (in the *Life of Antony*), and Macarius.[86] Once again, receipt of the Spirit has a prerequisite: Ammonas tells his readers that 'because your hearts are upright, you are able to acquire for yourselves this divine power . . . so that every work which is of God may be easy for you'. If his readers conquer vainglory and make their bodies acceptable, 'and abide living with [the body's] Creator', they can 'receive the divine power, which is better than all these things'.[87] (Grace is never mentioned in the text.) At the same time, Ammonas asks his readers 'to give yourselves to bodily toil and toil of heart, and stretch your thoughts up to heaven night and day, asking with all your heart for the Holy Spirit, and this will be given you', just as it was given to Elijah, Elisha, 'and all the other prophets'.[88] For Ammonas, the Spirit comes in two stages: first as the Spirit of repentance (which connects Ammonas with Antony), then as the Paraclete. The Paraclete is given only to perfect souls. Only after the Spirit of repentance has called a number of souls and completely purified them does it bring the Holy Spirit, who then fills them continuously with fragrant scents and sweetness.[89] As long as 'the righteous have the divine power with them, none can hold them back':

> The effect of this divine power, so long as it resides in a man, is that he despises all dishonour, and all honour from men, hates all the needs of this world, hates all the comforts of the body, cleanses his heart of every foul thought and all the wisdom of this world, and makes supplication with fasting and tears night and day.[90]

Several aspects of Ammonas' understanding of power and the Spirit may be difficult for us moderns, which is a good reason to attend to them; they may startle our presuppositions. These are precisely the characteristics that closely connect his letters with *Ad filios Dei:* (1) we must be 'upright' to receive the power; (2) the power causes trials and tribulations; and (3) God at times withdraws the power for our spiritual edification. With Antony, Macarius, and Ammonas, early monastic spirituality places great emphasis on the believer's righteousness and effort. When he or she turns to God, God is prepared to help the believer advance even further in the spiritual life. But for all three monastic writers, progress does not come without great effort, even suffering. The Devil wages war on the believer and wearies the heart (8). This is one of the chief themes of *Ad filios Dei*, of the *Life of Antony*, and of all monastic literature. Ammonas now explicitly links these trials with the gift of the Holy Spirit:

> But I want you to know what trial is. You know that trial does not come upon a man unless he has received the Spirit; and once he has received the Spirit he is handed over to Satan to be tried. But who hands him over? The Spirit of God. For it is impossible for Satan to try a faithful man unless God delivers him to be tried.[91]

Ammonas then goes on to say that this is the same Spirit who drove Jesus out into the wilderness after his baptism and allowed the Devil to tempt him (see Mk 1:12). The very trials the believer undergoes, then, are brought about by the Spirit and are imitations of Christ. Such an understanding may trouble us, but it is one that requires incredible faith. As the writer of the *Fifty Spiritual Homilies* bluntly and memorably puts it: 'Where the Holy Spirit is, there follow, as a shadow, persecution and struggle'.[92]

This is not a spirituality for the faint-hearted. As if 'persecution and struggle' were not enough, God at times deliberately withdraws the Spirit from the believer. The author of *Ad filios Dei* makes this clear:

> When the good God sees that the heart has been strengthened against its enemies, then he removes the power hour by hour and, once the power has become like a rudderless ship, listing aimlessly, allows the enemies to wage war through licentiousness and with the pleasures that come from seeing and the pleasures of spiritual pride and haughtiness.
>
> When the heart grows weary beneath the assaults of the enemies, then the good God, taking thought for his creature, once again sends the holy power to him and strengthens his heart and soul and body and all the

rest of his members by means of the <yoke> of the Paraclete. . . .

Then the good God begins to open "the eyes of the heart" so that the person might know that God is the one who strengthens him. Then the person acknowledges God and renders honor to God with great humility and contriteness of heart.[93]

The author of *Ad filios Dei* does not give the reason for God's withdrawal of power, but Ammonas does (sharing this belief with the *Life of Antony*): 'This is a sign of His activity and happens with every soul that seeks and fears God. He departs and keeps at a distance until He knows whether they will go on seeking Him or not'.[94] Humility, then, is one of the most important lessons the Spirit teaches: we cannot go it alone. God teaches the believer to 'know that God is the one who strengthens him. Then the person acknowledges God and renders honor to God with great humility and contriteness of heart'.[95] 'Great humility of soul' then teaches a person to be humble 'before everyone and all of creation, and not to be concerned about the failings of others'.[96] These are cardinal virtues of early monasticism: humility above all else, humility before others *and* the creation, and a humble refusal to stand in judgement of others.

If this seems like an unduly solitary struggle, it is not. The monk, 'whom God has taken to himself',[97] is never alone, despite his name ('monk' means 'solitary') and reputation: the good God, the holy power, and the Paraclete are always with him, guiding, exhorting, prodding, strengthening, comforting. This is, finally, the abiding and deeply felt message of *Ad filios Dei*. This understanding in turn takes us back to the watchful voice that speaks to Antony: 'Antony, I was here, but I waited to see your struggle. And now, since you persevered and were not defeated, I will be a helper to you always and I will make you famous everywhere'.[98] Some, Ammonas realistically says, will now fail: 'they become carnal and only wear the habit while denying its meaning'; the gate is narrow and the road is hard that leads to life.[99] Others, however, will beseech God with 'tears and fasting', and 'God in his grace will give them a greater joy than before'.[100] Perhaps this spiritual understanding can help us make sense of the otherwise difficult phrase in *Ad filios Dei* that ligatures weeping and gladness: 'the good and compassionate God sends to him holy power and strengthens his heart and gives him weeping and gladness and rest in his heart' (9).[101] Complacency is not an option on the authentic spiritual journey. The choice, these monastic writers remind us, is between fire and fire.

The Virtues of Saint Macarius

The Virtues of Saint Macarius, a collection of bohairic Coptic sayings by and about the great monastic leader of Scetis, preserves paragraphs 7–17 of *Ad filios Dei*.[102] Whoever assembled the *Virtues* in antiquity knew, then, that *Ad filios Dei* was attributed to Macarius. But is there more than this attribution to suggest that *Ad filios Dei* should indeed be assigned to Macarius? To answer the question, we turn once again to the three signature terms of the work: 'the good God', 'the Paraclete', and 'the power' (or 'holy power'). All three terms, rare in other monastic literature, do in fact occur in the *Virtues*. 'Power' and the goodness of God are important terms in the *Virtues*, but it is the text's emphasis on the Paraclete and the Holy Spirit and its close association of Macarius with the Spirit that closely connects it with *Ad filios Dei*.

For Macarius, Christ is the soul's 'good King', while Christ himself speaks of 'my good Father' and stands in 'the Father's goodness'.[103] God, Christ, the Paraclete, the Trinity, and Macarius himself all possess power.[104] Macarius, 'through the power of the Paraclete', wore humility like a cloak,[105] and in one of the coptic *Sayings of Saint Macarius* not found in the greek alphabetical collection, Abba Sisoës says that he 'saw the power of God going with' Macarius.[106] The Paraclete, too, is an important figure in the *Virtues*: Macarius tells his disciples that the Paraclete is at work in Antony's prayers, and Christ speaks of 'my good Father and the Holy Spirit Paraclete'.[107] But the Paraclete and the Spirit are associated particularly with the saint himself: Macarius speaks through the mouth of the Paraclete, which dwelt in him.[108] The conclusion of the work especially emphasizes Macarius' relationship with the Spirit: Abba Poemen, in a grand summing up, says that Macarius 'possessed a prophetic spirit' and was a Spiritbearer.[109] He possessed also the 'consolation of the Consoler' (Paraclete), that is, the Holy Spirit, which 'came down upon everyone' around him.[110] Macarius not only possessed the Spirit and the power of God, he also caused those near him to be visited by them.

Although *Ad filios Dei* has connections with the letters of Antony and Ammonas, the close association of the Holy Spirit with Macarius in the *Virtues of Saint Macarius* seems to place them most closely within the same provenance and milieu as *Ad filios Dei*. Therefore it seems reasonable to concur with Antoine Guillaumont that *Ad filios Dei* either comes from Macarius himself or from his spiritual descendants and community, a community that especially valued the movements of the Spirit and believed that the Spirit's continuing presence among them was due in large part to the graces of Saint Macarius the Great.

Ad Filios Dei
('To the Sons of God')[111]

FROM SAINT MACARIUS OF EGYPT

That it is necessary for a person to practice abstinence on account of the evil deeds he has done, and to turn with all his heart to God; that if he patiently endures the painful things that happen to him, little by little the grace of God will come upon him.[112]

1. When a person[113] turns to what is good[114] and abstains from evil and devotes himself to learning about himself[115] and regrets the things he has done in times of careless indifference, and seeks God with his whole soul,* then the good God[116] makes him sorrowful for what he has done.

* Dt 6:5, Mt 22:37

2. Afterwards, once again through his mercy and compassion, God grants to him bodily mortification through fastings and vigils and the recitation of large numbers of prayers and renunciation of the material world, and [allows him] to bear up under reprovals and to hate all bodily refreshment and to love weeping.[117]

3. Afterwards, God gives him weeping and sorrow and bodily abasement and [teaches him] not to be concerned about the failings of others but rather to be concerned only about his own failures and to be mindful of the day of his departure from

this dwelling place and how it is necessary to meet God,[118] and to picture before his heart the punishments,[119] and the honors bestowed on those who have loved God.

4. When these things are given to him and he begins to contend[120] and strive by means of fastings and vigils and, in a word, with all the means profitable for his soul, then come our enemies,[121] sowing wickedly contrived thoughts,[122] placing weakness in him;[123] as a result, he is not strong enough to keep even a short fast but instead counts the minutes[124] while the enemies say to him, 'How long will you be able[125] to endure this suffering?' and 'Your body is weak', and 'It is great suffering for God to indwell a human being, especially you, who have committed so many sins', and 'How many of the sins you've committed will God forgive you?'

5. But if his heart has not accepted knowledge[126] from them, again they come with specious arguments, saying to him, 'If, indeed, you *have* sinned, nevertheless *you* have repented of your sins', and they make him mindful of certain people who have sinned and have not repented, sowing spiritual pride in his soul.[127]

6. Not in order to give him real praise but to give him empty praise. And they make him eager for works that he is not able to carry through on, fastings and vigils and many other things that I am not able to number, making sure that he wears himself out doing them. Perhaps they are able to make him go off course because of them. As it says in Proverbs: 'Do not swerve to the right or to the left'.*[128]

* Prov 4:27

7. But if God, who is good,[129] sees that his heart has not followed any of these blandishments, that,

[as David said,] 'You have tried my heart, you have examined me by night, you have tested me by fire, and no wickedness has been found in me',* [then God helps him and saves him].¹³⁰ ¹³¹Why did he say 'at night' rather than saying 'during the day'? Because these are the wiles of the Enemy, as Paul proclaims: 'We are not children of night but of the day'.* Thus the Son of God is the day, while the Devil is night.

* Ps 16:3

* 1 Th 5:5-8

8. But if his heart passes by these temptations and wars, then [the Devil] begins to unleash against him the war with fornication¹³² and attraction to males. The heart is exhausted by these wars, so that as a result the person is unable¹³³ to govern his efforts to protect his chastity. [The enemies] whisper to him, as we said earlier, about how long and dragged-out time is.¹³⁴

9. But if the heart grows weary and faint-hearted in these matters so that it becomes enfeebled on account of what it has suffered in these wars, then the good and compassionate God sends to him holy power¹³⁵ and strengthens his heart and gives him weeping and gladness and rest in his heart.¹³⁶ As a result, he becomes stronger than his enemies; they fear the power indwelling him, and do not wish [to contend with it].¹³⁷ As Paul proclaims, 'Strive, and you will receive power'.* For this is the power that Peter spoke about when he said 'an inheritance that is imperishable and unfading, kept in heaven for you, who are being protected by the power of God through faith'.*

* Acts 1:8, Lk 13:24

* 1 Pt 1:4

10. When the good God sees that the heart has been strengthened against its enemies, then he removes the power hour by hour and, once the power has become like a rudderless ship, listing aimlessly, allows the enemies to wage war through

licentiousness and with the pleasures that come from seeing and the pleasures of spiritual pride and haughtiness.

11. When the heart grows weary beneath the assaults of the enemies, then the good God, taking thought for his creature, once again sends the holy power to him and strengthens his heart and soul and body and all the rest of his members[138] by means of the <yoke>[139] of the Paraclete.[140] As he says, 'Take my yoke upon you and learn from me, for I am gentle and humble in heart'.*[141]

* Mt 11:29

12. Then the good God begins to open 'the eyes of the heart'* so that the person may know that God is the one who strengthens him. Then the person acknowledges[142] God and renders honor to God with great humility and contriteness of heart, as David says: 'A sacrifice to God is a contrite spirit'.* For from the sufferings of those waging war humility takes root in the heart, and contrition.

* Eph 1:18

* Ps 51:17

13. Then the power begins to reveal heavenly things before the heart and how to pray and recite the psalms and the honors that will come to those who persevere. [The power also reveals] that however many sufferings the person endures, these are insignificant compared with the gifts that God gives to him, as the apostle says, 'The sufferings of the present time are not worth comparing with the glory about to be revealed to us'.*[143] Then it begins to reveal before the heart the punishments of those being punished and many other things that I am unable to declare, but the one striving will know by experience.[144]

* Rom 8:18

14. Then the Paraclete places laws in the pure heart[145] of the soul and of the other members, and great humility of soul, and [instructs the person] to

place himself beneath everyone and all of creation, and not to be concerned about the failings of others, and to see with the eyes what is right, and [instructs the person about] guarding the tongue,* and healing the feet to walk straight[146] and the hands for working righteousness,[147] worshiping with prayers, and bodily mortifications and vigils—these things [the Paraclete] places in him in due measure and for discernment,[148] not to cause trouble and confusion, but to bring order and stability.

* Jas 3:5, 3:8

15. But if the understanding denigrates the arrangements of the Spirit, then the power once again withdraws and henceforth wars break out in the heart, and disturbances, and the passions of the body disturb the person on account of the movements that the enemies sow.[149]

16. But if the heart turns about and holds fast to the commandments of the Spirit, it knows that it continuously abides with God. For this is its tranquility: 'Lord, to you I have cried out, and you have healed me'.[150]*

* Ps 30:2

17. I am offering my own opinion[151] that if man does not possess great humility in his heart and in his body and does not use moderation in all things and submit to reproval and constrain himself in everything and keep his death before him day after day[152] and renunciation of the material world and renunciation of all fleshly things, he cannot keep the commandments of the Spirit.

NOTES

[1] Much of this biographical section is drawn from Antoine Guillamont, 'Macarius the Egyptian, Saint', *The Coptic Encyclopedia* (New York: Macmillan, 1991) 5.1491, and Hugh G. Evelyn White, *The Monasteries of the Wadi 'N Natrûn*, volume 2, *The History of the Monasteries of Nitria and Scetis* (rpt. New York: Arno, 1973) 60–72.

[2] Years later, his thievery as a young camel driver was still a reproof, and means of humility, for him. See Alphabetical Apophthegmata Macarius the Great 31; Benedicta Ward, trans., *The Sayings of the Desert Fathers*, CS 59. rev. ed. (Kalamazoo: Cistercian Publications, 1984) 134.

[3] See the *Life of Antony* 3–4; on village ascetics, see E. A. Judge, 'The Earliest Use of Monachos for "Monk"' (Papyrus Collection Youtie 77) and the Origins of Monasticism', *Jahrbuch für Antike und Christentum* 20 (1977) 72–89.

[4] 'La plus belle époque du monachisme égyptien'. Antoine Guillaumont, 'Les moines des Kellia', in P. Miquel, et al., *Déserts chrétiens d'Égypte* (Nice: Culture Sud, 1993) 29.

[5] Alphabetical Apophthegmata Macarius the Great 1 (Ward, CS 59:124). See Chapter Two for a summary.

[6] Alphabetical Apophthegmata Macarius the Great 3 (Ward, CS 59:126).

[7] Alphabetical Apophthegmata Sisoes 28 (Ward, CS 59:218).

[8] The *Life of Macarius of Scetis* asserts that he was a priest *before* he came to Scetis; see Tim Vivian, *Saint Macarius the Spiritbearer* (Crestwood, New York: St Vladimir's, 2004).

[9] See Rufinus, *Ecclesiastical History* 2.4; Palladius, *Lausiac History* 17; and Alphabetical Apophthegmata Macarius the Great 2 and 4 (Ward, CS 59:125, 128).

[10] See Father Matta el-Meskeen, *Coptic Monasticism and the Monastery of St. Macarius: A Short History* (Cairo: the Monastery of St Macarius, 1984) 27–31, 53–54.

[11] For a full and judicious account of the material about Macarius, see Evelyn White, cited above, note 1. White, 465–468, makes a strong case that the *Life of Macarius of Scetis* consists, for the most part, of 'some fragments of surviving tradition floating in a sea of pious imagination'. (468). Nevertheless, there are undoubtedly historical elements in the text. For a translation, see Vivian, *Saint Macarius the Spiritbearer* (above, n.8).

[12] E. Amélineau, ed., *The Life of Maximus and Domitius*, *Histoire des monastères de la Basse Égypte*, Annales de Musée Guimet 25 (Paris, 1894) 263.

[13] See Cassian, *Conference* 15.3.1; *Historia Monachorum* 30.

[14] See el-Meskeen (above, note 10), and Chapter Two above.

[15] Although there is no doubt that the *Apophthegmata* were compiled and edited later, there is also no doubt that they have their origins in fourth century Nitria and Scetis; for a good recent discussion, see Douglas Burton-Christie, *The Word in the Desert: Scripture and the Quest for Holiness in Early Christian Monasticism* (New York and Oxford: Oxford University Press, 1993) esp. 76–103, on the origins of the *Apophthegmata*, and Part III on spirituality.

[16] For a good discussion, see Lucien Regnault, *La vie quotidienne des pères du désert en Égypte au IVe siècle* (Paris: Hachette, 1990) esp. 109–116. There is now

an english translation by Étienne Poirier, Jr.: *The Day-to-Day Life of the Desert Fathers in Fourth-Cenury Egypt* (Petersham, MA: St Bede's Publications, 1999).

[17] Alphabetical Apophthegmata Macarius the Great 28 (Ward, CS 59:133).

[18] Alphabetical Apophthegmata Macarius the Great 19 (Ward, 131).

[19] Alphabetical Apophthegmata Macarius the Great 23 (Ward, 132). See Chapter Three above, where novices at the Monastery of Saint Antony are covered with burial shrouds before their ordination as monks.

[20] Regnault, 233.

[21] Alphabetical Apophthegmata Macarius the Great 18 (Ward,CS 59:131); see also 40 (Ward, 137–138).

[22] According to Athanasius, Antony advised his monks to live as though they were to die each day; see *Life of Antony* 19.2.

[23] Regnault, 113.

[24] Alphabetical Apophthegmata Macarius the Great 35 (Ward,CS 59:136). Three good appreciations of early monastic spirituality are Roberta Bondi, *To Love as God Loves: Conversations on Prayer with the Early Church* (Philadelphia: Fortress, 1987); Alan Jones, *Soul Making: The Desert Way of Spirituality* (San Francisco: Harper and Row, 1985); and Kenneth Leech, 'God of the Desert', Chapter 5 of *Experiencing God: Theology as Spirituality* (San Francisco: Harper and Row, 1985).

[25] Good introductions may be found in Henry Barclay Swete, *The Holy Spirit in the Ancient Church: A Study of Christian Teaching in the Age of the Fathers* (London: Macmillan, 1912); and Stanley M. Burgess, *The Spirit and the Church: Antiquity* (Peabody, MA: Hendrickson, 1984). Burgess often closely follows Swete. See also Louis Doutreleau, ed., *Didyme l'Aveugle: Traité du Saint-Esprit* (Paris: Cerf, 1992) 17–92.

[26] See Burgess, 95.

[27] His most sustained exposition on the Spirit may be found in *De principiis (On First Principles)* 1.3.

[28] *Contra Celsum* 4.95; and *Commentary on John* 2.6.

[29] *De principiis* 1.3.5; Frederick Crombie, trans., *The Ante-Nicene Fathers* (rpt. Grand Rapids: Eerdmans, 1979) 4.253.

[30] *De principiis* 1.3.5; Crombie, 253, slightly altered. See also 1.3.7

[31] The Melitians were a rigorist group opposed to the perceived laxity of the bishop of Alexandria towards those who had lapsed during the Great Persecution (303–312). They counted a number of bishops and were particularly strong in the Nile delta.

[32] See David Brakke, *Athanasius and the Politics of Asceticism* (Oxford: Clarendon, 1995). A striking wall painting from Tebtunis (now, sadly, lost) shows Athanasius enthroned with Antony and Pachomius at his right and left hands; see C. C. Walters, 'Christian Paintings from Tebtunis', *The Journal of Egyptian Archaeology* 75 (1989) 191–209, esp. plate XVII.

[33] Burgess, 95; see Doutreleau, 26–28; and C. R. B. Shapland, *The Letters of Saint Athanasius Concerning the Holy Spirit* (New York: Philosophical Library, 1951) 18–34.

[34] Burgess (above, n. 25), 95.

[35] *Letter to Serapion* 4.1. For an english translation of the letters to Serapion, see Shapland (above, n. 33).

[36] *Letter to Serapion* 1.23-24; the quotation is from Shapland, 35. See Burgess, 117; Doutreleau, 26–32; Shapland, 34–43.
[37] *Letter to Serapion* 1.17.
[38] *Letter to Serapion* 1.19; Shapland, 112–113.
[39] See Swete (above, n. 25), 221–225; Doutreleau, 55–92. Didymus' *On the Holy Spirit* survives only in Jerome's latin translation; see Doutreleau for a french translation. As far as I know, there is no english translation.
[40] For an english translation, see David Anderson, trans., *St. Basil the Great: On the Holy Spirit* (Crestwood, NY: St Vladimir's, 1980). The quotation is from *On the Holy Spirit* 77.
[41] Basil, *On the Holy Spirit* 46.
[42] For a good brief discussion of Basil and the Spirit, see Anthony Meredith, *The Cappadocians* (Crestwood, NY: St Vladimir's, 1995) 29–35. John McGuckin, *Saint Gregory of Nazianzus* (Crestwood, NY: St Vladimir's, 2001), 196, argues that Gregory pressured Basil 'to make explicit' his pneumatology; see 196–218. McGuckin notes, 218, that Basil 'never calls the Spirit God outright, and certainly never affirms the Spirit's consubstantiality with the Father and the Son'.
[43] For an english translation, see Pseudo-Macarius: *The Fifty Spiritual Homilies and The Great Letter*, trans. George A. Maloney (New York: Paulist, 1992). Maloney, 6–11, provides an up-to-date discussion of the question of authorship. Columba Stewart, *'Working the Earth of the Heart': The Messalian Controversy in History, Texts, and Language* (Oxford: Clarendon, 1991) 70–71, places the Pseudo-Macarian writings in Syria or Asia Minor in the 380s. See also Vincent Desprez, *Le monachisme primitif: Des origines jusqu'au concile d'Éphèse*, Spiritualité orientale 72 (Bégrolles-en-Mauge: Bellefontaine, 1998) 401–414. Jon Dechow, however, believes that similarities between the *Homilies* and origenist positions held in Egypt support the traditional attribution of the *Homilies* to Macarius the Great; see his *Dogma and Mysticism in Early Christianity: Epiphanius of Cyprus and the Legacy of Origen* (Macon, GA: Mercer University Press, 1988) 308. On the other works, see Guillaumont and Evelyn White, cited above n. 1.
[44] Guillaumont, 1491, and Guillaumont, 'Le Problème des deux Macaire dans les Apophthegmata Patrum', *Irénikon* 48 (1975) 41–59, 51. G. L. Marriott, 'Macarius of Egypt: His Epistle *Ad Filios Dei* in Syriac', *The Journal of Theological Studies* 86 (1968) 42–44, is more optimistic, saying that 'competent scholars unanimously ascribe' the letter to Macarius. Gennadius of Marseilles, writing some ninety years after Macarius' death (476–479) in *De viris illustribus* 10 (PL 58:1065) has the following to say about Macarius and, possibly, *Ad filios Dei:* 'The Egyptian monk Macarius, famous for his miracles and his spiritual powers, wrote only one letter to the younger people of his monastic profession, a letter in which he teaches that a person can serve God perfectly who, by understanding that he is contingent on his creation, bends himself to all tasks; by struggling and by entreating God's help against everything that is comfortable in life, winning through to a natural purity, he will obtain continence as a reward due to his nature'.
[45] Werner Strothmann, ed., *Die syrische Überlieferung der Schriften des Makarios*, 2 volumes (Wiesbaden: Harrossowitz, 1981) 2.50-55, supplies a german translation.
[46] See Guillamont, 5.1491. There is supposedly an armenian version of *Ad filios Dei*, but I have been unable to locate it.

⁴⁷ It does, however, have some strking resemblances with the arabic version of paragraphs 78–85 of the *Ascetic Discourse* of Stephen of Thebes; see Chapter Eight below.

⁴⁸ Actually two handfuls, or nine times, in the collection translated by Benedicta Ward, *The Sayings of the Desert Fathers* (CS 59:7, 19, 59, 68, 87, 123, 162, 186, 210).

⁴⁹ The only other use of 'the good God' that I have noticed in monastic literature occurs in the *Life of Samuel of Kalamun* 22, which dates to the seventh-eighth centuries. See Anthony Alcock, ed. and trans., *The Life of Samuel of Kalamun by Isaac the Presbyter* (Warminster: Aris & Phillips, 1983): Coptic, 20; English, 97, line 27: 'according to the command of the good God'.

⁵⁰ Two inscriptions from the monastery of Apa Jeremias at Saqqara speak of the 'virtues' *(naretê)* of the Spirit (which the editor of the text translates as 'powers'. See G. W. H. Lampe, *A Patristic Greek Lexicon* (Oxford: Clarendon, 1961) 225B(D3), a possible reference to Is 11:2. The phrase occurs elsewhere as the virtues (or powers) of the Holy Spirit. See Sir Herbert Thompson, 'The Coptic Inscriptions', in J. E. Quibell, *Excavations at Saqqara*, volume 4: *The Monastery of Apa Jeremias* (Cairo: IFAO, 1912) #203 (pp. 59–60 and p. 60 n. 1), and #324 (p. 101). These Virtues, ten and twelve of them, are pictured in two wall paintings at Bawit; see Marguerite Rassart-Debergh and Jacques Debergh, 'A propos de trois peintures de Saqqara', in Hjalmar Torp, et al., eds., *Acta ad Archaeologiam et Artium Historiam*, volume 9 (Rome: Bretschneider, 1981) 193–201; and Jean Clédat, *Le Monastère et la necropole de Baouît* (Cairo, IFAO, 1904–1906) 1:13 and 23, fig. 12. See also the Appendix on Ama Sibylla in this volume, pp. 376–393.

⁵¹ This is true also for the 'Rules' of Saint Basil the Great.

⁵² For earlier examples of divine power coming as a guiding angel or the Holy Spirit, see Shepherd of Hermas, *Mandate* 6.2; Origen, *On First Principles (De principiis)* 3.2.4, and *Homilies on Luke* 35.3-5 (Sources chrétiennes 87: 414-418). For the concept of one's 'invisible companion', see Peter Brown, *The Making of Late Antiquity* (Cambridge, MA: Harvard University Press, 1978) 68–71, 89–91. I wish to thank David Brakke for these references.

⁵³ In the *Life of Antony* 35.5, the Lord is 'the power of God the Father'. In the New Testament, see Mt 1:23; Rom 1:16, 8:31; 1 Cor 1:18, 1:24; Acts 8:10.

⁵⁴ An english translation may be found in Vivian, *Saint Macarius the Spiritbearer* (above, n. 8); *Ad filios Dei* in fact appears as paragraph 5 of the *Virtues*. It is time now in the study of early egyptian monasticism to redefine what we mean by 'representative'. In the past, the *Apopophthegmata* have been considered normative, but the recent publication and reassessment of Antony's *Letters* (see n. 63 below) has forced scholars to broaden their view.

⁵⁵ Maloney (above, n. 43), 19. The most thorough recent study of the spiritual vocabulary of Pseudo-Macarius is Stewart (above, n. 43), esp. Chapters 3–5.

⁵⁶ Macarius, Homily 1.2 (Maloney, 38); *The Great Letter* (Maloney, 257).

⁵⁷ Macarius, Homily 44.5 (Maloney, 224).

⁵⁸ Macarius, Homily 4.8 (Maloney, 53–54). This understanding of the Spirit ultimately has its origins in Paul; see 1 Cor 3:16 and 6:19. In Rom 8:9 Paul says that if a person 'does not possess the Spirit of Christ, he is not a Christian'.

⁵⁹ On sin, see Stewart (note 43, above) 74–77.

⁶⁰ Macarius, Homily 18.10 (Maloney, 145). See Stewart, 203–223.

[61] Par. 1: *epignôsis*, 'learning'; par. 5: *gnôsis*, 'knowledge'; par. 12: *gnô*, 'know'; par. 12: *epignôskei*, 'acknowledges'; par. 17: *gnômên*, 'opinion'.

[62] Bohairic Life 10; *Pachomian Koinonia*, volume 1, *The Life of Saint Pachomius and His Disciples*, ed. and trans. Armand Veilleux (Kalamazoo: Cistercian Publications, 1980) 30. Veilleux comments, 268 n. 2 (SBo 10) that '"Until you get to know yourself" is a beautiful expression of the aim of monastic *ascesis*'.

[63] Samuel Rubenson, *The Letters of St. Antony: Monasticism and the Making of a Saint* (Minneapolis: Fortress, 1995) 59 and 63.

[64] Rubenson's revised edition of 1995 is preferable to the one published in Lund in 1990 *(St. Antony: Origenist Theology, Monastic Tradition, and the Making of a Saint)* because it contains a translation of the letters. On Antony's authorship of the letters, see *Letters* 35–42. See 59–88, where Rubenson connects Antony's letters with the platonic and origenist traditions, and his conclusions on 185–191.

[65] See Rubenson, 'Christian Asceticism and the Emergence of the Monastic Tradition', in Vincent L. Wimbush and Richard Valantasis, eds., *Asceticism* (New York & Oxford: Oxford UP, 1995), 49–57: 'It thus seems safe to regard the letters as our main source for what can be termed the School of St. Antony, shaping lower Egyptian monastic theology' (53). For criticism of Rubenson's tendencies to elevate the letters at the expense of the *Life of Antony* and the *Apophthegmata*, and to overestimate the origenist tradition, see Graham Gould, 'Recent Work on Monastic Origins: a Consideration of the Questions Raised by Samuel Rubenson's *The Letters of St. Antony*', *Studia Patristica* 25 (1993) 405–416, and "The Influence of Origen on Fourth-Century Monasticism: Some Further Remarks," in Gilles Dorival and Alain Le Boulluec, eds., *Origeniana Sexta: Origène et la Bible/ Origen and the Bible* (Leuven: University Press, 1995) 591–598. See also Jan Pollok, 'The Present State of Studies on *The Apophthegmata Patrum*: An Outline of Samuel Rubenson's and Graham Gould's Perspectives', in Marek Starowieyski, ed., *The Spirituality of Ancient Monasticism* (Cracow: Tyniec, 1995) 79–89.

[66] *Ad filios*, 9.

[67] See also Evagrius of Pontus, *Chapters On Prayer* 62: If the Spirit 'should find our spirit praying to him out of love for the truth he then descends upon it and dispels the whole army of thoughts and reasonings that beset it'. Evagrius Ponticus, *The Praktikos and Chapters on Prayer*, trans. John Eudes Bamberger, CS 4 (Kalamazoo: Cistercian Publications, 1981) 65.

[68] Boniface Ramsey, *John Cassian: The Conferences* (New York: Paulist, 1997) 459.

[69] Cassian, *Conference* 13.8.4; trans. Boniface Ramsey, *John Cassian: The Conferences*, Ancient Christian Writers, 57 (New York: Paulist, 1997) 474. For a sensible discussion of Cassian's entire thought on grace and free will (and not just the naughty bits), see Ramsey, 459–464 and, for bibliographical suggestions, 463. Cassian sought a middle way between those, like Pelagius, 'who ascribe everything to free will'(13.17.1) and those, like Augustine, who ascribe everything to grace; see *Conferences* 13.11-18 (Ramsey, 476–491).

[70] *Life of Antony*, 10.1-2. Quotations from the *Life of Antony* are from Tim Vivian and Apostolos N. Athanassakis, trans., *The Life of Antony*, CS 202 (Kalamazoo: Cistercian Publications, 2003).

[71] Antony, Letter 1.77-78 (Rubenson, *Letters*, 202).

[72] Rubenson, *Letters*, 80. 'The Spirit does not enter a soul that has an unclean heart, nor a body that sins. It is a holy power, far from any deceit' (Letter 4.14;

Rubenson, 211). Rubenson points out that this emphasis on purity and worthiness may also be found in Origen (*On First Principles* 1.3.7) and Didymus the Blind.

⁷³ Rubenson, *Letters*, 16.

⁷⁴ The fact that *Ad filios Dei* was undoubtedly written first in Greek is not a barrier to this possibility; the *Fifty Spiritual Homilies* attributed to Macarius, although Syrian in origin, were written in Greek.

⁷⁵ Letter 1.15-16.

⁷⁶ Letters 3.12, 5.5, 5.23.

⁷⁷ A variant reading here is 'earthly material nature'; see *Ad filios Dei* 17.

⁷⁸ Antony, Letter 5.33 (Rubenson, 214).

⁷⁹ A variant reading here adds 'the struggle', a common metaphor in both *Ad filios Dei* and the *Life of Antony*.

⁸⁰ Antony, Letter 1.18-19 (Rubenson, 198).

⁸¹ Antony, Letter 1.23-26 (Rubenson, 198).

⁸² Antony, Letter 1.30 (Rubenson, 199), 1.50 (200), 1.53 (200), and 1.59 (201).

⁸³ See, for example, the letter by Eusebius of Caesarea to his parish reporting on the Creed of Nicea, in J. Stevenson, ed., *A New Eusebius* (London: SPCK, 1957) 366. See also J.N.D. Kelly, *Early Christian Creeds* (London: Longmans, 1950) 215–216, for the creed of Nicea and 298 for that of Constantinople.

⁸⁴ Antony, Letter 6.82 (Rubenson, 221–222).

⁸⁵ In the coptic *Life of Macarius the Great*, the holy power belongs to Christ. See M. Chaîne,'La double recension de l'Histoire Lausique dans la version copte', *Revue de l'orient chrétien* 25 (1925–1926) 232–259, 250; and for an english translation, Vivian, *Four Desert Fathers* (Crestwood, NY: St Vladimir's, 2004).

⁸⁶ For an english translation of Ammonas' letters, see Derwas J. Chitty, rev. by Sebastian Brock, *The Letters of Ammonas* (Oxford: SLG Press, 1979; distributed in the United States by Cistercian Publications). References to Chitty in parentheses are to page, not letter, numbers.

⁸⁷ Ammonas, Letter 2 (Chitty, 3) and Letter 3 (Chitty, 4).

⁸⁸ Ammonas, Letter 8 (Chitty, 9).

⁸⁹ Johannes Tromp, 'Two References to a Levi Document in an Epistle of Ammonas', *Novum Testamentum* 39:3 (1997) 235–247; the reference is to p. 237. I wish to thank Graham Gould for this reference.

⁹⁰ Ammonas, Letter 2 (Chitty, 3).

⁹¹ Ammonas, Letter 13 (Chitty, 19).

⁹² Homily 15.12 (Maloney, 112).

⁹³ *Ad filios* 10–12.

⁹⁴ Ammonas, Letter 9 (Chitty, 11–12).

⁹⁵ Paragraph 12.

⁹⁶ Paragraph 14.

⁹⁷ Paul of Tamma, *De Cella* 6; Tito Orlandi, ed., *Paolo di Tamma: Opere* (Rome, C.I.M, 1988) 88. See Chapter Five below.

⁹⁸ *Life of Antony*, 10.3.

⁹⁹ See Mt 7:14.

¹⁰⁰ Ammonas, Letter 9 (Chitty, 12).

¹⁰¹ See Tim Vivian and Apostolos N. Athanassakis, 'Spiritual Direction from the Early Monastic Mothers and Fathers on Observing a Holy Lent: Chapter III of the

Greek *Systematic Apophthegmata*, "On Compunction"', *Sewanee Theological Review* 44:1 (Christmas 2000) 60–78.

[102] For the text, see E. Amélineau, ed. and trans., *Histoire des monastères de la Basse-Égypte*, Annales du Musée Guimet, 25 (Paris: Leroux, 1894) 122–125. For a translation of the *Virtues*, see Vivian, *Saint Macarius the Spiritbearer* (above, n. 8).

[103] Amélineau, 175, 137, 130; Vivian, 129, 100, 94.

[104] Amélineau, 196, 134, 202, 200, and 148; Vivian, 145, 98, 148, 148, 109.

[105] Amélineau, 202; Vivian, 68, 87.

[106] E. Amélineau, *Monuments pour servir a l'Histoire de l'Égypte chrétienne, Histoire des monastères de la Basse-Égypte* (Paris: Leroux, 1894) 221. For a translation of these sayings, see Vivian, *Saint Macarius the Spiritbearer* (above, n. 8).

[107] Amélineau, *Histoire*, 121, 137; Vivian.

[108] Amélineau, *Histoire*, 200; Vivian.

[109] In a striking coptic saying of Macarius (not found in Greek), a skull tells Macarius he is a Spirit-bearer. See Amélineau, *Monuments*, 225; Vivian, 72–74.

[110] Amélineau, *Histoire*, 202; Vivian, 149.

[111] Translated from the greek text edited by Werner Strothmann (above, n. 45), 2:xvi-xxii. In referring to versions of *Ad filios Dei*, I will use the following abbreviations: Gk = Greek, Syr = Syriac, Boh = Bohairic Coptic, Lat = Lat.

[112] The Syr MSS offer a number of titles, most attributing the work to Macarius; E, F, and G leave the letter unattributed. Four of the MSS (B, E, G, I, K) call *Ad filios Dei* simply 'the letter', while five (A, R, S, W, and Z) say it is the first letter and three (D, F, L) call it the fifth.

[113] Greek (Gk) *ho anthrôpos*. This 'person' is never referred to as a monk. Like Saint Basil in his 'Rules', the *Fifty Spiritual Homilies* addresses its audience as Christians, not monks.

[114] Gk *to agathon*, rather than the platonic *to kalon*.

[115] Gk *epignôsin heautou* echoes the famous platonic dictum *gnôthi seauton*, 'know thyself'. See paragraph 5 on accepting 'knowledge' from enemies. Self-knowledge was also an important part of Middle Platonism, Stoicism, and the thought of Philo of Alexandria.

[116] 'The good God': *ho agathos theos*. See Lk 18:19: 'Jesus said to him, "Why do you call me good? No one is good but God alone"'. Syr lacks 'good'.

[117] Weeping is recommended often in the *Apophthegmata* (though not in the *Life of Antony*); see for example Poemen 119 (Ward, CS 59:184): 'He who wishes to purify his faults purifies them with tears and he who wishes to acquire virtues, acquires them with tears; for weeping is the way the Scriptures and our Fathers give us'. Gk to love weeping: Syr that he love weeping more than laughter: Lat that he may prefer groaning to laughing.

[118] This is a common theme in the *Apophthegmata* and in the *Life of Antony*; see, for example, *Life* 19.5; and Alphabetical Apophthegmata Evagrius 4 (Ward, CS 59:64): 'Always keep your death in mind and do not forget the eternal judgement, then there will be no fault in your soul'.

[119] There may be an echo here of Ezk 43:11 (LXX). The depicting of eternal punishment, absent here, was a favorite one in egyptian monastic and coptic literature and art.

[120] 'Contending' or 'fighting' (*agônizesthai*) is an important theme in the *Life of Antony*; see, for example, 5.7 and 13.5.

¹²¹ In the *Apophthegmata* it is always 'the Enemy', that is, Satan, rather than 'enemies'; the *Life of Antony* usually uses the singular, although twice (21.2 and 37.1) 'enemies' is a synonym for 'demons'.

¹²² For the image of sowing, see Jesus' parable in Mt 13:3-9, and its explication in 13:18-23.

¹²³ 'Weakness' translates *adunamis*, literally 'powerlessness'. God sends 'power' *(dunamis)* in paragraph 9. Power and powerlessness form an important theme in the *Life of Antony*; see, among many examples, 9.9-9.10, 10.4, and 74.8.

¹²⁴ This seems to suggest *accidie*, spiritual restlessness or boredom; see *Life of Antony* 16.3.

¹²⁵ Gk *dunasai*, cognate with *dunamis*.

¹²⁶ Gk: *gnôsis*, knowledge; Syr: these things.

¹²⁷ 'Spiritual pride' translates *kenodoxia*, 'vainglory', which Macarius plays on in the first sentence of paragraph 6, where 'praise' renders *doxa*, which also means 'glory' (as in doxology).

¹²⁸ 'Swerve' and 'go off course' translate different forms of the verb *ekklinein*.

¹²⁹ In Antony, Letter 3.20 (Rubenson, 207), Christ is called 'the goodness of God': 'Through the word of his power he gathered us from all lands'.

¹³⁰ Syr and Lat identify the quotation as David's; Gk lacks the attribution. This sentence is anacolouthic in Gk. Lat and Syr complete the thought; I have used their readings to complete the Gk sentence. The original thought here is similar to that in paragraph 10 of the *Life of Antony*, where Antony, after being severely attacked by the demons, has a vision and asks of it: 'Why did you not appear from the beginning so you could stop my sufferings?' And a voice came to him: 'Antony, I was here, but I waited to see your struggle. And now, since you persevered and were not defeated, I will be a helper to you always and I will make you famous everywhere'.

¹³¹ The coptic text preserved in the *Virtues of Saint Macarius* begins here.

¹³² In the *Life of Antony* 6.2-3, the Devil, who is 'the spirit of fornication' (Hos 4:12), attacks Antony with this temptation.

¹³³ Gk *adunaton*; God is about to send power *(dunamis)* in paragraph 9.

¹³⁴ See paragraph 4. Gk lacks a final sentence; Syr: And they bring to him the weakness of the body; Boh: As a result, great suffering and weariness come over the body.

¹³⁵ In Letter 4.14 (Rubenson, 211), Antony refers to the Spirit as 'a holy power'.

¹³⁶ This unusual (to us) apposition of weeping and gladness has a parallel in Antony, Letter 3.32 (Rubenson, 208): 'the time we have reached is a time of joy, as well as grief and tears'.

¹³⁷ Pseudo-Macarius commonly uses language of indwelling for the Spirit; see Stewart, 203–223.

¹³⁸ In Antony, Letter 1.30 (Rubenson, 199), the Spirit 'leads each member of the body back to its original condition'.

¹³⁹ Gk 'members': Lat, Boh, and Syr 'yoke'. 'Yoke' makes more sense with the quotation that follows and thus preserves the original reading. 'Members' was probably accidentally repeated in Gk.

¹⁴⁰ A passage from the *Fifty Spiritual Homilies* strikes a similar chord: 'For the heart directs and governs all the other organs of the body. And when grace pastures the heart, it rules over all the members and the thoughts' (Homily 15.20; Maloney, 116).

[141] The theme of the waxing and waning of the Spirit in a person occurs in a homily by Saint Bede (673–735): 'The Spirit partly remains and partly leaves, perhaps to return again later. . . . He withdraws for a time so that they do not always have the ability to cure the sick, raise the dead, cast out demons, or even prophesy'. Quoted by Hugh Feiss, *Essential Monastic Wisdom: Writings on the Contemplative Life* (San Francisco: HarperSanFrancisco, 1999) 64.

[142] 'Acknowledges' translates *epignôskei* whereas 'know' immediately above renders *gnô*, both cognate with *gnôsis*, 'knowledge'. The root of these related words is *gno*.

[143] Antony also quotes this verse in *Life* 17.1.

[144] Gk: 'but the one striving will know by experience'; Syr, Boh lack.

[145] Literally: 'in the heart of purity'.

[146] Literally: 'the healing of the feet towards straightness'. See, among others, Ps 107:7, Prv 3:6, Is 40:3, Wis 10:10, Mt 3:3. On healing see par. 16.

[147] Literally: 'the hands towards righteousness'. See perhaps Is 42:6. On healing see par. 16. In Antony, Letter 1.50, 53, and 59 (Rubenson, 200–201), the Spirit instructs the eyes, tongue, and hands in purity.

[148] Discernment, *diakrisis*, is important in the *Life of Antony*; see 22.3, 38.5, 44.1.

[149] In Antony, Letter 1.43-44 (Rubenson, 200), if the soul disobeys the Spirit, evil spirits stir up 'movements' 'until the soul grows weary' and asks for help from the Spirit. In Letter 1.35 (Rubenson, 199), Antony identifies 'three movements of the body', the third of which is caused by evil spirits. For Cassian (who here uses Greek, *Conferences* 7.4.2), the mind *(nous)* is 'always changeable and manifoldly changeable'.

[150] Syr, Boh, Lat add 'as David says' before the quotation.

[151] 'Opinion': *gnômên*, cognate with *gnôsis*, 'knowledge'.

[152] In *Life of Antony* 19.2, Antony exhorts his followers to heed Paul's words (1 Cor 15:31), 'I die daily', and says, 'If we too live our lives like this—as though we are going to die each day—we will not sin'. In *Praktikos* 29 (Bamberger, CS 4:24), Evagrius of Pontus says that 'our holy and most ascetic master', Saint Macarius the Great 'stated that the monk should always live as if he were to die on the morrow but at the same time that he should treat his body as if he were to live on with it for many years to come'; *Praktikos* 29; CS 4:24.

5

Saint Paul of Tamma and the Life of the Cell

Introduction

> 'A brother came to Scetis to visit Abba Moses and asked him for a word. The old man said to him, "Go, sit in your cell, and your cell will teach you everything"'.
> — Alphabetical Apophthegmata, Moses 6*

SAINT PAUL OF TAMMA

PAUL OF TAMMA, as Tito Orlandi has observed, 'is one of those figures of Egyptian monasticism of whom the great Greco-Latin tradition (Palladius, Cassian, *Historia Monachorum, Apophthegmata*) has left no memory'.[1] At first this may not seem all that important, until one remembers that this same tradition knows nothing of Saint Shenoute, one of the greatest coptic monastics and saints. Paul, like Shenoute, wrote in Coptic, and therefore his works did not pass into the greco-roman monastic tradition. As a result, he is generally unknown.[2] But Paul's life and writings deserve our attention, both for what they reveal about early egyptian monasticism and for what they still have to contribute to christian spirituality.[3]

Paul's extant writings consist of three or possibly four short, fragmentary, pieces—'On Humility' [H], 'On Poverty' [P], a letter [L], and 'An Untitled Work' [U]—and a longer work, *On the Cell* (itself incomplete).[4] He may have written nine or ten works or more; taken together, these may have formed an 'Asceticon', or collection of ascetic writings.[5] His *Life* exists in some coptic fragments and ten arabic manuscripts, almost all of them still unpublished.[6]

The coptic-arabic Synaxery also contains an account of his life under 7 Babeh (October 17).[7]

Paul was born in Tamma (or Tammah) in the nome of Koeis (Kynopotis/al-Qays) in the vicinity of Dahrūt, on the left bank of the Nile opposite Sharūnah.[8] Unfortunately, we have no dates for him. According to his *Life*, at eighteen he wished to become a hermit and withdrew to the mountain of Touho (Theodosiopolis/ Ṭaḥāal-A'mīdah), where he became the disciple of Hyperichus. Fifty-four years later, Ezekiel, the future narrator of Paul's *Life*, became his disciple. The *Life* is mostly concerned with a long journey that Paul and Ezekiel make up the Nile from Touho as far as Shmin (Panopolis/Akhmīm). The two visit anchorites in Middle Egypt, probably a group headed by the priest Isidore, and also call upon Abba Apollo at Bawit. Many wondrous events take place along the way. The most striking of these is a series of occurrences unique in coptic hagiography: Paul dies six or seven times because of his excessive ascetic practices and is revived by the Lord each time.[9]

Another story connects Paul with Saint Bishoi, the founder of the famous monastery at Scetis (Wadi al-Natrun). When Scetis is attacked by barbarians in 407–408, Bishoi leaves with John the Little. John goes to Klysma, while Bishoi eventually settles in Ansina (Antinoë), where he and Paul live together. God assures Paul that just as in life the two were inseparable, so in death they will be together. After they die, three months apart, Abba Athanasius of Antinoë comes (by river) to get Bishoi's body. But when he reaches the area where Paul is buried, his boat stops and will go no further. An old monk named Armenius, 'dwelling in that place on a rock', comes out to the boat and asks why it won't move. When the travellers say they don't know why, Armenius tells them that 'it is because of the body of Abba Paul. . . . For he had made an agreement with the saint Abba Bishîyeh [Bishoi] during his life that they should be together while they lived in this world, and after their deaths their bodies should not be separated the one from the other'. So the travellers take both saints and place them together in a new shrine, 'and their bodies gave healing to all the sick down to our own day'.[10] The arabic Synaxery says that the bodies of Paul and Bishoi eventually came to Scetis, 'where they are still together'.[11] Apollo appears to have lived late into the fourth century (see Chapter Six) and Bishoi was active at the turn of the fifth century, so, if the details pertaining to them in the *Life* are historically accurate, Paul knew both and belongs to the fourth and fifth centuries.

Orlandi has suggested that the *Life* of Paul comes from a 'specifically Middle-Egyptian tradition' which existed in the area from Memphis to Shmin (Panopolis/Akhmīm), whose best-known figures are Paul, Apollo, Phib, Anup, Pamoun (or Amoun) and Aphu.[12] This group belongs to the fourth century and is distinct from the monks of Scetis, Kellia, and Nitria to the north and Pachomius and Shenoute to the south.[13] Paul is the only one of this group from whom we have writings.[14] These works, 'even if it should be necessary to date them later in the fourth century, . . . are precious testimony to what the monks themselves thought about their spiritual goals, about the meaning of their life, and what they taught their disciples'.[15]

Paul's feast day in the Coptic Church is 7 Babeh (17 October).

FOUR SHORT WORKS

The roots of Paul's writings are as old as the wisdom tradition of ancient Israel and Egypt. Many of the scriptural allusions in them are to the wisdom tradition of the Old Testament—Psalms, Proverbs, and Sirach—and Paul begins *On the Cell* by exhorting his disciple to 'be wise' (Coptic *sabe* = Greek *sophos*).[16] These roots are also as deep as the words of Jesus and Paul (references to the Gospels and Paul are prominent) and as wide spreading in the desert soil as the *Sayings of the Desert Fathers*, a confluent spirituality of patient waiting upon the Lord and advice on how to do it: 'Listen concerning the way you have asked about. Be attentive; stand with the Lord. If you keep these words, you will be one of the elect in all things' (H 1).

These words, though written, spring from an oral tradition. There exists an unspoken prologue to the words, a scene that takes place before we hear the first words uttered. Paul is the wise man (*rmnhêt* in Coptic), the trusted elder to whom a disciple has come for 'a saving word', advice, encouragement, instruction, comfort, even reproval, on how to live life in God.[17] This is serious business: 'the ways of life come from these precepts' (H 210). Some of

Paul's answers, his responsive words, are quotations from Scripture (from the Septuagint whose canon includes the 'Deuterocanonical' books not considered canonical in the Authorized Version[18]) some are from the monastic 'canon' of oral wisdom that was christian Midrash, Talmud, and second canon.[19] Paul's writings also share form, if not content, with the hellenistic egyptian 'wisdom' tradition as it is represented by *The Teachings of Silvanus* and *The Sentences of Sextus.*[20]

Some of Paul's words are seasoned with salt and sea-wind: 'Be like the master sailors piloting their ships as you watch the wind to see what direction it is taking you, whether it is a good wind or bad that is coming' (U 1). Some are flavored with earth: 'Do not act like farm animals being driven by someone, but act like the person driving the animals' (U 109). Some are egyptian *koans:*

> 'Do not be like the thorny acacias that grow on the mountain, which is God. Instead, be like a reed growing in the water, which is the abyss' (U 203-204);

> 'It is good that your suffering continue, keeping you safe' (H 11); 'Do not give rest to your thoughts until rest comes to you without rest' (L 3).

Some are words of warning:

> 'Do not crow over your brother's ways, for the person who rejoices over his neighbor's ways alienates himself from the Lord and God will be angry with him' (H 27).

And some are a benediction:

> 'And the Holy Spirit will illumine all your members, and the twelve Virtues will dance in the midst of your soul, and the Cherubim and Seraphim will shelter you beneath their wings' (H 9).

Paul's world has been made familiar by the *Apophthegmata;* it is the world of the monastic cell, Scripture, meditation, and *ascesis,* monastic discipline and training whose end is, not itself, but union with God: 'Now then, my son, observe all the saints, see how they are one with God' (P 5). The virtues sown and cultivated here are the familiar monastic virtues of poverty, humility, and repentance. The fruit that will come from the desert ground being prepared by the monk is rest, peace (mton, greek hesychia).²¹

Paul, like most monks, believed he was at war, at war against the Devil (whose aim is to corrupt and defeat, and ultimately spiritually to kill the believer, thus robbing him of salvation), at war with his passions (the impulses that pull one far from God). War and struggle are not just metaphor in this monastic world; it was a daily experience (H 31, U 117, L 4): 'The demons openly wage war against man in the desert'.²² If love seems lacking in this literature, love is nonetheless its leitmotif. The love Paul explicates is, to paraphrase Gabriel García Márquez, love in a time of war. It is the love a sergeant has for his soldier as he trains him and thus tries to save him when he is alone and explosed to heavy gunfire.²³ In a war zone, survival is uppermost on a soldier's mind. For Paul, survival is eschatological. As a result, salvation is what is of utmost importance here (P 3). We make a serious mistake if we think this war zone is 'merely' spiritual, somehow secondary to the world's real concerns. Victory and defeat are eternal. Salvation is the goal of the monastic struggle (P 3); to relax discipline in oneself or to coddle one's disciples would be a deadly caricature of love. The battle being waged here is for keeps; it is eternal.

The orthography and inflection of this saving discourse is Coptic, but the ascetic vocabulary, at least in origin, is Greek.²⁴ 'Vigilance' is the watchword in these works, and Paul symbiotically uses a number of coptic and greek words to express this central monastic concern. Coptic *roeis* and *hareh* (= Gk *phulassein*), 'watch, guard, pay attention' (H 1, U 110; H 6, H 12 [twice], U 116); čôsht, 'watch, pay close attention to' (P 5, U 1); čôeksobte, 'stay prepared' (H 12). Greek: nêphê (= nêphein), 'pay careful attention' (U 109); *proseche*, 'give attention to' (H 14);²⁵ *proskarterei*, 'persist' (U 117); *hupomine*, 'patiently remain' or 'endure' (L 2); *prokopê*, 'progress' (L 8). Two consecutive sentences in 'An Untitled Work' nicely demonstrate this symbiosis of Greek and Coptic (in what follows in parentheses, key greek words are in italics while key coptic words are in roman type):

117. Sitting in your cell, persist *(proskarterei)* with your prayer (shlêl) and your fasting *(nêstia)* and the struggle *(agôn)* taking place in your heart (hêt) and you will have the qualities of the pure of heart (ptbbo mphêt).

118. Because without peace *(eirênê)* and purity (tbbo)....

The 'fundamental attitude' here is that of paying attention to oneself (Greek: *prosochê*), to what is going on in the heart *(hêt)*, and it is a central concern of monastic spirituality that links Paul's spirituality both to the *Life of Antony*, written originally in Greek, and to Antony's *Letters*, probably written originally in Coptic,[26] and ultimately to the socratic-platonic dictum *gnôthi seauton*, 'know thyself'. Paul's method of scriptural exegesis also seems indebted to the greek and alexandrian tradition of Philo, Origen, Eusebius, Didymus, and Athanasius. Paul uses 'the Origenist hermeneutical principle of interpreting scripture with scripture'.[27] As Mark Sheridan has concluded in his comments on Paul's writings, 'the spirituality of Coptic monasticism'—at least with regard to the development of the interior life—'is no different' from 'the heart of Greek monasticism', and this points to his important, unifying, conclusion:

> Rather than to assume that there were radically different types of monasticism in Egypt with different sources of inspiration, it might be a better working hypothesis to assume that there was a common tradition about the nature of the spiritual life, understood perhaps in varying degrees, and that it was this that permitted the term 'monachos' to be applied to ascetics in very different external forms of monastic life.[28]

What is of ultimate value in Paul's writings, of course, is not how they relate to scholarly hypotheses or various forms of monastic life, then and now. What matters is the direction in which Paul's words are pointing the reader: to reflection, self-scrutiny, discipline, prayer, peace, and, finally, union with God. In that spirit, these writings should be read not as one reads an academic article, an essay, a novel, or even poetry; they should be read, as Paul intended, meditatively, slowly, on the lips and in the heart, like the psalms that

Paul read quietly aloud as he sat in his cell. What Jeremy Driscoll has cogently said about the writings of Evagrius of Pontus applies equally well to the works of Paul of Tamma:

> These are texts written in the short, cryptic style of the Bible's Wisdom literature, texts designed to promote not only prolonged meditation but likewise the actual practice in life of the subject matter of the given proverb. These are words from a desert master given to disciples ready to expend the effort in mind and action that will lead to the word's deepest meaning.[29]

Guarding our souls with meditation and prayer, Paul insists, keeps us prepared day and night (H 12). As a result, he says, it is written in the Psalms that 'a fire will burn in my meditation' (H 13, Ps 38:4). 'Let your manner be peaceful, with your heart like a fire against sin' (U 205). With such small fires, carefully tended and banked, watched and nourished, we can, as the monastic hope has it, become all flame.[30]

ON THE CELL

If the christian canon had remained open on into the fourth and fifth centuries, *On the Cell* could easily, and justifiably, have become part of the Church's wisdom literature, along with Proverbs, Ecclesiastes, The Song of Songs, Sirach, and the Wisdom of Solomon.[31] The main concern of *On the Cell* is the teaching and learning of wisdom—the monastic, biblical, wisdom that leads to salvation. 'Wisdom' and 'teaching', in fact, are etymological brethren in Coptic: a 'wise person' is *sabe* and 'wisdom' is *mntsabe*, the equivalent of the greek *sophia*. 'To teach' in Coptic is literally 'to make wise': *tsabo;* the same word, used as a noun, means 'teaching, instruction'. *Sbo* means 'to learn'. Words of wisdom and teaching occur seventeen times in *On the Cell*.[32]

The opening words of *On the Cell* could have come from Proverbs or Sirach—or from *The Teachings of Silvanus* and *The Sentences of Sextus:* 'My son, obey God and keep his commandments, and be wise and remain in your dwelling' (1).[33] For Paul, wisdom is to be found in the cell, because that is where one will find God: 'You shall be a wise man in your cell, building up your soul as you sit in your cell . . . while the fear of God surrounds you day and night' (77). The 'wise man in his cell will be hidden' from evil (49) because he understands its ways (50); 'the one who is in his cell is wise' (75[II]) and God 'knows his end' (75). He holds 'on to teaching with all humility' (21). In a striking series of images taken from Old Testament iconography, the wise man in his cell becomes 'the incense of God', (52) 'the altar of God', and 'the true and perfect "tent with the golden urn [in it], with manna, [and] Aaron's rod that budded, and the tablets of the covenant [Heb 9:11, 9:4]"' (68). So transformed, 'a wise man in his cell is the city of blessings . . . the dwelling place of the virtues'. The 'Spirit is perfected within him' (76). As a result, his cell, though on earth, enjoys the incense of heaven; it 'is always filled with a sweet smell from the fruit of his good works' (54).

On the Cell takes us as deep into the mysteries of ancient desert eremitism, its heart and soul, as we at the beginning of the twenty-first century are likely to be vouchsafed passage. The world here is far removed from the cenobitic structures and practices of pachomian monasticism. On the Cell emphasizes solitude—even uncomfortably, to the exclusion of all else. In 18, Paul seems to offer a definition of this virtue: 'But only humbly flee to yourself in humble knowledge, because it is the time for withdrawal'. This sentence sounds some of the key themes (and terms) of all early monastic literature: humility, knowledge (sooun = Gk gnosis), self-knowledge, and withdrawal (anachôrêsis).[34] Solitude, in fact, is so important that its requirement causes tension with its coeval monastic virtue of charity. Paul fears that the demons may mislead the monk into leaving the cell out of compassion to save someone (62). He insists that the life you save is in fact your own: 'Be afraid for the person whom you will save [that is, it seems, yourself], fleeing inward in the knowledge that it is the time for withdrawal' (113). 'Flee to yourself alone', Paul concludes (116).

This spirituality may at first seem solipsistic; it is in fact just the opposite: On the Cell points the monk away from self-centeredness and towards union with Christ; although alone, the monk entrusts himself to Christ and to God.[35] Paul bluntly reminds his disciple of the misdeeds of society: 'the saints and our Lord died at the hands of men'. And he goes on to relate cryptically that 'I have suffered more on account of the war with men than the war with the desert' (115). Solitude, however, is not flight but necessary instruction; it is not a reward for the virtuous but spiritual exercise and healing (58) for the weak: 'You know your weakness', he tells his disciple. Yes, there are other ways to God, Paul acknowledges, but you know which path is required for you (65): 'One person has one way, for another there is another way—to the cell for you!' The second recension of the text pointedly adds here: 'Remain where God put you'. Here all is solitude and silence, the monastic cell, the monk, and God; by contrast, the world of the *Apophthegmata*, with its narrative energy, seems bustling and gregarious.

On the Cell 77–81 summarizes Paul's teaching on the necessity of being alone with God:

> 77. You shall be a wise man in your cell, building up your soul as you sit in your cell, while glory is with you, while humility is with you, while the fear of God surrounds you day and night, while your cares are thrown down, while your soul and your thoughts watch God in astonishment, gazing at him all the days of your life.
>
> 78. Do not look toward man.
>
> 79. Also, do not let a man look toward you.
>
> 80. Allow yourself only one out of a thousand as an advisor [Sir 6:6] and you will be at peace all the days of your life.
>
> 81. You shall test the teaching that you follow, walking alone with God at your side.

In 'On Humility' 14–18, Paul uses Sirach 6:6-16 to extoll what at first seems to be the ideal of spiritual friendship with another person or adherence to an 'abba', a monastic elder and teacher. The verses cited above from *On the Cell*, however, suggest that this rare friend is, in fact, God, an identification that the *Teachings of Silvanus*, which also uses Sirach 6:6, makes explicit: 'entrust yourself to God alone as father and as friend'.[36] Silvanus elsewhere identifies Christ as the 'faithful friend' of Sirach 6:15.[37] Silvanus still sees the necessity of having a human counselor;[38] in *On the Cell,* however (and apparently in 'On Humility', if the reading suggested above is correct), Paul has gone beyond Silvanus to urge that the only friend and counselor a monk requires is God. In *On the Cell* 82 Paul both symbolizes and actualizes this understanding by using the figure of Elijah to demonstrate that being alone with God is indeed to have bread in the wilderness: 'For Elijah was at the river Chorath [alone, God was with him, and the raven ministered to him]' (see 1 Kings 17:1-7).[39]

The world of the cell as taught by Paul of Tamma is—almost— unimaginably different from our own, unless the person reading *On the Cell* now lives in a monastery; and perhaps even then. Prayer, meditation, chant, and weekends spent (or gained) at retreat centers are, happily, popular today; but how many even of those who have discovered and embrace monastic spirituality refer to themselves as 'wretched' and 'poor' and gain their self-understanding through these terms? The world of Paul of Tamma is one of spiritual, eschatological, and, presumably, physical, poverty. And it is poverty on monastic, not modern, terms. Not lack of wealth, poverty; not squalor, poverty; not crime, poverty. Giving up everything for the kingdom of God.[40]

For Paul, drawing perhaps on Ps 70:5 (LXX: Ps 69:6), the monk is the person who is poor. 'You who are poor', he addresses his disciple over and over again (9, 10, 23, 27, 69, 72, 125). He also seems to identify himself as poor (121). For 'poor' Paul uses two words that are interchangeable: *ebién* and *héke*. *Héke,* which is derived from *hko,* 'to be hungry', most commonly translates greek *ptôchos;* *ebién* means 'poor', but can also suggest 'wretched'.[41] Twice (27 and 69) Paul uses the two words together: 'poor and wretched'. Paul closely connects poverty with withdrawal from the world, *anachôrêsis:* 'Blessed is the person, poor and wretched, who withdraws' (69). Such a person 'is a friend of God just like Abraham'; he is one of the Lord's servants and prophets (69–71). His place is in the desert: 'the pride of the poor monk is the desert and instruction in humility' (13). For Paul, poverty is Christ-centered: 'Although our Lord was very rich, he became poor for our sakes [15; 2 Cor 8:9]'. Poverty is, literally, the imitation of Christ. As such, it is also eschatological, and the cell becomes the kingdom of God, both present and future. It is a kingdom realized now: 'A poor man who remains in his cell is a king and a lord. Honor him, for God is dwelling in him' (119). In language reminiscent of the Psalms, Paul declares that 'the Lord has made [the solitary] king, he has clothed him in beauty; the lord has clothed him with power, he has girded him with it' (120). His is a kingdom whose hope and reward also lie ahead: 'For if you wear poverty in this world [and humility, you will be] with the Son of God [in his kingdom]' (87). 'Blessed are you who are poor', Jesus said, 'for yours is the kingdom of heaven' (Lk 6:20). Paul of Tamma took Jesus at his word: 'You [sg.] who are poor, if you cling to the Lord alone, the Lord will also remain with you and have you rule with him' (9).

The kingdom is not, however, easily gained. As with the *Life of Antony*, the *Apophthegmata*, and other early monastic literature, *On the Cell* testifies that the spiritual life is warfare waged against Satan and his minions. Paul advises his disciple not to turn his back on the Devil (34) and warns that 'the demons openly wage war against humans in the desert' (60). War, however, is waged not just with the Devil; in a rare, and poignant, personal statement, Paul confesses that 'I have suffered more on account of the war with men than the war with the desert' (115). Spiritual warfare is also waged within: the interior sins Paul warns against are not the common monastic ones of fornication and sexual thoughts, but spiritual pride (100–101) and listening to gossip (33). Like Antony, Paul counsels his charges not to fear, but to trust in the Lord: 'Do not be afraid of the demons. I have waged war with them in the desert and God has scattered them with his love, not with my strength' (110). In Paul's vision of the spiritual life, the monk will be 'strong and victorious in battle' (104), and will 'go up to the Lord in victory' (8).

If victory *(jro)* and glory *(eoou)* are the fruits and rewards of the monastic life, this is only because the earth is first tilled, sowed, watered, and cared for with labor *(hise,* which can also suggest suffering), humility *(thbbio),* and patient endurance *(hupomonê).*[42] All of these are borne in solitude.[43] Paul does not dwell on labor and suffering, mentioning it only a few times; he gives much more emphasis to humility, which seems to be for him the chief of the monastic virtues: 'Now, then, give yourself to humility as you sit in your cell, and you will be with God always' (122). Solitude, however, is the ground of monastic well-being: 'So, therefore, flee to yourself alone' (116). Elijah (82), Agabus (83), and Andrew (117) were alone, where they found favor with God. In a seeming paradox, peace comes because the monk is not really alone: 'Now, then, you shall be alone *[mauaak]*, placing your hope in God' (92). But 'if you cling to the Lord alone *[mauaaf]* the Lord will also remain with you and have you rule with him' (9).[44] This 'paradox' offers a central monastic truth: the more a person is alone (with God), the less he or she is alone: 'You shall test the teaching that you follow, walking alone with God at your side' (81). For Paul, the monk should be like the 'true widow' of 1 Tim 5:5 'who remains alone and perseveres in petition and fasting' (90). The reward of such solitary practice is peace *(mton)*: the monk who perseveres will be able to resist evil; 'his heart delights in God. God will give him peace in his cell' (50).

Peace is a blessing, a favor from God; it comes from God's grace. The coptic word *hmot* encompasses all these meanings—blessing, favor, grace—and *hmot* lies at the heart of Paul's spirituality. Paul does not systematically explicate grace, nor is he concerned with its theological tensions. For this monk in the desert, grace is a given; it becomes almost the abiding spirit that watches over monks, the invisible presence that dwells within both cell and solitary. For Paul, the cell provides grace (15), and the gift is not to be rejected (31). The demons, however, will try to take it away (62). But God places his grace in the human heart (123). As Paul exhorts his monk, '[give yourself] to the grace of the cell. All healing will take place for you there' (58).

The need for healing, and its promise, implies illness, lesion, disrepair. The genius of monasticism, and its gift, freely offered, is its understanding of the human condition. In monastic spirituality, past (sin, the fall) is truly prologue, not predestination. *On the Cell* literally abounds with the future tense. Despite its austerities (not dwelled upon), it is a work of deep hope. God is always present. So are the saints, those on earth and those in heaven. If the monk only opens his spiritual eyes he will see that though best alone he is never alone. Old Testament images populate *On the Cell* like guardian angels bringing promise. Therefore, although *On the Cell* is a work of deepest solitude, it is also a celebration of the most profound communion possible with God and the entire communion of saints:

103. You shall be saved, therefore, O man of God, from the evil spirit, and you shall not become a mountain burning and harsh.

104. You shall on the contrary be a mountain fat and strong [Ps 67:16 (LXX)] and God will want to dwell in you, and the chariot of God will be twice ten thousand in you [68:17], and your sweet fragrance will be manifest in heaven and will spread in the midst of the saints while you are an example for those on earth because you are strong and victorious in battle.

1. The Life of Paul of Tamma

FRAGMENT 1[45]

The Monks Visit Apa Pamoun

. . . the remaining pieces . . . will put them in my father's basket. I drank the water that was in the jug; we prayed; we left that place. We came south where it was completely mountainous . . . [rule] of our fellow monks.[46] We heard a [voice] softly calling to us: 'You, Paul of Tamma, and Ezekiel, from Tekouinerôt, come in, you who are holy to the Lord! It is good that you have come to us, Apa Paul of Tamma, whom the Lord has raised [from the dead]. . . . help us here today'.

My father said: 'It is good to see you, Apa Pamoun, who is known by his many-colored garment, like that of Joseph, the righteous king'.[47] Then he asked him who had shaved his head.[48]

He said: 'My father, Apa Hêllên. Remember me, my holy father. . . .'

My father [asked]: 'Where do you celebrate the *synaxis* on the Sabbath and the Lord's day?'[49]

Apa Pamoun replied: 'It is John the Virgin who celebrates the synaxis with me on the Sabbath and the Lord's day. . . .'

FRAGMENT II[50]

The Monks Visit Apa Apollo

. . . Apa Apollo. We found him sitting on a throne,[51] teaching his children from the commandments of life. When he saw my father Apa Paul, he jumped down from his throne, embraced him, kissed him, and said: 'It is good that you have come to us today, athlete of Christ, Apa Paul, whom the Lord has raised from the dead five times; what is more, he will raise you again, just as he has told you, and the seventh time that he raises you will be on the day of the resurrection of all the saints'.

When Apa Apollo had said these things, he had all the people gather together; he went to the church and we celebrated Communion with the holy sacrifice. He dismissed the brothers to the refectory but led us to the *diakonia* and had them prepare something for us to eat.[52] But my father refused, because he had been fasting for three days during Lent. But our father Apa Apollo continued to entreat him, saying, 'Please do as I ask, my father, and eat with me so God's grace will be upon my dwelling and my monastery today on account of you. You know, my beloved father, that it is not what enters a person that defiles him.* So then, my father, please do as I ask and eat with me'.

So my father stretched out his hand to eat with Apa Apollo,[53] while I ate with Papohe.[54] We ate together, along with the other brothers who were with us, namely Apa Paêse and Apa Nishčrôou and Apa Soures and Apa Pita. When we had finished eating that evening, our father Apa Apollo went into our midst and stood and clapped his hands together, saying, 'He who has received wing, let him fly away'. At that hour Apa

* Mk 7:15

Paêse flew away; he went to the mountain of Hače. Apa Nishčrôou also flew away; he went to the mountain north of Antinoë. Apa Pitta [sic] flew away, too; he went to the mountain of Sioout.[55] When dawn arrived, our father Apa Apollo escorted us to the south of the monastery. He embraced us, and saw us off in peace.

Paul and Ezekiel Visit Apa Aphou

We walked south where it was completely mountainous until we came to the mountain of Terôt-Ashans, to the south of Kôs.[56] We found antelope below in the valley and there was a monk in their midst.[57]

My father approached him and greeted him with a kiss and said to him, 'What is your name?'

He said, 'Aphou is my name. Remember me, my father Apa Paul, so the Lord will bring me to a perfect end'.

My father said to him, 'How many years have you been here?'

He said, 'For fifty-four years'.

My father again asked, 'Who clothed you in the monastic habit?'

He said, 'It was Apa Antony of Scetis'.

My father said to him, 'What do you live on traveling with these antelope?'

He said, 'My food and the food of these antelope is one and the same, namely, the plants of the field and green vegetables'.

My father said to him, 'Don't you freeze in the winter and get exhausted in the summer?'

He said to him, 'If it is winter, I sleep in the midst of these antelope so that they warm me with the breath from their mouths. If it is summer, they gather close together and provide shade for me so that the burning heat does not bother me'.

My father said to him, 'Truly you are worthy to be called "Apa Aphou the Antelope!"'[58]

At that very hour, a voice came to us: 'This is his name for all the generations of the earth'.[59]

Paul and Ezekiel Visit Apa Phib

We marvelled at what had so suddenly taken place. We embraced him and took our leave of him. We walked south to the mountain of Peshčepohe and found a cave to our west. My father knocked on the rock three times according to the rule of our fellow-monks, and immediately we heard a small voice saying, 'Bless me, my holy fathers'. And so he came out and opened the door for us. We prostrated ourselves before him and greeted him with a kiss. His body had become very feeble on account of hunger and thirst, and he took us into the cave. We prayed, we sat down, we spoke of the greatness of God.

My father said to him, 'What is your name?'

He replied, saying, 'Phib is my name, and I am from Perčoush in the nome of Touhô'.[60]

My father said to him, 'How many years has it been since you came here?'

He said, 'It's been eighteen years'.

My father said to him, 'How long will you remain here?'

He again said to him, 'This is my dwelling place while I am alive and when I am dead'.

My father said to him, 'What do you eat? What do you drink? Who ministers to you?'[61]

Saint Apa Phib answered, 'From the time I was little when I left home, up to the present, in every place where I have lived, when I have completed my forty-day fast, each time I have found a loaf of bread and a jug of water placed before me and, as God is my witness, during that time a single loaf has been appointed for me each time. But since you have come to visit me today along with your disciple, look, God has sent us food for three! Now then, rise, let us taste a little bread according to the commandment of God'.[62]

So we got up, we stretched forth our hands, we prayed, we stretched out [our hands for the bread], we ate a single loaf of bread together and we drank a little water. We took our leave of our father Apa Phib. He escorted us out in peace.

Apa Paul Defeats the Devil

We went south where it was completely mountainous until we came to the mountain of Meroeit and found ourselves a dwelling place there. While I was sitting in the dwelling alone, a man suddenly came to the entrance; he called to me, and I went out to see who it was. That man said to me, 'Are you Ezekiel?'

I said to him, 'Yes, I am'.

He said to me, 'Let me enter your dwelling so I can have a word with you; I do not want the brothers to hear what I am saying and become afraid'.

I welcomed him inside because of his fine manner of speaking.

He said to me, 'My brother Ezekiel, do you know what has happened?'

I said, 'No'.

He said to me, 'I have come, walking in the desert for seven hours since yesterday, I with some other men, looking for rocks from which we could make bath powder.[63] We found highwaymen in the mountain; we took up our implements in our hands and were barely able to escape their clutches alive. And when we fled their hands, we came upon a great man who had been bound and thrown down into the valley and we released him. That man said to us, "Leave me here, but if you go to the mountain, you will find this certain dwelling; call inside: 'Ezekiel, your father says "Come to me in the desert, for thieves have robbed me; they have tied me up, wishing to kill me, but God has rescued my soul from their hands"' ". We asked him, "What is your name?" He said to us, "My name is Paul, and I am from Tamma in the nome of Koeis"'.

I, Ezekiel, when I heard these words, I was troubled because he had spoken the name of my father and his village.

That man spoke to me again, 'Get up, follow me so I can take you to him, for I see that you are afraid'.

I walked with him in the middle of the desert. We walked, completing the first day and the second. I said to him, 'Aren't we there yet?'

He said, 'No'.

We spent a third day walking in the desert. I said to him again, 'Haven't we reached him yet?'

He said, 'Look, we're approaching him now'.

While he was speaking to me he changed shape and became a huge Ethiopian;[64] his eyes were filled with blood, his whole body bristled with spines, and he gave off a foul odor like a billy goat. He said to me, 'Don't you know who I am, Ezekiel?'

I said to him, 'No'.

He said to me, 'I was the one who dried up the well that time. Your father beat me until I filled it up like it was before. I suffered putting up with you and your father. You two have not gotten very smart'.

I said to him, 'Why, you're the Devil, whom the Lord punishes for all the evil you've done to the servants of Christ!'

But he rushed at me like a ferocious lion, wanting to kill me, and I cried out, 'Father, help me!' Immediately my father heard my voice as though he were right by me. He got up immediately and through the grace of God came to me. When my father drew near to him, the Devil suddenly changed and took on the form of a monk wearing a skin and carrying some small sheaves of palm branches. He went up to my father and prostrated himself at his feet according to the rule of our fellow monks. Immediately my father traced a line around him so he would not be able to move this way or that, for he knew that it was the Devil. He grabbed him and bound him hand and foot and rolled him down into the valley. We left him and went our way.

I said to my father, 'What was it that you did to that shameless creature?'

My father said to me, 'God delivered him to me so I could punish him as I saw fit since he dared to tempt us'.

After my father said these things, we rose and went to our dwelling, glorifying God. My father passed forty days and forty nights without eating or drinking, sitting on a brick inside our dwelling, gazing into the window as though into a mirror. He did not shut his eyes for those forty days until they burst and poured blood to the ground. But the holy archangel came from heaven—it was Michael—at first light on the Lord's day at the end of the forty days. He sealed my father with the sign of the cross and released him from all his suffering, and his eyes returned to normal. Michael ascended to the heavens in glory. We celebrated the *synaxis* with the brothers who were there with us. We ate with them on the Lord's day and left them in peace.

*The Encounter with Apa Pshai-nte-Jeremias
and the Dead Idolators*

We went south towards the cave of Sioout. We found ourselves a small dwelling place there and my father performed a great act of religious devotion.[65] It happened one day that a great saint of God came to see us; his name was Apa Pshai-nte-Jeremias, and he lived on the mountain of Pkôou, to the east of the River. We greeted one another with a kiss, we prayed, we sat down, we spoke of the greatness of Christ and the ways of life[66] of the saints. When we had finished considering these things among ourselves, we got up and walked in the mountain. We found a cave filled with corpses; they were all those of idolators. When the saints reached the place where the bodies were, they stood and prayed over them. They raised all of them to life, numbering six hundred males and fifty-four females. The saints said to them, 'What are you doing here?'

One of them answered and said, 'Listen to me, saints, so I can explain to you our wickedness and wrongdoing. We were all from one tribe, worshiping a beast whose name was 'the wolf'; we cared for him at all times, offering up as a sacrifice to him small children who had reached three years of age. He would give us courage, saying, "Do this for me like this", and other things even more evil than these, things I do not wish to talk about. Now, then, my holy fathers, have mercy on us and baptize us as Christians, because we are in great distress'.

The athlete of Christ, Apa Pshai-nte-Jeremias, replied, 'Arise. Let us pray to God so he will listen to us concerning this matter'.

My father said, 'Let us pray'.

They got up and together we called upon God, speaking thus: 'Merciful and compassionate God, who has sent your only-begotten son, Jesus Christ our Lord, who died for his creation, having made the world free through the water of holy baptism, show compassion for these your servants who stand before you here today, who look to your mercy and compassion, that they may receive. . . .'

Fragment III[67]

'. . . their sins'. While the [saints] were saying these things, the pagans stood and marvelled. Suddenly, the Lord Jesus came forth from heaven, with Peter and Paul following him. They stood in our midst and the Saviour said to the saints, 'Peace be with you, my [peace I] give to you'.*

* Jn 14:27

They said, 'You who know everything before it takes place, we wished for your mercy to come upon these pagans, that you might baptize them with the seal of holy baptism'.

The Saviour answered and said, 'This I shall do, O . . .'.

There was a great lake of water churning up wave after wave like the River, and immediately he baptized all of them in his holy name and gathered them all together for his holy body and pure blood. He said to them, . . .

Apa Pshai[-nte-Jeremias?] disappeared. He left us without our knowing where he had gone. My father said to me, 'This saint came to us for the sake of . . . these pagans'. We walked south until. . . .

APPENDIX

The Coptic-Arabic Synaxery Saint Paul of Tamma[68]

[THE SEVENTH OF BABEH]

On this day* Anba Paul of Tamma fell asleep. He dwelled on the mountain of Antinoë in Upper Egypt; with him was his disciple Ezekiel, who testified to his virtues. Through the great love that he bore for Christ and on account of the excesses of his asceticism, he killed himself seven times.

* October 4

The first time, he tied himself upside down to a tree. He remained hanging there for forty days until all of his blood flowed out through his nose and mouth. Then he delivered his soul into the hands of the Lord; then the Lord returned his soul to him.

Another time, he plunged himself into the sea [the Nile?], hoping that the crocodiles would eat him, but they did not touch him at all. He remained lying face down in the water for many days until he died.

Another time, he buried himself in the sand and died; his disciple was standing by his side, weeping for him. God sent his angel who brought him back to life and consoled him.

Another time, he rolled down the side of a mountain where the rocks were as sharp as knives; they pierced his body and sides. He died immediately.

Another time, he threw himself off the top of a high boulder upon an enormous rock whose tip was like a sword. He was cut in two.

Another time he bound himself by the legs and remained that way for forty days, then he died.

Each time, the Lord Christ raised him up. Then the Lord appeared to him, consoled him, and said, 'Paul, my beloved, what your soul has suffered is sufficient'. He responded, 'Master, allow me to mortify myself for your holy name as you mortified yourself for the human race. You, who are God and Son of God, died for our sins although we are undeserving'. God comforted him and strengthened him.

When our father Anba Bishoi went to the mountain of Antinoë, he met with Saint Anba Paul and said to him, 'The Lord Christ intends for your body, Anba Paul, to be placed with the body of Anba Bishoi'. When Saint Anba Paul died for the seventh time, his body was placed with that of Saint Anba Bishoi, as had been told to him. When they wanted to transport the body of Saint Anba Bishoi to the mountain of Scetis (I mean the monastery of Saint Anba Macarius),[69] they took the body of Saint Anba Bishoi and left the body of Anba Paul. The boat on which the body lay remained immobile and would not sail. They realized that it was because of the body of Anba Paul. They took him, put him with the other, and conveyed them to Scetis and he is with the body of Anba Bishoi until this day.[70]

May their prayers be with us! Amen.

II. Four Short Works

On Humility
On Poverty
A Letter
An Untitled Work

On Humility[71]*

* De humilitate

1. Listen concerning the way you have asked about.[72] Be attentive; stand with the Lord. If you keep these words, you will be one of the elect in all things.

2. For it is written: 'Glory will go before those who are humble'.* And again, 'The wisdom of the humble person lifts high that person's head'.* And again, 'Whom will I look upon except the person who is humble and gentle and who trembles at my words?'*

* Prov 29:23?
* Sir 11:1

* Is 66:2

3. And again it is written: 'The bones of the humble will rejoice with you in every way'.[73]* And again, 'The prayer of a humble person is immediately heard'.*

* Ps 50:10 (LXX); 51:8
* Sir 4:6?

4. Again it is written: 'Look on my humility and my suffering and forgive all my sins'.*

* Ps 24:18 (25:18)

5. See what sort of thing humility is: If you acquire it, you have acquired everything.

6. And again: Keep your body holy and the holy angels will come to you and give you joy, and you will see God.

7. It is written: 'I have seen the Lord of Hosts with my eyes'.*

* Is 6:5

8. Again it is written: 'I heard you with the hearing of the ears and just now I saw you with my eyes'.*

* Job 42:5

9. And the Holy Spirit will illumine all your members, and the twelve Virtues will dance in the midst of your soul, and the Cherubim and Seraphim will shelter you beneath their wings.[74]

10. For it is written: 'Blessed are the bodies of virgins, for the reward for their purity will not perish'.[75]* And beget silence.**

* Mt 10:42
** cf Prov 17:28, Zeph 1:7

11. It is good that your suffering continue, keeping you safe.

12. For thus it is written: 'The person who protects himself, guarding his soul with meditation[76] and prayer, stays prepared day and night'.[77]

13. For it is written: 'A fire will burn in my meditation',* and 'Unless your law is with me in my meditation, I will perish in my humility'.*

* Ps 38:4 (LXX)
* Ps 118:92 (LXX)

14. Moreover, Paul commanded Timothy: 'Give attention to your reading until I come'.* And do not allow yourself numerous friends, and you will always be at peace.

* 1 Tim 4:13

15. For it is written: 'If your concerns are many, you will not loosen the hold of sin'. 'Let your advisors be one in a thousand',* and 'A faithful friend is a life-giving medicine',* and 'The beauty of a faithful friend is a trusted weight and measure'.*

* Sir 6:6
* Sir 6:16

* Sir 6:15

16. 'A faithful friend is beyond price'.[78]*

* Sir 6:15

17. If you keep a faithful friend by your side, he will remain faithful when you are afraid and he will strengthen you and give you courage.[79]

18. He will cause you to be a worker and will make you a citizen,[80] and he will be a strong wall for you to lean against, and he will be a shade tree for you to rest under in all your troubles. He

will be strength and power and consolation for you. He will find you during your affliction. You will find him there when you are in distress; he will bear all your sufferings.

19. If you place all your sufferings on him, he will bear them.

20. Moreover, my son, zealously seek gentleness, for it is written concerning our father Moses: 'He was more gentle than everyone on earth'.*

* Num 12:3

21. And it is written: 'The gentle will inherit the earth'* and again, 'Guard your heart with all vigilance'.* Indeed, the ways of life come from these precepts.

* Mt 5:4
* Prov 4:23

22. If you cast evil thoughts from your heart, your whole body will feel relief[81] and your mind[82] will abide on the heights of virtue.

23. For it is written: 'My son, do not give into every passing desire so that the spirit of falsehood may not turn in your direction'.*

* Sir 6:2?

24. And do not follow your desires but restrain yourself from the things you desire and 'the Jerusalem of heaven will be for you a holy city and as a result no stranger will enter it. And at that time the mountains[83] will pour forth sweetness and the hills will flow with milk and all the springs[84] of Judah will produce abundant water and a stream will come forth from the house of the Lord and it will water the thorn bushes with rivers of water. Egypt will become desolate' (that is, your enemies), 'and the Lord will dwell in Zion'.[85]*

* Joel 3:17-21 (LXX)

25. You wretch,[86] do not let your belly lord it over you and you will be a child of the Most High and will inherit the Kingdom and its goods and you will reign with Christ for ever.

26. Do not turn God away for the sake of your belly. For he spoke in Ezekiel, saying: 'They defiled me before my people for handfuls of barley and for pieces of bread'.* * Ezk 13:19

27. Do not crow over your brother's ways, for the person who rejoices over his neighbor's ways alienates himself from the Lord and God will be angry with him and as a result will hand him over to his enemies and will humiliate him just as that person acted wickedly in what he did to his brother. Thus the Lord has spoken.

28. These are the words that the Lord said concerning the sons of Haman: 'Since you rejoiced over my holy places because they had been defiled and rejoiced over the house of Israel because it had been destroyed and rejoiced over the house of Judah because it had been taken prisoner, I will now hand you over to the sons of Kedem and they will receive your inheritance'.* * cf Est 3-9

29. And do not be a hypocrite, looking for the word of the Lord from a godly person.

30. For God has spoken through the prophet: 'They will come to you and sit before you and hear your words but they will not obey them because their mouths speak lies and their hearts follow their polluted ways'.* * Ezk 33:31

31. Therefore, my son, fight for yourself from now on, for I have done my utmost for you. . . .

On Poverty [87]

*De paupertate

1. Before all else, 'fear God and keep his commandments'.*

*Qo 12:13

2. These, then, are the commandments of God, my son. You shall keep them. Walk in poverty and an unencumbered life, without worries and needs, and you will remain at peace.[88]

3. Therefore, my son, since poverty and need are holdovers from passion,[89] not worrying about these things is what saves[90] a person.

4. Do not look for a lot of work and you will know how you are doing, and do not multiply your thoughts and you will remain at peace and will not be confused.

5. Now then, my son, observe all the saints, see how they are one with God.

6. For it is they who walked in estrangement and poverty and want, rejected by everyone, until they defeated the Adversary, 'wandering in deserts and mountains and caves and holes in the ground, in need, afflicted, suffering, those of whom the world was not worthy'.*

*Heb 11:38

7. Remember, then, that our Saviour came in poverty; he laid down the ways for us so that we might follow in his footsteps and become imitators of him, as it is written: 'Be imitators of me as I am of Christ',* and also [imitate] his other apostles.

*1 Cor 11:1

On Poverty

8. For when he was about to send them forth, he did not give them a multitude of commandments to follow but gave them only the commandment of poverty.

9. As it is written in the Gospel according to Matthew: 'When you go forth to preach, do not acquire for yourselves gold or silver or copper in your belts, nor two tunics, nor sandals'.* These are all words he spoke concerning poverty.

* Mt 9:9-10

10. Therefore, do not walk with anyone so that you will not lose your way and become confused; what is more, do not allow friendship between you and someone to give worldly satisfaction so that your poverty is destroyed and brought to nothing and you backslide.

11. Since, therefore, a poor man. . . .

Letter[91]

1. . . . stand before . . . the Lord God Almighty.

2. You shall eat your little bit of bread and drink your little bit of water, my beloved, patiently remaining[92] in your dwelling in poverty, and God will have confidence in you.

3. Do not give rest to your thoughts until rest comes to you without rest. Let them be dead while you live with God.

4. Do not neglect what is on the left;[93] do not confide in those who . . .; do not cease . . . rest . . . war.

5. Indeed, now is the time to endure temptation since the elect and the blessed receive "the crown of life," as James said.* Because you have worked at these things, my son, you have become the beloved of the unicorn.[94]

* Jas 1:12

6. The voice of the turtledove has called out in your land within our midst,[95]* within your place of rest, Amen, so that you might be perfected, my beloved, bearing fruit a hundredfold* as you pray for me, for my salvation, and for all of us together.

* cf Sg 2:12

* Mt 13:8

7. Placing confidence in your obedience, I have written to you, knowing that you will carry out the things that I have written to you.*

* see Phlm 21

8. Indeed, my lord, there is greater progress for you and for me too and for the one who will listen.[96]

9. Blessed is Christ who gives us victory.

10. The honor is God's. Amen.

11. The letter of Apa Paul. Surely his blessing will be upon us. Amen.

An Untitled Work ('Sitting in Your Cell') [97]

100. [Sitting] in your cell,[98] be like the master sailors piloting their ships as you watch the wind to see what direction it is taking you, whether it is a good wind or a bad wind that is coming.[99]

101. Be strong in war and cry out: 'Arise, north wind! Come, south wind! Blow upon my garden so its fragrance may be wafted abroad like incense'.[100]*

* Sg 4:16

102. Sitting in your cell, my son, do not be like the hypocrites.*

* cf Mt 6:5, 16

103. Do not grow weary praying and you will be heard.

104. When you are weary, wait for relief.

105. My son, give yourself to God with all your might* and he will fight for you and protect you; he will give you strength and will fight against those who fight against you.

* cf Mt 22:37, Dt 11:1

106. Because without God you will not be able to do anything.[101]

107. But if a person prays to God, God will give him strength and watch over him; he will fill him with wisdom and understanding and will guide him with his own counsel.

Sitting in Your Cell

108. Sitting in your cell, do not be idle.

109. Pay careful attention to how you sit in your cell. Do not act like farm animals being driven by someone, but act like the person driving the animals.[102]

110. Sitting in your cell, keep careful watch over yourself.

111. Do not put your body in a cell while your heart is elsewhere.[103]

112. Instead, make your body a temple for God* and direct your thoughts to him and you will acquire a sound way of thinking.

* cf 1 Cor 3:16, 2 Cor 6:16, 2 Th 2:4

113. Sitting in your cell, do not think highly of yourself: neither exalt yourself in the counsels of your heart nor think you are the only one deserving praise, for God hates those who think they are the only ones deserving praise.

114. 'But he regards the prayer of the humble'.*

* Ps 101:18 (102:17)

115. Sitting in your cell, allow nothing to chain you down. Let the day's matters be enough for the day* and you will remain at peace.

* cf Mt 6:34

116. But with regard to sin, watch yourself that you do not sin.

117. Sitting in your cell, persist with your prayer and your fasting and the struggle[104] taking place in your heart and you will have the qualities of the pure of heart.

118. Because without peace and purity. . . .

200. [Do not] show arrogance to anyone but bear everything for the sake of the love of God.*

* cf Gal 6:2, Col 3:13, 2 Thess 3:5

201. Be kind, my son, because 'those who are kind will dwell on the earth and the innocent will remain on it',* because 'love is kind'**.¹⁰⁵

* Prov 2:21
** 1 Cor 13:4

202. It says: 'If you see anything, be kind and innocent and you will find the glory of God'.

203. Do not be like the thorny acacias that grow on the mountain, which is God.

204. Instead, be like a reed growing in the water, which is the abyss.¹⁰⁶

205. Let your manner be peaceful, with your heart like a fire against sin.

206. Do not let your heart grow slack.

207. On the contrary, be sober in everything.

208. Do not let your heart lord it over you but on the contrary be the master of your heart.

209. Do not follow your heart but let your heart follow you.

210. Do not obey your heart but on the contrary let your heart obey you.

211. Do not let your heart be your god but on the contrary let your heart obey God.

212. You want to obey God, my son, but you will not want to obey your desire and thus will not obey God.¹⁰⁷

213. God's wish for you is for you to keep his commandments.*

* cf Ex 20:6, Lev 26:3, Dt 5:10

214. For if you keep his commandments, everything you do will be powerful and what you do will be perfect, for his commandments are not burdensome.

215. He cries out again: 'Come to me everyone who is weary and burdened, and I will give you rest'.*

* Mt 11:28

216. And again he cries out against certain people who are afflicted with vanity, as it is written: 'What is wrong with those who suffer? They are afflicted with vanity'.

217. And again: 'My iniquities have risen over my head, they have weighed me down like a heavy burden'.*

* Ps 37:5 (38:4)

218. For we see that if a person clings to God, he stops being burdened with sin; the word of the Saviour is fulfilled concerning him: 'If you continue in my word, you will know the truth, and the truth will make you free'.*

* Jn 8:31-32

219. It says: 'God will free you from your sins because God is the one who cleanses us'.*

* cf Sir 38:10, 1 Jn 1:7?

220. Because it is written: 'The one who cleanses and those who are cleansed. . . .'

III. On the Cell[108]

1. My son, obey God and keep his commandments, and be wise and remain in your dwelling, which is your delight, and your cell will remain with you in your heart as you seek its blessing, and the labor[109] of your cell will go with you to God.

2. Your cell will bring you to Lake Acherousia,[110] and will take you into 'the assembly of the first born who are enrolled in heaven'.*

* Heb 12:23

3. 'My son, keep my words and store up my commandments . . . ; keep them for your life'.*

* Prov 7:1

4. Pride in your cell will give you glory in the midst of the saints in the house of God.[111]

5. The patient endurance of the poor person[112] will not perish.*

* cf Ps 9:19 (LXX); (9:18 NRSV)

6. Now then, my beloved, whom God has taken to himself, embrace him in patient endurance.[113] Do not lose heart. Do not neglect God's grace until with joy and certainty you ascend to God.

7. Truly, the lion leaves the desert and erases his pawprints with his tail. If he prevails over the person who has come out after him, he goes up in complete confidence.[114]

8. Now then, do not let your heart grow slack while you are in this world until you go up to the Lord in victory.[115]

On the Cell

9. You* who are poor,[116] if you cling to the Lord alone, the Lord will also remain with you and have you rule with him.

* (sing.)

10. Now then, you who are poor, you shall worship God with all your heart and with all your thoughts and with all your strength* and with your words, and you shall place your heart in your dwelling as you do in God,[117] for you will bear[118] his commandments in this way. And do your utmost to go up on the Lord's day without being commanded to do so.[119] God will rule over you and you will profit from him as you profit from your cell.

* Dt 6:4-5,
Mk 12:30, Lk 10:27

11. Because there is no lion on the mountain, in humility you will have as much joy in your heart as the person who celebrates a festival.[120]

12. For there is no festival like the worship of God in your dwelling.

13. For you will find God in your cell. And his favor is very great and the pride of the poor monk is the desert and instruction in humility.

14. The poor person, therefore, who is humble will be called Josedek among the prophets.[121]*

* cf 1 Chr 6:15
and Sir 49:12;
Jer 23: 6 and 9

15. For our Lord, although he was very rich, became poor for our sakes,* and if you receive the grace that the cell provides, you will reach God.

* cf 2 Cor 8:9

16. For the cell has no need of testimony,[122] because the testimony of the saints is constant mourning.

17. If they mock you, saying, 'Why do you trouble yourself like this?' patiently say in return, 'This "trouble" is edification for me'.

18. But only humbly flee to yourself in humble knowledge, because it is the time for withdrawal,[123] and your cell will become for you a [ ].[124]

19.[125]

* cf Rom 11:33

20. Know that you are wealthy on account of the depths of the wisdom that will be yours in love.*

* Rom 11:33

21. Hold on to teaching with all humility and in addition say to yourself: 'O the depths of the riches and wisdom!'[126] and rule with God.*

* cf Eph 2:19, Gal 4:26, Heb 12:22

22. . . . in the world . . . afflicting . . . become 'citizens with the saints and members of the household of God' 'in the heavenly Jerusalem', which is 'the mother of us all'.[127]*

* cf Prov 28:15, 2 Sam 17:8

23. Now then, you who are poor, you shall look boldly upon your enemies like the roaring lions and like a bear that has had her cubs taken away from her.*

24. Lower your eyes to the image of God, like these sheep.

* cf Jas 3:5-8

25. Do not let your mouth give you so much difficulty that, in its lack of restraint, it delivers you into the hands of your enemies.*

26. For great and numerous are its slaughters and the deadly snares that come from it.[128]

27. May its madness not visit you, poor and wretched as you are.

28. May the disturbing spirit not happen upon you.

29. May the lying spirit not be in you lest the Lord destroy you.

30. May the world's entanglements not seize you, my beloved.

31. You shall not reject the grace that your cell offers so that . . . you.

32. For I have undergone great suffering for your sake until God shows you mercy . . . [the] Devil . . . me for your sake. God, therefore, has wished. . . .¹²⁹

33. Do not give ear to anyone who speaks troubling things to you that cause you to be disturbed and forsake your cell.

34. For you will know God in your cell. Keep him with you and the Devil will depart from you, which will allow you to tame him.

35. Therefore, my beloved, do not allow him behind you in the contest¹³⁰ lest he mock you and give you trouble.

36. O cell, the monk's tester and teacher!*   * cf Hos 5:2 (LXX), Jer 6:27

37. O cell, the anchorite's wealth!

38. The thoughts of the wise man sitting in his cell are judgements.

39. A wise man in his cell is the winnower of the impious, and he will drive a wheel over the wicked one.¹³¹*   * cf Prov 20:26 (LXX)

40. Place your thinking and your speech below every person so that you are at peace and you will be at peace with everyone, keeping these words, while victory is [with you] on the day of [battle].¹³²

41. Do not offer a sacrifice w[ith] the sons of those whom 'I turned back on the day of battle' because 'they did not keep God's covenant'.*   * Ps 78:9-10

cf Num 22-24

42. Moreover, you have heard about Balaam, the son of Beor, who died in battle on account of his disobedience—in which I, too, share.[133]*

43. Now then, my beloved, you shall renounce disobedience and withdraw to your [cell], living in purity.[134]

44. For God is limitless. A wise man [in] his cell is without [measure].[135]

45. For his name is in heaven. His countenance casts forth rays of light from Jerusalem. The people behold him in this time of famine.

46. He who has come upon these gifts of grace will know them.

47. The measure of a wise man sitting in his cell is the Lord.

48. For he is like God because he is invisible.

49.[136] The wise man[137] in his cell will be hidden from the coming evils.[138]

50. For the wisdom of a wise man[139] understands God's ways. His heart delights in God. God will give him peace in his cell.

51. Do not forsake God. Do not forsake your cell.

52. For the incense of God is a wise man in his cell.

53. The altar of God is a wise man in his cell.[140]

54. For his cell is always filled with a sweet smell from the fruit of his good works.

55. The glory of God will appear to him there.

On the Cell

56. The angel of the Lord appeared to Zacharias within[141] the altar of incense.* * See Lk 1:11

57. The angels entered Lot's house.* The angel entered[142] the house of Tobias and Tobit [and his wife].[143]* He also entered the house of Manoah.[144]*
* Gen 19:3
* cf Tob 5:10
* cf Jdg 13

58. Now, then, [give yourself][145] to the grace of the cell. All healing will take place for you there.

59. You shall not[146] walk to your cell without [learning][147] about deceitfulness.

60. For the demons openly wage war against humans in the desert.

61. For they are stripped naked before God. Therefore there is no pity in them towards the person who is sitting alone in peace.[148]

62. Therefore, when you arrive at the blessing of the cell,[149] watch yourself on the right[150] because they wage war against you with compassion to save someone so they may take away the blessing of the cell from you.[151]

63. O Lot, save yourself [from] the mountain![152] Who, then, will have mercy on a dwelling in the desert and weep for me?[153]

64. Place your thought downward,[154] believing that there is a purpose[155] for the image of God.

65. You know your weakness.[156] One person has one way, for another there is another way—to the cell for you![157]

66. And you will find the daughter of Phanuel[158] beside you; she is a woman who worships God night [and] day[159] and prophesies concerning the Lord with all who look for the redemption of Jerusalem.* * cf Lk 2:36-38

67. O cell, there is no way to measure your honor! The true and good tent[160]* shall be the person of God who sits in it.

* cf Heb 9:11

68. A wise man in his cell is the true and perfect 'tent with the golden urn [in it],[161] with manna, [and] Aaron's rod that budded, and the tablets of the covenant'.[162]*

* cf Heb 9:11, 9:4

69. Blessed is the person, poor and wretched, who withdraws;[163] he is a friend of God just like Abraham, because the Lord will not do anything that he has not revealed[164] through his servants and his prophets.[165]*

* cf 2 Kings 17:23

70. Indeed, God spoke with him[166] beside the tree of Mamre while he was sitting at the door of the[167] tent at midday.*

* cf Gn 18:1

71. He also spoke with Solomon in the house he had built.* Elijah, too, at the river Chorath.[168]**

* cf 1 Kings 9:1-2
** cf 1 Kings 17:1-7

72. Now then, you who are poor, the honor of the poor man in his cell is very great.[169]

73. Wise stranger, it has been said: 'Flee from yourself!' God will speak with you and will forgive you in your cell.[170]

74. He[171] spoke with Abimelech, who was king, in his house. He forgave him.[172]*

* cf Gn 20

75. As for a wise man in his cell,[173] God is the one who knows his end, and the Lord is the one who has said: 'Blessed are those who mourn for they are the ones who will be comforted'.*

* Mt 5:4

76. A wise man in his cell is the city of blessings;[174] he is the dwelling place of the virtues and[175] the Spirit is perfected within him.[176]

77. You shall be a wise man[177] in your cell, building up your soul as you sit in your cell,[178] while glory[179] is with you, while humility is with you, while the fear of God surrounds you day and night, while your cares[180] are thrown down, while your soul and your thoughts[181] watch God in astonishment,[182] gazing at him[183] all the days of your life.

78. Do not look toward man.

79. Also,[184] do not let a man look toward you.

80. Allow yourself only one out of a thousand as an advisor* and you will be at peace all the days of your life.

* Sir 6:6

81. You shall test[185] the teaching that you follow, walking alone[186] with God at your side.[187]

82. For Elijah was at the river Chorath [alone, God was with him, and the raven ministered to him].[188]*

* cf 1 K 17:1-7

83. The prophet was also walking alone; he took Paul's belt and bound himself.[189]*

* cf Acts 21:11

84. Now then, fight bravely for your dwelling[190] for it is what will remain with you.

85. A spirit of God also snatched Philip away[191] and he was found in Azotus.* And we are also built upon the foundation of the apostles and the prophets.[192]*

* cf Acts 8:39-40

* cf Eph 2:20

86. Now, then, God will remain with you as you walk[193] and he will look for you [in your cell][194] and mysteries of God will be revealed to you there as they were to Cornelius in his house.[195]*

* cf Acts 10

87. For if you wear poverty in this world [and humility, you will be] with the Son of God [in his kingdom].[196]

88. Desire the blessing of your cell all the days of your life for it will remain with you.

89. [197]There is no measure to the [honor] of the cell, and its mysteries are without number.[198]

90. Therefore, the <true> widow who remains alone and perseveres in petition and fasting[199] is very great.[200]

* 1 Tim 5:6

91. 'But the pampered woman is dead even while she lives'.*

92. Now, then, you shall be[201] alone, placing your hope in God, and your glory will be great in the presence of God, and your honor in the midst of the saints.[202]

93. You shall not speak with people as you remain back in your cell. Neither disturbances nor the cowardice of the demons shall drive you out of it, as your mind becomes conformed to God in your cell.

94. Do not cling to weakness,[203] for weakness begets weakness.[204]

95. And, moreover, do not walk with someone whose strength comes from an arrogant tongue.[205]

96. Know that being troubled is weakness.[206] Do not allow it entrance.

97. Do not walk with a poor man who has grown slack, who is lacking[207] God's mercy, lest you become like him.

98. You shall rather cling to a land of mountains, a land of valleys, one that the eyes of the Lord watch over always.[208]*

* cf Dt 11:11-12: [Dt 11:11 (Lxx) continues: You shall drink rain water always]

99–102 (I)

99. Blessed be Christ who gives [you] the victory![209]*

* cf 1 Cor 15:57

100. The honor belongs to God forever. Amen.[210]

101. The Letter of Apa Paul of Tamah concerning the cell.

102. May his blessing come upon us. Amen. 99.[211]

99–125 (II)

99. Let your labor be between you and God so God will reveal himself in the resurrection and glorify you in him in the midst of all the righteous and the saints.

100. Do not welcome vainglory, for you will not be able to bear its wiles and mad lies as it plants lying thoughts within you.

101. If you give your heart to it in lying dreams, it makes progress,[212] persisting in vain thoughts; as a result, it leads some astray among those who welcome the spirit that loves the saying written thus:

102. 'When the liar speaks, he speaks according to his own nature, for he is a liar and also its father'.*

* cf Jn 8:44

103. You shall be saved, therefore, O man of God, from this evil spirit, and you shall not become a mountain burning and harsh.*

* cf Rev 8:8?

104. You shall on the contrary be a mountain fat and strong* and God will want to dwell in you, and the chariot of God will be twice ten thousand in you,* and your sweet fragrance will be manifest in heaven and will spread in the midst of the saints while you are an example for those on earth because you are strong and victorious in battle.

* cf Ps 67:16 (LXX)

* Ps 67:18 (LXX) = 68:17

105. As a result, it will come to be written about you: 'The mountain of the Lord will be revealed' and 'the house of God will be on the mountaintop'.*

* cf Mi 4:1 and Is 2:2

106. This honor shall be yours, you who fight! You shall receive a crown of joy* from God for your sufferings as you sit in your cell.

* cf 1 Pet 5:4

107. For someone has said: 'Fighting the good fight, I have finished the race, I have kept the faith. Now, therefore, there is reserved for me the crown of righteousness, which the Lord, the righteous judge, will give me on that day, and not only to me but to all who have longed for[213] his appearing',* and to all who contend.[214]

* 2 Tim 4:7-8

108. Therefore you shall give yourself to God as you sit in your cell.

109. You shall stand against your enemies and drive them out with the name of the Lord your God as you sit in your cell.

110. Do not be afraid of the demons. I have waged war with them in the desert and God has scattered them with his love, not with my strength.

111. As for me, I am weak and I am powerless.[215] God alone is mighty.

112. So therefore do not be afraid of the demons. For they are powerless before him.

On the Cell

113. Instead be afraid for the person whom you will save, fleeing inward in the knowledge that it is the time for withdrawal.[216]*   *cf Rom 13:11, 1 Cor 7:29

114. For David withdrew and was saved.* Withdraw earnestly on your own behalf.   *cf 1 Sam 19:18

115. For the saints and our Lord died at the hands of men, and I have suffered more on account of the war with men than the war with the desert.

116. So, therefore, flee to yourself alone.

117. For Andrew was found walking alone in the city of the cannibals.[217]

118. For if you find the way to remain in your cell, which will save you from vainglory because you will be a stranger to arrogance, you will be rescued from all these things and you will be strong in battle at all times just as Joshua the son of Nun. While the [dew] is upon you in your dwelling, God is looking after you.

119. A poor man who remains in his cell is a king and a lord. Honor him, for God is dwelling in him.

120. The Lord has made him king, he has clothed him in beauty; the lord has clothed him with power, he has girded him with it.

121. Thus you have listened to the honor of the poor man sitting humbly in his cell.

122. Now, then, give yourself to humility as you sit in your cell, and you will be with God always.

123. Now, then, my beloved, God will surely place this grace and this blessing in your heart for you.

124. Blessed is Christ who gives the victory!* The honor belongs to God. Amen.[218]   *cf 1 Cor 15:57

125. You who are poor, give yourself to patient endurance, being humble, and you will come upon this honor, and your mind[219] will think heavenly things, not earthly things, and you will believe in the saints that come to you, and you will be like the disciples of Christ Jesus. His is the glory and the power for ever. Amen.

NOTES

* *The Sayings of the Desert Fathers*, CS 59, translated Benedicta Ward SLG (Kalamazoo: Cistercian Publications, 1975) 139.

[1] Tito Orlandi, ed. and trans., *Paolo di Tamma: Opere* (Rome: C.I.M., 1988) 10.

[2] To give just one example, Paul is not mentioned in Lucien Regnault's fine book, *La vie quotidienne des pères du désert en Égypte au IVe siècle* (Hachette: Paris, 1990), now translated as *The Day-to-Day Life of the Desert Fathers in Fourth-Century Egypt* (Petersham, MA: St Bede's, 1999), nor is *On the Cell* cited in chapter seven, 'Le séjour en cellule', 95–108. That chapter nevertheless provides good background for fourth-century monasticism and *On the Cell*. Paul may be unknown in the West, but the Coptic Church has preserved his name in its liturgy. In 'The Commemoration of the Saints', which takes place during the Sunday Eucharist, 'our father Abba Paul of Tammoh and Ezekiel his disciple' are remembered. See *The Coptic Liturgy (of St. Basil)* (Cairo: J.B.P.H., 1993) 254. Ancient inscriptions at the monastery of Apa Jeremias and elsewhere invoke his name; see Sir Herbert Thompson, 'The Coptic Inscriptions', in J. E. Quibell, *Excavations at Saqqara (1908–9, 1909–10)*, volume 4: *The Monastery of Apa Jeremias* (Cairo: IFAO, 1912) #203 (p. 61 and 61 n. 9) and #240 (p. 75).

[3] Emile Amélineau published two fragments of Paul's *Life* in 1889, but Orlandi essentially 'discovered' Paul and edited his extant works in 1988. There is no comprehensive study of either Paul's life or writings. A brief introduction is that of René-Georges Coquin, 'Paul of Tamma, Saint', *The Coptic Encyclopedia*, ed. Aziz S. Atiya (New York: Macmillan, 1991): 6:1923-1925. See also Orlandi, 'La vita di Paolo di Tamma e i monaci del Medio Egitto' and 'Le opere di Paolo di Tamma', in Alberto Camplani, ed., *L'Egitto Cristiano: Aspetti e Problemi in Età Tardo-Antica* (Rome: Institutum Patristicum Augustinianum, 1997) 68–70 and 70–71. Mark Sheridan has recently drawn attention to the spirituality of Paul's writing in 'The Development of the Interior Life in Certain Early Monastic Writings in Egypt', in Marek Starowicyski, ed., *The Spirituality of Ancient Monasticism. Acts of the International Colloquium held in Cracow-Tyniec, 16–19th November 1994* (Cracow: Tyniec, 1995) 91–104, and 'Il mondo spirituale e intellettuale del primo monachesimo egiziano', in Camplani, ed., *L'Egitto Cristiano* 177–216, esp. 201–207.

[4] Enzo Lucchesi believes that 'An Untitled Work' *(Opus sine titulo)* does not belong to Paul on codicological grounds; see Lucchesi, 'Une version copte du Sermo Asceticus d'Étienne le Thébain', *Analecta Bollandiana* 115.3-4 (1997) 252, and 'À propos d'une édition récente des oeuvres de Paul de Tamma', *Studia*

Notes 191

Orientalia Christiana Collectanea 28 (1995) 161–166. Much of 'An Untitled Work' has parallels with portions of the *Ascetic Discourse* of Stephen of Thebes. See Chapter Eight, below.

⁵ There was apparently another work, 'On Judgement', of which only the title survives. A papyrus fragment dating to the sixth century states that an unnamed author who died on 7 Babeh (Paul's date of death) wrote four works: 'On the Place of Retreat', 'On Dwelling in the Desert', 'On Disbelief', and 'On Spiritual Weariness'. See Michel Pezin, 'Nouveau fragment copte concernant Paul de Tamma (P. Sorbonne inv. 2632)', in Jean-Marc Rosenstiehl, ed., *Christianisme d'Égypte: Hommages à René-Georges Coquin*, Cahiers de la Bibliothèque Copte 9 (Paris-Louvain: Peeters, 1995) 15–20. Pezin suggests, 20, that these works taken together form an 'Asceticon'. See Lucchesi, 165–166.

⁶ For a discussion, see Orlandi, 10–13, and Coquin, 1925.

⁷ René Basset, *Patrologia Orientalis* 1.3, no. 3, 321–322.

⁸ For its location, see Wolgang Kosack, *Historisches Kartenwerk Ägyptens* (Bonn, 1971), Blatt 2: Mittelägypten.

⁹ The coptic account has six, the arabic seven; see Basset; Coquin, 1923–1925; and Orlandi, 11.

¹⁰ See H. G. Evelyn White, *The Monasteries of the Wâdi 'N Natrûn*, Part II, *The History of the Monasteries of Nitria and of Scetis* (rpt, New York: Arno, 1973) 159. For John, see Maged S. Mikhail and Tim Vivian, trans., 'Life of Saint John the Little', *Coptic Church Review* 18:1-2 (Spring/Summer 1997) 1–64.

¹¹ Basset, 322.

¹² For accounts of Apollo and Amoun, see *Historia Monachorum* 8–9; *The Lives of the Desert Fathers*, trans. Norman Russell (Kalamazoo: Cistercian Publications, 1980) 70–81. For Phib, see Chapter Six, below.

¹³ Wall paintings at Bawit show Apollo with his disciples, Phip and Anup, sitting on a bench. At Saqqara, 'a particularly interesting painting brings together Onnophrius (or Abu Nofer) and his disciple Paphnutius, Macarius (of Wadi Natrun), Apollo, Phib, and Amoun (of Bawit)'; Marguerite Rassart-Debergh, 'L'art des "fils des pharaons"', in P. Miquel, et al., *Déserts chrétiens d'Égypte* (Nice: Culture Sud, 1993) 131. Rassart-Debergh, with Jacques Debergh, has provided a full discussion of this painting in 'A propos de trois peintures de Saqqara', in Hjalmar Torp, et al., edd., *Acta ad Archaeologium et Artium Historiam Pertinentia* (Rome: Giorgio Bretschneider, 1981) 11.187-203. See also Chapter Six, below. The painting is now preserved in the Coptic Museum in Cairo; for a color illustration, see Nabil Selim Atalla, *Coptic Art*, Volume 1: *Wall-Paintings* (Cairo: Lehnert & Landrock, n.d.) 14–15. On Apollo, see the excellent article by René-Georges Coquin, 'Apollon de Titkooḥ ou/et Apollon de Bawit?', *Orientalia* 46 (1977) 435–446.

¹⁴ Orlandi, 12–13.

¹⁵ Sheridan, 'Development' (above, n. 3), 96.

¹⁶ For the text, see Orlandi, 88. Much of *On the Cell* is concerned with wisdom and being wise; see *On the Cell* 44, 47, See 49, 50, 52, 53 below.

¹⁷ See Chapter One for examples.

¹⁸ The works translated here contain a number of sentences that begin with 'it is written' (H 10, H 12, P 216, P 220), but the allusions or quotations do not seem to belong to biblical works. H 10 quotes from the *Acts of Paul and Thecla*. *On the Cell* 2 contains a clear reference to Lake Acherusia from the *Apocalypse of Paul* 22 along with a quotation from Heb 12:23; by its context, Paul seems to have

expected his reader to recognize the allusion to the *Apocalypse of Paul*. *On the Cell* 117 alludes to a scene from *The Acts of Andrew and Matthias*; see D. R. MacDonald, ed., *The Acts of Andrew and Matthias in the City of the Cannibals* (Atlanta: Scholars Press, 1990).

[19] As far as I can determine, none of the 'sayings' attributed to Paul have direct parallels with the *Apophthegmata*, which underlines Paul's independence from the traditions of Nitria, Kellia, and Scetis.

[20] The *Sentences of Sextus* is a collection of ascetic sayings used by Origen, Basil, and Evagrius. Both it and *The Teachings of Silvanus* are found in the Nag Hammadi 'gnostic library'. For texts and translations, see *The Teachings of Silvanus*, trans. Malcolm Peel, in *Nag Hammadi Codex VII*, ed. Birger A. Pearson (Leiden: Brill, 1996) 249–369; Pythagoras Sextus, *The Sentences of Sextus*, ed. Henry Chadwick (Cambridge: Cambridge University Press, 1959); 'The Sentences of Sextus', trans. Frederik Wisse, in *The Nag Hammadi Library in English*, ed. James M. Robinson (San Francisco: Harper & Row, 1977) 454–459.

[21] See P 4 and *On the Cell* 61. For a discussion of the importance of peace and quiet in monastic thought, see J. Mark Sheridan, '"Steersman of the mind": The Virgin Mary as Ideal Nun (an interpretation of Luke 1:29 by Rufus of Shotep)', *Studia Patristica* 30, ed. Elizabeth A Livingstone (Leuven: Peeters, 1997) 226 and n. 5.

[22] *On the Cell* 60; Orlandi, 94. See the *Ascetic Discourse* of Stephen of Thebes 67a-d, Chapter Eight below.

[23] For Evagrius of Pontus, *On Teachers and Disciples* 3, the spiritual director is 'a director of battle' who 'does not allow someone to be wounded'. See Graham Gould, 'An Ancient Monastic Writing Giving Advice to Spiritual Directors (Evagrius of Pontus, *On Teachers and Disciples*)', *Hallel* 22 (1997) 96–103. In *On Teachers* 10, Evagrius says that the director arms, sheathes, protects, equips, places swords in his soldiers' hands, and disposes troops. In the coptic version of the *Lausiac History* of Palladius, Macarius the Great is referred to as a 'commander-in-chief among his soldiers', who had supplied the monks 'with all the arms of combat against the Devil', See Tim Vivian, *Four Desert Fathers* (Crestwood, New York: St. Vladimir's Seminary Press, 2004). Such use of military imagery is also found in Cassian and has antecedents both in Saint Paul and the Stoics; see Abraham J. Malherbe, *Paul and the Popular Philosophers* (Minneapolis: Fortress, 1989) 91–96.

[24] Sheridan, 'Development'(above, n. 3), 97–99, and 'Il mondo spirituale', 202–204, has pointed this out; in the discussion that follows I have elaborated on some of his observations.

[25] For further discussion of the importance of *prosoché*, see Sheridan, 'Steersman' (above, n. 21) 268–269.

[26] Sheridan, 'Development' (above, n. 3), 97, 101. On Antony's *Letters*, see Samuel Rubenson, *The Letters of St. Antony: Monasticism and the Making of a Saint* (Minneapolis: Fortress, 1995).

[27] See Sheridan (n. 3 above), 'Development', 99–103, and 'Il mondo spirituale', 204–207; the quotation is from the latter, 206.

[28] Sheridan, 'Development', 104.

[29] Driscoll (below, n. 31), 62.

[30] 'Abba Lot went to see Abba Joseph and said to him, "Abba, as far as I can I say my little office, I fast a little, I pray and meditate, I live in peace as far as I can, I purify my thoughts. What else can I do?" Then the old man stood up and stretched

General view of the Monastery of Saint Antony.

(All photos by the author.)

The Monastery of Saint Antony with the Galala Mountain Range in the background.

Interior views of the Monastery of Saint Antony; in the photo below, the keep is at the right.

Interior views of of Deir Anba Bishoy.

Front entrance of the Monastery of Saint Antony
with the ancient pulley and watchtower.

Abouna Maximous seated before an old millstone.

Entrance to the Cave of Saint Antony.

Father Lazarus in his hermitage.

Wall paintings of Saint Mary in the Church of Saint Antony before and after cleaning.

Wall painting of John the Little (John Kolobos).

Wall painting of Christ in Majesty.

Earlier wall painting, perhaps from the 6th c., perhaps of Saint Paul.

Wall painting of Saint Antony the Great and Saint Paul the Hermit, showing cleaning.

his hands towards heaven. His fingers became like ten lamps of fire and he said to him, "If you will, you can become all flame'". Alphabetical Apophthegmata Joseph of Panephysis 7; Benedicta Ward, trans., *The Sayings of the Desert Fathers: The Alphabetical Collection*, CS 59, rev. ed. (Kalamazoo: Cistercian Publications, 1984) 103.

[31] The wisdom tradition was very important in earlier egyptian and monastic spirituality, as is demonstrated by the scholia on the biblical wisdom books (Proverbs, Ecclesiastes, and Song of Songs) by Origen and Evagrius Ponticus, both of whom 'identified an order of spiritual progress in the progression from one of these biblical books to the other'. See Francesca Cocchini, 'Il Progresso Spirituale in Origene', and Jeremy Driscoll, 'Spiritual Progress in the Works of Evagrius Ponticus', both in *Spiritual Progress: Studies in the Spirituality of Late Antiquity and Early Monasticism*, ed. Jeremy Driscoll and Mark Sheridan (Rome: Pontificio Ateneo S. Anselmo, 1994) 29–46 and 47–84, respectively; the quotation is from Driscoll, 51.

[32] See 1, 20, 21, 38, 39, 47, 49, 50, 52, 53, 68, 73, 75, 76, 77, 81.

[33] See, for example, *The Teachings of Silvanus* 87,4-5 and 91,25-30.

[34] Knowledge, *gnosis*, and self-knowledge connect Paul to the letters of Saint Antony.

[35] As Mark McIntosh, *Mystical Theology* (London: Blackwell, 1998) 7, has noted, 'the experience of an individual person was [not] unimportant in this early conception of spirituality. . . . personal experience is not in itself the goal of spirituality. Individuals are not so much seeking to discover their own feelings as to live into the knowledge and love of God through the hard work of being members one with another of the Body of Christ'.

[36] *Teachings of Silvanus* 97.3–98.22. This portion of Silvanus was transmitted separately in antiquity under the name of Saint Antony the Great and may well have been used by Paul; see Wolf-Peter Funk, 'Ein doppelt überliefertes Stück spätägyptischer Weisheit', *Zeitschrift für ägyptische Sprache und Altertumskunde* 103 (1976) 8–21.

[37] *Teachings of Silvanus* 110.14-16.

[38] *Teachings of Silvanus* 97.19-21. I wish to thank David Brakke for these insights and identifications.

[39] This image of bread supplied by a raven in the wilderness or desert was transferred to Saint Paul the Hermit and Saint Antony by Saint Jerome in his *Life of Paul the First Hermit* 10; see Paul B. Harvey, Jr., 'The Life of Paul, the First Hermit, by Jerome', in Vincent Wimbush, ed., *Ascetic Behavior in Greco-Roman Antiquity: A Sourcebook* (Minneapolis: Fortress, 1990) 366. In the wall painting depicting this scene at the Monastery of Saint Antony, the bread has become a eucharistic symbol; see Elizabeth S. Bolman, ed., *Monastic Visions* (New Haven: Yale UP, 2001).

[40] As L. S. B. MacCoul observes, 'Paul of Tamma and the Monastic Priesthood', *Vigiliae Christianae* 53 (1999) 316–320, 319, 'What Paul of Tamma for his part was saying was that *all* [emphasis added] a monk needs to do to share in the eternal priesthood is remain poor and humble in his cell, not receive ordination and thereby become enmeshed in all-too-worldly episcopal politics'. Given what was required to abide in one's cell in early monasticism, as witnessed by Paul, Evagrius, and the *Apophthegmata*, one might certainly say "All?"

[41] Ps 70:5 (69:6) uses *ebiên* and *ptôchos*. The author of *The Teachings of Silvanus* often addresses his disciple as 'O wretched one' or 'O wretched soul'; see, for

example, 85,22; 86,8; 104, 8-12. This seems to show the influence of the Stoic-wisdom diatribe; see Peel (above, n. 20), 253.

[42] Victory: 8, 40, 99, 104, 124; glory: 4, 55, 76, 92, 99; suffering: 1, 32, 99; humility: 11, 13, 18, 21, 77, 87, 122, 125; patient endurance: 5, 6, 125.

[43] Solitude: 81, 82, 83, 90, 92, 116, 117.

[44] In Coptic *mauaa-* means 'alone', with, in these examples, the second *(k)* and third *(f)* person singular pronoun suffixes added.

[45] Translated from E. Amélineau, ed., 'Vie de Paul de Tamoueh', *Monuments pour servir à l'histoire de l'Égypte chrétienne: Mémoires publiés par les membres de la mission archéologique française au Caire* (Paris, 1888) 759–760. Section titles are those of the translator.

[46] The monks apparently knock at the entrance of a dwelling; see below, the beginning of 'Paul and Ezekiel Visit Apa Phib'.

[47] This monk must be the same Pamoun whom Abba Pambo visits in 'The Life of Apa Cyrus'. There he is identified as 'pa-m-porek', 'my beloved brother of the many-colored coat which is like the coat of the righteous man Joseph' (see Gn 37:3). See 'The Story of Abba Pambo' in Tim Vivian, trans., *Journeying into God: Seven Early Monastic Lives* (Minneapolis: Fortress, 1996) 31.

[48] That is, who made him a monk.

[49] By the late fourth century, the practice of celebrating the Eucharist on Saturday and Sunday was widespread among egyptian monks; see Regnault (above, n. 2), *La vie quotidienne*, 177–188.

[50] Translated from Amélineau, *Monuments* (above, n. 45) 760–769.

[51] *Thronos* usually indicates a bishop's seat; see Chapter Six below.

[52] *Diakonia* here must = *diakonikon*, a part of a church, that is, a sacristy or vestry or, as a separate building, a chapel; see G. W. H. Lampe, *A Patristic Greek Lexicon* (Oxford: Clarendon, 1961) 351B.

[53] The same expression occurs in the novel *Palace Walk* by Naguib Mahfouz, which is set in modern Cairo: "The brothers . . . restrained themselves and pretended not to see the delightful array [of food] . . . until their father put out his hand to take a piece of bread." See Naguib Mahfouz, *Palace Walk* (New York: Doubleday, 1990) 20.

[54] The *Life of Phib* (see Chapter Six below) is narrated by Papohe 'the steward', who is closely associated with Abba Apollo.

[55] These are identifiable locations in Middle Egypt: Hace (Hagje) and Sioout are southeast of Antinoë and northwest of Tamma and Titkooh. See Kosack (above, n. 6), 32, 35, and *Karte des koptischen Ägypten*, Blatt 2, Mittelägypten, at grid 5K.

[56] Terôt-Ashans (Dairut) was just northeast of Bawit; see Kosack, 33, and *Karte des koptischen Ägypten*, Blatt 2, Mittelägypten, at grid 4J.

[57] On the theme of monks living peacefully with animals in the desert, see Regnault (above, n. 2) 209–221. As Regnault points out, 221, these animal stories emphasize paradise regained: 'the saints, by their submission to God and their humility, shared in the privilege of Adam in paradise before the fall'.

[58] A Paphnutius at Scetis had the nickname 'Bubalus' or 'Bubalis', which means 'wild ox' or 'buffalo'. See Vivian, *Paphnutius*, 47–48.

[59] The questions asked here are reminiscent of those that Pambo asks on his journey; see Vivian, *Journeying into God*, 31, 33.

⁶⁰ See Chapter Six below for the *Life of Phib*.

⁶¹ R.-G. Coquin cites Paul's 'astonishment' in this passage to support his belief that 'Egyptian monks scarcely conceived the anchoritic life without the presence and aid of a companion, at one and the same time both disciple and servant'. See René-Georges Coquin, 'L'évolution de la vie monastique', *Dossiers Histoire et Archéologie [Chrétiens d'Egypte au 4e siècele: Saint Antonie et les moines du désert]* 133 (December 1988) 60–65, at 63.

⁶² This motif of God supplying extra bread may be found in the *Life of Onnophrius* and the *Life of Paul the First Hermit* 11 by Saint Jerome; see Vivian, *Journeying into God*, 183, and Harvey, Jr., 'The Life of Paul' (above, n. 39) 366–367.

⁶³ *Konia*, literally 'dust', could also be ashes or powder from ground rock which was sprinkled over athletes after they competed or could be used as a dry bath.

⁶⁴ The belief that the Devil and demons took the form of Ethiopians was common in early monastic literature; as Regnault points out, 201, 'the form that they seem to have especially effected was that of male or female Ethiopians, whose swarthy color evoked the blackness of malice', For his catalogue of Ethiopians in monastic literature, see 201–202, and on the Devil and demons in general, 189–207. For a general study, see Peter Frost, 'Attitudes toward Blacks in the Early Christian Era', *The Second Century* 8 (1991) 1–11. For further references, see Boniface Ramsey, trans., *John Cassian: The Conferences*, Ancient Christian Writers, 57 (Mahwah, NJ: Paulist, 1997) 73–74; Cassian, *Conferences* 1.21.1 and 2.13.7.

⁶⁵ *Pôlutia* = Gk *politeia*. In monastic literature, *politeia* usually means 'way of life'. Here, however, it seems to be suggesting a specific act. A parallel use occurs in the 'Appendix ad Palladium', *Patrologia Graeca* 65:136C: 'They said concerning a certain old man in the Thebaid, Abba Antianou, that he did many *politeas* in his youth . . .'. See Lampe, 1114 (G.).

⁶⁶ Again *pôlutia*.

⁶⁷ Translated from Amélineau, *Monuments* (above, n 45) 835–836.

⁶⁸ Translated with the assistance of Maged S. A. Mikhail from René Basset, ed. and trans., *Le Synaxaire arabe jacobite (redaction copte), Patrologia Orientalis* 1.3 (Turnhout: Brepols, 1980) 321–322.

⁶⁹ In Arabic, as in Coptic, 'mountain' can also mean 'monastery'. Deir Anba Maqar, the Monastery of Saint Macarius, is one of the ancient and modern monasteries in the Wadi al-Natrun (Scetis); see Chapter Two.

⁷⁰ The sense of this last paragraph is clear, but its awkwardness shows probable wear and tear either from numerous revisions or from the juxtapositions of slightly different manuscripts.

⁷¹ Translated from Orlandi, *Paolo di Tamma* (above, n. 1) 126–132.

⁷² See H 21.

⁷³ Psalms are given first according to the numbering in the Septuagint (LXX), then with the NRSV numeration in parentheses.

⁷⁴ The Virtues are well represented in monastic wall paintings at Bawit and Saqqara; at the former, one painting shows twelve Virtues surrounding Ama Sibylla while another has ten around her. For a full discussion and photographs, see Marguerite Rassart-Debergh, 'A propos de trois peintures de Saqqara', 'B. Des murs et des Vertus: la cellule 709', 193–201, and Plates I and II following p. 206. See also Stephen of Thebes, *Ascetic Discourse* 37 (Chapter Eight below) and the Appendix on Ama Sibylla in this volume.

75 See *Acts of Paul and Thecla* 6; Edgar Hennecke, *New Testament Apocrypha*, ed. Wilhelm Schneemelcher (Philadelphia: Westminster, 1964) 2:355. I am grateful to David Brakke for this reference.

76 'Meditation', *meleta*, suggests prayerful and quiet recitation of Scripture, especially the Psalms, rather than meditation in the modern sense.

77 'Stays' and 'continue' both translate čō.

78 The *Teachings of Silvanus* 110.14-16 identifies Christ as the 'faithful friend' of Sir 6:15.

79 In the Coptic, the word 'heart' *(hêt)* occurs three times in compound words in the second half of this sentence, whereas it is only faintly available once in English in 'courage' (French *coeur*).

80 Coptic/Gk: *politeutês*. Politeia, 'citizenship', came also to mean a monastic 'way of life'.

81 Coptic *asai* and its greek equivalent *kouphizesthai* suggest both relief and lightness, as in the english phrase 'all your burdens will be lifted'. See 'An Untitled Work' 214–215, 217–218.

82 'Mind' and 'thoughts' both translate *meeue*.

83 'Mountains' *(ntouiê)* may suggest 'monastic communities' here since in coptic monastic literature 'mountain' *(toou)* can also mean 'monastery' or 'monastic community'.

84 'Pour forth', 'flow with', and 'springs' in Coptic all use variants of the verb *shouo*, 'to flow, pour'.

85 Sheridan points out ('Development' (n. 3, above), 101) that from the time of Philo 'Egypt' 'was commonly held to represent the human body as the seat of the passions'. See 'An Untitled Work', 111. In *On Teachers and Disciples* 14, Evagrius considers monks to be 'those who have fled the land of Egypt'. See Gould (above, n. 23) 103.

86 Coptic *ebiên* = Gk *ptôchos*. This may be a technical term, meaning the monastic poor (the root meaning of the term), but it may also be a term of opprobrium, 'wretched', as I have rendered it here because of the context.

87 Translated from Orlandi, *Paolo di Tamma* (above, n. 1) 122–125.

88 Coptic *mton* literally means 'rest', but can also equal Gk *hesychia*.

89 Coptic/Gk: *pathos*.

90 Or: heals *(toujo)*.

91 Translated from the text in Orlandi, *Paolo di Tamma*, 86.

92 Or, possibly, 'enduring': *hupomine*.

93 Or: the things of the left hand. In *On the Cell* 62 Paul exhorts his reader to 'guard yourself on the right'; See Sheridan (above, n 3), 'Development', 102–103, and 'Il mondo spirituale', 206–207. Pachomius tells his monks that demons can come from the left; see Armand Veilleux, trans., *Pachomian Koinonia*, vol. 3, *Instructions, Letters, and Other Writings of Saint Pachomius and his Disciples*, CS 47 (Kalamazoo: Cistercian Publications, 1982) 39.

94 See Ps 28:6 (LXX): 'his beloved will be like a son of the unicorns'. Eusebius, in his commentary on the Psalms, understood 'the beloved' as Jerusalem and, as Sheridan observes ('Development'[n. 3], 100–101), 'Jerusalem was commonly held to be a figure of the individual soul and, as such, the dwelling place of God'. See 'On Humility' 24. On a wall at Kellia is a drawing of a unicorn, clearly identified as *monocheiros*, the same greek word (though misspelled) as is used here (spelled correctly: *monokerôs*); see Rassart-Debergh (above, n. 74), 136, and

figure 69 on 151. Rassart-Debergh comments, 136, that hermetic and patristic literature delighted in expounding on the unicorn's symbolism, that it 'sometimes represents the virginity of Mary and sometimes the sacrifice of Christ'.

[95] The Septuagint has 'our land'. I take 'your land within our midst' (literally: 'within us') to mean the cell of the person to whom the letter is addressed; he dwells within their midst.

[96] The context is not clear: is 'my lord' the person to whom Paul is writing, or is it the Lord? In the story of Abba Pambo, Pambo addresses an elder as 'lord'; see Vivian, *Journeying into God*, 31. 'Progress' *(prokopê)* may link this sentence with Phil 1:25 and 1 Tim 4:15.

[97] Translated from Orlandi, *Paolo di Tamma* (above, n. 1) 116–121.

[98] This phrase may also be found in the *Ascetic Discourse* of Stephen of Thebes. For the text, see Edouard des Places,'Le "Discours Ascétique" d'Etienne de Thèbes . . .' (see bibliography) 35–59; see the translation below, Chapter Eight, #36–39, #43–44, #46, #52, #66, #71. Sayings 100–112 and 200–220 of 'An Untitled Work' have parallels with sayings in the *Ascetic Discourse* 38–43 and 72–74.

[99] Metaphors of sailing are common in egyptian monastic literature, not surprising in a country dominated by the Nile; for one example, see Alphabetical Apophthegmata Syncletica 9 (Ward, CS 59:232-233). For a discussion of boats and sailing in monastic art and literature, see Rassart-Debergh (above, n. 74) 168–173, and plates 82–84 (on 170–171).

[100] Gregory of Nyssa, *Homilies on the Song of Songs*, says that the north wind symbolizes evil and the south wind the Holy Spirit.

[101] 'Be able' renders shčmčom; 'strength' and 'might' translate čom.

[102] See *The Teachings of Silvanus* 86,1-4 (Peel (above, n. 20), 283): 'Be not an animal, with men pursuing you; but rather, be a man, with you pursuing the evil wild beasts'.

[103] Literally: 'while your heart is in Egypt'. If we locate Paul in Middle Egypt, then 'Egypt' would have referred to Lower Egypt, the area around Babylon (Cairo) and the delta. 'Egypt' may also represent here the body and its passions; see 'On Humility' 24.

[104] Coptic/Gk: *agôn*, which can also be translated as 'contest' or 'fight'; see 1 Tim 4:10, 6:12; 2 Tim 4:7.

[105] 'Kind' *(chrêstos)* was probably pronounced the same as *christos*, 'Christ'.

[106] 'Abyss' is *pnoun* whereas God (in 203) is *pnoute*.

[107] 'Want' and 'desire' translate *ouôsh*, as does 'wish' in the next sentence.

[108] Translated with Birger A. Pearson from the text in Orlandi, 88-101 (I) and 102-115 (II). There are two extant recensions of *On the Cell*, which Orlandi has indicated with 'I' and 'II'. For a discussion of textual matters, see Orlandi, *Paolo di Tamma*, 3–10. Ellipses indicate gaps in the coptic text.

[109] Coptic: *hise*.

[110] In the *Apocalypse of Paul* 22–23, 'Paul' records the following vision: 'And after that he took me up away from that place where I had seen these things and, behold, a river whose waters were very white, whiter than milk. And I said to the angel: What is this? And he said to me: This is Lake Acherusia where the city of Christ is, but not every man is allowed to enter into that city. For this is the way which leads to God; and if there is anyone who is a fornicator and ungodly and who turns and repents and brings forth fruit worthy of repentance, first when he

has come forth from the body he is brought and worships God and (he) is handed over from there at the command of God to the angel Michael and he baptizes him in Lake Acherusia. Thus he leads him into the city of Christ with those who have not sinned. And I marvelled and blessed the Lord God because of all I had seen.

(23) 'And the angel answered and said to me: Follow me and I shall lead you into the City of Christ. And he stood by Lake Acherusia and put me in a golden boat and about three thousand angels were singing a hymn before me until I reached the city of Christ'. See 'Apocalypse of Paul', trans. H. Duensing, in Wilhelm Schneemelcher, ed., *New Testament Apocrypha* (rev. ed., Louisville: Westminster/ John Knox, 1992) 2:726-727. 'Acherousia' is clearly based on Acheron, the river in southern Epirus in Greece where an ancient lake once lay and where the entrance to Hades was reputed to be; see N.G.L. Hammond and H. H. Scullard, *The Oxford Classical Dictionary* (2nd ed.; Oxford: Clarendon, 1970) 4. The *Apocalypse of Paul* does exist in a sahidic Coptic version; see E. A. Wallis Budge, ed. and trans., *Miscellaneous Coptic Texts in the Dialect of Upper Egypt* (2 volumes, rpt., New York: AMS, 1977) 1:534-574 (Coptic), 2:1043-1084 (English). It is interesting to note that 'Lake Acherousia' occurs four times in the coptic text (1:537 l. 28, 1:563 ll. 22 and 30, 1:564 l. 1) with four different spellings and that none of the spellings matches the one in *On the Cell*; the closest (Budge, 1:563, l. 22) is *archêerousa*. This raises the intriguing question of whether Paul used the greek or coptic version of the *Apocalypse of Paul*.

[111] 'House of God' and 'house of the Lord' are common expressions in the Psalms, referring to the Temple.

[112] Coptic *ebiên* = Gk *penêtôn* (LXX); see 9 and 10 and the note at 9.

[113] 'Patient endurance' translates *hupomonê*, a very important monastic virtue.

[114] 'Complete confidence' translates *parrêsia*, an important virtue in the New Testament, in John and Paul especially, which passed into monasticism.

[115] 'Victory' translates *oujro*, which also means 'strength', and is etymologically related to *tajro*, translated as 'certainty' at the end of 6.

[116] Coptic: *ô pebiên* (see 5). *Ebiên* can mean either 'poor' or 'wretched', literally or metaphorically, and can be the equivalent of Gk *penês*, *ptôchos*, or *talaipôros*; see Ps 69:6 (LXX = NRSV 70:5): 'I am poor and needy', which uses *ptôchos* and *penês*. See 13 for 'the poor monk'; 'poor' there is *hêke*. 'O wretch' or 'you wretch' in English does not fit the context here, although *ebiên* may suggest that the monk is wretched in the eyes of the world, and thus the term may be a self-designation. In 69, the monk is the one who 'withdraws' *(anachôri)*; he is 'poor and wretched'—and 'blessed', 'a son of God'; in 97, 'poor man' seems to be a synonym for 'monk'. See *The Teachings of Silvanus*, 86,8; 104,11.

[117] 'Place your heart': *ka pekhêt*, which Paul may intend as the opposite of letting one's heart grow slack (8) or losing heart (6), both *ka pekhêt ebol*.

[118] 'Bear' (*phori* = Gk *phorein*) seems unusual here, though Prov 3:16a (LXX) says 'he bears [*phorei*] law and mercy on his tongue'.

[119] Literally, 'without a command of God', taking *nte-* as a genitive. See Orlandi, 139, for the sentence's grammatical difficulties.

[120] Orlandi, 140, notes that the grammar of this sentence is problematic in Coptic. It seems in part to be a summary of Is 35:9-10: 'No lion shall be there. . . . And the ransomed of the Lord shall return. . . . everlasting joy shall be upon their heads'.

121 Sheridan, 'Development' (above, n.3), 100, points out that the allusion here is primarily to Jer 23:6 and 9 (vss. 7-8 are missing in the Septuagint) and that 'the citation is unintelligible . . . unless one knows that the name Josedek (and precisely in this phrase), has already been interpreted to mean "righteousness" . . . or "the just of God"'. This citation and same interpretation may be found in Eusebius and Didymus the Blind and 'obviously suggests contact with the Alexandrian exegetical tradition'. See further L.S.B. MacCoul, 'Paul of Tamma and the Monastic Priesthood', *Vigiliae Christianae* 53 (1999) 316–320.

122 Coptic/Gk: *martyria*, which can also mean 'martyrdom'.

123 'Withdrawal' (*olk* < *ôl*) may be the coptic equivalent of Gk *anachôrêsis*.

124 See 113. The end of the sentence, *noupê*, is corrupt.

125 This sentence is so fragmentary that it is untranslatable.

126 When completed, Rom 11:33 says: 'O the depth of the riches and wisdom and knowledge of God!'

127 See also 2 Es 10:7 where Zion is 'the mother of us all'.

128 For the image of the snare, see Sir 5:14.

129 Presumably Paul is speaking here, though it is also possible that it is Christ.

130 Coptic/Gk *agôn*; contesting was an important part of monastic spirituality.

131 The second part of the sentence literally reads 'will drive over them an evil wheel'. We have changed the text to make better sense and to accord with the passage from Proverbs. The context seems to suggest that the Devil is being referred to. 'Wicked' (*pethoou*), which is lacking in the Septuagint, is singular and thus probably refers to Satan.

132 As Orlandi notes, 141, the emendation *[pole]mos*, 'war, battle', could also be *[peiras]mos*, 'temptation', but see 41 below.

133 Although Balaam does not die in battle in Num 22-24, his death is recounted in Jewish legends.

134 Literally: be in withdrawal of purity in your [cell].

135 'Measure': *shi*. In the *Life of John the Little* 16, John has suspended or weighed *[afesh shiêt]* all of Scetis from his finger. Scetis, *shi hêt*, means 'to weigh the heart'. See Mikhail and Vivian, 'The Life of John the Little'. 28. See 47 above.

136 On the Cell II (hereafter 'II') begins here at 49. Where I is deficient and the lacuna can clearly be supplied from II, brackets have not been used.

137 II: a wise man.

138 Or: the evil ones.

139 II: the wise man.

140 II lacks this sentence, probably, as Orlandi notes, 145, because the scribe's eye jumped from 'his cell' (*tefri*), the last word in 52, to 'his cell', which is the first word in 54.

141 For 'within', II has 'at the right side'. Orlandi suggests, 145, that the scribe changed the reading of I to conform with Lk 1:11.

142 II: also entered.

143 Corrected from II, which has the better reading; I has 'Tobit in his house'. Tobit's wife appears in 5:18.

144 II: The angel appeared to Manoah and his wife; Manoah and his wife became the parents of Samson.

145 I is deficient here; the translation follows II.

146 I lacks 'therefore'.

147 I: *cbô*; II: *ji cbô*.

¹⁴⁸ II: towards God's servants sitting in their cells.
¹⁴⁹ II lacks this first clause.
¹⁵⁰ The 'Instructions of Saint Pachomius' 56, declare to the monk that 'demons come to you from the right, while to all other men they clearly come from the left'. See Veilleux, *Pachomian Koinonia*, 3:39. See also Zech 3:1 where Satan stands at Joshua's right hand in order 'to accuse him'. Sheridan, 'Development' (above, n. 3) 102–103, suggests connections here once again with Didymus and the alexandrian exegetical tradition.
¹⁵¹ The sense seems to be that the demons get the monk, through misguided mercifulness, to leave the cell to show compassion to someone in need. So we have here an expression of the tension in monasticism between the twin requirements of solitude and charity.
¹⁵² See Gn 19:19-20 (LXX): 'I will not be able to be saved on the mountain'.
¹⁵³ II: in a desert place and run and weep for me?
¹⁵⁴ II: Place your thought below everyone.
¹⁵⁵ Gk: *skopos*.
¹⁵⁶ II continues: Save yourself from the mountain! [see 63] Remain where God put you.
¹⁵⁷ The sentence is very elliptical (much more so in Coptic than in our rendering), but the sense seems to be: One person prefers one way of life while another prefers another way, but the cell is best for you.
¹⁵⁸ II: Anna, the daughter of Phanuel.
¹⁵⁹ II: day and night.
¹⁶⁰ II lacks 'true'.
¹⁶¹ 'It' is feminine in Coptic and can refer either to cell or tent.
¹⁶² II: It is the glory of a wise man sitting in his cell with the golden urn in it, with manna in it, with Aaron's urn in it and the tablets of the covenant. ('Urn' [*čelmai*] must be a mistake for 'rod' [*čerôb*]).
¹⁶³ *Anachôri = anachôrei*.
¹⁶⁴ II uses the negative conjunctive here instead of the negative first perfect.
¹⁶⁵ II: his servants the prophets.
¹⁶⁶ II: Abraham.
¹⁶⁷ II: his.
¹⁶⁸ The LXX has 'river Corrath' whereas the NRSV has 'Wadi Cherith'.
¹⁶⁹ II: Moreover, with regard to you [the same applies to you?], you who are poor, your honor as you sit in your cell is very great.
¹⁷⁰ The text of I is corrupt, and II does not help; see Orlandi, 144.
¹⁷¹ II: He also spoke.
¹⁷² II: He forgave him in his house.
¹⁷³ II: The one who is in his cell is wise.
¹⁷⁴ II: The one who is in his cell is wise, he is the city of blessings.
¹⁷⁵ II: for.
¹⁷⁶ That is, within the dwelling place or, possibly, 'in him', in the wise man.
¹⁷⁷ II: Therefore, be a wise man.
¹⁷⁸ II lacks 'in your cell'.
¹⁷⁹ II: your glory.
¹⁸⁰ II: the cares of your body.
¹⁸¹ II: mind (singular).
¹⁸² II: your soul and your mind staring.

[183] II lacks 'gazing at him'.
[184] II lacks 'also'.
[185] II: Test.
[186] II *mauaak* instead of I *ouak*, with the same meaning.
[187] II: while God walks at your side.
[188] The lacuna is supplied from II.
[189] The prophet is Agabus.
[190] II: for the blessing of your dwelling. 'Blessing', as Orlandi notes, 149, is probably a scribal addition.
[191] II: Philip also was snatched away by the spirit of the Lord.
[192] So II; I is deficient: And . . . upon the foundation . . . of the apostles and prophets.
[193] II: walk alone.
[194] 'In your cell' is Orlandi's suggestion (II: in your dwelling), although 'he will look for you alone' *(mauaak)* is also possible.
[195] There appear to be lacunae in the text of I, but II, with essentially the same text, suggests otherwise.
[196] I is grammatically incomplete; the words in bracket are supplied from II. II has "therefore" at the beginning of the sentence.
[197] I lacks 'for' at the beginning of the sentence.
[198] II: without number are its mysteries.
[199] II: prayer, petition, fasting.
[200] The text is corrupt: it reads 'the man of the widow', but ends with *she (te)* is very great. 'The man of the widow' *(prôme . . . [ntech]êra)* may well be a corruption of *techêra name*, 'the true widow' (see I Tim 5:5).
[201] II: You shall remain.
[202] II: and your honor and glory will be great in the midst of the saints.
[203] 'Weakness' translates čôb, related to 'cowardice' *(mntčabhêt)* in 93.
[204] II lacks the second part of the sentence.
[205] II has a slightly different word order with essentially the same meaning.
[206] II: Know that weakness has disturbed you. Orlandi believes, 149, that I 'probably has the genuine reading,' and that 'being troubled is weakness' offer's Paul's definition of arrogance.
[207] Or: in need of *(efshaat)*.
[208] The land is the promised land. The agreement between I and II ends here.
[209] See 124 (II) below.
[210] See 124 (II) below.
[211] "99" ϙⲑ is an isopsephism. 'Amen' is ⲁ (1) + ⲙ (40) + ⲉ̄ (50) + ⲛ (8) = 99 (ϙⲑ).
[212] *Prokoptei*. *Prokopê*, 'progress', is a seminal term and central theme in early monastic spirituality.
[213] Literally: loved.
[214] 'Contend' and 'fight' *(mishe)* both translate Gk *agônizomai* (2 Tim 4:7), a key term in early monastic spirituality. 'Fight' above translates *agôn*.
[215] 'Powerless' translates atčom, and 'strength' translates čom.
[216] See 18 above. 'The person whom you will save' may well be the monk himself.
[217] See D. R. MacDonald, ed., *The Acts of Andrew and Matthias in the City of the Cannibals* (Atlanta: Scholars Press, 1990).

[218] See I.99-100 above.
[219] Or: heart *(hêt)*.

6

Monks, Middle Egypt, and Metanoia:
The Life of Phib by Papohe the Steward

Introduction

IN RECENT YEARS, the fourth- and fifth-century pioneers of christian monasticism have become increasingly better known: Antony, Macarius, Amoun, Evagrius, the Tall Brothers in Lower Egypt; in Upper Egypt, Pachomius and Shenoute. Much less appreciated are the monks of Middle Egypt, especially the remarkable Abba Apollo.[1] Although the *Historia Monachorum* includes some monastics of Middle Egypt in its narratives, these monks apparently left no outstanding written works like the *Apophthegmata* or the writings by and about Pachomius and Shenoute.[2] In fact, the monks of Middle Egypt may be best known today, at least by scholars, because of the excavations of their ruined monasteries, especially those at Bawit and Saqqara.[3] The *Life of Phib*, then, provides an important addition to the fragmentary history of the monks of Middle Egypt.

The *Life of Phib*, translated below, is from a sahidic coptic manuscript in the Morgan Library dated to 994.[4] Papyrus fragments in the British Library suggest that the *Life* was part of a larger composition.[5] The copto-arabic *Synaxary* gives just a few details from the coptic text (noted in the translation below).[6] An arabic version translated from a different coptic text may be found in the National Library in Paris and in the library of the Monastery of Saint Antony by the Red Sea.[7]

The 'Life' of Phib is a misnomer; indeed, the piece could be re-titled 'The Death of Phib', since Phib (Abib in Arabic) is important not for his life but for what occurs after his passing. The *Life of Phib* is also more about Apollo than Phib and was probably originally part of a *Life of Apollo*.[8] At some point, an editor added portions to the latter in order to focus attention on Phib, his death, and the

205

unique feast day celebrated in his honor.⁹ Tito Orlandi has reasonably suggested that paragraphs 3–4 and 6–17 formed the original *Life of Apollo*.¹⁰ Paragraph 3 commences with what looks like the beginning of a work (perhaps an encomium) on Apollo: 'Listen to me, my beloved brothers in the Lord, and I will tell you of the great works and living teachings of our blessed father, Apa Apollo, the man of God'. It is here that the narrator, Papohe, first identifies himself, although the first person was already used in paragraph two. Paragraph one offers a generic encomiastic introduction, while paragraph two introduces Phib as the subject.

Papohe is a disciple of Apollo (whom he calls 'my father'), and Phib's appearances in paragraphs four and five seem to be afterthoughts or insertions: 'Our beloved brother Apa Phib the holy was there with him [Apollo]' (par. 4), and 'There too was Apa Phib, a person who loved quiet at all times' (par. 5). The subject of paragraph four, in fact, bounces back and forth between Apollo and Phib, which makes one suspect that the parts about Phib are later additions. The fact that Phib dies, rather unceremoniously, part way through the narrative (par. 10) increases the suspicion that the original text was about Apollo, and that Phib's feast day (not his death) marked an important event in the life of Apollo's monastic community.

Papohe, the narrator of the *Life* as we now have it, was the disciple of Apollo and steward of the community. Since the *Life of Paul of Tamma* also associates Papohe closely with Apollo and since he is present throughout the text, the attribution of the narrative to him appears to be reliable.¹¹ According to Papohe, Phib was from the nome of Shmoun and stayed with Apollo five years (par. 2) before dying at Titkooh (par. 10).¹² Phib's dates are unknown; all we can say is that he lived in the fourth century. After just two brief paragraphs on Phib, Papohe exclaims,

> Listen to me, my beloved brothers in the Lord, and I will tell you of the great works and living teachings of our blessed father, Apa Apollo, the man of God, who offered his body as a holy sacrifice to God, who became a dwelling place for the Father and a place of rest for the Son and a place of assembly for the Holy Spirit (par. 3).

The subsequent 'Life of Apollo' has two purposes: first, it wishes to claim Apollo as the 'father' of the monastery (or, rather, monastic community) of Titkooh; second, it wishes to give the divine origins of the *metanoia*, or day of repentance and absolution, that came to be associated with Phib's feast day.

The *Life of Phib* also seems to show the transition from scattered anchoritic and semi-anchoritic communities to a larger, more centralized community gathered around the figure of Apollo and the feast day of Phib (pars. 16–17).[13] This situation, in fact, provides some of the strongest evidence for monastic practices in Apollo's community that can be corroborated outside the *Life*. In paragraph sixteen the brothers build a church and they 'continued to gather in it every day before they ate their bread'. Such a custom was not observed in semi-anchoritic communities, where all the monks assembled together only on Saturdays and Sundays. It would be feasible only in a cenobitic community. The *Historia monachorum* reports that the members of Apollo's community (five hundred of them, it says) all shared a common life and ate at the same table (8.18). It goes on to say, in agreement with the *Life of Phib*, that those who lived with Apollo 'do not take any food themselves until they have assisted at the Eucharist and received Communion'.[14] This daily Communion, the *Historia* relates, was made at the express commandment of Apollo: 'He also said, "Monks, if possible, should communicate daily in the Mysteries of Christ"'.[15] This agreement between the *Historia monachorum* and the *Life of Phib* not only illustrates one aspect of the (now cenobitic) community but also testifies to the historical trustworthiness of at least some details of the *Life*.

Apollo was born around 305, and lived most of the fourth century.[16] His monastic activity centered around Hermopolis Magna in the Thebaid (Shmoun; al-Ashmunein in the Middle Sa'id) between modern-day al-Minya and Asyut (Lycopolis).[17] According to the *Historia monachorum*, 'when he was eighty years old he established on his own a great monastery of five hundred perfect men' at Bawit, about fifteen miles south of Hermopolis.[18] In addition to the *Historia monachorum*, Apollo is very well known from epigraphic and iconographic evidence found along the entire Nile valley of Middle and Upper Egypt, from Saqqara (Memphis) in the north, to Bawit, to Esna (Latopolis), south of Thebes (Luxor).[19] His companions are usually Phib and Anoub, who figure in the *Life*.[20] A number of inscriptions from the Monastery of Apa Jeremias at Saqqara list Apollo and Phib, Apollo and Anoup, or Apollo, Anoup and Phib. One striking inscription ranks the three saints of Bawit (Apollo, Anoup, and Phib) right after the Trinity, Michael, and Gabriel, and before Apa Jeremias, the founder of the monastery.[21]

Although the ancient sources show some confusion about chronology and location with regard to Apollo, there is no doubt that Apollo of Bawit is the same person as Apollo of Titkooh, who figures prominently in the *Life of Phib*.[22] Bawit and Titkooh may well be different designations for 'one and the same monastery'.[23] The monastery at Titkooh (Titkôis in Greek), if separate from Bawit, may have bordered the Libyan desert near Titkooh, which itself may have lain between Sanabu and Mîr in the south of the Hermopolite nome.[24] The monastery at Bawit also bordered the Libyan desert to the north, directly west of Dairout.[25] The site of the Monastery of Apa Apollo at Bawit 'is a kôm on the edge of the desert at the foot of cliffs about two kilometres west of the modern village of Bawit, and twenty-eight kilometres south-west of al-Ashmunein on the west bank of the Nile'. It was founded at the end of the fourth century, rebuilt in the sixth century, and destroyed in the second half of the twelfth century.[26] A number of monastic communities, it seems, wanted to have the honor of having Apollo as their founder; the *Life of Phib* attempts to claim Apollo exclusively for Titkooh, and adjusts the facts accordingly.[27] The papyri definitely speak of a later (sixth-seventh century) Monastery of Abba Apollo 'on the hill of the village Titkois in the Great Hermopolite nome'.[28] This monastery was well enough established that the monks had property or sold products in nearby villages and had become money lenders.[29]

In the *Life*, Apollo's coming to Titkooh is divinely sanctioned and ordained. Christ appears to the monk and tells him to go to Titkooh, which God has given him as an 'inheritance': God 'placed there the bones of your companion, Apa Phib, so you too would abide there' (11). Christ informs Apollo: 'Everyone who keeps your commandments I will give to you as children in my kingdom. Everyone who perseveres in your work and service will be your children in my Father's house' (12). When Apollo and Papohe arrive at Titkooh, the monks welcome them 'with great rejoicing' and tell them of a 'mystery' they have seen: a trumpet awakened them from sleep, informing them that 'the good shepherd who has pastured his sheep in the pasture of life has come'. Accompanying the celestial trumpet, a choir of angels 'spent the entire night singing and dancing' over the grave of Apa Phib, exalting Titkooh as 'the mountain of the Lord'. The monks proclaim Apollo as their shepherd and ask to be his children. Apollo humbly answers that if this is God's will, so be it (all 14).

Phib's future, according to the *Life*, is also divinely ordained. Phib relates to Apollo that when he was living at home as a child he was shepherding the family's flock one day when a 'holy old man of God' passed by. Because it was late, Phib invited him to eat and spend the night. In the morning, Phib 'prostrated himself' (Coptic *paht*, an important term; see below) before the old man and asked for his blessing. The old man says only one, startling, thing: 'There will be a day for the forgiveness of sin in your name' (7). We learn about this prophecy in a 'flashback' wherein Phib tells Apollo the story of his encounter with the old man. In the narrative Apollo has just looked Phib over and likened him to the lamp hidden under a bushel basket (Mt 5:15): 'There is no gift of the forgiveness of sin on your day each year'. At hearing this, Phib immediately prostrates himself (paht ⌀). Apollo tells him to get up, that it is the Holy Spirit who has prophesied, and that he is to preserve this 'mystery' until its meaning is made manifest (6). Phib then asks to speak, Apollo grants him permission, and he tells Apollo that, when he was a boy, an old man had indeed revealed that there would be a day of repentance in his name (7). This narrative structure serves several purposes: it underscores both Apollo's prophetic insight (6) and the divine plan for Phib (7). It also, perhaps unintentionally, highlights the monastic tension between humility (seen in Phib) and the requirements of fulfilling a divinely-appointed charism, especially as mandated by those in authority (seen when Apollo tells Phib not to hide his lamp).

Later (this is before Apollo's 'triumphant entry' and apparently before the revelation of the trumpet), Apollo and Phib visit Titkooh, where Phib dies and is buried (10). Apollo and Papohe journey on, and it is only later, when they have left Titkooh, that Christ tells Apollo of Phib's inheritance at Titkooh (11). Apollo tries to shuffle out of his role and hand it over to Papohe, who, he says, is a better steward than he.³⁰ Like someone in the Old Testament tapped on the shoulder by God for service, Apollo seems to be saying, 'Why me, Lord?' Dramatically, this evasion precedes an astonishing revelation: Christ tells Apollo that before the incarnation, as he was preparing to come to earth, his Father declared to him that the day of his birth and the day of his resurrection would be days of absolution *(eleutheria)* 'for the forgiveness of sin'. In addition, the Father declared, 'I will reveal a holy place on the earth and at the end of time I will establish there an act of repentance *[metanoia]* . . . a feast day . . . and a day for the forgiveness of sin for everyone who believes in your name'. Then Christ tells Apollo, 'the gift that my Father gave to me I now give to you also'. This holy place is Titkooh, where the name of Apa Phib will be proclaimed. 'Do not be afraid', Christ assures Apollo, 'I am with you everywhere; I will give you a great and famous name, and all the people will listen and will come to your site for this gift and will worship at your holy place' (all 12).

With such divine approbation, Apollo instructs his monks to build a small church 'over the body of our blessed brother Apa Phib'. So many people throng to Titkooh, however, that Christ instructs Apollo to build a large church; then the Saviour 'walked with him and instructed him concerning the entire boundary of the church. He told him its length and its breadth' (16). Finally, Christ appoints Archangel Michael as the monastery's protector, and ascends into heaven. When Phib's feast day, the twenty-fifth of Paope [4 November, Gregorian] draws nigh, Apollo instructs his monks to send for their brothers in 'all' the monastic communities so they can celebrate an Agape feast: 'When we gathered together on the twenty-fourth of Paope we passed the whole night . . . with rejoicing and gladness, celebrating a great *synaxis* with psalms in gladness and rejoicing in the Spirit' (17). In the morning a young monk, Zachary, dies. After they bury him they pray together and prostrate themelves *(paht* ⌧*)* for a long time; then Apollo declares, 'Truly, God has forgiven the sins of everyone who prostrates himself *(paht* ⌧*)* here today as on the day they were born' (18). Many believe. Some of the brothers, however, do not. Suddenly up jumps Zachary, his burial cloths falling away. He exclaims, 'One is God, Christ Jesus our Lord!' and repeats what Apollo declared.

When he had said these things, he went to sleep, and immediately the linens wrapped around him again. The multitude that saw him were amazed and their hearts were strengthened. They knew that the act of repentance [metanoia] was from God and that God had bestowed the gift of the forgiveness of sins on our brother Apa Phib (18).

The *Life of Phib* theologizes and liturgizes two common early monastic actions: prostration and *metanoia*.[31] A number of descriptions of prostration occur in the *Apophthegmata*. In some cases, prostration is simply a gesture of respect for one's abba, the acknowledgement, it seems, that the abba possesses something holy (a usage found also in the *Life of Phib*; see paragraphs six and seven). For example, Abba Isaac, a disciple of Poemen, prostrated himself before the old man when he saw him have an ecstatic experience.[32] But prostration can also be a *metanoia*, an act of repentance: an unnamed monk prostrated himself before Abba Zeno when the old man alerted him to his sinfulness.[33] In both coptic and greek sources, the offer of *metanoia* shows that the person is sorry or is begging forgiveness but it can also suggest humility rather than sinfulness. In the coptic *Life of Macarius of Scetis*, for example, Macarius goes to Antony: 'Abba Macarius implored him [nafti ho] and with tears begged him [nafti metanoia] to let him stay with him . . . and Abba Antony, not wishing to cause him grief, allowed him to stay with him. Then Abba Macarius asked his forgiveness [afti metanoia]'.[34] In a greek fragment dealing with John the Little, however, the use of *metanoia* brings with it the request for forgiveness (even if, as in this case, the 'sin' is not great).[35] One time at dinner John snapped at a talkative old man and rebuked him by leaving the table. John's disciple went to him and asked, 'Why, abba, did you offend the old man so he went away sad?' John replied,

> It is far better and mightier and more seemly and suitable not to provoke God. . . . For a monk talking while he eats is no different from a young porker or tom cat, for the young pig grunts while it eats and the tom cat purrs loudly while it eats. (But) I will go [to]

this old man and ask his forgiveness [*ballô metanoian*] and he will forgive me [*sunchôrei moi*]; he will benefit from this and I will sit undisturbed and you will go to your cell without being harmed.[36]

More penitently, in the *Virtues of Saint Macarius*, a monk accused of theft asks the forgiveness *(afti metanoia)* of his community.[37] In the *Life of Phib*, both 'prostration' (18) and *'metanoia'* (12, 18) have evolved into liturgical terms for an act of repentance and consequent absolution.

If we had only the *Life of Phib* for evidence, it would be impossible historically to corroborate the details of the hagiographical account that exalts Apollo, Phib, and their monastic community, and recounts, by liturgizing prostration and *metanoia*, the divine establishment at Titkooh of what seems to be the equivalent of Ash Wednesday and the Day of Atonement. As we have seen above with regard to the custom of daily Communion in Apollo's community, the *Life* contains details which appear to be historical; these combine, however, with a theological and hagiographical etiology that lies outside the customary expertise of the historian.[38] But, in fact, we have supporting evidence that such a *metanoia*, or day of repentance and absolution, *was* celebrated in late antiquity—not only at Titkooh, but, apparently, throughout Middle Egypt.

The evidence for this metanoia is substantial. A fragmentary liturgical calendar from Oxyrhynchus (probably from a monastic community there) that dates to 535–536 has this instruction for 25 Pahopi, Phib's feast day: 'to [the church of] Saint Serenus, day of repentance [*metan(oias)*]'.[39] In the five months of instructions that the calendar preserves, this is the only example of a *metanoia*. Far to the south, at Sūhāj (Sohag, near Akhmim), the monks at the White Monastery, founded by Saint Shenoute, celebrated 25 Paope as 'the feast of prostration/repentance [pah<t>s] (in the name) of (Apa) Apollo and Apa Phib'.[40] Another papyrus fragment merely mentions 'the feast of Apa Apollo and Apa Phib'.[41] An inscription at Bawit speaks of 'our beloved father Apa Apollo, friend of the angels, and our beloved father Anoup the confessor [*homologitis*], and our beloved father Apa Phib, he of the saving repentance *[pa tmetanoia noujai]*'.⁴² The manuscript of the *Life of Phib* comes from Edfu (Apollonopolis Magna in the southern Thebaid);⁴³ it and these papyrus fragments and inscriptions demonstrate that the rite of *metanoia/pahts* was known in the south at the White Monastery at Sūhāj (Sohag) and at Edfu, at Bawit in the Thebaid, and north at Oxyrhynchus.⁴⁴ It was celebrated on a feast day associated with Apollo and Phib, a day of repentance *(metanoia)* and prostration *(pahts)*. Further evidence, considered below, demonstrates that the rite was known and practised as far north as Saqqara, just south of Babylon (Cairo), at the monastery of Apa Jeremias.

What was this singular ritual?⁴⁵ Liturgical prostration was apparently practised by the monks of Kellia in Lower Egypt, although it is not clear whether the action was explicitly associated with penitence. At their weekend *synaxis*, or communal worship, the monks recited a number of psalms, each of which was followed by a prayer said standing up and then a moment of prostration; the celebration of the Eucharist concluded the service.⁴⁶ Despite the lack of direct liturgical connection here between prostration and penitence, the earliest monks clearly acknowledged their sinfulness: 'Abba Antony said to Abba Poemen, "This is a person's great work: always to accept the blame for his own sins before God"'; Abba Matoës declared that 'the closer a person comes to God, the more he sees himself a sinner'.⁴⁷ Declarations like these demonstrate that the monks believed the desert to be the dwelling place of sinners, not saints, because it was in the desert that one stood most nakedly before God.⁴⁸ As Matoës continued, 'It was when Isaiah the prophet saw God that he declared himself "a person of unclean lips"' [Is 6:5]. Sinlessness was not something to be achieved; sin and repentance would be one's constant companions throughout the monastic journey. This understanding was part of the monks' awareness that even at the end of the monastic life they had only just made a beginning: Antony, at the conclusion of the saying quoted above, advised others to expect temptation to their last breath. As Hermann Dörries has noted, the monks' theological and empirical bases for these convictions lay within themselves, in the devices and desires of their own hearts, which they knew all too well:

In the face of God's holiness the conception soon dies out that sin is a matter of individual, avoidable deeds which could be atoned away with a shorter or longer period of time [that is, as within the Church's developing penitential system].⁴⁹ Beneath the deeds there lies the ground from which they ascend—tempting thoughts. These above all, these λογισμοί [*logismoi;* see Chapter One, above], which are mentioned over and over again, are the targets of the monastics' struggle. To succumb to them ever again is guilt; always to remain exposed to them is ineluctable.⁵⁰

Given such an understanding, it is not surprising that the monks developed a liturgical rite of repentance. The surprise, in fact, is that we do not see more evidence of it in the sources. The *Life of Phib* assumes that monks are sinful and in need of atonement; the work offers no theological (or even pastoral) discussion concerning the rite. It is a given, like the sand on the ground and the everpresent sun in the desert sky. The *Life* clearly shows that the monasteries of Middle Egypt developed such a liturgical act of repentance and that it became associated with the feast day of Apa Phib; it also suggests that this liturgical practice originated in monasteries connected with Apa Apollo.⁵¹ Surviving sources show that it was described with both greek and coptic terms: *metanoia*, 'repentance', and *paht ⳿*, *pahts*, 'prostration'.⁵² It is likely that, in the bilingual world of late antique Egypt, the terms were symbiotically doing double duty, and that each influenced the meaning of the other. As the *Life of Phib* shows, prostration *(pahts)* was the outward and visible sign of an interior action: repentance *(metanoia)*.⁵³

The *Life of Phib* demonstrates that for at least some monks of late antique Egypt, the days of Christ's birth and resurrection were considered the primary days of 'absolution for salvation and the forgiveness of sin' and that the *metanoia* granted on Phib's feast day was seen as a 'gift' given by Christ from the plenitude of forgiveness that came with his incarnation and resurrection (12). R.-G. Coquin thus terms the rite a *mikra metanoia* (μικρὰ μετάνοια) or 'small act of repentance'. In later coptic tradition, the feast day persisted, but the specific act of prostration seems to have been lost. The entry for 25 Babeh in the arabic synaxary says that 'if someone prays a prayer today in the name of Saint Anba Phib, Christ the Saviour will forgive his sin, *as promised*' (emphasis added).[54] Eventually the feast was no longer celebrated.[55]

Archeological evidence may provide us a snapshot, as it were, of what the *Life of Phib* describes. A wall painting found at the ancient monastery of Apa Jeremias at Saqqara, south of Babylon (Cairo), seems to depict this rite of prostration and repentance.[56] The painting shows the standing figures of Onnophrius, Macarius, Apollo,[57] and another figure whose name, unfortunately, has been lost, but who is, in all likelihood, Apa Phib.[58] In front of the last figure (Phib?) is a smaller figure who is bent over, touching the feet of Apa Apollo and the last figure in an act of prostration. Scholars have made a number of suggestions regarding this prostrating figure and the meaning of the painting.[59] R.-G. Coquin, however, convincingly argues that the prostrating figure is a monk and that, since he is touching the feet of *both* Apollo *and* the last figure (Phib), he is in fact performing the act of *metanoia* associated with the two saints, the feast day described in the *Life of Phib*:

> It seems to us therefore that this monk was represented in this position of repentance and touching the feet of the two saints at the same time . . . as the symbol of the whole community of anchorites assembled by Apollo, performing the rite established by the founder for the feast day of Apa Phib and for the monastery church where the body of his friend reposed.[60]

If Coquin is correct—and I believe he is—then this painting preserves a vivid depiction of the rite of repentance described in the *Life of Phib*. Two significant changes have, however, taken place: in the *Life of Phib*, the entire community prostrates itself on Phib's feast day and thus gains his intercession for the forgiveness of their sins. In the painting, the members of the community (as represented by the penitent monk) prostrate themselves at the feet of Apollo and Phib, although there is no mention in the *Life* of prostration before Apollo. It seems likely, though, that the prostration by the community depicted in the *Life* took place at Phib's tomb (see 12) or, to be more precise, on top of it: Apollo, at Christ's command, ordered a church to be built on top of Phib's grave

(16). The painting, therefore, represents with human figures the veneration that took place at Phib's tomb, but intercession in both ritual and painting would still come from the saint—or saints. This is the second change. Originally, it seems, Phib was the sole intercessor; later, probably after his death, the great Apollo, not surprisingly, became co-intercessor with his disciple Phib.

This evidence appears to be decisive. Coquin and other scholars have, however, overlooked one more crucial and fascinating piece of evidence from the same monastery of Apa Jeremias at Saqqara, one that complicates the picture (both literally and figuratively) of a rite of prostration. An inscription there speaks of the rite, but makes *Jeremias*, not Apollo or Phib, the 'remover of sins':

> O Father, O Son, O Holy Spirit, Apa Jeremias, Apa Enoch, Ama Sibylla,[61] our father Peter, our father Paul, our father John: this is the place where our lord and father Apa Jeremias prostrated himself *[pahtf]* until he removed the sins of the people of the whole world. May [his] holy blessing descend upon us. Amen, Amen, so be it, Amen.[62]

This inscription would seem to show that individual monasteries adapted a rite of prostration for the forgiveness of sin to their local saints, whether Apollo, Phib, or, as in this case, Jeremias.

What is fascinating at Saqqara is that a painting at the monastery shows Apollo (and Phib?) as the intermediaries, while an inscription there demonstrates that Jeremias led his community in the rite and thereby gained intercession for his people. Perhaps the painting reveals that the monks were aware of the origins of a ritual of repentance with Apollo and Phib as intermediaries while the inscription shows that Jeremias took their part as intercessor at Saqqara. Scattered bits of evidence demonstrate the authority that these monastic leaders had. According to the *Life of Paul of Tamma*, Apollo taught his children while sitting on a thronos, which normally designated a bishop's chair.[63] The inscriptions at Saqqara plentifully show that Jeremias occupied an equally exalted position. It seems reasonable to suppose that Jeremias' community continued to honor the feast day of Phib while Jeremias led them in the rite. Perhaps the painting is older than the inscription and shows the early ritual custom at Jeremias' monastery (with Apollo and Phib as intercessors), while the inscription is later and shows how the rite developed as the power of intercession was transferred from Phib and Apollo to Jeremias. Or, quite probably, the inscription was written after Jeremias' death (since it uses the past tense) and located intercessory power in the saint *post mortem*. At this remove we do not have enough evidence to delineate either the chronology of the ritual or its particulars and the belief that lay behind it. Nevertheless, the painting and inscription at Saqqara do clearly demonstrate that an act of repentance, associated with Phib and Apollo, was known at Jeremias' monastery and that an act of prostration for the removal of 'the sins of the people of the whole world' was practised there.[64]

Throughout Middle Egypt, then, from the White Monastery in the south to the monastery of Saint Jeremias in the north, painting, papyrus, and inscription powerfully illustrate how the 'cult of the saints' in monastic Egypt in late antiquity was particularized in a specific religious ritual, the rite of prostration for the forgiveness of sins. They demonstrate how sanctity and holiness—and even salvation—could reside in God's elect. But we need to remember that these sources point further, and deeper: the *Life of Phib* strongly emphasizes that Phib's feast day is a 'gift' or simulacrum of the great acts of forgiveness that have come with Christ's incarnation and resurrection.[65] Intercession, the *Life* makes clear, comes *from* Christ, *through* his saints. Many coptic monks of late antiquity had this hope and belief, and they enacted it in ritual throughout Middle and Upper Egypt on the feast day of Apa Phib.

The Life of Phib [66]

The Life of Our Holy Father Apa Phib the Holy Anchorite, which Papohe, the Disciple of the Perfect and Blessed Apa Apollo, Narrated. Blessed Apa Phib Went to His Rest on the Twenty-Fifth of Paope[67] in the Peace of God.

May His Blessing Be Upon Us.
Amen.

* Ps 112:6; 111:7 (LXX)

* cf Prov 10:7, Ps 92:12 (91:13)

1. Truly what the holy psalmist David says is true when he cries out, 'The righteous will be remembered forever'.* And again, 'The righteous person will be exalted like a spreading palm tree, like a cedar in Lebanon'.* What the psalmist said was fulfilled concerning this saint.

2. There was a brother whose name was Apa Phib,[68] who was from Sinemoun in the Shmoun nome.[69] He went to my holy father Apa Apollo and became a monk at his side. They remained together about five years. After <Apa> Petra <went to his rest,>[70] the two of them committed themselves to each other on the mountain of Titkooh.[71] It was there that he went to his rest. The two of them were together, performing great ascetic practices;[72] multitudes of men were counted with them and they did not send them away in spite of their numbers.

The Life of Apa Phib

3. Listen to me, my beloved brothers in the Lord, and I will tell you of the great works and living teachings of our blessed father, Apa Apollo, the man of God, who offered his body as a holy sacrifice to God,* who became a dwelling place for the Father and a place of rest for the Son and a place of assembly for the Holy Spirit. I, Papohe, the most unworthy steward, was living as a small child in the house of my parents. God sent his angel who took me from my father's house and led me north on the paths of righteousness. He brought me to the good shepherd, the saver of souls.* I came into port into the harbor of salvation where there are no thieves;[73] I am talking about our beloved father, blessed Apa Apollo, the true Israelite, in whom there was no deceit.*

* cf Eph 5:2

* cf Jn 10:11

* cf Mt 6:19, Jn 1:47

4. On this mountain, before the Lord revealed his glory to him, I knocked at his door and he immediately came out to see me; his face was relaxed and smiling, for my father was in every way a gentle person before God and his fellow human beings, especially towards all good persons. He gladly tested me to see if I measured up and made me a monk with him.[74] I was worthy to remain beneath the shadow of his holy prayers and his fatherhood.* Our beloved brother Apa Phib the holy was there with him. The two of them lived the monastic life[75] together with great ascetic practices and great acts of devotion,[76] and there were numerous men with them. Apa Phib was a person who loved quiet, wishing to remain in the desert at all times living the monastic way of life.[77] My father was a person of peace who loved the entire image of God as a single person.[78] The brothers gathered around him like bees collecting honey in their mouths, listening to his words of life and his holy commandments, becoming children of the great God who was present through our father.

* cf Pss 17:8, 36:6, Is 49:2, 51:16, among others

5. I remained a year with them on this mountain. Afterwards, we traveled from there and continued walking where it was completely mountainous, like wild beasts. The brothers had heard about my father every place we stayed and would come to him and receive spiritual edification from him. He would tell them the contents of their souls, comforting all of them with his sweet words, while they gave glory to God.[79] I remained a year by my father's side. There too was Apa Phib, a person who loved quiet at all times. My father was an ascetic. I myself would walk ministering to their worldly needs, concerned with the stewardship for the saints. Therefore he called me Papohe the steward.

6. One day while the three of us were together, giving glory to God, my father turned to Apa Phib, his face glad. He said to him, 'I see that you love quiet, my son, and that you hate human vainglory. It is written in the Gospel, "It is impossible for a city to be hidden when it is set upon a mountain, nor is a lamp lit and placed under a bushel basket; rather, it is placed on a lampstand and gives light to everyone in the house".* You, then, are the hidden lamp, my son, which will be placed on the lampstand where it will give light to everyone in the house and will spread its incense throughout the world. It will be a gift for the forgiveness of sin each year on your feast day'.

Immediately Apa Phib prostrated himself and entreated my father.[80] Then my father answered and said, 'Get up, my son, it was not I who spoke but the Holy Spirit, who prophesies concerning things that will happen before they have happened. Now, therefore, keep this mystery until it is made manifest. For it is written in the Deuteronomy of Moses, 'The things that are hidden belong to the Lord your God but those that are manifest belong to you and your children'".*

* Mt 5:15

* Dt 29:29

7. Apa Phib answered and said, 'Command me and I will speak to you. Do not be angry with me. Truly I shall not speak out of a desire for greatness nor with vain love of glory; no, I marvel at the Holy Spirit who is in those who are honorable before God and who agree with each other in what they say'.

Blessed Apa Apollo said, 'Speak, my son'.

Apa Phib answered, saying, 'One day when I was little, living in the home of my parents, I was shepherding their sheep in the field when a holy old man of God passed by me in the field. Since evening had already come, I invited him into the sheepfold.[81] I repeatedly begged him to eat some bread. He obeyed me and ate the bread. I did this small kindness for him.[82] He slept beside me until morning. When morning had come, he was about to leave and I prostrated myself[83] before him so he would bless me and he did so, and he also said to me the very words that you spoke to me: "There will be a day for the forgiveness of sin in your name". Now, then, I marvel at this for I do not know what will happen. One day I was worthy to have the Lord call me to your fatherhood. Now as it pleases the Lord, may his good will be done'.

8. Apa Apollo, the athlete of Christ who gives victory to his right hand and his left, answered, 'Listen to me and I will speak this word to you, for it was the Lord who spoke to me. I will not arrogantly speak but I will explain to all of you what will happen to all of us together. My Saviour said to me these words that Paul used while writing to the Corinthians concerning brother Apollo: "I strongly urged him to come to you and perhaps now is not the time for him to come to you. But he will come if he finds the opportunity"'.[84]* (The Holy Spirit, therefore, continued to urge my father to come now. My father answered

* cf I Cor 16:12

that he was coming if he found the opportunity.)[85] 'Now, then, my children, we are ready to bear everything that the Lord will command us. His <will> be done.[86] Glory be to him for ever and ever. Amen'.

9. After all these things, we went to a mountain of the desert opposite a village called Tahrouj.[87] We found some holes in the rock there and made some small dwellings and stayed in them and lived the monastic life with numerous ascetic practices.[88] All the brothers, when they heard that my father was there, went to him. They heard the words of life from his mouth. There was, however, no water in that desert place. My father said to me, 'Papohe, my son, dig in the earth and we will see that God will give us water for the sake of the brothers <who are coming>[89] to us'. When we dug down four cubits, a spring of water rushed up, good and very sweet, with water for us to drink.[90] We spent two years drinking from it with those who came to us. Then my father said to me, 'Let us make a well and place it at the disposal of the brothers who come to us. Surely the Lord has shown us that "every place you dwell, I will have it remain for ever"'.*

* cf I K 8:13

10. When we had finished digging the well, we left to go to the place in Upper Egypt called [the Monastery of] Apa Pamin.[91] While we were walking, we came to the mountain of Titkooh, this mountain where God granted his blessing for eternal life.[92] We visited some God-loving brothers on that mountain. They showed us great kindness.[93] Our beloved brother Apa Phib went to his rest there on the twenty-fifth of Paope at the third hour of the day.[94] We were grief-stricken, very sad and discouraged at our loss. We buried him there.

11. Afterwards, we left that place and went to the monastery of Apa Pamin. We stayed there a few days, and the brothers gathered around us; there was a multitude of them. Afterwards, the Saviour appeared to our father; he spoke with him, saying, 'Peace be with you, my friend and honored and beloved companion[95] of my Father. Behold! The time has come for you to reveal my glory and for my name to be glorified on earth through you. Arise, therefore, and go to the mountain of Titkooh and stay there, for my Father has given it to you as an inheritance. For this reason I placed there the bones of your companion, Apa Phib, so you too would abide there'.

He answered and said to the Saviour, 'Look, here is a man who is able to care for stewardship of this sort. For I am a man who renounces all such things. I beg you, my Lord, if I have found favor in your sight, do not have me do this'.

12. The Saviour answered and said to him, 'Apollo, my chosen one, this is what the Father has determined for you from the beginning so he can establish your name there. When I came down to this world from my Father, he spoke to me with compassion, "My Son, do not be sad that you are going down to the world, which is filled with suffering and groaning. Concerning your suffering,[96] my Son, I will appoint the day that you are born from the holy virgin Mary as a day of absolution for the forgiveness of sin for the world.[97] For everyone who has faith in your cross and the resurrection of your flesh I will tear up the bond of indebtedness that they have incurred because of their sins* and I will give them to you, my beloved Son. And on the day of your glorious resurrection I will allow there to be a day of absolution for salvation and the forgiveness of sin for the whole world.[98] And I will reveal

* cf Col 2:14

a holy place on the earth at the end of time and I will establish there an act of repentance[99] for salvation and a feast day for my saints throughout the world and the forgiveness of sin for everyone who believes in your name".

'The gift that my Father gave to me I now give to you also; moreover, I will establish it there and they will proclaim the name of your holy companion,[100] Apa Phib. Do not be afraid, I am with you everywhere; I will give you a great and famous name, and all the people will hear of you and will come to your site for this gift and will worship at your holy place. All the people will come and say, "Come, let us go up to the mountain of the Lord and to the house of the God of Jacob, and he will tell us his way and we will walk in it"', just as Isaiah the prophet spoke.* It is also written, "There will be an altar of the Lord in the land of Egypt and a pillar to the Lord at its borders".* The place that I have given you is the altar and the pillar is the body of my servant \<Phib\>.[101] See now, I have shown you everything that will happen to you in all the designs of my Father. Be strong concerning what I have told you and do not let your heart doubt. I will place great blessings upon your sanctuary in every way and I will have your children called the lamp-bearers of Christ. Everyone who keeps your commandments I will give to you as children in my kingdom. Everyone who perseveres in your work and service will be your children in my Father's house'.

13. Immediately my father called me and told me all the words the Saviour had told him. As I listened to them I was astounded and said to him, 'My father, if this is what pleases the Lord, let us do it. Let us follow the Lord and keep his commandments. Those who do everything that the Lord commands are good; they are very elect and honored and they will enter the house of the

* Is 2:3

* Is 19:19

Lord together. We will follow the path that he has appointed for us, just as he wishes'.

14. After all these things we rose and left in order to go to the mountain of Titkooh, the mountain where God commanded[102] us to go, which he had prepared for my father Apollô, and we went up to the mountain across from a village called Taparooue.[103] We visited some God-serving brothers who showed us great kindness.[104] We slept there until morning. When morning had come, we went north to Titkooh. When the brothers there heard that we had come, they came out to greet us with great rejoicing and welcomed us to their community. We told them the mystery that we had seen and they were amazed and said to us, 'We too beheld a mystery: when we were sleeping at night we heard the sound of a trumpet sounding forth, crying out with a loud voice three times like this: "Look! The good shepherd who has pastured his sheep in the pasture of life has come!" Afterwards, a choir of angels spent the entire night singing and dancing over the body of blessed Apa Phib, singing a hymn with the angels answering them [sic]: 'This mountain is going to rejoice and be glorified. This is the mountain of the Lord, the exalted mountain, the established mountain, the fertile mountain. This is the mountain where God has wished to dwell forever. This is the house of God, the dwelling place of the righteous". When we heard these things, we were very afraid and spent the night gathered together until morning, praising God the Father of our Lord Jesus Christ and marvelling at what we had heard. Now God our Saviour has sent you to us! You are the shepherd who pastures all of us, young and old, in goodness. Behold! Our bodies and our souls are in your hands. Be for us a father and we will be your children'.

15. My father answered, saying, 'If what you wish is of God, we will do as you say'. And we gathered together doing the work of twenty men in front of my father. My father was occupied with the word of God and the teaching and canons of our holy fathers the apostles while I was responsible for the needs of the brothers. Great powers and wonders occurred by means of my father, for his name became famous throughout the surrounding area and people brought to him all who were sick and he cured all of them. Our numbers increased little by little and we grew in God. God did great good things through my father.

16. We continued our work and built a small church over the body of our blessed brother Apa Phib. The brothers continued to gather in it every day before they ate their bread.[105] Afterwards the Saviour appeared to my father; he spoke with him, saying, 'Peace be with you, my honored friend and companion. I am with you. Behold! I will bring throngs of people to you and they will become very numerous. Arise and build a great church as I instruct you so the people will have it as a dwelling place'. The Saviour walked with my father and instructed him concerning the entire boundary of the church. He told him its length and its breadth. The Saviour said to him, 'Behold! I have appointed for you Michael the Archangel, for it is he who will minister to your site. Michael's words will be your words. Bring in Papohe to serve as deacon'. When the Saviour had said these things, he ascended into heaven.

17. Afterwards, my father called me and told me all these words. We built the church according to the measurements he instructed. When we had increased and grown in numbers, my father said to me, 'Behold! The day of our blessed brother Apa Phib is nigh. Let us send for the brothers in

all the monastic dwellings[106] and let us celebrate an Agape with them with joy and rejoicing because it is the Saviour who said these things concerning him: "'I will reveal my glory each year on his feast day when my name is glorified in all the earth'".

I did as my father told me. I sent brothers to all the monastic dwellings. I gathered all the brothers together on the holy day that the Lord appointed for our brother Apa Phib. When we gathered together on the twenty-fourth of Paope we passed the whole night of the twenty-fifth of Paope with rejoicing and gladness, celebrating a great synaxis with psalms in gladness and rejoicing in the Spirit.

18. When morning came, a young brother named Zachary went to his rest. He was a sweet child in everyone's eyes and my father loved him very much on account of the good things he did for the brothers. We took him into the church. The brothers continued to attend to him until they buried him, for it was the sixth hour.[107] When they had buried him, we rose right away and prayed together, and my father had us prostrate ourselves[108] a long time on our faces. Afterwards, my father rose and stood and spoke to the brothers, 'Truly, God has forgiven the sins of everyone who prostrates himself[109] here today as on the day they were born'.[110]

Some of the brothers did not believe, while others believed him. Up jumped young brother Zachary who had died! He sat up and the burial linens fell off him. He got up and stood and walked this way and that. Truly, he cried out, 'One is God, Christ Jesus our Lord!' Everyone standing there was amazed and he said, 'Believe me, God-loving people, God has forgiven the sins of everyone standing here today as on the day they were born. And whoever prostrates himself[111] here today will have his sins forgiven in the name of our brother Apa Phib. This is a great mystery, my brothers and God-loving fathers'.

When he had said these things, he went to sleep, and immediately the linens wrapped around him again. The multitude that saw him were amazed and their hearts were strengthened.[112] They knew that the act of repentance[113] was from God and that God had bestowed the gift of the forgiveness of sins on our brother Apa Phib. To the glory of the Holy Trinity, the Father and the Son and the Holy Spirit, for ever and ever.

NOTES

[1] Two other representatives of monasticism in Middle Egypt are Paul of Tamma and John of Shmoun. For the former, see Chapter Five. For the latter, see Gérard Garitte, 'Panégyrique de saint Antoine par Jean, évêque d'Hermopolis', *Orientalia Christiana Periodica* 9:3 (1943) 100–134, 330–365, and Tim Vivian, trans., 'John of Shmūn: An Encomium on Saint Antony of Egypt', in Tim Vivian and Apostolos N. Athanassakis, trans., *The Life of Antony* (Kalamazoo: Cistercian Publications, 2003).

[2] The *Apophthegmata*, though they may have been edited in Palestine, have their origin in Scetis in Lower Egypt; the Apollo who has three sayings in the Alphabetical Collection is not the same person as the Apollo of Middle Egypt.

[3] For introductions to these monasteries, see 'Bawit', *The Coptic Encyclopedia*, ed. Aziz S. Atiya (New York: Macmillan, 1991) 2.362-372, and 'Dayr Apa Jeremiah (Saqqara)', *The Coptic Encyclopedia* 3.772-779, and the bibliographies in each article.

[4] M 633, 47–68; see H. Hyvernat, *Bibliothecae Pierpont Morgan codice coptici photographice expressi* (Rome, 1922) volume 56; A. van Lantschoot, *Recueil des colophons des manuscrits chrétiens d'Egypte* (Louvain: Bibliothèque du Muséon, 1929; rpt. Milan, 1973) fasc. 1, no. 114, pp. 201–202, and fasc. 2, pp. 80–81. For the edited text, see Tito Orlandi, *Vite dei Monachi Phif e Longino*, Testi e documenti per lo Studio dell'antichità 51; Milan (Cisalpino-Goliardica, 1975), with an italian translation by Antonella Campagnano. For a description of the codex, see Orlandi, 13–14 and, on the date, 14.

[5] See Bentley Layton, *Catalogue of Coptic Literary Manuscripts in the British Library Acquired Since the Year 1906* (London, 1987) 157–158.

[6] R. Basset, ed., *Le Synaxaire arabe-jacobite*, Patrologia Orientalis 1 (1904) 366–369 under 25 Babah (or Babeh) [November 4 (Gregorian)]. The synaxary says only that Phib died, that there was a rite of forgiveness on his feast day, and summarizes the story of the dead monk Zachary (see paragraph 18 below).

[7] René-Georges Coquin, 'Phib, Saint', *The Coptic Encyclopedia* 6.1953-54. See G. Troupeau, *Catalogue des manuscrits arabes*, vol. 1, *Manuscrits chrétiens* (Paris,

1972–1974) 38–63. BN arabe 4787, fols. 126v–158r, and BN arabe 4888, fols. 139r–175r.

⁸ The best previous discussion of Phib and Apollo is by René-Georges Coquin, 'Apollon de Titkooh ou/et Apollon de Bawit?', *Orientalia* 46 (1977) 435–446. The arabic synaxary shows that Apollo (Aboulou) and Phib (Abib) shared the same feast day, that of Apollo being celebrated on this day 'following the custom of Upper Egypt'. The synaxary also says very little about Phib; it gives most of its attention to Apollo, recounting his miraculous birth and his relations with Macarius the Great. See Basset, ed., 366–369.

⁹ For Phib's and Apollo's relation to Paul of Tammah, see Chapter Five.

¹⁰ Orlandi, 16. See Coquin, 'Apollon de Titkooh', 435; Layton, 157–158.

¹¹ See Amélineau, ed., 'Vie de Paul de Tamoueh', 761.

¹² According to the *Life of Paul of Tamma*, Phib was from Perčoush in the nome of Touhô, and lived as a hermit for eighteen years on the mountain of Peshčepohe where he expected to die. See Amélineau, ed., 763.

¹³ See Orlandi, *Phif*, 16. S. J. Clackson, *Coptic and Greek Texts relating to the Hermopolite Monastery of Apa Apollo* (Oxford: Griffith Institute-Ashmolean Museum, 2000), 8, suggests that 'the monastery of Apa Apollo described in the *[Historia Monachorum]* and the *Life of Paul of Tammah* was an Antonian-type laura', but adds that 'Titles like "archimandrite", which is recorded in the texts as well as in inscriptions . . ., may, however, be associated particularly with pachomian and post-pachomian monasteries like the White Monastery [of Saint Shenoute the Great]'. She then adds that 'Archaeological evidence, especially the vestiges of a surrounding wall, suggests that the monastery was essentially a *coenobium*'. Outer walls, however, do not preclude semi-anchoritic monks living outside the walls. Chackson's different types of monasticism may in fact suggest different stages at the monastery.

¹⁴ *Historia Monachorum* 8.50; trans. Norman Russell, *The Lives of the Desert Fathers: The Historia Monachorum in Aegypto*, CS 34 (Kalamazoo: Cistercian Publications, 1981) 77.

¹⁵ *Historia Monachorum* 8.56; Russell, CS 34:78.

¹⁶ The travellers of the *Historia Monachorum*, who made their trip around 394, seem to have visited Apollo (chap. 8) when he was in his late 80s; see 8.2.

¹⁷ On this area, see Stefan Timm, *Das christlich-koptische Ägypten in arabischer Zeit*, 6 volumes (Wiesbaden: L. Reichert 1984–1992) 1:198-220. A list, possibly from the ninth century, of twenty-four churches in the Shmoun area includes (no. 5) one named after 'Apa Apollo'; see Timm, 1:206.

¹⁸ *Historia Monachorum* 8.2; Russell, CS 34:70. For a thorough discussion, see Coquin, 'Apollon de Titkooh', 435–438.

¹⁹ See Coquin, 'Apollon de Titkooh', 436, for references.

²⁰ A fresco inside the ancient church at the Monastery of Saint Paul (Red Sea) shows Apollo and Apip (Phib); see Nabil Selim Atalla, *Coptic Art*, volume 1: *Wall-Paintings* (Cairo: Lehnert & Landrock, n.d.) 101. On Apollo, Phib, and Anoup, see now S. J. Clackson, *Coptic and Greek Texts relating to the Hermopolite Monastery of Apa Apollo* (Oxford: Griffith Institute - Ashmolean Museum, 2000) 6.

²¹ See Sir Herbert Thompson, 'The Coptic Inscriptions', in J. E. Quibell, *Excavations at Saqqara (1908–1909, 1909–1910)*, volume 4: *The Monastery of Apa Jeremias* (Cairo: IFAO, 1912) 47–125: Apollo and Phib (#185, 203, 219, 226, 251), Apollo and Anoup (#204, 329), and Apollo, Anoup and Phib (#222, 240). An

inscription at Bawit (Room XVIII, East Wall, #XI) lists 'God, the Son, the Holy Spirit, Michael, Gabriel, Raphael, *oumarihama* [Miriam? Mary?], Apa Apollo, Apa Phib, Apa Anoup, Apa Jacob the father of the monastery *[topos]*, Apa Isaac the *hêgoumenos*. . . . .; see Jean Clédat, *Le Monastère et la Nécropole de Baouît*, Mémoires publiés par les membres de L'Institut Français d'Archéologie Orientale du Caire 12 [one volume in two parts] (Cairo: IFAO, 1904) 96. See among many others #XIV, p. 85, and II, p. 107.

[22] See Orlandi, *Phif*, 15, who cites W. E. Crum and Martin Krause as already having made this identification, and his conclusions on 18.

[23] Clackson (above, n. 20), 3, and 14. Clackson works from the presumption that the two monasteries and sites are the same.

[24] On Titkooh, see Marie Drew-Bear, *Le nome Hermopolite: Toponymes et sites*, American Studies in Papyrology 21 (Missoula, Montana: Scholars Press, 1979) 300–330; for Bawit on a map, see Carte 2 (partie Sud).

[25] J. Gascou, 'Documents grecs relatifs au monastère d'Abba Apollôs de Titkôis', *Anagennesis* 1.2 (1981) 219–230, at 219–220.

[26] Clackson, 6; see the map on xvi. Clackson's book focusing on coptic and greek texts from the hermopolite monastery of Apa Apollo offers a fascinating look at such day-to-day activities as tithing, taxation, and landholding from the sixth to the eighth centuries.

[27] See Coquin, 'Apollon de Titkooh', 438. Since Apollo and Phib travel to various monastic communities, and since a number of these seem to claim Apollo as their founder, one wonders if they form some sort of 'multicommunity system' like the pachomian *koinonia* with Apollo as their charismatic leader. See James E. Goehring, 'Monastic Diversity and Ideological Boundaries in Fourth-Century Egypt', *JECS* 5 (1997) 61–83; repr. in Goehring, *Ascetics, Society, and the Desert: Studies in Early Egyptian Monasticism* (Valley Forge: Trinity, 1999) 196–218.

[28] Μοναστηρίου Ἄπα Ἀπολλῶτος ὄρ[ου]ς κώμης Τιτκώεως τοῦ μεγάλου Ἑρμοπολίτου νομοῦ; Basil G. Mandilaras, *The Byzantine Papyri of the Greek Papyrological Society* (Athens: The Greek Papyrological Society, 1993) 39. See also 44–45 for a discussion of this passage. See also 53, 109, and 111 for other references to the monastery.

[29] See the references cited above and Gascou, 'Documents grecs', who publishes two papyrus fragments; the second, dated to 540, concerns the price of wine agreed to by a monk of the monastery of Titkois. See especially now Clackson.

[30] Earlier (par. 5), Apollo calls him 'Papohe the steward'. The inscription at Bawit calls Papophe 'Apa Papohe the Steward'.

[31] For the institutionalizing of repentance in the pachomian koinonia, see Bernadette McNary-Zak, 'Pachomian Remission', *Coptic Church Review* 23:4 (Winter 2002) 107–110.

[32] Alphabetical Apophthegmata Poemen 144 (PG 65:358).

[33] Apophthegmata Nau 509, quoted in Columba Stewart, 'Radical Honesty about the Self: the Practice of the Desert Fathers', *Sobornost* 12 (1990) 25–39, 31–32.

[34] E. Amélineau, 'Vie de Macaire de Scété', *Histoire des moines de la Basse-Égypte* (Paris: Leroux, 1894) 85. It is interesting that Amélineau freely and reasonably translates the first example of *metanoia* in the passage cited as an act of prostration: 'le suppliait à genoux'.

³⁵ Analogously, see the *Virtues of Saint Macarius* (Amélineau, 157), where Evagrius asks the forgiveness *(-ti metanoia)* of Macarius.

³⁶ René Draguet,'A la source de deux apophtegmes grecs (PG 65, Jean Colobos 24 et 32)', *Byzantion* 32 (1962) 53–61; the quotation may be found on p. 56. *Ballein metanoian* is common in the Systematic Apophthegmata; see, for example, 5.36, 5.37, and 6.26.

³⁷ Amélineau, *Virtues*, 164. When Macarius comes to the monastery, the brother 'asked the old man's forgiveness just as Abba Macarius asked forgiveness of the brother, and they accepted forgiveness from each other' (Amélineau, 165).

³⁸ The most striking contrast is that historically Phib does not seem to have been very important or to have been a person of outstanding qualities (although he did love quiet, which would have been highly regarded among monks) while hagiographically he is chosen by God as a youth to have a day of forgiveness celebrated in his name (par. 7).

³⁹ Coquin, 'Apollon de Titkooh', 442.

⁴⁰ Coquin, 'Apollon de Titkooh', 443: *psha ntapah<t>s napollô mn<a>pa pehieib*. Coquin, 443, has emended *pahs* to *pah<t>s* (see W. E. Crum, *A Coptic Dictionary* [Oxford: Clarendon, 1939] 283AB) by means of a papyrus fragment that, unfortunately, has no provenance: *tpahts <n>ap<o>l<l>ô*, 'the prostration/repentance of Apollo'.

⁴¹ Coquin, 'Apollon de Titkooh', 443.

⁴² Clédat, 119–120 (Room XX, #1).

⁴³ Orlandi, 13.

⁴⁴ An inscription from Bawit, Apollo's monastery (see n. 21), describes Phib as a 'man of penitence *[metanoia]* for salvation', a phrase echoed by the *Life*; see J. Clédat, ed., *Mémoires de l'institut français d'archéologie orientale* 12.119.

⁴⁵ Coquin, 'Apollon de Titkooh', 438: 'assez singulier'.

⁴⁶ See Antoine Guillaumont,'Les moines des Kellia aux 4ᵉ et 5ᵉ siècles', in 'Saint Antoine et les moines du désert', *Dossiers Histoire et Archéologie* 133 (December 1988) 7–8; for the service, see also Guillaumont, 'Les moines des Kellia', in Myriam Orban, ed., *Déserts Chrétiens d'Égypte* (Nice: Culture Sud, 1993) 37–38.

⁴⁷ Apophthegmata Antony 4 and Matoës 2.

⁴⁸ Columba Stewart believes that 'the dominant values' in early monasticism were 'humility and obedience, rather than penitence and pardon'. See his excellent article, 'Radical Honesty about the Self', 25–39. But perhaps it was precisely humility that prepared one to acknowledge sin, do penance, and seek pardon.

⁴⁹ For a discussion of this system, see Tim Vivian, *St. Peter of Alexandria: Bishop and Martyr*, Studies in Antiquity and Christianity (Philadelphia: Fortress, 1988) esp. Chapter 3 and the works cited there.

⁵⁰ Hermann Dörries, 'The Place of Confession in Ancient Monasticism', F. L. Cross, ed., *Studia Patristica* 5.3, Texte und Untersuchungen 80 (1962) 284–311, esp. 284–298; this article is a translation by Hans Frei of Dörries' article in *Judentum—Urchristentum—Kirche: Festschrift für Joachim Jeremias*, Zeitschrift für neutestamentliche Wissenschaft und die Kunde der älteren Kirche [henceforth ZNW], Beiheft 26 (Berlin, 1960) 235–259. This is not the place to discuss the subject in full; for a good introduction, see Dörries.

⁵¹ Coquin, 'Apollon de Titkooh', 443, describes it as 'cette innovation d'Apollon', but the extant evidence does not conclusively demonstrate this.

[52] *Eleutheria,* Greek for 'absolution', is followed by the redundant coptic *nka nobe ebol,* 'the forgiveness of sins' (par. 12), one of the signs that the *Life* was translated from Greek into Coptic; see Coquin, 'Apollon de Titkooh', 441.

[53] See Coquin, 'Apollon de Titkooh', 440; Crum, 283AB.

[54] Emphasis added. Thus, without an act of prostration, the rite seems to have come full circle. In par. 12 of the *Life of Phib,* Christ does not specifically enjoin prostration: 'I will reveal a holy place on the earth at the end of time and I will establish there an act of repentance for salvation and a feast day for my saints throughout the world and the forgiveness of sin for everyone who believes in your name'. The synaxary was probably edited in the fourteenth century; see Basset, ed., *Le Synaxaire arabe-jacobite, Patrologia Orientalis* 1 (1904) 367, and René-Georges Coquin and Aziz S. Atiya, 'Synaxarion, Copto-Arabic', in *The Coptic Encyclopedia,* 7:2171-2190.

[55] In the Coptic Church today, the celebration of Maundy Thursday, especially the partaking of the Eucharist that day, comes closest to a day of forgiveness. A separate rite, the *sagda,* or 'prostration', is celebrated at Pentecost at the ninth hour, but it emphasizes the descent of the Holy Spirit and does not involve the forgiveness of sin.

[56] The painting is now in the Coptic Museum in Cairo. A black and white photograph of the painting as originally discovered may be found in J. E. Quibell, *Excavations at Saqqara* (1906–1907) (Cairo: IFAO, 1908) volume 2, Plate XLIV, with a description on p. 64. Quibell did not supply a color representation because, he opined, the painting 'was not worth reproducing in colour'. Unfortunately, the painting was subsequently damaged in removal; a photograph of it in its current state may be found in Atalla, 15. Photographs of the painting in both states may be found in Paul van Moorsel and Mathilde Huijbers, 'Repertory of the preserved wallpaintings from the monastery of Apa Jeremiah at Saqqara', *Acta ad archaeologiam et artium historiam pertinentia,* ed. Hjalmar Torp, et al. (Rome: Bretschneider, 1981) 9:131-135 and Plates IV–V. Marguerite Rassart-Debergh and Jacques Debergh, 'A propos de trois peintures de *Saqqara', Acta,* ed. Torp, et al., 9:187-201, discuss the painting and provide drawings of it. Rassart-Debergh, following Quibell's notes, has reconstructed the painting by adding to the right of Onnophrius (our left) another penitent and a tree; see her 'La décoration picturale du monastére de Saqqara. Essai de reconstitution', in *Acta,* ed. Torp, et al., 41 and Fig. 15.1 (p. 40).

[57] Rassart-Debergh and Debergh, 191, suggest that the painting originally showed Onnophrius, Paphnutius, Macarius, Apollo, Phib, and Amoun; at some point, they argue, a monk retouched the painting and effaced the name of Amoun.

[58] *Peiwt apa [fib] pouêêb etenhot,* 'Father Apa [Phib] the faithful priest'. There are three spaces available for the name, so 'Phib' *(fib)* seems probable, as W. E. Crum long ago suggested. See Coquin, 'Apollon de Titkooh', 445; Rassart-Debergh and Debergh, 190. The last figure is a priest, which might argue against it being Phib, since no literary text calls him a priest. Coquin, 445–446, believes that Phib was in fact a priest and argues that a rite of repentance in his name makes better sense if he was a priest, but it also seems possible that Phib's priesthood could have been bestowed on him *ex post facto* by hagiography and tradition.

[59] Rassart-Debergh and Debergh, 190, believe that it is Anoub who is at the feet of Apollo and Phib, since 'Apollo, Phib, and Anoub in effect constitute the

"triad" of Bawit', and are found together in numerous inscriptions at Bawit and Saqqara; see their article for earlier suggestions. Interestingly, 'Anoub' seems to have been mistakenly inserted for 'Phib' in par. 12 of the Life.

⁶⁰ Coquin, 'Apollon de Titkooh', 446. Van Moorsel and Huijbers, 9.131, 133, follow Quibell (Saqqara II.64) and agree with Coquin by terming this figure a penitent. They state, 132 n.3, that cleaning has made some writing visible near the fourth figure and hope to address the problem of identification in a future article.

⁶¹ Ama Sibylla was apparently not a monastic but rather a mythological figure, a coptic metamorphosis of the Sibyl. She is invoked in over sixty inscriptions at Saqqara and was pictured at Bawit with the Virtues of the Spirit. For a discussion, see the Appendix at the end of this volume.

⁶² Sir Herbert Thompson, 'The Coptic Inscriptions', in Quibell, *Excavations at Saqqara*, volume IV, #188 (p. 55). The relevant sentence in Coptic is *paipe pma ntapenjoei[s] niôt apa ierêmias pahtf hij[ôf] shantefbi nnobe mplaos mpkosmos têref mmau*.

⁶³ For the text, see Amélineau, 'Vie de Paul de Tamoueh', 760; see 'Fragment II' of the *Life of Paul* in Chapter Five above. For *thronos*, see W. G. H. Lampe, *A Patristic Greek Lexicon* (Oxford: Clarendon, 1961) 655A.

⁶⁴ In a fragmentary papyrus from the sixth or seventh century, a monk, 'Petre, (the) humble monk of (the Monastery of) Apa Apollô', writes to a woman asking her to bring wine, possibly for the agapê of Apa Phib *(nakapê apa Phib)*; see Clackson, #4, pp. 120–121.

⁶⁵ One might note here the emphasis on the incarnation and resurrection, not the crucifixion. Until quite recently, crucifixes were extremely rare in coptic Christianity.

⁶⁶ Translated from the text edited by Orlandi, *Phif*, 20–36.

⁶⁷ Arabic Babeh; November 4 (Gregorian).

⁶⁸ 'Phib' is spelled 'Phif' *(fif)* throughout the text, which is the spelling Orlandi uses, but since 'Phib' is the more commonly used spelling, I have decided to adopt it. 'Phib' originally meant 'of Ibis'. Its spelling varies widely in the papyri, though usually with 'beta'; see Mandilaras, 74.

⁶⁹ Sinemoun is otherwise unknown. On Shmoun, see n. 17 above.

⁷⁰ The text is corrupt, but the British Library fragments say that Apollo had a spiritual brother, Petra; after his death, Apollo and Phib joined together. See Coquin, 437.

⁷¹ The 'mountain' is spelled 'Titkooh' here, although in the rest of the *Life* the spelling is Tkooh; since Titkooh is the usual spelling, it has been adopted here. Titkooh lay in the nome of Hermopolis Magna (Shmoun); see Timm, 6.2700. In Coptic, 'mountain', *tooh*, can also mean 'monastic community', so throughout the *Life* it may well have a double meaning; see 'Mountain and Desert: The Geographies of Early Coptic Monasticism', in Tim Vivian, *Histories of the Monks of Upper Egypt and the Life of Onnophrius*, rev. ed. (Kalamazoo: Cistercian Publications, 2000) 18–26.

⁷² *Polutia* (Gk. *politeia*) usually means 'a (monastic) way of life', but here is used in the plural; see Lampe, 1114A(G).

⁷³ On thieves and their absence, see Mt 6:19-20. Coming into the security and safety of port is a common image in late antiquity.

⁷⁴ 'Tested' is literally 'weighed' *(shi)*. John the Little was said to equal all of Scetis in virtue; the image used in the *Life of John the Little* 16 (Apophthegmata John the

Little 36) is of John balancing *(shi)* with a single finger a scale holding the virtues of all the other monks. See Maged S. Mikhail and Tim Vivian, trans., 'Life of Saint John the Little', *Coptic Church Review* 18: 1 & 2 (Spring/Summer 1997) 28. 'Scetis' itself is Coptic for 'to weigh the heart' *(shi hêt);* see the *Life of John the Little* 3; Mikhail and Vivian, 21.

[75] Coptic: *poluteue.*
[76] Coptic: *polutia.*
[77] Coptic: *poluteue.*
[78] Coquin, 441, says this phrase does not make sense, that it represents the ancient editor's bungled rendering of Greek into Coptic. Coquin, however, believes that the phrase refers to Phib whereas the subject seems to have shifted suddenly to Apollo. Might it be a reference to the Alexandrian and Coptic insistence on the single nature of Christ (so-called 'Monophysitism')? The paragraph might have originally been about Apollo, since the portions about Phib seem like additions.

[79] The giving of spiritual counsel (usually by an elder to a younger monk) is extremely important in early monasticism: in the *Apophthegmata Patrum,* Abba Paphnutius reports that he went to see elders twice a month, walking some 12 miles (Paphnutius 3; PG 65:380), and Abba John the Little used to sit in front of the church on weekends so that monks might approach him about their thoughts (John Colobos 8; PG 65:205). So customary was this practice that Macarius the Great was bothered when two young foreigners did not come to tell him their thoughts (Macarius 33). See also Chapter Eight below, and Stewart, 'Radical Honesty', 25–39.

[80] 'Prostrated': *afpahtf.*
[81] Father Lazarus, a hermit at the Monastery of Saint Antony by the Red Sea and formerly an Australian, showed me his places of prayer, one of which was modeled on an australian sheepfold; he pointed out to me as I sat in it how snug it was and good at keeping out the wind. See Chapter Three above.
[82] Literally: I did a little good for him. This sentiment and action occurs elsewhere in the *Life* (10, 14), seemingly associated with the giving and eating of bread, and appears to be an important part of monastic hospitality, here projected back to Papohe in his youth.
[83] Coptic: *ai**paht**.*
[84] The name Apollo (Apollos) in the New Testament is spelled the same as the name of the monk.
[85] This parenthesis seems to point to Apollo's coming to Titkooh; see pars. 11–14.
[86] Reading *pefouôsh marefshôpe* (with which par. 7 concludes) instead of *pefouoeish marefshôpe.*
[87] Tahrouj (Greek Teruthis, Arabic Dahrut or Dayrut) was in the nome of Oxyrhynchus (al-Bahnasa), east of Bawit, near the west bank of the Nile; see Timm, 2.493, who reports that in the byzantine era there was a monastery in the area of Tahrouj and that coptic economic documents from the Wadi Sarga often name Tahrouj in connection with wine deliveries. See also Clackson, 8, and text 33, pp. 96–97.
[88] 'Monastic life': -*poluteue;* 'ascetic practices': *polutia.* See par. 4 and the notes there.

Notes   235

⁸⁹ Reading <etnêu> with Orlandi, which was omitted because of homeoteleuton with nesnêu preceding it.

⁹⁰ In the *Life of Antony* 49.7, Antony 'came to a very high mountain, and at the foot of the mountain was very clear water, sweet and very cold'. Finding water would be one of the first priorities for any monastic community. A cubit *(mahe)* was a measurement based on the length of the forearm, about eighteen inches. So the well here was approximately six feet deep.

⁹¹ Pamin (if this is the same person referred to here) was a monk of the early fourth century who is associated particularly with al-Ashmunein; his tomb was the site of a cult and healing and numerous inscriptions demonstrate his renown. See René-Georges Coquin, 'Pamin, Saint', *The Coptic Encyclopedia* 6.1878.

⁹² 'Granted' uneasily renders coptic *hôn*, which would normally mean 'commanded'. Coquin suggests, 442, that *hôn* represents Gk. *sunchorein*.

⁹³ See n. 82.

⁹⁴ About 9 AM.

⁹⁵ I have not translated Gk. *melos* ('member') here, which occurs after 'companion', and have silently omitted it hereafter (see n. 100). This usage also occurs in the coptic *Life of Macarius of Scetis*; see Vivian, *Saint Macarius the Spiritbearer*.

⁹⁶ Literally 'the suffering *(hise)* of your suffering' *(skulmos)*. The Coptic *(hise)* seems to be a redundant translation of the Greek *(skulmos)*. See Coquin, 'Apollon de Titkooh', 441.

⁹⁷ 'Absolution': Coptic/Gk *eleutheria*. Lampe (449B) cites the Liturgy of Gregory of Nazianzus (PG 36.728A), which has a prayer of absolution before communion: *euchê tês eleutherias*. 'For the forgiveness of sin': Coptic *nka nobe*. This phrase is probably redundant, a coptic translation of Gk. *eleutheria*, which precedes it.

⁹⁸ See n. 97; here *eleutheria* and *nka nobe* are joined by 'and'.

⁹⁹ Coptic/Gk *metanoia*.

¹⁰⁰ Coptic *shbêrmelos*, which is a 'curious expression' (Coquin, 440), a hybrid of Greek and Coptic. It is attested, however, in the Nag Hammadi texts and in a coptic martyrdom; see Coquin, 440 n. 31.

¹⁰¹ The text has 'Anoub', but this must be a mistake.

¹⁰² Coptic *hôn*; see n. 92 above.

¹⁰³ This village is attested in ancient documents; see Timm, 6:2510.

¹⁰⁴ See notes 82 and 92.

¹⁰⁵ If the monks had a single meal, it was normally taken at the ninth hour or about 3 p.m. According to the *Historia Monachorum* 8.50, this was when the monks of Apollo's community ate, when they were not fasting.

¹⁰⁶ *Toou*, literally 'mountains'; see n. 71 above. This is probably the meaning, rather than 'monasteries'. The community was most likely a semi-anchoritic one where the monks lived in scattered monastic dwellings and gathered together on Saturday and Sunday. But see n. 27 above.

¹⁰⁷ About noon.

¹⁰⁸ Coptic: *-paht-*.

¹⁰⁹ Coptic: *paht-*.

¹¹⁰ This seems to suggest that the monks became as free of sin as on the day they were born.

¹¹¹ Coptic: *paht-*.

[112] The arabic synaxary (Basset, 368) gives a shortened version of this story; in it Zachary is not named, being only 'a monk who had died'.
[113] *Metanoia.*

7

Humility and Resistance in Late Antique Egypt: The Life of Longinus

Introduction

A THEOLOGY AND SPIRITUALITY OF HUMILITY

THE *LIFE OF LONGINUS*, in the judgement of its modern editor, may have only one historical event in it.[1] Thus the *Life*, by modern standards, is hagiography, which too often is treated by historians as the illegitimate offspring of history, deserving little attention and no inheritance. Even when hagiography is begrudged insight into the minds and feelings of its ancient audience (one of the historian's chief duties), it is still too often accorded third-cousin status. But what ancient Christians thought, felt, and believed matters, both within history's large, but finite, circumference, and even more within the illimitable community of saints. Within both compasses past is prologue, but within the communion of saints past is also eternal present, as the saints in heaven and the saints on earth blend in one chorus of unceasing praise. This is a spiritual reality understood very well by the author of the *Life* (pars. 34–36).

The *Life of Longinus*, therefore, contains several realities, and thus possesses diverse gifts. It may be read profitably as history for the insights it offers into a particular time, place and situation, in this case monastic Egypt in the fifth and sixth centuries, shortly after the Council of Chalcedon (451). It may be read as historical theology for what it tells us about the beliefs of egyptian monks *vis-à-vis* the Tome of Leo and its christological definitions. It may also be read spiritually. This last, I believe, is the way its original author intended it to be heard: as a sustained parable on humility—humility that glorifies God, not itself; humility so profound that it is capable, when God works through 'the truly humble', of effecting miraculous signs and wonders. Apa Longinus, the hero of the *Life*, is firmly grounded in the monastic milieu of late antique Egypt. The scene that has him (incognito, like a shakespearian hero) suffering reproof, patiently sitting outside the gate of the monastery and doing menial chores, is wonderfully vivid (14–16). Yet for the author of the *Life*, what truly matters here is not the hero *as* hero—like some monastic John Wayne—but the virtues of patience and humility that he embodies, indeed incarnates. Longinus is like the saints painted on the walls of coptic monastic churches. They are seemingly indistinguishable from one another; we are not being invited to look at them as individuals but as representatives of holiness. For the author of the *Life of Longinus*, Apa Longinus represents what it means to be holy.

Holiness, for the author of the *Life*, is found not in miracle but in humility. As Apa Longinus says in one apophthegm or saying not in the *Life*: 'Humility is stronger than any power or authority'.[2] The author of the *Life* may, in fact, be writing both an encomium on humility and a cautionary tale about the dangers of miracles. Miracles cause glory to be misdirected: people see wonderworkers and give glory to them rather than to God. Such misplaced adulation, the *Life* cautions, is merely 'the empty praises of men' ('vainglory', 13). Apa Longinus twice flees its clutches. Vainglory is a form of idolatry, it is honor given to the creature rather than to the Creator. In a parallel situation, probably added later (31), Apa Longinus proclaims to the emperor's servants that he and his monks will honor the Almighty *(pantôkratôr)* rather than the Almighty's image, the emperor, the supreme ruler *(autokratôr)*.

Another caution sounded by the author of the *Life* is that humility, one of the chief monastic virtues, may also be one of the shortest and surest paths to vainglory. Crowds come and heap honors and glory on Apa Lucius and Apa Longinus (12), and who would not be tempted to bask, at least for a moment, in that false light?

The struggle between humility and vainglory takes place both on a large theological field and within each person spiritually. Theologically, vainglory is idolatry; spiritually, it is 'the rule of all the passions'. It obscenely begets the love of money, anger, vanity, and envy, 'the evil wild beast' (38). For the author of the *Life*, the antidote to empty human praise is 'great and godly silence' (13). The most valued adjectives in the *Life of Longinus* are 'peace' and 'quiet' (8, 14, 19), while idolatrous vainglory comes with the clamor of crowds; mob rule, even in a monastery (18), is bad, both theologically and spiritually. The *Life* quietly assumes the symbiotic monastic practices of work and prayer (20–21), which come from and create silence. But silence is not solipsism. After fleeing two monasteries, Apa Longinus finally arrives at his spiritual home, a small cell near the sea—where he immediately begins to help others (19):

> He was at peace in the cell, making rope, and he labored with his handiwork so he could find a way to give to those in need by means of his handiwork, making himself in this regard like the holy apostle Paul, who says, 'My hands served my own needs and the needs of my companions', and 'It is more blessed to give than to receive' (Acts 20:34-35).

The peace Longinus finds is soon broken. Shipowners come to him for the rope he makes so they can use it on their vessels as benediction and protection; three monks come to be his disciples; and, as before, the sick and diseased seek out the saint for healing. But a profound change has taken place: the spiritual peace that Apa Longinus has found not only cures physical ailments, it also seems to heal the great theological and spiritual defect of vainglory and idolatry. Now when people are healed, instead of mistakenly glorifying Longinus, as had occurred earlier (12, 18), they give glory to God (22–25). The words of God are true: God does glorify those who give glory to him and he does exalt the humble (16; 1 K 2:30, Job 5:11). At Apa Longinus' death, the poor, the young, the ill, the married, and the monastic lament his passing with tears; his only concern 'for all of them, whether monk or lay person, was to bring them to salvation, presenting all of them as saints for the Lord Jesus Christ' (39). Whatever our historical judgement concerning the 'facts' of Apa Longinus' life, it is clear that the author of that *Life* saw in the example of 'this truly humble one' deep and abiding values for the salvation of the human person.

Fragments of a History

Reading the *Life of Longinus* historically is like looking at the wall painting mentioned earlier. The painting, a badly damaged image from the fifth or sixth century seen at a long-abandoned coptic monastery, has several figures, one or two of whom may be identified, but most of the inscriptions have been effaced, and the damage is so extensive that the action or scene being depicted cannot be determined with certainty.[3] There is no doubt that Longinus, like the painting, existed. The *Apophthegmata*, or *Sayings* of the Desert Fathers and Mothers, include eighteen sayings attributed to the saint, six of which appear in his *Life* (22, 25a, 25b, 26, 27b, and 28).[4] It seems that the individual sayings attributed to Longinus circulated separately before being included in the *Life* and that the *Apophthegmata* and the *Life of Longinus* are independent of one another.[5]

The *Life* contains further connections with the *Apophthegmata*. In the Sayings, Lucius teaches the Euchites (ascetics who eschewed work for constant prayer) about the necessity of both work and prayer, and in one saying Apa Longinus asks Apa Lucius about three thoughts.[6] One apophthegm also connects Lucius with Apa Theodore of Enaton, who comes on stage in the *Life* when he visits Apa Longinus with regard to a wayward brother (27c).[7] This Theodore may have been a companion of Apa Or and a disciple of Amoun; he went to Enaton in 308 and was still alive in 364.[8] Thus the *Apophthegmata* clearly associate Longinus, Lucius, and Theodore, and connect the latter two with the monastery of Enaton (so-named because it lay at the ninth milestone west of Alexandria).[9] It is interesting to note that the superscription to the *Life* says that Longinus 'was from the Laura of the Enaton of Alexandria' but that the *Apophthegmata* are silent on this matter. The *Life* clearly shows that Longinus left Enaton and lived in a cell by the sea (19). The silence of the *Apophthegmata* on his relationship with the laura may therefore reflect the real historical situation. The desire of the monks in the *Life* to make Longinus *hegoumenos*, or superior, of Enaton (29) at first appears to be pious fiction. It might, however, accurately portray the crisis brought about by the imposition of the Tome of Leo on the monks by the prefect of Alexandria, and the monks' turning to

Longinus for a trusted leader (see below). The *Life* says that after the chalcedonian crisis, Longinus 'spent another twenty years as head of the monastery of the laura' (38). So he may, in fact, as the *Life* represents, have come to Enaton, stayed briefly, left, founded his own community, returned to Enaton during crisis, and stayed on as its superior. The silence of the *Apophthegmata* on his provenance, however, does not allow confirmation for his connection with Enaton.

Most of the *Life of Longinus*, as outlined in Part I above, consists of theological and spiritual reflection on the themes of humility and vainglory. In all probability this material makes up the earliest stratum of the work. At some point, a later editor added the anti-chalcedonian section that so strongly shapes the end of the *Life* (29–37).[10] Whatever its editorial history, this section provides a fascinating glimpse into events and, importantly, feelings that occurred in Egypt after 451, when the Council of Chalcedon accepted the Tome of Leo with its definition of the two natures of Christ, and the subsequent decision by the emperor to impose that decision on the Christians of Egypt.[11] The reaction of egyptian monks to these episcopal and imperial decisions makes up paragraphs 29–37 of the *Life of Longinus*, the lone section of the *Life* that its editor believes has historical basis.[12]

These events took place in 457.[13] Emperor Marcian died on 26 January of that year; in the eyes of those opposed to Chalcedon, he had forced 'the bishops to affirm in writing that he who was crucified was not God', thereby ushering in the time of Anti-Christ.[14] Dioscorus, anti-chalcedonian patriarch of Alexandria, had died in 454, and Proterius, a chalcedonian, had succeeded him. From this point on, ancient Church historians, not known for their disinterestedness and objectivity, disagree. A pro-chalcedonian, Evagrius Scholasticus, reports that at Marcian's death, the people of Alexandria, 'an obscure and promiscuous rabble', 'renewed their feud against Proterius with still greater exasperation and excessive heat'.[15] Although Alexandria had a (chalcedonian) bishop in Proterius, another (anti-chalcedonian) was now consecrated, Timothy Aelurus ('the Cat' or 'the Weasel'). He had been a monk, then a priest under Dioscorus; on March 16 he was seized by the people, clergy, and monks of Alexandria, who wanted to make him bishop. John Rufus, an anti-chalcedonian historian, reports that 'the blessed ascetic and great prophet Longinus, abbot of the monks', was their 'head and chief, waking and rousing them according to the will of God'. According to John, 'multitudes of the holy monks gathered', both those from Alexandria and those living in monasteries outside the city.[16] In the words of Zacharius of Mytilene, an anti-chalcedonian chronicler, these monks and people set Timothy 'on the throne of Mark'.[17] Evagrius, by contrast, says that the people of Alexandria took 'advantage of the prolonged absence of Dionysius, commander of the legions, in Upper Egypt', and elected Timothy bishop, 'though Proterius was still bishop and discharged the functions of his office'.[18] Timothy, Evagrius charges, was 'guilty of an adulterous outrage on the church' because she already had 'her rightful spouse', Proterius, 'who was performing the divine offices in her, and canonically occupied his proper throne'.[19] Theodore Lector, another chalcedonian historian, charges Timothy with killing Proterius.[20]

Not surprisingly, matters soon turned violent. According to Zacharius, Timothy organized opposition to the Council of Chalcedon. General Dionysius then imprisoned Timothy, and 'many were killed'. Timothy was then removed from the city, 'and there was a great tumult, and slaughters were matters of daily occurrence'. Here Longinus enters the story: after 'confusion . . . had prevailed in the city for many days', Dionysius 'brought a certain monk Longinus, celebrated for chastity and virtue, and he entrusted Timothy to him, that he might restore the bishop to the city and to his church, upon the condition that the fighting should cease, and that there should be no more slaughter'. Timothy returned to his church and Proterius to his. When Easter came, 'children without number were brought to Timothy to be baptized . . . but only five were brought to Proterius. And the people were so devotedly attached to Timothy that they drove Proterius out . . . and slaughter ensued'.[21] Evagrius, as might be expected, has a different version: Dionysius 'had occupied the city with the utmost dispatch, and was taking prompt measures to quench the towering conflagration of the sedition', when 'some of the Alexandrians, at the instigation' of Timothy, killed Proterius 'by thrusting a sword through his bowels'.[22]

According to Zacharius, Longinus was something of a mediator, and Proterius, the chalcedonian bishop, suffered nothing worse than exile. Evagrius does not mention Longinus, although he had access to Zacharius' account.[23] Longinus may, however, have played a more substantive role, one certainly accorded him by the *Life* and seconded by John Rufus and Timothy Aelurus. In a pastoral letter written sometime before 478 and preserved only in Ethiopic, Pope Timothy speaks of 'Abba Longinus, the martyr [or: witness] who tore down the *Tome* of Leon [sic], the heretic, and threw it away (and) who died (just) before this day.'[24] Poor Proterius, it seems, was lynched and burned in the Hippodrome on 28 March, an event recorded in gruesome detail by Evagrius.[25] According to the *Life of Longinus*, it was Acacius, the prefect of Egypt, who tried to force the monks of Enaton to subscribe to the *Tome of Leo* and it was Longinus who led the opposition to 'that abominable ordinance' (29–30).[26] After the monks, led by Longinus, defeated the emperor's soldiers without bloodshed (33-34), Longinus led monks and soldiers together to the tombs where the holy fathers of Enaton lay buried and asked them (36),

> 'My holy fathers, is it truly the wish of God that we accept the Tome of Leo and subscribe to it?' Immediately a voice arose from the tombs where the bodies of the saints lay, three times saying 'Anathema to ungodly Leo's Tome! Do not speak his name nor be in communion with anyone who accepts that ordinance! Anathema to those who subscribe to the Tome of Leo! Anathema to Leo's blasphemous act, for it is full of blasphemy against the divinity of Christ because it divides Christ into two natures instead of maintaining the unity of Christ!'

A number of soldiers immediately laid down their weapons and became monks; the other soldiers returned to Alexandria, 'proclaiming the wonders they had seen'. The citizens of the city went to the praetorium, seized Acacius, 'and burned him in the middle of the city'. When Proterius (unnamed), 'the bishop of that false teaching, saw the uproar taking place, he took off his ecclesiastical garments and put on layman's clothing and left the city. He fled on account of the fear that had seized him and he has not been found to this day' (37).

The accounts agree that someone, either the prefect Acacius or the patriarch Proterius, died for Leo's sin, was burned to death for the blasphemous act of compelling support for the Council of Chalcedon.[27] According to the *Life of Longinus*, the horrible death of Acacius was a judgement from God (the author of the *Life* seems compelled to justify it) and thereafter 'the Church boldly proclaimed the doctrines of the orthodox faith and advanced through the encouragement and intercessions of the Holy Spirit' (37). In reality, however, the conclusion was neither so simple nor so salutary for the (anti-chalcedonian) Orthodox of Egypt: Emperor Leo I expelled Timothy from Alexandria in 458.[28] If Longinus did in fact lead the monks of Enaton for another twenty years, as his *Life* says, he did so within sight of a hostile, chalcedonian, governor and patriarch in Alexandria, a mere nine miles away.[29]

The Life of Longinus [30]

The Life and Ascetic Practice of Our Holy Fathers
and Glorious Ascetics Apa Longinus and
His Spiritual Father Apa Lucius.
They Completed Their Glorious Lives
on the Second of Mshir.
In the Peace of God. Amen.

Prologue

1. It belongs to us with tongues of flesh to sing the praises of those who bear flesh who have completed their earthly way of life. Through their way of life they have reached the heights of human achievement and through their accomplishments they have attained the greatest heights possible for those burdened with flesh, almost as if they bore no flesh. What tongue of flesh will be able to do them honor? Men such as these have need of an incorporeal tongue to sing their praises, just as they also completed their angelic ways of life. Fleshly burden hindered none of those heavenly beings who were on earth from completing their way of life and becoming the equal of angels, as the holy apostle said: 'But our citizenship is in heaven, from where we expect our Saviour and Lord, who will transform our humility to be like the body of his glory'.[31]*

* Phil 3:20-21

2. Therefore, when I wanted to set forth the history[32] of Saint Apa Longinus and his spiritual

father Apa Lucius, who completed their ways of life (not to speak of their contests and struggles),[33] I was at a loss since I knew my own weakness and the lofty virtues of those saints. Like someone standing under a very high rock who attempts to lift that rock or climb on top of it, I am completely at a loss as to how I shall be able to climb on top of that rock.[34] Indulge me when I say that the rock is Christ, for the place where the saints dwelled was in fact the saints' Lord. For he who did not refrain from going up the mountain with Peter and John also did not refrain from living with Apa Longinus and his father Apa Lucius where they lived.[35] And indeed just as that vision [of Christ's transfiguration] showed Peter and John who it was that had ascended that rock, thus it also showed Apa Lucius and Apa Longinus the upright faith, which many attained through them, as I will reveal as we proceed.

3. But since I know my own inferiority, I wish to be silent about the history of those saints on account of their exalted nature and my own inferiority. But then judgement stares me in the face and threatens me thus: 'Is not such fearfulness pleasing to God? If, as you so thoroughly declare, they were saints and counsellors and their entire way of life was as completely exalted as you say and their life has the power to edify those who listen to it, why do you choose to be silent and not speak to us about the life of those saints? Even if you are unable to tell us about the way of life of those saints filled with every virtue, at least tell us what you can in humility lest you seem envious of those whose souls will profit from listening to the life of those holy counsellors and who will in some small measure follow them'.

4. The herald of truth, Paul the teacher, especially enjoins, 'Remember your leaders, those who

spoke the word of God to you; consider the greatness of their way of life, and imitate their faith'.³⁶* Since God knows that the saints will profit everyone who listens to the life of those who conducted their lives according to the will of God, he wrote to us through the Holy Spirit of the life of the patriarchs and the other saints, those in the Old Testament and the New, so that we might not only listen to them but also imitate their character and ourselves inherit the promises that God made to those who love him. Thinking therefore on these things, I realized that it was encumbent on me to begin the history of the saints and call to mind for us their ways of life, knowing with certainty that 'the memory of the righteous is a good memory', and that 'good renown delights the heart',* and especially that 'the people delight in speaking of the righteous', as the wise Solomon says.'³⁷*

* Heb 13:7

* Prov 10:7, 15:30

* Prov 29:2

THE LIFE AND ASCETIC PRACTICE OF OUR HOLY FATHER APA LONGINUS WHO WAS FROM THE LAURA OF THE ENATON OF ALEXANDRIA

Longinus' Origins;
He Becomes a Disciple of Apa Lucius

5. His story is as follows: He was from a city of Lycia, as one reckons earthly birth,³⁸ but he was a citizen of the heavenly Jerusalem since his citizenship was in heaven,³⁹ according to the word of the wise Paul.* From his youth he loved the philosophy of the monastic life.⁴⁰ He went to a monastery in his native region of Lycia called the monastery of Apa Hieronikos. When he was worthy of the holy monastic habit at that monastery, he put himself in the hands of a great ascetic by the name of Apa Lucius, who was adorned

* cf Heb 12:22

with the word of the holy Scriptures and discernment, the mother of all virtues.[41] Apa Lucius instructed Longinus in all faith and discipleship befitting the monastic life.

Apa Lucius Decides to Leave the Monastery

6. After he had spent some time in the monastery living the monastic life[42] and practising the virtues of Christ (which are humility and gentleness and renunciation and other virtues like these), the superior of that monastery, a tranquil and peaceful man, went to his rest and another had to be appointed in his place. As a result, a disturbance broke out in the monastery church, and this was its cause: all the monks knew Apa Lucius and everyone looked to him to be their superior to replace the one who had gone to his rest. When the holy one understood that he was the cause of the disturbance, he chose to leave them; that is, he left the monastery so it might have peace. He especially did this because, like his Saviour, he never ceased pursuing humility.

7. Thinking these things, he called his disciple Apa Longinus and said to him, 'My son, we know that it is a weighty matter to leave our monastery while we are alive, but so I am not the cause of a disturbance of this sort so that judgement come upon me, I think it is good that we withdraw someplace by ourselves, as it is written in Proverbs: "It is better to live in a corner of the rooftop than to live in a new house or a place plastered over with fighting".* It is more profitable for us, therefore, to withdraw someplace by ourselves so we can be occupied with the salvation of our souls, on account of which we have renounced the world and everything in it, than to remain here and watch our monastery fall into

* Prov 21:9 (LXX)

ruinous error'. This was the reason they left their monastery; or rather, it was the divine plan of God that arranged things so he might reveal the good gifts of his goodness that steward our bodies and souls through his elect and so many might be saved through them.

Lucius and Longinus Perform Miracles at the Shrine of Saint Theoctistus

8. After they left their monastery, they came to a quiet village in that region of Lycia and lived in a church in that village named after the honored saint and martyr Theoctistus.[43] This did not come about merely by chance but so the wonders of God might be manifested, just as they are manifested through the interpretation of the honored name of the martyr Theoctistus, which indicates what is going to take place in his oratory through these saints. For Theoctistus is translated 'that which is built through God', in that he caused these saints, through their ascetic practices and many contests, to be edified in the name of the martyr.[44] They edified numerous souls through the wonders and healings that God worked there through them. While they were living there, many came from the surrounding countryside bringing those who were sick, especially those possessed by unclean spirits,* laying them in the cemetery there. And they obtained healing through the prayers of those saints.

* cf Mk 1:32, Mt 8:16

The Healing of a Possessed Woman

9. One woman was possessed by an unclean spirit that was very powerful. This woman was creating a great disturbance and disorder on account of the demon inside her; as a result, she

ripped the clothing of everyone who approached her and also tore at their bodies. When they brought her to the servants of God and begged them to pray over her so she might obtain healing through their entreaty, she began to tear at and attack those around her. Then she fell at their feet and continued to be convulsed by the evil spirit inside her and was foaming at the mouth. Then she cried out with a loud voice and appeared to be dead. Then blessed Lucius had compassion for her. He began to pray, and laid hands on her. He ordered his disciple Longinus to pray also and lay hands on her and seal her with the sign of the cross. When they did this, the demon immediately left her and she got up as someone gets up from sleep, cleansed of the scourge that possessed her. And so from that day until her death she ministered to those who were sick at the *martyrium*. This, then, was the first sign* that God worked through them after they left their monastery and came to live in that church.

* cf Jn 2:11

Luicius and Longinus Raise a Dead Youth

10. I will also recount another wonder that God did through his servants. There was a man from the surrounding countryside there who had a noble son whom he had raised to adulthood from a child. There was a woman named Flavia who entrusted to the parents of that youth a document which they gave to their son to protect. When the youth died suddenly, his parents did not know where the document was. That woman, Flaviana, went to recover her deposit, that is, the document that she had entrusted to them. When they were at a loss regarding it and could not find it because they did not know where the young man had put it, she threatened with great anger that she would make them her slaves

if they did not restore her document to her. Then the parents of the youth, when they continued to be hounded by that woman, left their beloved child unburied and hurried to where the saints were living, with a great crowd following them, that is, their relatives and neighbors. They prostrated themselves at the feet of Apa Lucius and Apa Longinus, imploring them, 'Ask the Lord Christ, whose servants you are, to reveal the soul of our child who has died so we might learn from him where he placed the document that the wife of the rich man entrusted to us, because she is now threatening to make us slaves if we do not find the document and give it to her!'

11. When the blessed ones heard this story from the young man's parents, they felt pity for them on account of the love and compassion of Christ that was in them; they immediately arose and followed them without hesitation or being bothered at all. When they reached the house where the dead youth was, they went inside to where the deceased lay and knelt down and prayed that God might wish to manifest a miracle through blessed Apa Longinus who was filled with virtues. Suddenly he was filled with the Holy Spirit. He seized the child's hand in front of the crowd and spoke thus: 'God, who raised Lazarus,* will also on this occasion now restore your spirit to you so you may tell us where you put the document belonging to the rich man's wife so she will not take your parents as slaves'. And immediately the spirit returned to the young man; he rose up and sat and opened his mouth. With everyone standing there listening, he told them where the document had been placed in the house. And his parents asked him other things that they did not know and he gave them an account of everything they asked him, and so he immediately lay down again. When the people of Lycia saw this miracle

* cf Jn 11:1–12:19

that had taken place through the saints, they glorified God, who alone works such wonders.

Because of their Renown, Lucius and Longinus Decide to Flee

12. When the news of their fame spread through that region, whole crowds brought to them their sick who were afflicted with every kind of illness in order to have them pray over them and heal them, and they bestowed great honors on them. When the saints were surrounded by excessive crowds that bothered them and the glory that they gave them, on account of their great humility they did not esteem it. Finally, they decided to secretly flee and get away from the crowds there. When those living around the saints found out, they kept constant watch so they would not be deprived of their blessing and their presence among them. For the saints were the pride of that whole region on account of the multitude of miracles that took place through them.

Lucius Sends Longinus to Enaton

13. Then blessed Lucius took his disciple aside and said to him, 'We can not continue enduring the empty praises[45] of men like this, nor is it good for our souls. Therefore, my son, listen to me. Arise and secretly go to Alexandria. I hear that there is a monastery in the western part of that city called Enaton that possesses great and godly silence.[46] Seek out a man from Corinth whose name is Gaius; he is the superior of the cenobium that he himself founded there. Remain in that monastery with him and I have faith in the Lord God our Saviour that, wherever you are, he will not deprive me of the opportunity of physically

being there with you. And even if I have to go a long time without you, I have faith in the Lord that I will no doubt come to you so we can complete our course together somewhere that the Lord determines for us as he wishes. Wherever you are, my son, flee the empty praises of men, and go to the *martyrium* of Saint Menas and first pray, then go to Enaton and stay in the monastery of Apa Gaius'.[47]

Apa Longinus Comes to Enaton

14. When he had said these things, they prayed, then embraced one another, and in this way Apa Longinus left Apa Lucius. When blessed Apa Longinus came to Alexandria, he sought out at the ninth milestone[48] the monastery of Apa Gaius and some religious[49] gave him directions. When he came to the monastery, he quietly knocked at the door.[50] When the gatekeeper opened the door, he asked Apa Longinus, 'Where are you from, and what is the reason for your coming here?' The truly humble one, Apa Longinus, answered, 'I am from the region of Lycia and I have come here to be a monk', for on account of his great humility he did not claim to call himself a monk. He wore no cowl or scapular[51] nor a habit[52] such as foreign monks wear, but only a *kolobion* and *pallium* and belt;[53] these were the only things that he was wearing when he entered the monastery. His hair had grown a little long on account of the many days he had spent traveling on the road. As a result, they did not immediately recognize him as a monk. The gatekeeper said to him, 'How can you be a monk here? Truly, the canon of our psalmody is long and our customs regarding eating and sleeping and the other requirements entail great pain and suffering.'[54] There

is no comfort in them. Here, take some bread as a blessing.⁵⁵ The Lord be with you'.

15. Noble Longinus did not gainsay what the gatekeeper had said with a single word to him but when he heard the word 'blessing', which means bread that has been blessed, he patiently waited at the door a number of days, making himself like that other saint, Antony the Great, who went to the anchorite Paul the Great after patiently enduring great suffering on the desert road. That great one did not accept him right away, but blessed Antony patiently waited at the door, saying, 'I sought and I found, and I believe that it will be opened to me'.⁵⁶* Longinus, too, since this same Spirit dwelled in him and he believed these things in his heart, patiently waited at the door until he attained that which he believed in his heart would come with great patience. When the gatekeeper continued to come outside each day to do his assigned duties and found Apa Longinus sitting by the door with great patience, he reported it to the *hegoumenos*⁵⁷ of the monastery, saying, 'There's a young man, a foreigner, at the door of the monastery; he's been there a number of days, saying, "I want to become a monk". I rebuffed him numerous times, but he's been patiently waiting there all this time'. The superior answered, saying, 'Since you have seen his patience, bring him in with you inside the gates so he may help you with your duties, performing all the tasks you give him'.

* cf Mt 7:7; Lk 11:9

16. So the gatekeeper brought him inside the gates, as the father of the monastery had commanded. Not only did Longinus do everything that the gatekeeper ordered, but everything that the brothers would order he did with great enthusiasm⁵⁸ and perfect obedience. And he remained patient like this, doing things of this sort,

for two years or more, and he did not tell the brothers in any way that he was a monk. But God, who always glorifies those who give glory to him,* and reveals the things that are hidden,* and exalts the humble,* spoke with a mouth that is true, saying, 'A lamp will not burn when it is placed under a basket, but when it is placed on a lampstand, it gives light to everyone in the house'.* He did not want his chosen one to remain hidden but revealed him as one who truly shines: he placed him on a spiritual lampstand so he would give light not only to those around him but also to those far away from him. He gave light to them through his abundant fruits and his achievements, as the narrative will make clear for us as the discourse proceeds.

* 1 K 2:30
* Dan 2:22
* Job 5:11

* Mt 5:15

A Merchant from Lycia Recognizes Apa Longinus

17. A merchant from Lycia, Apa Longinus' homeland, who knew him well when he was living at his monastery, happened to come to Alexandria on business. When he came to the monastery of Saint Menas, he prayed and then desired to go to the monastery of blessed Gaius the priest, as was his custom, since the monastery was known for its great faith. When he arrived at the monastery, he received a blessing from Apa Gaius and asked him to pray for him. While he was sitting at the door of the church, Saint Gaius spoke to him at length concerning teachings from the holy Scriptures for the salvation of his soul. The merchant stared: he saw Apa Longinus, who had raised the dead youth and performed numerous miracles in Lycia. But now he doubted whether it was really Longinus, or was someone who resembled him. In fact, Longinus' hair had grown so long over time and was so unkempt that the merchant did

not recognize him with certainty. But from the time he was little Apa Longinus had had a mark on his face and the merchant observed with certainty now the mark on his face. He said to Saint Gaius, 'You have a great man in this monastery who has done many powerful things'.

18. The superior said to him, 'Whom among the brothers are you talking about?' The merchant said to him, 'I'm talking about the one sweeping in front of the gate, for he is Apa Longinus, who is famous in Lycia, he and his spiritual father, Apa Lucius. He raised the dead and cast out many demons from people and did numerous other healings that God worked through him in that country. As a result, when his fame spread through that land and he was being glorified by everyone, he left his spiritual father and fled and secretly came here, fleeing from the empty praise of men'. When he finished saying these things about Saint Apa Longinus, the latter was still sweeping the area in front of the gate. Then the *hegoumenos* called him and said to him, 'Why did you hide from us? You didn't tell us that you're a monk'. Immediately Apa Longinus, whose heart was truly humble, prostrated himself at the feet of Gaius the priest and asked his forgiveness, 'Forgive me, my father'. And immediately the superior ordered them to shave from his head the hair that had grown so long. He prayed over him and clothed him in the cowl and scapular in accordance with the monastic habit of Alexandria. When the brothers in the monastery heard all these words concerning Apa Longinus, they gathered around him as around a great and perfect saint and began to glorify him exceedingly.[59] But when Saint Apa Longinus saw that he was being glorified by men, his heart was grieved, especially when he remembered the instructions his spirit-

ual father had given him to flee from the empty praises of men.

Apa Longinus Leaves the Monastery

19. Then he took counsel within, saying, 'I renounced my homeland on account of human glory and separated from my father. So how can I stay here where crowds of this sort glorify me?' Therefore, he left that monastery. Some God-loving men built a small cell for him near the monastery by the sea. He was at peace in the cell, making rope,⁶⁰ and he labored with his handiwork so he could find a way to give to those in need by means of his handiwork, making himself in this regard like the holy apostle Paul, who says, 'My hands served my own needs and the needs of my companions', and 'It is more blessed to give than to receive'.⁶¹* Many came to him from among the great shipowners and bought the ropes that he made with his holy hands; they used them as crosses in the midst of their sails as blessing, believing that by doing this his prayers would be with them as protectors and that the Lord would save their ships wherever they went. After a few days, three monks came to him and became his disciples.⁶²

* cf Acts 20:34-35

Apa Lucius Rejoins Apa Longinus

20. One night while he was sitting with his disciples meditating on the word of God and working with his hands,⁶³ he fell asleep on his seat where he was working, thinking of David, the holy singer of psalms, who says, 'I will not give sleep to my eyes, slumber to my eyelids, rest to my brows, until I find a place for the Lord, a dwelling place for the God of Jacob'.* While he

* Ps 131:4-5 (132:4-5)

was sitting at night, sleep weighed him down, and he went into a trance, as if a man stood before him speaking to him, 'Hurry, get up, and go to the seashore! There you will find your father, Apa Lucius. He has come to you from his homeland'. And so he immediately got up; without speaking to any of his disciples, he went to the harbor, the place that he had been told about in the revelation. He found Saint Apa Lucius and immediately climbed up into the boat. After they greeted one another, the old man said to Apa Longinus, 'Did I not tell you, my son, that I trusted in Christ that wherever you would go, I would come to you?' Then they glorified God because he had allowed them to see one another again and because the Scripture was fulfilled: 'The deer met and saw one another's face; they came forth in a group and not one of them perished, for the Lord was the one who commanded them and his spirit was the one bringing them together'.[64]* Rightly indeed the great trumpets of the prophets called men of this sort 'deer' since deer are lovers of the desert and track down the race of snakes as enemies. So it also is with these saints who flee the disturbances of cities and who are hidden in desert places and who at all times track down spiritual serpents, that is, the spirits of evil.

* Is 34:15-16 (LXX)

21. The two of them walked and together went inside. His disciples were sitting while they meditated and worked. When they saw Saint Apa Longinus walking with his father, they were amazed and got up with great joy. They greeted one another and after they prayed, sat down. Apa Longinus said to them, 'This is your father from this day on'. Then he told them what he had seen in the vision concerning Apa Lucius. Saint Apa Lucius had Apa Longinus teach him how to make the ropes. So they continued to serve God with great zeal, living together in great peace, each

one keeping to every aspect of his regimen. As a result, the news of their monastic practices and sober life filled the great city of Alexandria and all the surrounding countryside.

Apa Longinus Heals a Woman with Cancer[65]

22. For example, a woman who had a disease in her breast called 'cancer' by physicians heard about Apa Longinus the Great, that the Lord worked cures through him. She arose in faith and went to him. (She had told the doctors all her symptoms and none of them had cured her.)[66] When she went to the seashore, she came upon Saint Apa Longinus gathering wood on the shore of the sea as was his custom. She asked him, 'Where is the servant of God, Apa Longinus?'

He said, 'What do you want with him?'

She told him about her illness. But he said to her, 'What do you want with that guy? He is nothing'. Then he made the sign of the cross where she was ill, saying, 'My Lord Jesus Christ do with you according to your faith'.* The woman believed and turned to go home. When she had gone just a little ways, she was healed of her illness. When she entered the city, she told everyone about the cure that had happened to her through the saint. They asked her, 'What sort of person was this man?' She told them about the mark on his blessed face.[67] When they told her it was Apa Longinus who had healed her, the woman gave glory to God.

* cf Lk 7:50, 8:48

23. Who would be able to relate all the healings and miracles that God did through Apa Longinus! If I wished to relate each of the healings, I would not have the time. But I will speak of a few of them so I may satisfactorily complete the discourse up to this point, being selective because some are

unbelieving concerning the large number of miracles.⁶⁸ For many came to him from the city of Alexandria and its environs, wishing to know where he was, and people came to him ill with every kind of illness and he healed every one of them.

Apa Longinus Heals a Demoniac

24a. One day a woman came to him with her child who was possessed by a demon; his face was contorted on account of the workings of the demon and it convulsed him every day, afflicting him. His mother implored the saint to pray over him. He held out his hands and prayed, saying, 'Lord Jesus Christ, who works our health and salvation, if you so wish, bestow healing on this child'. And so he blew into the face of the child.* Immediately the demon left the child and his face returned to normal. They ran to their house, glorifying God.

* cf Jn 20:22

The Miracle of the Rainstorm

24b. When they saw so many coming to them, the need arose to supply some bread on account of the needs of the visitors and those coming to see them. When the bread was laid out in the sun, a great rainstorm suddenly poured down. Immediately Saint Apa Longinus stood and prayed, saying, 'God of all and Creator⁶⁹ of creation, command this rainstorm to pass us by!' And immediately the clouds dispersed from where the bread lay, and not a drop of rain fell on it. His prayers had acted as protection⁷⁰ over where the bread lay, and not a drop of rain fell on it.

Apa Longinus Heals a Woman with a Diseased Hand [71]

25a. Again one time when he was sitting in his cell making ropes and meditating on the word of God, a woman came to him with an illness in her hand that the doctors call *aniatos*, that is, incurable. She came up behind his cell and implored him, saying, 'Please pray for me!' but he threatened her so she would go away from his cell. She remained at the door of his cell, however, afraid to speak. When he understood in the Spirit the great suffering that she endured, he got up and closed the shutters of the window she was looking through and said to her, 'Go in peace. May the Lord grant you healing'. And the woman was healed from then on.

Apa Longinus' Cowl Heals a Demoniac [72]

25b. One day a man came to him to receive his blessing and begged him to give him his cowl so it might be protection for him. When he got it, he left him. When he returned home, there was a man there possessed by a demon, and when the demoniac saw the man coming with the cowl of Apa Longinus, the demon threw the demoniac to the ground and cried out, saying, 'Why have you brought Apa Longinus here to persecute people?'* Those in the house were astounded at what the demon said and the man carrying the cowl was also amazed and perceived that this was happening on account of Apa Longinus' cowl. And immediately he took it and placed it on the man possessed by the demon, saying, 'In the name of God and with the prayers of my father Apa Longinus, come out from him!' And immediately the demon came out of him. When the

* cf Mk 1:24

people saw what had taken place, they glorified God, who works miracles like these through his saints.

An Elder Comes to Apa Longinus to Die [73]

26. Again one day while he was sitting in his cell, there was sitting beside him an elder from the laura who had come to visit him. While they were talking about the heart of their souls, Apa Longinus suddenly got up as though someone had called him, left the cell, and went to the seashore. He found a boat that had come from Upper Egypt in which a saintly elder had ridden. When the elder saw him, he greeted him with a holy kiss. The elder raised his eyes to heaven, saying, 'Lord, did I not implore you to not let this saint know that I was coming to him because he would be bothered and would come outside?' The elder turned to Apa Longinus and said to him, 'My time is coming to leave this life. Therefore, the Lord sent me to you for you to lay your hands on my eyes'.[74] And so the two of them walked and went inside Apa Longinus' cell and after three days the elder went to his rest in good old age. Saint Apa Longinus laid hands on his eyes and he finished his life in good old age.

Apa Longinus Foresees the Death of His Disciple Arcadius

27a. Again one time when Apa Longinus was going into his cell with a disciple whose name was Arcadius (Arcadius was making a rope that Apa Longinus had told him to cut), Apa Longinus said to him, 'Arcadius, my son, hurry and finish, for God will be sending for you now'. When Arcadius had finished the rope, Apa Longinus took him by the hand, rolled up his mat, and turned his face toward the east, and immediately the disciple gave his spirit into the hands of God in peace.

The Prayers of Apa Longinus Drive Out a Demon [75]

27b. Again one day a demoniac was brought to Apa Longinus and he was implored to cast out the demon from him. Apa Longinus said to him in humility of heart, 'I do not know what I can do for him, but go to Apa Zenon and I believe that God will grant him healing'. When they went to Apa Zenon, they implored him to pray over the demoniac, and as Apa Zenon began to pray, the demon cried out, 'Do you think I'm going to leave because of you? But look! Apa Longinus is nearby, praying, and since I'm afraid of his prayers, I'll leave. But I am not going to answer to you!' When the unclean spirit had said these things, he left the man.

Apa Longinus Teaches about Passing Judgement [76]

27c. Again, there was one of his disciples who had done some inappropriate things. When Apa Theodore of Enaton found out, he came to Apa Longinus with another elder.[77] They implored him to expel the disciple. But Apa Longinus did not listen to them, thinking that perhaps his disciple would repent and God would forgive him; he did not desire the death of the sinner but hoped he would repent and live.* He said to them just these words: 'Woe to us because we renounce the world and have entered into the monastic life saying, "We are like angels", but in reality we are more evil than unclean spirits!'

* cf Ezek 33:11, Jas 5:20

*Apa Longinus Instructs a
Shipowner to Help a Debtor* [78]

28. Again one day a great shipowner came to Apa Longinus and brought a large amount of money to give him. But Apa Longinus accepted nothing from him, saying, 'We do not need things of this sort. What we make with our hands is sufficient. But please, get on your donkey and hurry and go to the steps of Saint Peter's [79] and you will find a man there wearing such and such clothing and also having a certain mark on his face (these things God just now revealed to me). Ask him, "Where are you from?" and "What is that in your hand?"'

The shipowner hurried and went, as the old man had ordered. When he came to the steps, he found the man whom Apa Longinus had told him about. He went up to him and spoke to him. But that man did not answer at all on account of his misery, but hastened to leave the city to do what he had resolved to do. When the shipowner saw the man's distress and how upset he was, he said to him, 'I have just now come from Enaton, from my father Apa Longinus. He's the one who sent me to you'. When the man heard the name of Apa Longinus, he stood up. The shipowner gave him the money. The man took it in his misery, saying, 'I am badly in debt and the moneylenders are dunning me for repayment. I haven't found any way to pay them. I decided to flee the city and strangle myself because of the numerous troubles hanging over me. So you'll know I'm telling the truth, look, here's the rope in my hand that I'm going to hang myself with'. And he showed him the rope in his hand. The shipowner was amazed at what Apa Longinus had said. He gave the gold to the man. The man went home.

The shipowner returned to Apa Longinus and told him everything that had happened. The old man said to him, 'Believe me, my son: whatever we have been careless about, even a little, God judges the two of us for the sake of that soul'.

APA LONGINUS DEFENDS THE ORTHODOX FAITH AGAINST THE COUNCIL OF CHALCEDON[80]

Apa Longinus Foresees the Imposition of the Tome of Leo

29. At that time when the emperor Marcian wanted to send a court official[81] to Alexandria with the Tome of the ungodly Leo,[82] he ordered the city of Alexandria, and especially the monks of Enaton, to subscribe to it.[83] But the Lord revealed this matter to Saint Apa Longinus three months beforehand; the Lord ordered Apa Longinus, through the revelation that was shown to him, to assemble together all the monks of Enaton and tell them what had happened. And he commanded him not to accept that ordinance[84] at all nor to subscribe to it. Apa Longinus gathered together everyone who was at the laura and told them what the Lord had revealed to him in the vision and ordered them to firmly adhere to the righteous ordinance[85] of the Lord and to fight to the death for the orthodox faith.

When they heard these things from Apa Longinus, they greatly rejoiced and deliberated with one another, saying, 'No one will be able to set at naught this abominable ordinance except him to whom the Lord has revealed this mystery and whom the Lord has told of the oppression that is ordained to come!'[86] Then they implored blessed Apa Longinus to be their father and leader and *hêgoumenos* of the monastery of Enaton.

The Letter of Acacius Commanding the Monks to Subscribe to Chalcedon

30. Three months later, the court official and that godless ordinance[87] arrived. The emperor instructed Acacius, the prefect ruling Egypt at that time, to force the monks at the laura to subscribe to the abominable Tome of Leo. The duke, when he read the emperor's letter, made a copy of it and sent it to the monks of Enaton, written thus: 'Acacius, prefect of Egypt, writing to the holy and God-loving monks[88] of the laura of Enaton, sends greetings. Since our lord emperor and supreme ruler[89] has made us worthy to receive his holy letter, which commands everyone to subscribe to the Tome of Leo, Bishop of Rome, and especially you who are righteous, O monks of Enaton, you will now accept the letter from the court official and you will carry out the command of our lord the emperor so that you will enjoy gifts and honors from him, the great benefactor and supreme ruler and fighter for our wise doctrine'.

The Monks of Enaton Refuse to Accept the Tome of Leo

31. When Saint Apa Longinus received the letter, he gathered together all the brothers and read the copy to them. When they heard it, they cried out as one, 'Anathematize that abominable ordinance and everything in it, ungodly Leo too, and everyone in communion with him!' Then they wrote a letter to the prefect, written thusly: 'You have submitted to the abominable ordinance of the supreme ruler; we, on the other hand, are obedient to the Almighty who through his providence cares for all of creation.[90] Therefore, let it be clear to Your Authority that there is no one among us, from the least to the greatest, who will

allow himself to take part in[91] or in any way obey that abominable ordinance and the lawbreaking and ungodly Leo. Instead, we are prepared, each and every one of us, to fight to the death for the established doctrine and the tradition of the saving faith of our holy and orthodox fathers that has been handed down to us.[92] In order not to write too many words to you, in sum, we think it better, and more profitable for our souls, to obey the ordinance of the Almighty rather than that of the supreme ruler'.

The Monks Go Out to Face the Duke's Army [93]

32. When the duke received the letter, he recognized its power. He and the emperor's official were very angry and outraged at the reply from the saints of Enaton. They together decided for the official to send his army to kill and slaughter the monks of Enaton. But the Lord, who sets aside the designs of rulers,[94]* revealed the plan to the holy elders Apa Lucius and Apa Longinus. They gathered together all the brothers and Apa Longinus said to them, 'I entreat you, my brothers, let none of you be troubled. Listen to me: each of you take some palm branches from the palm trees and go together to meet the ruler before he comes to us'. These words pleased the brothers and they took palm branches from the palm trees and went to the place called 'Lithazomenon' outside the city.[95] The whole chorus of monks waited there; no one dared to go into the city because their father had ordered them not to.

* Ps 32:10 (33:10)

The Miracle on the Battlefield

33. Then the emperor's officer came to wage war against the monks. When his troops reached the

monks, he ordered the army to shoot arrows at the crowd of monks, so the soldiers shot their arrows at them. But what great miracle took place! The soldiers stood and shot their arrows at the chorus of monks and not one of them was harmed! And all of them said this hymn in unison: 'My trust is in the Lord; how will you say to our soul, "Flee to the mountains like a sparrow, for look, the wicked bend their bows, they have fitted their arrows to the string, to shoot their arrows secretly at the upright in heart,"'* and '"The wicked have drawn their swords, they have bent their bows, in order to attack someone who is poor and wretched, to slay the upright in heart.'⁹⁶ Truly their swords entered their own hearts, their arrows broke.'"* That mighty soldier, Apa Longinus, who fought to the death for the truth,⁹⁷ who showed that he dwelled under the shadow of the Almighty,* was not afraid to face the arrows flying through the air but made his profession of faith like a conscript, saying, 'His truth will surround you like these weapons, you shall not fear an arrow that flies by day'.*

* Ps 10:1-2 (11:1-2)

* cf Ps 37:15-16

* Ps 90:1 (91:1)

* Ps 90:6 (91:4-5)

Apa Longinus Speaks to the Soldiers

34. With these words on his lips,⁹⁸ the mighty old man approached the army with great courage⁹⁹ as the soldiers shot their arrows, and the arrows were flying on this side and that, but none of them reached the noble Apa Longinus. When the court official saw his great courage, he was amazed that none of the arrows touched him, nor were any of the brothers harmed in any way. The soldiers suddenly jumped from their horses, prostrated themselves at the feet of Apa Longinus, and worshipped him and the brothers who were with him, asking their forgiveness for their insolence. When Apa Longinus saw their repentance

and their faith, he spoke to the official and the soldiers, saying, 'You saw that we fought and were prepared to do battle for the faith of our fathers, even unto death.[100] We beseech you to go to the laura of Enaton, where our fathers are, so we may ask them in the presence of your authorities for satisfaction from you and, as they command us in your presence, we are prepared to follow their words'.

The Holy Fathers of Enaton Denounce the Tome of Leo from their Tombs

35. The brothers were astonished at the words that Apa Longinus was saying in front of the ruler and the army, and they were saying to one another, 'But there's no one left in the laura who did not come here, is there?' Then they approached their father Apa Longinus and said, 'Father, do you not know that all of us are here and not one of us is missing? How will we give trouble to these men and trouble them to come to the laura?'[101] He, however, did not say a single word to them since he knew what he was going to do. Then all of them followed Apa Longinus, the court official along with all the brothers. He walked in front of them until he brought them to the tombs where their fathers were buried, those who had been the elders before his time, who had preserved the saving faith with firmness until they completed their lives, as it was pleasing to God. Then he stopped in the middle of the tombs. He spread his hands and prayed and commanded them to pray with him. When he had finished his prayer, they all said 'Amen' together.

36. Apa Longinus opened his mouth and shouted aloud in front of them, saying, 'My holy fathers, is it truly the wish of God that we accept the Tome of Leo and subscribe to it?'

Immediately a voice arose from the tombs where the bodies of the saints lay, three times saying 'Anathema to ungodly Leo's Tome! Do not speak his name nor be in communion with anyone who accepts that ordinance! Anathema to those who subscribe to the Tome of Leo! Anathema to Leo's blasphemous act, for it is full of blasphemy against the divinity of Christ because it divides Christ into two natures instead of maintaining the unity of Christ!'

When the court official and the whole army gathered there heard that voice coming from the midst of the bodies of the saints, they were astonished, and they prostrated themselves at the feet of Apa Longinus and the other monks who were with him, asking them to forgive them and to pray for them so they might come to know the truth. And suddenly many from the army renounced[102] their military status and the empty duties of this way of life and became monks and submitted themselves[103] to the authority of Saint Apa Longinus on account of the fear that had seized them.

The Orthodox Faith Triumphs over the Tome of Leo

37. The court official and the other soldiers returned to the city, proclaiming the wonders they had seen. When the citizens of the city heard about the mighty works and wonders that had taken place through Apa Longinus, strengthened[104] in their faith they went as a group to the praetorium. They brought out the prefect Acacius, who had forced them to be in communion with the Tome of Leo, and burned him in the middle of the city. I am not saying he was condemned to death simply because of these actions, but because it was a judgement of God's justice, pronounced through the mouth of Apa Longinus the

Great and the brothers who were with him as a prophecy that our father David spoke in the tenth psalm, which he sang like this: 'Fire and sulfur are the portion of their cup'.[105]* When the bishop of that false teaching[106] saw the uproar taking place, he took off his ecclesiastical garments and put on layman's clothing and left the city. He fled on account of the fear that had seized him and he has not been found to this day.[107] The Church boldly proclaimed the doctrines[108] of the orthodox faith and advanced through the encouragement and intercessions of the Holy Spirit.

* Ps 10:7 (11:6)

Apa Longinus' Nature

38. After standing his ground in battle, blessed Apa Longinus spent another twenty years as head of the monastery of the laura. He was deemed worthy to place his hands over the eyes of his father Apa Lucius, just as Joseph had placed his hands over the eyes of Jacob.[109]* Apa Longinus shepherded the brothers in all knowledge[110] and commanded them to flee vainglory, that is, the rule of all the passions.[111] (From vainglory comes the love of money, which is the root of evil; the love of money begets anger; anger begets vanity; <vanity>[112] begets envy, the evil wild beast.)* He also taught them to devote themselves zealously to handiwork whenever appropriate and to celebrate the Eucharist[113] in the fear of God. He was an example to the monks in everything, nurturing all of them, whether through food for their bodies or through the teaching of the Lord. For he was in their midst like a bishop, and everyone who wanted to live in accordance with God's law looked to him and modeled their lives according to the virtues he exhibited. For who hated vainglory like that man? Or who reached the heights[114] in daily practice like him, as he kept his thoughts

* cf Gen 50:1

* cf Qo 5:10,
  1 Tim 6:10

humble? For he was humble in every way: he always looked at the ground as he walked,[115] which was a way of walking in wisdom. For he never bore at this time the false dress of lying and deception,[116] giving the external appearance of being pious while being filled inside with hypocrisy and lawlessness.[117] Who was patient like Apa Longinus, who was patient with those who stumbled in their transgressions until he restored them to their original condition?

The Death of Apa Longinus

39. Living the monastic life this way, he departed this life to be with the Lord whom he loved on the second of Mshir, going to his rest with all his fathers whom he resembled in his perfect and virtuous life, that is, the patriarchs and prophets and apostles and all the saints who did the will of God. How great was the grief on the day he went to his rest! Not only his fellow monks, but also the city and district of Alexandria,[118] especially those living in the surrounding countryside,[119] cried out with loud voices and with tears because such a father as this had left them. And their cries and tears mixed with a hymn that they sang, the old men seeking the staff of their old age, the young men seeking the bridle for their chastity, those who had become novices in monastic obedience seeking the one who would lead them into the kingdom of heaven, those who were married seeking the one who established the law for them, the poor seeking the one who cared for them, those seeking healing for their illnesses, whether of body or soul. In short, his concern for all of them, whether monk or lay person, was to bring them to salvation, presenting all of them as saints for the Lord Jesus Christ,

to whom be the glory, with the Father and the
Holy Spirit, consubstantial and life-giving, now and
forever and ever. Amen.

NOTES

¹ The anti-chalcedonian story in pars. 29–37; see Tito Orlandi, ed., *Vite dei Monaci Phif e Longino* (Milan: Cisalpino-Goliardica, 1975) 44.

² Systematic Apophthegmata XV.114; Jean-Claude Guy, *Recherches sur la tradition grecque des Apophthegmata Patrum* (Brussells: Société des Bollandistes, 1962) 241. Whoever the author of the *Life* was, he correctly understood the monastic tradition linking Longinus with humility; see also Systematic Apophthegmata XV.113 (Guy, 241).

³ For an example of such a painting, which conveys a sad sense of loss, see J. E. Quibell, *Excavations at Saqqara*, vol. 4, *The Monastery of Apa Jeremias* (Cairo: IFAO, 1912) Plate VII.

⁴ The alphabetical apophthegms may be found in Longinus 1–5, of which 3 and 4 occur in the *Life*; for an english translation, see Benedicta Ward, trans., *The Sayings of the Desert Fathers*, CS 59, rev. ed. (Kalamazoo: Cistercian Publications, 1984) 122–123. According to Jean-Claude Guy, the systematic collection attributes seven apophthegms to Longinus; see Guy, *Recherches*, 241. Lucien Regnault lists five sayings in the alphabetical collection, ten in the anonymous series, and three in the systematic collection; see Lucien Regnault, *Les Sentences des pères du désert* (Sablé-sur-Sarthe: Solesmes, 1976) 327.

⁵ Orlandi (above, n. 1), 44. For a parallel case, the Life of John the Little, see Maged S. Mikhail and Tim Vivian, trans., 'Life of Saint John the Little', *Coptic Church Review* 18:1-2 (Spring/Summer 1997) 1–64.

⁶ Lucius 1 (Ward, CS 59:120-121) and Longinus 1 (Ward, CS 59:122).

⁷ Theodore of Enaton 2 (CS 59:79).

⁸ See H. G. Evelyn White, *The Monasteries of the Wadi 'N Natrun*, volume 2: *The History of the Monasteries of Nitria and of Scetis* (1932; rpt. New York: Arno, 1973) 50, 52. Ward, CS 59:79, makes the identification and supplies the dates, but I have not found confirmation for the latter. See Or 1 (CS 59:246) and 8 (CS 59:247).

⁹ On this monastery, see Jean Gascou, 'Enaton, The', *The Coptic Encyclopedia*, ed. Aziz S. Atiya (New York: Macmillan, 1991) 3.954-958.

¹⁰ This can be seen from the ethiopic version, which includes only the equivalent of pars. 29–37; see Sylvain Grébaut, 'La Prière de Langinos', *Revue de l'orient chrétien* 15 (1910) 42–52. References here are to Grébaut's french translation. See Orlandi (above, n. 1), 45, for a discussion. As Orlandi points out, 42, what we have is the last stage of redaction, what he considers the union of many, originally independent, episodes. At some stage there was a 'Life' (pars. 5–39), with its own title, to which was added a homiletical prologue (pars. 1–4). The original 'Life' may itself be a composite of ascetic teaching on humility and vainglory combined with

276 Words to Live By

the anti-chalcedonian material. The *Synaxarium Alexandrinum* (2 Amsir) summarizes the *Life;* see Iacobus Forget, trans., *Synaxarium Alexandrinum* (rpt. Louvain: Imprimerie Orientaliste L. Durbecq, 1953 [1922]) 1.455-56.

[11] For a general discussion of the Council and its aftermath in Church history, see W. H. C. Frend, *The Rise of Christianity* (Philadelphia: Fortress, 1984) chapters 21, 23, and 24.

[12] See n. 1 above.

[13] For the context, see Frend, *The Rise of the Monophysite Movement* (Cambridge: Cambridge University Press, 1972) 143–183; for details on the story reported in the *Life, ibid.,* 155. See also Orlandi (above, n. 1), 44. On Alexandria and its propensity for turmoil, see Christopher Haas, *Alexandria in Late Antiquity: Topography and Social Conflict* (Baltimore: Johns Hopkins, 1997).

[14] John Rufus, *Plerophoriae* 7; F. Nau, ed., *Jean Rufus, Évêque de Maïouma, Plérophories,* Patrologia Orientalis 8.1 (Paris: Firmin-Didot, 1912) 18–20. John goes on to say (10; Nau, 25) that 'the day that the impious Marcian was proclaimed emperor and put on the crown, thick darkness suddenly covered the whole earth and sand came from on high; the darkness was like that which covered Egypt [see Ex 10:21-23]'.

[15] Evagrius Scholasticus, *Ecclesiastical History* 2.8; *The Ecclesiastical History of Evagrius,* ed. J. Bidez and L. Parmentier (Amsterdam: Hakkert, 1964) 55. The wonderfully worded translation is from *A History of the Church by Evagrius* (London: Samuel Bagster, 1846) 69–70.

[16] He specifically lists Enaton, Oktodekaton, and Eikoston, that is, monasteries that lay nine, eighteen, and twenty miles outside the city. John Rufus, *Peter the Iberian,* ed. R. Raabe, *Petrus der Iberer: Ein Charakterbild zur Kirchen- und Sittengeschichte des fünften Jahrhunderts* (Leipzig, 1895) 64. I wish to express my gratitude to Jennifer Hevelone-Harper for translating this section from Syriac.

[17] As Timothy II, he was the anti-Chalcedonian pope from 457–477. See Zacharius of Mytilene, *Syriac Chronicle* 4.1; F. J. Hamilton and E. W. Brooks, trans., *The Syriac Chronicle Known as that of Zachariah of Mytilene* (London: Methuen, 1899; rpt. New York: AMS, 1979) 64–66. Peter the Iberian and two other bishops laid hands on Timothy; see Frend, *Rise* (above, n. 13), 155.

[18] Evagrius, ed. Bidez and Parmentier, 56; *A History,* 70.

[19] Evagrius, ed. Bidez and Parmentier, 58; *A History,* 73.

[20] Theodore Lector, *Ecclesiastical History* 1.8; *Patrologia Graeca* 86.1: 169B. John Rufus, an anti-chalcedonian, has, as one would expect, a different view, charging that the Council of Chalcedon was 'assembled and directed by the Devil, and is the precursor of the Antichrist'. John Rufus, *Plerophoriae* 26 (Nau, ed., 67).

[21] Zacharius, *Syriac Chronicle* 4.1 (cited above).

[22] Evagrius, ed. Bidez and Parmentier, 56; *A History,* 71.

[23] It must be said that Evagrius is surprisingly fair here, citing Zacharius as corroboration 'that the greater part of the circumstances thus detailed actually occurred', but that the latter historian believed that events came about 'through the fault of Proterius' (ed. Bidez and Parmentier, 59; *A History,* 74).

[24] Getatchew Haile, 'An Ethiopic Letter of Timothy II of Alexandria Concerning the Death of Children', *Journal of Theological Studies,* NS, 38.1 (April 1987) 34–57, at 53.

[25] Evagrius, ed. Bidez and Parmentier, 56; *A History,* 71. See Frend, *Monophysite,* 155.

²⁶ Orlandi, 44, believes that Longinus was head of a group of monks who consecrated Timothy, while Frend, *Rise* (above, n. 13), 155, says that there was 'a small committee of monks and dissident clerics led by Longinus'. Neither the *Life* nor Zacharius supports these conclusions.

²⁷ It is not surprising that the anti-chalcedonian accounts—Zacharius of Mytilene and the *Life of Longinus*—agree that Proterius was not murdered; such a crime does not do their side honor. It is much better to have a miscreant government official die. The *Life of Peter the Iberian* makes Proterius and the 'commander' Dionysius the villains; it terms the latter 'a deadly and fiercely raging man'.

²⁸ Orlandi (above, n. 1), 44; Timothy did not return until 475 and died in 477.

²⁹ As Evagrius laconically concludes (ed. Bidez and Parmentier, 59; *A History*, 74): 'In consequence, however, of these proceedings, Stilas is sent out by the emperor to chastise them [that is, the Alexandrians]'.

³⁰ Translated from the text edited by Orlandi, 46–92. Paragraph divisions follow those of Orlandi, except for pars. 24, 25, and 27, which I have subdivided to better indicate individual pericopes. Section titles are my own and differ slightly from Orlandi's table of contents, 43.

³¹ 'Citizenship' translates *politeuma*, whereas 'way of life' renders *polêtia*. In the superscription, *polêtia*, 'ascetic practice', is paired with *bios*, 'life'.

³² Coptic *histôria* = Gk *historia*.

³³ 'Contests and struggles': -*athlôn* and -*agôn*, key greek terms in monastic spirituality, borrowed from athletic and military imagery, that depict the monastic undertaking.

³⁴ The rock is 'high' (*jose*) just as the virtues of the saints are 'lofty' (*jise*).

³⁵ The author of the *Life* is speaking of Mount Tabor and the Transfiguration; see Mt 17:1-3, Mk 9:2-13, Lk 9: 28-36.

³⁶ The attribution of Hebrews to Paul in late antiquity was nearly universal. 'Greatness' translates *jise*, as seen above, n. 34.

³⁷ The attribution of Proverbs to Solomon was also almost universal.

³⁸ Lycia was a mountainous country in southwest Asia Minor.

³⁹ 'Citizen': *politês*; 'citizenship': *politeuma*.

⁴⁰ The use of 'philosophy' for Christianity and then monasticism is a common patristic use.

⁴¹ The *Synaxarium Alexanandrinum* (Forget [above, n.10], 1:455) aptly summarizes: 'he loved Christ and fled human glory'.

⁴² Coptic/Gk *politeue*.

⁴³ The *Synaxarium Alexanandrinum* (Forget, 1:455) says they went to Syria.

⁴⁴ 'Theoctistus' is a compound of *theos*, 'God', and *ktistos*, from Gk. *ktizein*, 'to build'. 'Edify' in English retains the etymological remembrance of building: 'to build up'. In Coptic, 'built', in 'that which is built', is *kot-*, while 'edified' is *kôt*.

⁴⁵ Literally: vainglory, as it will be translated below.

⁴⁶ 'Silence': Coptic *ezechia* = Gk *hêsuchia*.

⁴⁷ Orlandi believes, 59 n. 13, that the command to pray at the martyrium of Saint Menas is an interpolation by the last redactor (see par. 17 below). The martyrium of Saint Menas was in the western desert of Mareotis (Maryut), near Alexandria. In 1960 Pope Cyril VI refounded Dayr Abu Mina near there; one can today see the two sites from each other. See Mounir Shoucri, 'Dayr Abu Mina', *The Coptic Encyclopedia*, 3:706-707. On Menas himself, see Martin Krause, 'Menas the Miracle Worker, Saint', *The Coptic Encyclopedia* 5:1589-1590. With regard to

the martyrium, Peter Grossmann believes that 'the crypt below the Martyr-church contained the grave of St. Menas and was the focus of his cult. According to the historical sources (written centuries after the saint's death whose facts are not always confirmed by archaeological evidence), the remains of St. Menas were contained in a shrine above ground, a tetrapylon styled mausoleum (encomium, eighth century, fol. 63-65). Only later, according to the sources, was he buried in a crypt. Archaeologists have found a later fourth century brick superstructure above the crypt, although it is not yet clear that this was in fact the tetrapylon, a building which rested on four pillars and was open from all sides'. See Peter Grossmann, *Abu Mina: A Guide to the Ancient Pilgrimage Center* (Cairo: Fotiadis & Co. Press-Cairo, 1986) 16.

[48] Coptic/Gk: *henaton*, the ninth mile marker, which was also the name of the monastery. Other monasteries were at the eighteenth (*oktôdekaton*) and twentieth (*eikoston*) milestones.

[49] Coptic/Gk: *eulabês*, which might also mean devout or pious men. But *eulabês* can suggest clergy or monastics as opposed to seculars; see Lampe 567B(2).

[50] 'Quiet' is almost an epithet attributed to Longinus; in par. 8 the village to which the saints flee is quiet.

[51] Coptic *anabolos* = Gk *analabos*.

[52] Coptic *hethos* = Gk *ethos*, which is interesting etymologically. *Ethos* means 'custom or habit', and seems to mean a monastic habit here, as in latin (*habitus*) and english usage, but Lampe (407AB) does not cite its use to designate a monastic habit. On monastic clothing see Paul van Moorsel, *Les Peintures du Monastère de Saint-Antoine près de la Mer Rouge*, La peinture murale chez les Coptes, Mémoires publiés par les membres de l'institut français d'archéologie orientale du Caire CXII (Cairo: IFAO, 1998) Chapter 6.2.B, 'Le vêtement monastique', 64–72.

[53] Thus Longinus was wearing a short-sleeve shirt (*kolobion*) and cloak (*pallion*).

[54] The Coptic *mmokhs mn ouhise* might mean 'toil and labor', but they equally suggest 'pain and suffering'.

[55] Gk: *eulogia*, which can mean 'benediction or blessing', and can refer to the consecration of the bread at the eucharist or the consecrated elements themselves, then a gift of bread that has been blessed (see Lampe 570A); see par. 15, and Chapter Nine, n. 104.

[56] According to Saint Jerome's *Life of Paul* 9, Antony remained outside Paul's door from nightime until noon 'and even longer', but the words attributed to him from Scripture by the author of the *Life of Longinus* are not in Jerome's account.

[57] *Hêgoumenos*, like *proestôs*, means the superior of the monastery.

[58] *Spoudê* is a monastic virtue as early as the *Life of Antony* 4.1.

[59] Coptic *epehouo*. *Houo* also suggests 'excessively', which our author undoubtedly intends. In the next sentence *houo*, 'especially', signals the instructions of Apa Lucius to flee such praise.

[60] Coptic/Gk *scholakin*, which occurs six times in the *Life*. The word, though certainly Greek in origin, is unattested. Its closest sources appear to be *scholê*, 'leisure, rest', and then 'study, attention', and *scholazein*, 'have leisure', then 'devote one's time to something, be intent on something' (see Lampe, 1360–61). Its meaning, therefore, seems to be 'a little [-kin] something to pass the time', analogous to Italian *passatempo* and modern Greek *kombolion*, the rope and beads ('worry beads') used to pass the time. Campagnano's translation of *gomena*,

'hawser', given the context, seems reasonable. Because of the uncertainty of the word's meaning, however, I will use the more generic term 'rope'.

⁶¹ The latter quotation Paul attributes to Jesus.

⁶² The *Synaxarium Alexanandrinum* (Forget [above, n.10], 1:455) omits virtually all of the events related above about Longinus at Enaton, saying only that he stayed there until, on the death of the abbot, he was made archpriest of the monastery because of his outstanding way of life.

⁶³ 'Meditating', *meletan*, usually means quietly reciting the scriptures, most often the psalms. As Douglas Burton-Christie has memorably put it,'And there is the slow, gentle hum—a kind of white noise in the desert—of words being ruminated, repeated ceaselessly, leading toward what Cassian described as a simplification of the mind and heart'. See his 'Oral Culture and Biblical Interpretation in Early Egyptian Monasticism', *Studia Patristica*, 30, ed. Elizabeth A. Livingstone (Leuven: Peeters, 1997) 144–150: 148. While practising this discipline of psalmody, the anchorites may have alternated work, standing prayer, and prostrations; see Luke Dysinger, OSB, 'The Significance of Psalmody in the Mystical Theology of Evagrius of Pontus', *Studia Patristica*, 30:177, and his references to Cassian, *Institutes*, 2.11-12, and Palladius, *Lausiac History* 22.5-8 and 43.2-3.

⁶⁴ The LXX has *echinos*, 'hedgehog', instead of 'deer'. Since our author says deer track down snakes, perhaps he associated *echinos*, 'hedgehog', with *echidna*, 'adder, viper'.

⁶⁵ See Alphabetical Apophthegmata Longinus 3 (Ward, CS 59:123) for another version of this story.

⁶⁶ This parenthesis, added by the editor of the *Life* (it is not in the saying represented by the *Apophthegmata*), is reminiscent of Mk 5:26.

⁶⁷ See par. 17.

⁶⁸ See *Life of Antony* Preface 3.

⁶⁹ Coptic *dumiourgos* = Gk *dēmiourgos*, 'Demiurge'.

⁷⁰ On Longinus' 'protection', see par. 19 above.

⁷¹ See Systematic Apophthegmata 19.7 (Guy, 241; Regnault, 106).

⁷² See Systematic Apophthegmata 19.9 (Guy, 241; Regnault, 106).

⁷³ See Systematic Apophthegmata 18.12 (Guy, 241).

⁷⁴ On laying hands on the eyes, see par. 38.

⁷⁵ See Alphabetical Apophthegmata Longinus 4 (Ward, CS 59:123).

⁷⁶ This is a common theme in the *Apophthegmata*; see the index in Ward, CS 59:261, under 'Judgement'.

⁷⁷ This Apa Theodore has three sayings attributed to him in the *Apophthegmata* under Theodore of Enaton (Ward, CS 59:79).

⁷⁸ See Systematic Apophthegmata 18.11 (Guy, 241).

⁷⁹ John Moschus, *Pratum spirituale* 73, says that a soldier in Alexandria lived at a monastery near the steps of Saint Peter's. This presumably refers to the Church of Saint Peter in the western part of the city, dedicated to Bishop Peter I (d. 311). Peter had apparently had a cemetery built there and a church dedicated to the Virgin. [See *John Moschos: The Spiritual Meadow*, translated John Wortley, CS 139 (Kalamazoo: Cistercian Publications, 1992) 55f.] According to Peter's *Passio*, he was brought there and buried after his martyrdom, and thus the church came to be called Saint Peter's; see Tim Vivian, *Saint Peter of Alexandria: Bishop and Martyr* (Philadelphia: Fortress, 1988) 77. On the site, see Henri Leclercq, 'Alexandrie,

Archéologie', in Fernand Cabrol and Henri Leclercq, eds., *Dictionnaire d'archéologie chrétienne* (Paris: Letouzet et Ané, 1907–53) 1:1118 and 1142.

[80] Another version of this story appears in an encomium of Macarius of Tkow, which is falsely attributed to Dioscurus of Alexandria; in it, the protagonist is Longinus, but the episode takes place not at Enaton but in an unnamed monastery in Lycia. Enaton seems to be the original locale of the story, not Lycia; see Orlandi, 44, for a discussion. The ethiopic version begins here; see Grébaut, 'La Prière de Langinos'.

[81] Gk: *magistrianos*, an official of the staff of the *magister officiorum*.

[82] Leo, in our author's view, is *asebês*, 'ungodly, impious', the opposite of *eusebês*, 'pious, godly', which has the added connotation of 'orthodox'. Both sides of the chalcedonian dispute used 'the language of orthodoxy' to fortify their own position and assault that of their enemies; see James E. Goehring, *Ascetics, Society, and the Desert: Studies in Early Egyptian Monasticism* (Harrisburg, Pennsylvania: Trinity, 1999) 245–246.

[83] Marcian was Emperor of the East from 450–457. The Council of Chalcedon, which accepted the Tome of Leo as defining the orthodox faith, bestowed on the emperor the title 'Protector of the True Faith'.

[84] Coptic/Gk *dogma*.

[85] Coptic/Gk *dikaiôma*, which may have sounded like a combination of *dikaios*, 'just, righteous', and *dogma*, as opposed to the *dogma* of the emperor.

[86] See *Life of Antony* 82.4-8, where Antony foresees the persecution of the Church by Arians. Such foresight about Chalcedon is a common occurence in the *Plerophoriae* of John Rufus.

[87] Here the Tome is *atnoute*, the coptic equivalent of *a-theos*, 'without God'.

[88] The monks are *mainoute*, the opposite of *atnoute*.

[89] 'Supreme ruler' is *autokratôr*; see the next note.

[90] There is a deliberate juxtaposition here and at the end of the paragraph: 'Almighty' translates *pantôkratôr*, whereas 'supreme ruler' is *autokratôr*; 'cares for' renders -*euergetai*, whereas 'benefactor' (an appellation of the emperor in par. 31) is *euergetês*.

[91] Coptic/Gk -*koinonei*, translated above as 'communion'.

[92] According to Apa Theodore, Pachomius had praised Athanasius, 'who struggles for the faith even to the point of death'. See SBo 134; Armand Veilleux, trans., *Pachomian Koinonia* (Kalamazoo: Cistercian Publications, 1980) 1 (CS 45) 192.

[93] The *Synaxarium Alexanandrinum* (Forget [above, n. 10], 1:456) omits entirely the events of pars. 32–35, resuming with the scene related in par. 36.

[94] God sets aside the 'designs' (*shojne*) that the officials had 'decided' on (*ji shojne*); the Lord defeats the plans of the earthly lord.

[95] *Lithazomenon* literally means 'stoned'. John Moschus, *Pratum spirituale* 69 [CS 139:51ff], says that an Abba Palladius had his monastery there

[96] 'Poor and wretched' (-*hêke* and -*ebiên*) may well be a conscious self-understanding and self-designation (see Ps 69:6 (LXX = RSV 70:5); see Paul of Tamma, *On the Cell* 5, 9, 13, 69, and 97, Chapter Five above.

[97] See n. 91 (par. 31) above.

[98] Coptic/Gk -*meleta*, the same word translated as 'meditate' earlier.

[99] 'Courage' translates *mntjarhêt* while 'mighty' renders *jôôre*; *jar* and *jôôre* both come from *jro*, 'be strong'.

Notes 281

[100] On the role that 'the faith of the fathers' played in the chalcedonian conflict, see Goehring (above, n. 82), 246.

[101] This sentence is a bit awkward in Coptic. 'Give trouble' translates *-oueh hise*, which may be a translation of Gk *kopon parechein*; 'trouble' renders Coptic/Gk *-skullei (skullein)*, which is essentially a synonym of the first verb, with the added sense of 'annoy'. The verbs together are redundant, and it is unlikely that the Gk text used both in such close proximity.

[102] 'Renounced', Gk *apotasse*, is often the word used for monastic renunciation of the world; see the last sentence Longinus speaks in par. 27.

[103] Coptic *hupotakê* (= Gk *hupotagê*), playing on *apotasse*; they share the same root TAG.

[104] Coptic *-tajro*; see n. 98 above.

[105] This is one of the rare instances in monastic literature (the only one I recall seeing) where the number of the psalm is given.

[106] Gk *hairesis*.

[107] The ethiopic version ends here.

[108] Coptic/Gk *dogma*, which above has been translated as 'ordinance' and 'tome'.

[109] See par. 26.

[110] Gk *epistêmê*, which might also mean 'discipline'; see Lampe 535A(II).

[111] The *Apophthegmata* preserve a striking saying by Apa Longinus on the passions (Ward, CS 59:123): 'A woman knows she has conceived when she no longer loses any blood. So it is with the soul, she knows she has conceived the Holy Spirit when the passions stop coming out of her. But as long as one is held back in the passions, how can one dare to believe one is sinless? Give blood and receive the Spirit'.

[112] Instead of 'vanity', which should follow in progression, the coptic text repeats 'anger', but the scribe probably skipped over 'vanity' and saw 'anger' and so mistakenly repeated it.

[113] Gk *sunaxis*.

[114] There is a sly play on words here: 'heights' renders *-jose*, which Apa Longinus reaches through his aversion to vainglory; above, vainglory leads to vanity and arrogance, *jasi nhêt. Jose* and *jasi* come from the same root, *jise*, 'to elevate, exalt, raise high'. Early monastic spirituality often emphasizes 'the heights of humility'.

[115] Embedded in this clause in Coptic is *paht*, which means 'to bend oneself', and can mean 'to prostrate oneself' as a sign of humility and deference, which occurs several times in the *Life*. On prostration, see Chapter Six above.

[116] 'Dress' renders *schêma*, which can also suggest the monastic habit.

[117] 'Lawlessness', *anomia*, may also suggest 'unlawful opinion', therefore 'heresy', the opposite of *eusebês*, 'pious', which often carries the added connotation of 'orthodox' (see n. 82 above), an important virtue to the writer of the *Life*.

[118] Coptic *tosh*, translated as 'district' here, may more specifically mean 'nome' or 'diocese'.

[119] Is this a suggestion that the city was strongly chalcedonian while the outlying areas were anti-chalcedonian?

8

The Ascetic Discourse of Stephen of Thebes

Introduction

STEPHEN OF THEBES

Although a number of works are attributed to Stephen of Thebes, we know virtually nothing about him. Joseph-Marie Sauget, a modern editor of his work, has reflected on this fact:

> That an individual completely ignored by history was able to survive complete oblivion thanks solely to the preservation of his literary work is not a surprising development. This seems, in fact, quite normal when we are dealing with an ascetic, whether anchorite or cenobite, whose entire life aspired to humility, detachment from the world, and flight from vainglory. Along with many others of his monastic brethren this was, at all events, the fate of Stephen of Thebes, whose name no chronicle seems to have preserved, about whom no disciple has recorded, for purposes of edification, even the briefest of accounts.[1]

Stephen was a monk. He wrote in Greek, which indicates some level of formal education. The *Ascetic Discourse* demonstrates that he was also a monastic teacher, with enough experience of the ascetic desert to pass that way of life on to a disciple. Presumably he was from Thebes (Luxor) or lived there as a monk. We have no dates for him. This paucity of information has led one scholar (too skeptically in my mind) to doubt his existence.[2] The monk who copied the *Ascetic Discourse* in 885 at the Monastery of Saint Sabas in Palestine identified it as belonging to Stephen of Thebes. The question remains, however: Why is Stephen *of Thebes* not known in our sources before the ninth century?[3] In Stephen's case, eremitical silence only deepens historical silence.

In addition to the *Ascetic Discourse (Logos Askêtikos)*, three other works are attributed to Stephen: *Precepts (Entolai)*, *Regulations (Diataxis)*, and 'Precepts for those who Desire to be Saved'.[4] All of these are problematic. The *Diataxis* and *Entolai*, greek works of only a few pages, are really extracts from precepts attributed to Saint Antony and Saint Isaiah of Scetis, while the 'Precepts' is a slavic translation from Isaiah's works.[5] Therefore, only the *Ascetic Discourse* can claim Stephen as its author. Although we know very little about Stephen, and nothing of his dates, his connection in manuscripts with Isaiah of Scetis and Paul of Tamma seems to place him in the fifth century. His thought and way of life is certainly at home with theirs, and the style and tone of the *Ascetic Discourse* is strikingly similar to Isaiah's *Logoi*.[6]

THE ASCETIC DISCOURSE

Stephen's *Ascetic Discourse* exists most fully in Greek,[7] with less complete arabic[8] and georgian versions having been published.[9] There are also syriac extracts,[10] as well as coptic fragments.[11] Portions of the *Discourse*, #38–43 and 72–74, are also incorporated within 'An Untitled Work' attributed to Paul of Tamma (Chapter Five above; see the discussion below), and #78 from the arabic version made its way into the ethiopic monastic collection.[12] Stephen's work, therefore, had wide diffusion in the christian east. The earliest-known arabic manuscript, translated directly from Greek, though not complete, is well attested and forms the base of the published arabic edition.[13] It was copied in 885 at the Monastery of Saint Sabas in Palestine by a certain Isaac and made its way thence to Mount Sinai. The *Discourse* was known to Copts at the beginning of the thirteenth century. Around 1230, al-Safi ibn al-'Assal published an epitome of it. It is also attested in two fifteenth-century manuscripts.[14] The georgian version comes from a tenth-century manuscript containing other ancient monastic texts, including letters by Antony, Ammonas, and Arsenius, and represents less than half of the greek text. It too journeyed to Sinai from Saint Sabas'.[15] Thus Stephen, though little known to us, was recognized far and wide in antiquity and was associated with some of the greatest monastic luminaries.

STEPHEN OF THEBES AND PAUL OF TAMMA

There is, as was mentioned above, a very close correspondence between Stephen's *Ascetic Discourse* and a fragmentary, untitled work attributed to Paul of Tamma.[16] One scholar has argued that the untitled piece can not belong to Paul, in spite of the attribution in the manuscripts.[17] Paragraphs 100–112 and 200–220 of Paul's 'An Untitled Work' parallel #38–43 and 72–74 of the *Ascetic Discourse*. Paragraphs 113–118, however, the remaining portion, do not show any correspondence with #44–71 of Stephen's work; equally, #44–71 of the *Ascetic Discourse*, a large portion of the work, has no parallels with Paul's 'Untitled Work'. Given that the *Ascetic Discourse* was written in Greek, one would normally assume that *it* was written first and that Paul's 'Untitled Work' was a coptic translation. But the fact that sections of each work show no correspondence with the other might suggest that each is dependent on an earlier, greek, source. What does a closer look at the two texts reveal?

A close comparison of the two works suggests that Paul's 'Untitled Work' is a translation of portions of Stephen's *Ascetic Discourse*. It is possible, of course, that the latter could be a translation of the former, but examples of greek translations from coptic are extremely rare; more decisively, the Greek gives no indication of being a translation. For the most part, 'An Untitled Work' closely follows the *Ascetic Discourse*, even in duplicating repetition of words and in using the same greek vocabulary.[18] There are places, however, that clearly demonstrate the secondary nature of the Coptic: in paragraphs 102 (= #39) and 112 (= #43) a saying in Greek is converted into a scriptural allusion in Coptic where there was none before. (One assumes here that such changes would not go in the other direction: references to Scripture are not normally dropped.)

Finally, and most conclusively, there are examples of the coptic text having expanded the Greek.

1) In #72 of the *Ascetic Discourse*, the admonition 'Do not obey your heart but have your heart obey you so you may be obedient to God' has been expanded into two sentences in paragraphs 210–211 of 'An Untitled Work': 'Do not obey your heart but on the contrary let your heart obey you. Do not let your heart be your god but on the contrary let your heart obey God';

2) #72 of the *Ascetic Discourse* contains the gnomic sentence 'Do not be like the trees in the mountain that produce dry, bitter fruit but be like the reeds in the water that produce soft, juicy fruit'. In paragraphs 203–204 of 'An Untitled Discourse' this becomes 'Do not be like the thorny acacias that grow on the mountain, which is God. Instead, be like a reed growing in the water, which is the abyss'. The Coptic adds two explanatory glosses ('which is . . .') symbolically interpreting 'mountain' and 'water'. Moreover, these glosses contain a play on words in Coptic: 'God' is *pnoute* while 'abyss' is *pnoun*.

These examples show that 'An Untitled Work' is for the most part a translation of the *Ascetic Discourse*. As a result, we have the unusual situation where Paul is better attested historically than Stephen, yet Stephen's work appears to offer the primary text.

STRUCTURE AND SPIRITUALITY OF THE DISCOURSE

At first glance, the *Ascetic Discourse* seems to be a potpourri or, less pleasing, a hodgepodge, with little discernible structure. The numbering of the text, apparently ancient, does not help matters: it is often haphazard and occasionally chaotic. On closer inspection, however, one sees that the *logoi*, short pithy sayings, are like the sayings of the desert fathers and mothers, the *Apophthegmata*, or the 'centuries' of Evagrius of Pontus. On a larger level, too, the *Discourse* does reveal a structure, dividing into two unequal sections: #1–78 provide monastic counsel (all the parallels with Paul of Tamma occur in this section); #79–108, half the length of the first part, continue this counsel with spiritual exegeses of Scripture. Such a structure may also be found in the *Logoi* of Isaiah of Scetis.[19]

This view, however, may obscure the trees for the sake of the forest, the trees in this case being the individual sayings, with their roots deep in Scripture. *All* of the *Ascetic Discourse* is spiritual exegesis of Scripture. If we look below the surface, we will see the *Discourse* at a subterranean level, where it gets its nutrients, where it is in fact an interlocking network of scriptural roots. Such rootedness places Stephen's writing squarely within the monastic world of the *Apophthegmata* and the *Life of Antony*, to name just two of the most famous examples.[20]

The modern edition of the *Ascetic Discourse* comprises twenty-three pages, and in those pages there are around one hundred fifty references to the Bible.[21] The world of the *Discourse* is the universe of the Bible. Although direct quotations occur far less often than do indirect references and allusions, the Bible is assumed in every sentence, almost every word. But it is the Bible read 'spiritually', allegorically and topically, in a way by which biblical 'facts' point to deeper 'spiritual' truths. Stephen's first sentence provides a perfect illustration of both his method and his spirituality. This is the word remembered and kept alive in the present; the word becomes pregnant with meaning and association and is ever giving birth. Stephen is

> making a text memorable, that is to say, operative over time in the deepest parts of the consciousness of the one to whom the word is given. The word is re-membered again and again in the monk's heart, and it continues to bear fruit there.[22]

At work here, we must remember, is the monastic practice of rumination on Scripture in the desert. There 'prayer without ceasing'—that is, the constant uttering of Scripture on the lips—becomes the outward and visible sign of an inward and spiritual grace, transforming not only 'the deepest parts of the consciousness' but also the very fabric of one's physical reality. In other words, one's entire being.

'First of all, child', Stephen declares, 'renounce the world. Renounce your country, your parents [see Gn 12:1]. Renounce what is material and visible, that is, the cares of this world [see Mk 4:19, Lk 8:14], so you may see the good kingdom of heaven'. The monk, suffused with Scripture, knowing large parts of it by heart, would immediately hear in Stephen's exhortation to renounce parents and country God's call to Abraham. But Abraham is not some remote figure: in obeying God's call to renunciation, the monk *actually becomes Abraham*. And he–like Abraham—would know God's promise (Gn 12:2): 'I will make of you a great nation, and I will bless you, and make your name great, so that you will be a blessing'. This, then, becomes the subtext, the foundation, of the entire *Discourse:* the monastic life entails renunciations, hardships, and privations, even hand-to-hand combat, *but it is a blessing. It is God's calling.* The monk, therefore, does not 'go it alone', but like Abraham, Moses, Isaiah, and all the saints (# 25-28), he lives within the embrace of salvation history.[23]

But mimesis and identification, as deep as they are with Abraham, go much deeper yet. 'Observe your teacher', Stephen says, 'how he walked in humility, providing us with an example so we might follow closely in his footsteps' (# 24). That teacher, as the scriptural allusions (Mt 11:29 and 1 Pt 2:21) have undoubtedly made clear, is Christ.[24] Stephen opens his *Discourse* with 'renounce' *(apotassou)*, the clarion call of monasticism; he repeats it twice in the first sentence and seventeen more times in the first eight sentences. In that single word the disciple would hear not just Abraham but Christ: 'None of you can become my disciple if you do not give up *[apotassetai]* all your possessions' (Lk 14:33). These possessions, 'material and visible', are 'the cares of this world'; the monk would surely recall that such cares, in Jesus' parable, choke the seeds that fall, not on good earth, but on thorns (Lk 8:14). Stephen will later return to this image and promise (#92): the monk 'is sown in good earth, bringing forth fruit a hundredfold'.

The monastic vocation, like following Christ, is not (or should not be) a part-time vocation. The monk is 'someone who bears the cross' (#60). At the beginning of his call to his disciple, Stephen may also be pointing to Jesus' call to the kingdom of God in Luke 9:59-61. Those whom Jesus calls make excuses: one wants to bury his father, and Jesus rebukes him, saying, 'Let the dead bury their own dead'. Another responds, 'I will follow you, Lord; but let me first say farewell *[apotaxasthai]* to those at my home'. Jesus replies, 'No one who puts a hand to the plow and looks back is fit for the kingdom of God'. This is a saying to which Stephen will return (#95): 'Put your hands to the plow and do not turn back, but give your attention to what lies ahead [Phil 3:13], crying out and saying, "I will not give sleep to my eyes and slumber to my eyelids and rest to my temples until I find a place for the Lord, a dwelling place for the God of Jacob [Ps 132:4-5]"'. These scriptural framing devices provide Stephen's words with a cosmic, even eternal, canvas: the duty of the monk is to obey Christ's invitations to renunciation and to find within a dwelling place for God, to establish the kingdom of heaven.

Assumed here is the platonic and christian view that 'the material and visible' is not what is real; what is real, what the monk will see, is the invisible reality of the kingdom of heaven. This kingdom, Stephen insists, 'is not here or there but, in fact, "is within you"' (#78, Lk 17:21). With this assumption as a starting point, Stephen can pursue another seeming paradox (which is, in fact, not a paradox but a spiritual reality): the necessity of 'acquisitions'. Stephen's disciple would have understood at the outset the need to abandon everything but God, but such renunciation, in the monastic world of spiritual plenty, leads to numerous and rich possessions. This is one of those 'surprises' so common in Jesus' parables and in the *Apophthegmata*, unexpected words that grab the listener by the ear, or the throat, and demand attention.[25] Although (or, precisely, *because*) the monk gives up everything, he is to acquire *(ktênai)* 'good shame' (#10), 'good obedience' (#18), 'the habit of godliness' (#19) and wisdom (#99); 'whoever has acquired for himself the fear of God has acquired all good gifts. Whoever has the fear of God has a treasury filled with good things' (#51: Gn 22:12, Prov 1:7; see Sir 1:16-17). Although the monk gives up all desires, he is to 'long for every good word' (#32) and to 'profit' *(kerdainein)* from words, situations, and people (#33, 48, 58, 59, 100). With striking imagery, Stephen sums up this spiritual inversion: 'Renounce your desires and longings so you may purchase for yourself Christ, the root of all good things'. Such purchase (literally, *redemption*) has its prophetic basis in the Old Testament: 'I will divide my possessions with those who love me and their treasuries I will fill with good things' (#99, Prov 8:21).

Such treasure is a pearl of great price (#98), both valuable and costly. It can be acquired only by warfare. Not by murder and massacre, common to both Stephen's world and ours, but through spiritual warfare. Images of ancient monks sitting quietly at work and prayer are accurate but potentially misleading; they provide only a partial view, an exterior one. The interior is made more readily visible by all the images of fighting and warfare that one finds in early monastic literature. As Stephen says, the kingdom is within. In another seeming paradox—or spiritual reality—the kingdom is also the soul's bloody battleground. Barbarians are at the gate, but for Stephen the gate that needs guarding is the entry to the soul, and the barbarians are evil thoughts (#37, 63). King David is the 'type' *(tupos, prosôpon)* of this warfare: just as David 'physically battled with his enemies', the monk spiritually battles the evil thoughts that wage war against him (#67a–67b). The outcome, however, is never in doubt: God empowers the faithful to defeat their enemies, and they have Christ's promise as their sword and shield: 'I have given you authority to tread on snakes and scorpions, and over all the power of the Enemy, and nothing will hurt you' (#67c, Lk 10:19). The monk is to be like Joshua in battle: 'The enemies that wage war against you are the evil thoughts. Therefore ask for power for yourself, my son, and you will defeat those who do battle against you'. This is because 'God has not given us a spirit of cowardice, but rather of power and love' (#67d, 2 Tim 1:7).

'War is Peace' is modern doublespeak, pilloried by George Orwell in *1984* as he cast a cold eye on both fascism and communism. Now, after the end of the Cold War, it nevertheless remains the mantra of numerous dictators, politicians, and military-industrialists. In their mouths it is the great lie. But for Stephen of Thebes it is a spiritual truth: 'Fight, therefore . . . so you may remain at peace, and complete purity will surround you, for God loves holiness and for that reason he says, "I am holy and I am at peace in those who are holy", and "Blessed are the pure in heart, because they will see God"' (#107; Lev 11:44, Is 57:15, Mt 5:8). Such language, in the 'material and visible' world, can become the rhetoric of warlords, so we should exercise extreme caution in using it. It cannot be used against others, or against 'the other'. It cannot be used even against the self, although some misshapen forms of Christianity do so. It can only be used, as Stephen wisely teaches, *within* the self, within the human soul that is both battleground and kingdom. From within that place which has no earthly counterpart (here metaphor and language break down), neither kingdom nor battlefield, Stephen exhorts his disciple to 'pursue peace with everyone and the holiness without which no one will see the Lord' (#107, Heb 12:14). In closing, Stephen offers one final, paradoxical, image (with its origins probably in Jesus' admonition to be 'wise as serpents and innocent as doves'), one that is deeply moving, yet unsentimental, because it is hard won:

> Therefore, child, fight, so you may always remain in holiness, whether with your eyes or whether with your heart, so you may return to your original nature, like the little children about whom God has said, 'for to such as these belongs the kingdom of heaven' (#108, Mt 19:14).

Stephen, A Monk of Thebes
Ascetic Discourse[26]

RENUNCIATIONS

[1] First of all, child, renounce the world. Renounce your country, your parents.* Renounce what is material and visible, that is, the cares of this world,* so you may see the good kingdom of heaven. [2] Remove the veil from your heart so you may see;[27]* renounce the visible so you may see the invisible. [3] Let your heart have a watchman within so you will know what is moving you within,[28] because solid food is for the perfect, those who by means of tenacious observance[29] have, through training, acquired the ability to discern good and evil.[30]* Such discernment is the heart's watchman.† [4] Child, fear God[31]‡ and renounce arrogance. Renounce evil, renounce envy, renounce vainglory, renounce slander, renounce wordiness, [5] renounce [the desire for food and][32] what your eyes covet, renounce doubt, renounce puffed-up pride, renounce small-minded pettiness, renounce impatience and anger, renounce grumbling and being agitated.[33] [6] Child, do not be stubbornly assertive; renounce laughter and the desires of your belly, and do not get distracted. [7] Renounce making a mockery of people, and do not be contentious in any matter. Renounce wickedness and <religious frenzy>.[34] [8] Get rid of <empty>[35] worry and do not become listless.[38] Renounce lack of self-control. Do not give into your fears, lest you fall in battle.

* cf Gn 12:1
* cf Mk 4:19, Lk 8:14

* cf 2 Cor 3:12-16

* cf Heb 5:14, 1 Cor 3:2

† cf Ps 141:3 (140:3)

‡ see, among many, Gn 22:12, Dt 6:13, Ps 2:11, Prov 1:7

Flee from Various Sins

[9] Son, be <straightforward>[37] in all your works and words, for God loves <straight>[38] talk. [10] And do not be pleasure-loving nor shameless in appearance, but rather acquire for yourself good shame. Do not be inattentive, lest you die before your time.* [11] Child, do not be a lover of money, for this is the root of all evil.* [12] Do not be a dissembler,[39] nor desire what belongs to others. [13] Flee from sin, lest you become enslaved to desire. Do not be insatiable, but rather flee from sexual sin.[40] [14] Do not follow your fleshly desires but instead master them.* [15] Do not be a thief but keep away from lies. Do not be severe but gentle. [16] Child, do not be agitated and worldly, [17] and do not carry tales from place to place. [18] Child, acquire for yourself good obedience,[41] [19] and do not put on a false front[42] but acquire for yourself the habit of godliness. [20] Do not be an evil-doer or be deceitful; do not associate with crooks, for all such works belong to the old self.[43]

* cf Qo 7:17
* 1 Tim 6:10

* cf Eph 2:3

Be Gentle and Humble

[21] Child, fear God[44] and flee from all these things. Do not be rash but gentle, because 'the gentle will inherit the earth'.* [22] Be humble, for God is God of the humble.* [23] Humble your soul before God and the Devil will have no power over you. Be peaceful and humble with everyone. [24] Observe your teacher, how he walked in humility, providing us with an example so we might follow closely in his footsteps.[45]* [25] Son, observe all the saints, how they walked in humility. [26] Observe faithful Abraham, humbling himself and saying, 'I am earth and ashes'.* [27] Observe Moses,

* Mt 5:5
* cf Ps 25:9, Pr 3:4

* cf Mt 11:29, 1 Pet 2:21

* Gn 18:27

who says, 'I am slow of speech and a wisp of steam from a boiling pot'.* [28] Behold Isaiah, who cries out and says, 'All our righteous deeds are like a menstrual rag in your sight'.* [29] And the Saviour, teaching his followers, says, 'If you will do all these things, say, "We are worthless slaves; we have done only what we ought to have done"'.* [30] Those, therefore, who have sown upon good earth humble themselves before everyone, because the earth covers both the haughty and the humble and the eyes of the Lord watch over both.*

* cf Ex 4:10

* Is 64:6 (64:5 LXX)

* Lk 17:10

* cf Ps 102:19; Mt 13:8

Make Yourself Free for God

[31] Live your life without possessions, because poverty humbles a man.[46] Do not allow yourself anything except sufficient food and shelter; as for the rest, give it to those in need, as Christ commanded,[47]* so you will be free for God, and God will give you the knowledge to know him. [32] Make yourself free for God so your eyes may be uncovered. Son, abound in the work of God more than the work of the world.*

* cf Mt 5:42, 19:21

* cf 2 Cor 8:7, 9:8

Long for Every Good Word

[33] Long for every good word, and if you do not profit from a word, refuse to listen to it at all, for the Lord said in the Gospel, 'My sheep listen to my voice', and 'Whoever is from God hears the words of God'.* [34] Son, if you are sitting in the midst of your betters, wish to listen rather than speak.[48] Do not be reckless with your speech lest you become a braggart. [35] Be lord of your heart and bridle your tongue.* Do not eagerly listen to someone speak against someone else so you may be at peace with everyone, for all God's

* Jn 10:3, 27; 8:47

* cf Jas 1:26

saints are at peace and God dwells in them, for it is written, 'There is great peace for those who love your law'.* Those who love God, therefore, will be at peace with everyone. [36] Child, let every person be held in honor before you.

* Ps 119:165

Sitting in Your Cell

If you are sitting in your cell, do not allow your thought to wander outside.* Ask God, so you may know the things that are troubling[49] you. [37] Sitting in your cell, do not act like it is a tomb but rather behave like it is a banquet room filled with gold that has guards protecting it night and day. The 'guards' are the powers of God that protect your spirit,[50] that is, knowledge and faith and patience and abstinence, sincerity and innocence, purity and chastity, love, concord, and truth.[51] These are things that form a protective circle around a person so he won't lean to the right or the left.* This is the armor that a person puts on and with which he becomes powerful in battle and turns aside the enemy armies, that is, the evil thoughts that wage war with him.* [38] Child, if you are sitting in your cell, be like the skilled helmsman piloting his own vessel, carefully watching the wind to see what direction it is coming from, whether it is favorable or gusty.[52] Be strong in battle, crying out and saying, 'Wake up, north wind! Come on, south wind! Blow upon my garden and let my herbs give off their sweet odors!'[53]* [39] Sitting in your cell, do not act like a judge but make God your judge and jury.[54] [40] Do not grow weary of praying so God will hearken to you.[55] [41] When you are weary, hope for rest.[56] [42] Offer yourself to God with all your might* so God will fight for you* and pick you out and give you the power to do battle with those waging war against you, because without God

* cf Prov 7:12 (LXX)

* cf Prov 4:27

* cf Eph 6:11, 13

* Sg 4:16

* cf Lk 10:27
* cf Ex 14:14

you can do nothing,[57]* but if a person asks it of God, God gives him power and protection and knowledge and wisdom, and with his counsel God will guide him.[58]

* cf Jn 15:5

Keep a Close Watch over Yourself

[43] As you sit in your cell, do not wander around outside,[59]* but keep a close watch over yourself; furthermore, learn as you sit in your cell.[60] Do not be like an ox being driven but be like the person driving the ox.[61] As you sit in your cell, be on guard; do not have only your body in your cell while your soul is in Egypt, and do not be like the people who were in the desert while their souls were in Egypt.[62]* No, shut out the body, shut out your thoughts so you may build for yourself pious thought.[63] [44] If you sit in your cell and invite in idle words as you would a brother, do not hand over your heart to them so you may remain at peace, for manifold are the thoughts of the cell. [45] As you sit, have a psalm on your lips,[64] and if you stop, be on guard lest the enemies lead you astray. But remain in purity and the Holy Spirit will be your friend. As you sit, pursue pious thought that comes from God so you may be victorious over all who wage war against you, for mindfulness of God, that is, pious thought, is ruler over the passions. [46] As you sit in your cell, call upon God so that the grace of the cell may be granted to you,[65] for great is the grace of the cell.

* Prov 7:12

* cf Ex 16:3

Dealing with Others

[47] As you sit, do not make it a habit to wait for someone, nor have someone else wait for you, so you may be at peace, but according to God's

commandment receive the person who comes to see you.* If a brother spends a Sunday with you, receive him[66] out of love for God. If a brother comes to the mountain[67] and you are living there before him, for the sake of God's love support him until he finds a cell, and supply the person who comes to you according to his need, because it is the same with you: if you leave your cell for the mountain,[68] you wish them to supply your needs. For this is the commandment of God; these are the works of the cell.

*cf Lk 10:7-8?

IF YOU LEAVE YOUR CELL

[48] Son, if you leave your cell, watch your heart, lest you shove off from shore with a full boat and return with it empty and you go about following what your eyes see and your ears hear. Therefore, be faithful, and if you see something, profit from it[69] so you come back at peace.

ACQUIRE THE FEAR OF GOD

[49] As you sit, therefore, be mindful of God at all times, and the fear of God will always surround you, [50] because the fear of God casts out from the soul all sin and all evil and all transgression.* [51] Whoever has acquired for himself the fear of God has acquired all good gifts.[70] Whoever has the fear of God has a treasury filled with good things,[71]* and on account of the fear of God everyone will turn away from evil. [52] Son, as you sit in your cell, let judgement be before you and you will do the works of life. Gird your loins with the teaching of God and you will trample down many enemies.* [53] Keep the commandments of God,[72] [54] and do not become a slave to your will on account of human glory. Protect yourself

*cf Sir 1:27

*cf Sir 1:16-17

*cf Eph 6:14;
Lk 12:35, 10:19

from the vainglory of people, lest God scatter your bones.* [55] Do all your work for the sake of God, for God is not so unjust as to not reward you for your works.* [56] Son, purify your work so God will listen to you; be eager to show yourself worthy in the presence of God.* Do not neglect yourself and procrastinate day after day; [57] the opportune time will slip away from you and you will curse the day you were born.*

* cf Ps 52:6

* cf Heb 6:10, Rm 2:6

* cf 2 Tim 2:15

* Job 3:1

Relationships with Others

[58] I command you, child, do not associate with a person from whom you cannot profit,[73] lest you fall on your face. Do not associate with someone who is hot-tempered or angry. Do not be in relationship with someone who is a slanderer, nor with someone who is talkative. Do not associate with an envious person, for 'the meek will inherit the earth'.* Do not associate with someone who is dissolute. Do not be friends with someone prone to violent moods. Nor be friends with someone who is friends with a woman. Pay attention here: with all your might, have no friendship with a woman! Do not associate with a monk who is not your equal, lest you lose ground. [59] If you allow yourself a friend, let it be a faithful person whose work surpasses your own, a person who is a friend of God, who does not heed the things of this world that distinguish people from each other.* Do not, on account of the things of this world, be friends with a person from whom you do not profit,[74] [60] but be friends with someone who is poor and a lover of God and humble and a stranger to this world, who protects his isolation[75] and who is girded with the fear of God, and poor, someone who bears the cross,* who watches his mouth.** [61] Son, be friends with everyone who fears the Lord.[76]

* Mt 5:5

* cf Acts 15:9; Rm 3:22, 10:12

* cf Lk 14:27
** cf Ps 141:3

Draw Near to God

[62] Do not put your faith in someone because of the things of this life, so you may remain free; cast your cares upon the Lord so the Lord may care for you.* Put your faith in God, child, because it is he who shepherds you and it is he who protects you. And again, it is he who watches over you, and it is he who strengthens your heart and who guides you, and it is he who sees to it that you have him as your helper.* [63] Child, bear fruit for the Lord, because it is he who sweetens your heart. And let his fire be yours* and you will burn up all those who wage war against you, that is, evil thoughts. [64] Draw near to God so he in turn may pay close attention to you;* listen to God so he in turn may listen closely to you. Flee to him so he may take possession of you, and he will teach you his law and knowledge, and he will be your guide. [65] Refer your heart to him so he in turn may come to your aid. Depend on him night and day, for he is the one who helps you. Delight in him and he will give you your heart's desires.* If you ask anything from God, do not hesitate, for God wants you to submit to him with all your heart.⁷⁷*

* cf Ps 55:22

* cf Ps 55:22

* see, among many, Ex 3:2, 19:18; Dt 4:24; Heb 12:29

* Jms 4:8

* Ps 37:4

* cf Ps 27:14

Embark on the Straight Path

[66] If you are sitting in your cell, have the narrow gate with you;⁷⁸* if you are sitting at table, have the commandment of God with you lest your face be dishonored on account of your belly.* If you wish, you will be disciplined like a child,⁷⁹ and if you wish, you shall. Be friends with affliction so you may be at peace, and do not hate laborious work, because through much hard toil a person shall live. [67] My son, I am instructing you as one who gives life, helping you to embark on the

* cf Mt 7:13

* cf Ps 34:5

straight path.⁸⁰* Do not be crooked but be honest in everything you do. Do not winnow in every kind of wind, and do not pursue every kind of work.

* cf Heb 12:13
(Prov 4:26)

Be Like David

Be established in what is written in the Scriptures and keep God's law in your heart at all times, as David cries out, 'If your law were not my practice, then I would have perished in my humiliation'. And again, 'I will rejoice at your words, like one who finds great spoils'.* Let the word of God be sweet in you, as David himself cries out, 'How sweet to my throat are your utterances, sweeter than honey to my mouth',* [67a] for David represents all those who love God.⁸¹ Take once more David as an example, pursued by Saul and crying out, 'I am a dead dog, a flea'.* All of this on account of his humility. Again, take David, pursued by his enemies, crying out and saying, 'I will pursue my enemies and overtake them and I will not turn away until they abandon their attack',* [67b] for David physically battled with his enemies, and he took courage in God because God was fighting for him on account of the intentions God had for him.

* Ps 119:92, 162

* Ps 119:103

* 1 Sam 24:14

* Ps 18:38
(17:38 LXX)

Be Courageous in Battle against Evil Thoughts

And you therefore, child, be steadfast in heart and cry out, 'I will pursue my enemies and overtake them'⁸²* (which are the evil thoughts that do battle with you, since it is God who empowers a person) until you do battle with those waging war against you. For he said to those who followed him, 'I have given you authority to tread on

* Ps 18:38

snakes and scorpions, and over all the power of the Enemy, and nothing will hurt you'.* [67c] Therefore do not say that the Saviour gave power only to the apostles. He cries out, 'that which I say to you, I say to everyone'.* Take on the courage of [Joshua, son of] Nun, who became powerful in war when he was drawn up in battle against [the one who seemed to be]⁸³ the Amalekite, and emulate the way in which he defeated him because Moses stretched out his hand.⁸⁴* So never say that the Lord is a prophet. Listen to the Apostle when he says, 'built upon the foundation of the apostles and prophets'.* [67d] And you, therefore, my child, by stretching out *your* hands, defeat those who wage war against you. If you fear God and sally forth to do battle with your enemies by a single path, they will fall before you on seven paths.⁸⁵ The enemies that wage war against you are the evil thoughts. Therefore ask for power for yourself, my son, and you will defeat those who do battle against you. For God has not given us a spirit of cowardice, but rather of power and love.*

* Lk 10:19

* Mk 13:37

* cf Ex 17:8-16

* Eph 2:20

* 2 Tim 1:7

PROTECT YOURSELF AGAINST THE DEVIL

[68] Therefore, child, do not be found asking God to teach you to wage war and to bind the Devil to your feet. Do not be found praying 'Lead us not into temptation',* for there are deeds that a person takes on himself and all by himself binds the Devil to himself. For the Devil lays traps and entices a person into doing works of love until he leads him into the trap,⁸⁶* surreptitiously suggesting to him works that lead into false <caves and thickets>.⁸⁷ [69] Therefore, do not confuse your will with love and mix together the bitter with the sweet.* Beseech God, my son, that you may be saved from the Devil's snares, for they deceive

* Mt 6:13

* cf I Tim 3:7, 2 Tim 2:26

* Jas 3:11

the godly with works of righteousness. Adam was utterly deceived by a pretext of righteousness, and he mixed together the bitter with the sweet. [70] Therefore protect yourself from giving 'sleep to your eyes or drowsiness to your eyelids' so you may be 'saved from traps like the gazelle and like a bird from a snare'.* Protect your heart in every possible way, for such snares bring an end to life.

* Ps 132:4 (see #95); Prov 6:5, Sir 27:20

Keep Your Thoughts to Yourself

[71] Therefore, whether you are sitting in your cell or whether you are in the midst of people, keep your thoughts to yourself. If you see anything, first decide for yourself whether you have taken the beam out of your own eye.* And when you see or hear something about someone, do not dwell on it but take up his trespass and put it on your own head, on account of what is written in Scripture, 'Mourn for the sufferings of others and consider that their deficiencies are [yours]'.[88]* [72] For if you consider your neighbor's deficiency your own, you judge no one, you condemn no one, you lord it over no one; instead, you bear everything on account of the love of God.[89]* Therefore, be kind, my son, because 'those who are kind will inhabit the earth and the holy will be found dwelling on it'.* And again, 'love does what is kind'.[90]** Therefore be innocent and kind so you may see righteousness.[91] Do not be like the trees in the mountains that produce dry, bitter fruit but be like the reeds in the water that produce soft, juicy fruit.[92] Make your face joyful for God, and let your heart be like fire against sin.[93] Do not let down your guard but be steadfast in everything.[94] Do not allow your heart to rule over you but rule over your heart.[95] Do not follow after your soul but have your soul follow you.[96]

* cf Mt 7:5

* cf Gal 6:2, Sir 7:34

* cf 1 Cor 13:7

* cf Prov 2:21; Ps 37:3, 9, 28-29

** 1 Cor 13:4

Do not obey your heart but have your heart obey you so you may be obedient to God.⁹⁷

Cling to God

[73] My son, defeat your desires so you may be obedient to God's will. This, then, is God's will: to keep his commandments. If you keep his commandments, you become powerful in all your works. And your work will be pure because his commandments are not burdensome.* For he cries out, 'Come to me, all you who are weary and are carrying heavy burdens, and I will give you rest'.* Again he cries out with regard to those who toil in vain, 'Why do those who toil toil in vain?'* And again, 'My iniquities are like a heavy burden; they have weighed me down'.⁹⁸* [74] For we know that if a person clings to God, God cleanses him so he may be relieved of his sins and the word of the Saviour take hold of him: 'whoever dwells in my word will truly be my disciple and will know the truth, and the truth will make you free'.⁹⁹* Since God is the one who cleanses a person (for it is written, 'He who sanctifies and those who are sanctified are all one',¹⁰⁰* and again, 'Every vine in me that does not bear fruit he removes' and 'every branch that bears fruit he prunes to make it bear more fruit',¹⁰¹*) [75] therefore cling to God,* my son, and you will flee from all evil works. Come to the aid of your soul and flee from sin like one fleeing the face of a snake. [76] If you wish to be without sin, do not get caught up in numerous works, because those who multiply works are sinners. If therefore you wish to live your life with a peaceful heart, do not get caught up in numerous matters. Keep your life simple so you may enter through the narrow gate.¹⁰²* [77] Observe all the saints, how they lived indigently without property, hungry

* Mt 11:30, 1 Jn 5:3

* Mt 11:28

* cf Qo 1:3
* Ps 38:4

* Jn 8:31-32

* cf Heb 2:11

* Jn 15:2
* Sir 2:3

* cf Mt 7:13-14

and thirsty, stripped naked and beaten, wandering in deserts and mountains and holes in the ground,* [78]¹⁰³ so you may know that we enter the kingdom of God through numerous afflictions,* for the Kingdom of God is not here or there but, in fact, 'is within you'.¹⁰⁴*

* cf I Cor 4:11, Heb 11:38
* Acts 14:22
* cf Lk 17:21

Exegesis of the Lord's Prayer*

* Mt 6:9-13

[79] On account of this, therefore, the Saviour also says to us, 'Our Father, you who are in heaven, hallowed be your name, your Kingdom come', and again the blessed apostle Peter says, 'Sanctify the Lord your God with <your> hearts',¹⁰⁵* [80] for if you keep holy the name of God, the Kingdom of God comes to you and dwells in you and all your work is in accord with God and you become like those in heaven above whose works [on earth] were pleasing to God.

* cf I Pet 3:15

[81] For he said, 'Your will in heaven be done on earth'¹⁰⁶ (since those who are considered worthy of that eternal age have no need either to marry or be given in marriage for they are no longer able to die but are like the angels in heaven),* [82] exhorting us, 'Purify your work so you may be like the angels in heaven and so the word of Scripture may be fulfilled in you: "your will be done in heaven as on earth"', which means, 'let your work be done on earth as in heaven'.

* Mt 22:30, Lk 20:34-36

[83] For it is written, 'Your will in heaven be done on earth. Give us today our daily bread'. Wherefore it is written, 'I am the living bread that has come down from heaven'.* [84] And again, 'The bread that I give you is my flesh for the life of the world'.* 'Give us today our daily bread', that is, his body and his word and his commandment. And 'forgive us our debts as we also forgive our

* Jn 6:51
* Jn 6:51

debtors', that is, the sins between us and him. Forgive us them, as we also forgive our debtors.

[85] 'And lead us not into temptation, but deliver us from evil, for yours is the kingdom and the power and the glory for ever'.¹⁰⁷ For it is God who empowers the person who obeys him, because 'yours is the power'. So that it is written, 'The Lord will give power and strength to his people'.*

* Ps 68:35

Son, Worker, Slave

[86] My son, if you love God, the spirit of truth* shows favor to you, for God grants the Holy Spirit to those who obey him.¹⁰⁸ [87] If therefore you are unable to be a son, be a worker, because the good worker receives his pay with confidence.* [88] But if you are unable to be a worker, be a slave, like David who cries out, 'I am a slave; give me understanding so I may learn your commandments'.* [89] But if you do not become a slave, mourn for yourself and cry out, 'I am weary with my crying and my throat is sore'¹⁰⁹ <lest>¹¹⁰ this saying be fulfilled for you: 'A slave who knows the will of his master and who has not gotten himself ready nor done his master's will will receive a severe beating,' and 'from him to whom much has been given even more will be asked',* for just as we have received great knowledge so will we be in great danger.

* cf Jn 14:17, 15:26, 16:13; Acts 5:32

* cf Lk 19:17

* Ps 119:125

* Lk 12:47, 48

Be Like Mary¹¹¹*

* Exegesis of Lk 10:38-42

[90] Listen, my son, choose for yourself the work of Mary, who in her work chose for herself the good portion. This is the good portion: that you believe in God and love to listen to his word like

Mary, and keep his commandments and be steadfast and love learning and be a cross-bearer and innocent and pure and powerful in battle. [91] Child, take care of your heart; watch your mouth. Be good and love people. Be without care; cast upon the Lord your cares.* [92] Watch yourself inside and out, that you judge no one[112] and wrong no one, because the person who prays addresses his prayers to God[113] and offers his praises to God.[114] Since he devotes himself to glorifying God at all times, 'he is dressed for action',[115]* he is a lamp-bearer who has oil in his flasks.* He is strong and powerful; his strength lies in God; he is a fighter against the Devil; he is a fruit-bearer for God; his heart is pure; he is God's temple; he is a sanctuary of the Holy Spirit;* he is a house built upon rock.* He is magnanimous; he is meek and intelligent and humble. He has a godly grief; he does not have a worldly grief.[116]* He openly and freely rejoices and is glad in God. He is peaceful, and his peace surrounds him. 'Forgetting what lies behind, and straining forward to what lies ahead', he takes off the old self and puts on the new.* He bears people's reproaches;** he is a tree that has sweet fruit; he is an innocent lamb; he is wise about what is good; he is truthful in everything he does, never foolish; he is moderate in speech, inclining neither to the left nor the right;* he is light inside and out;** he is sown in good earth, bringing forth fruit a hundredfold;* he is as firmly anchored as a lion;[117] he is perfect in everything he does.* [93] This is the good portion, which you acquire for yourself, son.[118] And do no work without God. Be like Mary in her work.

[94] But if you are not able to be Mary, carry out Martha's work, caring for the things of God, serving the saints. [95] <Choose>[119] for yourself

* Ps 55:22

* Lk 12:35
* cf Mt 25:4, Lk 12:3

* cf 1 Cor 3:16
* cf Mt 7:24

* cf 2 Cor 7:9-10

* Phil 3:13; Eph 4:22, 24
** cf Heb 10:33; Rom 15:3

* Prov 4:27
** Lk 11:34-36
* cf Mt 13:8
* cf Mt 5:48

work that you will persist in until it is finished. Put your hands to the plow and do not turn back,* but give your attention to what lies ahead,* crying out and saying, 'I will not give sleep to my eyes and slumber to my eyelids and rest to my temples until I find a place for the Lord, a dwelling place for the God of Jacob'.[120]*

* Lk 9:62
* Phil 3:13

* Ps 132:4-5

MAKE YOURSELF POOR FOR GOD; PURCHASE CHRIST

[96] For the person who seeks God does not pause until God hears him, for it is written, 'This poor person cried out and the Lord listened to him and saved him from all his afflictions'.* [97] See therefore that if a person makes himself poor for God, God quickly hearkens to him. [98] Haven't you heard that 'the kingdom of heaven is like a merchant in search of fine pearls; on finding one of great value, he went and sold all that he had and bought it'.* [99] If therefore someone says 'I have nothing to sell', he will say to you,* 'Go, renounce the desires of your wicked heart so you may buy for yourself the very costly stone, which is the Spirit of God.[121] Renounce your desires and longings so you may purchase for yourself Christ, the root of all good things, as it is written, "I will divide my possessions with those who love me[122] and their treasuries I will fill with good things", and again, "Bearing fruit is better for me than gold and expensive stone and the fruit I bear is better than precious silver."'*

* Ps 34:6

* Mt 13:45
* sic

* Prov 8:21, 19

ACQUIRE WISDOM

Therefore acquire for yourself wisdom, for it is written, 'Wisdom is mine, strength is mine', and again, 'The person who is sagacious in things is the person who discovers good things'.* [100] Therefore acquire for yourself wisdom and do not be foolish, because everything opposes the foolish man.* For the wise man profits from the good and he has nothing to do with evil since he is someone who discovers good things in his works.* [101] And the wise person draws the net ashore and selects the good fish for his baskets and throws the rancid ones away.* [102] Therefore be wise concerning good and innocent concerning evil,* for there are some who are wise concerning evil and innocent concerning good. Are these people wise concerning evil? These are the ones who see the good and forsake it and exalt the evil and associate with it. Everything you see with your eyes draw to the good and be innocent concerning evil, and the God of peace will quickly crush Satan beneath your feet, for 'human inclination inclines unerringly towards evil from youth'.* [103] Therefore draw your heart to the good at all times, taking thought for good things in the presence of both the Lord and other people, as it is written, 'We take every thought captive in obedience to Christ'.*

* Prov 8:14, 16:20

* Prov 14:7

* cf Prov 16:20

* cf Mt 13:47-48

* cf Mt 10:16

* Rom 16:20, Gn 8:21

* 2 Cor 10:5

BE SINGLE-MINDED

[104] Child, if you pursue godly thought, it flees to you;[123] if you sit in your cell, teach your heart to put your thoughts in order, for if you master your heart, you will thoroughly master all your passions, as it is written, 'All things are lawful, but I will not be dominated by anyone'.* Therefore do not be like a saddled beast of burden constantly led about by others from place to place,[124] [105] but when you come out of your cell, figure out who it is who is drawing you out. Examine your

* 1 Cor 6:12

work first so you may come out with one heart, because the fruit of the heart is concord.[125]

Do Not Waver

[106] Protect yourself from wavering, because many have thrown away their faith, even though they were very faithful. If you go forth single-mindedly[126] and all kinds of temptation seize you, do not waver. Whether you leave to carry out an order, or go with a brother to do so, whether you go away to sell a small article you've made and weariness overtakes you, do not waver, because temptations try a person in everything he does, 'for there is always a snare in the treasuries'.*

* Is 42:22?

Be Alert

Therefore, be alert. When you leave your cell, do not ignorantly go out like a wild donkey or they'll throw a halter around your neck and put fetters on your feet: the halter for your belly and the fetters for your eyes. If you have to go forward for battle, watch out for your eyes so you do not bring temptation back with you into your cell and you grow weary and cry out and no one hear you, all because you did not watch out for your eyes. Do you not know that it is through actions that some thoughts enter the heart and others leave it? It is your eyes that bring things into your heart, while your evil thoughts send them out. As it is written in the Gospel, 'From out of the heart come evil intentions'.[127]* [107] Fight, therefore, whether by means of your eyes or by means of your heart, so you may remain at peace, and complete purity will surround you, for God loves holiness and for that reason he says, 'I am holy

* Mt 15:19

*Lev 11:44, Is 57:15

*Mt 5:8

*Heb 12:14
*cf Jn 15:2

*Mt 19:14,
Mk 10:14

and I am at peace in those who are holy',[128]* and 'Blessed are the pure in heart, because they will see God'.* And again, 'Pursue peace with everyone and the holiness without which no one will see the Lord'.* For we know that if we bear fruit God prunes us.[129]* [108] Therefore, child, fight, so you may always remain in holiness, whether with your eyes or whether with your heart, so you may return to your original nature,[130] like the little children about whom God has said, 'for to such as these belongs the kingdom of heaven'.*

[109. To him be glory, laud, honor, and dignity forever and ever. Amen.][131]

APPENDIX

The Arabic Version of #77–85[132]

[77] Observe the saints, how they live without plenty in great poverty, hunger, thirst, and nakedness and all that accompanies such conditions, so you may know that one enters the kingdom of God through many tribulations.* [78] My son, if you desire entrance into the kingdom of heaven, accept tribulations, for the door is narrow.* And if one loves God with all his soul and all his heart* he must persevere in the fear of God. Fear begets mourning and joy in him, and through it he is given a great power, and his soul bears fruit. If God sees the beauty of a person's effort he receives him and forgives all his transgressions and places him with the angels and gives him a guardian to guard him in all his ways until he reaches the place of repose. If the Devil sees this guardian with him he will not be able to approach him, for he sees this power surrounding him.[133] [79] Now, beloved, attain this power so the Devil may fear you and you may be wise in all your deeds, and so grace may increase within you and fill you with the sweetness of the Holy Spirit. For this sweetness is sweeter than honey and many monks have not known how sweet it is because they did not acquire this divine power and did not perform its deeds. Consequently, God did not grant them this aid which he gives to those who implement his commandments at the present, for God

* Acts 14:22

* Mt 7:14
* Dt 10:12, 30:6; Jos 22:5

is not fooled by appearances.* [80] For this reason, my son, attain cheerfulness of heart so that divine power may abide in you, and all the days of your life will be spent in freedom and joy. [81] Know, beloved, that we have enemies who want to prevent us from ascending to the Lord. [82] Therefore it is imperative that we pray to God continually,* night and day, that they not find in us a reason to prevent us from ascending to God. [83] These demons cannot prevent the saints who have received this power—and it is with them—from ascending, nor can they approach them, because they see from that power and the deeds that result from it that it abides in each of the saints, [84] provided that each individual despises the honor of men and takes it for granted and does not heed their scorn or disdain and loathes the affairs of this world, which he considers loathsome, and despises physical sloth and purifies his heart from every impure thought. And if he asks God at all times, in fasting and in tears, to grant him mercy, God, the Good, the Virtuous, will not refrain or delay in granting him his request. [85] Let us beware so our deeds may not be offered to secure the praise of people lest God not accept our prayer and not grant us this power which he gave to his saints and the righteous, for the Book states that 'God disperses hypocrites and the insincere'.*

* Rom 2:11

* cf I Th 5:17

* cf Ps 52: 6 (LXX)

NOTES

[1] Joseph-Marie Sauget, 'Une version arabe du "Sermon Ascétique" d'Étienne le Thébain', *Le Muséon* 77 (1964) 367–406, at 367.

[2] Enzo Lucchesi, 'Une version copte du Sermo Asceticus d'Étienne le Thébain', *Analecta Bollandiana* 115 (1997) 252: 'un personnage sans réele consistance historique'. See also Lucchesi, 'À propos d'une édition récente des oeuvres de Paul de Tamma', *Studia Orientalia Christiana Collectanea* 28 (1995) 161–166.

[3] See Sauget, 373.

[4] For an overview, see Jean Darrouzès, 'Étienne le Thébain', in *Dictionnaire de Spiritualité*, 4 (Paris, 1961) 1525–1526; Khalil Samir, 'Stephen the Theban', *The Coptic Encyclopedia*, ed. Aziz S. Atiya (New York: Macmillan, 1991) 7:2154-2155; and Michel van Parys, trans., 'Étienne de Thèbes: Enseignement sur la vie monastique', in Paul Tirot, et al., *Enseignement des pères du désert: Hyperéchios, Étienne de Thèbes, Zosime*, Spiritualité Orientale 51 (Begrolles-en-Mauges: Bellefontaine, 1991) 60–62. There is also an italian translation, which I was unable to obtain, in L. Cremaschi, *Parole dal deserto: Detti inediti di Iperechio, Stefano di Tebe e Zosima* (Magnano: Edizioni Qiqajon [Bose], 1992).

[5] The *Diataxis* and *Entolai* were edited by K. I. Dyobouniotis, 'Étienne le Sabbaïte', *Hieros Syndesmos* 8 (16), no. 193 (May 15, 1913) 9–12, and no. 194 (June 1, 1913) 10–13. The *Diataxis* and the Slavic 'Precepts' contain *Logoi* 3 and 4 of Isaiah of Scetis; on the connections with Isaiah, see Sauget, 368; Lucchesi, 'Une version', 252; Samir, 2155; and van Parys, 61.

[6] It does not seem coincidental that some arabic manuscripts transmit Stephen and Isaiah together (see Sauget, 371); we have seen above the connection between the two in the greek works attributed to Stephen. On Isaiah, see Lucien Regnault, 'Isaiah of Scetis, Saint', *The Coptic Encyclopedia* 4:1305-1306, and the bibliography; on Paul, see Chapter Four above. For Isaiah's work, see L. Regnault and Hervé de Broc, edd., *Abbé Isaïe: Recueil ascétique*, Spiritualité orientale 7 (Maine & Loire: Bellefontaine, 1976).

[7] For the greek text, with a french translation, see Édouard des Places, 'Le "Discours Ascétique" d'Étienne d'Thébes: texte Grec inédit et traduction', *Le Muséon* 82 (1969) 35–59. There is another french translation of the Greek by van Parys, 65–86.

[8] For the arabic text, with a french translation, see Sauget, 375–401; for his discussion of the manuscripts, 369–372.

[9] For the georgian text, with a latin translation, see Gérard Garitte, 'Le "Discours Ascétique" d'Étienne le Thébain en Géorgien', *Le Muséon* 83 (1970) 73–93.

[10] Paris Syriac (karsuni) 293, 1493, ff. 137v–139v (Sauget, 371).

[11] Lucchesi, 'Une version', 252, reports that there are coptic fragments in Paris Coptic 132.1, 87. This manuscript, originally from the White Monastery and now in the Bibliothèque Nationale, is very fragmentary. I wish to thank Hany N. Takla, who was able to examine a microfiche of it; he reports that only a few scattered words are discernible, among them *titôn*, 'to fight, do battle', which does fit with language found in the *Discourse*.

[12] See Victor Arras, *Collectio Monastica*, CSCO 238–239, Scriptores Aethiopici 45–46; Louvain: Peeters, 1963), chapter 13[10]b: Ethiopic: CSCO 238:85-86; latin trans.: CSCO 239:63-64.

[13] Sauget, 369. In the Arabic, #67 is abbreviated, and #77–85 reflect a different text. For a translation, see the Appendix at the end of this chapter.
[14] See van Parys, 61; Sauget, 372.
[15] Nos. 11–49 and 67c–83 are missing, and there are other abbreviations. See Garitte, 73.
[16] For the coptic text of Paul's work, see Tito Orlandi, *Paolo di Tamma Opere* (Rome: C.I.M., 1988) 116–121; for an english translation, see Chapter Five above.
[17] Lucchesi, 'Une version', 252, and 'À propos d'une édition récente des oeuvres de Paul de Tamma', *Studia Orientalia Christiana Collectanea* 28 (1995) 161–166, who cites codicological reasons.
[18] Paul, pars. 103–104, *mperhise* and *ekhn hise:* Stephen, #40–41, *mē apokamēis* and *en kamatōi;* Paul, pars 201–2, *chrêstos:* Stephen, #72, *chrêstos.*
[19] See van Parys, 62.
[20] For two outstanding works on early monasticism and scripture, see Douglas Burton-Christie, *The Word in the Desert: Scripture and the Quest for Holiness in Early Christian Monasticism* (New York and Oxford: Oxford University Press, 1993), and Jeremy Driscoll, 'Exegetical Procedures in the Desert Monk Poemen', *Mysterium Christi: Symbolgegenwart und theologische Bedeutung. Festschrift für Basil Studer,* ed. Magnus Löhrer and Elmar Salmann (Rome: Pontificio Ateneo S. Anselmo, 1995) 155–178.
[21] I am indebted to des Places, supplemented by van Parys, for supplying most of the references in the translation below; I have been able to identify a few others.
[22] Driscoll, 158. Driscoll's insights have inspired my reading of Stephen.
[23] On renunciation, see Alphabetical Apophthegmata Antony 32–33; Benedicta Ward, trans., *The Sayings of the Desert Fathers: The Alphabetical Collection,* CS 59, rev. ed. (Kalamazoo: Cistercian Publications, 1984) 8.
[24] Christ is often teacher *(didaskalos)* in the New Testament; among numerous examples, see Mt 8:19, Jn 1:38, and Jn 8:10. Clement of Alexandria (150–215) 'hellenized' the teacher by making him an instructor *(paidagogos):* 'our Instructor is like His Father God, whose son He is, sinless, blameless, and with a soul devoid of passion. . . . Our Instructor, the Word, therefore cures the unnatural passions of the soul by means of exhortations'. *The Instructor* 1.2, trans. A. Cleveland Coxe, *The Ante-Nicene Fathers,* vol. 2, *Fathers of the Second Century* (Grand Rapids: Eerdman, repr. 1979) 209–210. Such healing of the passions would have naturally appealed to a monastic audience (see #4–8).
[25] See Driscoll (above, n. 20), 159, for his discussion of how Poemen uses surprise.
[26] Translated with Apostolos N. Athanassakis. 'Ascetic Discourse' is the greek title; the arabic (Ar) title is 'Extract from the Discourse of Saint Stephen of Thebes on the Monastic Life', while the georgian (G) simply has 'Teaching of the Monk Stephen'. Translated from des Places (above, n. 7) 36–59. The numbers in brackets are from his text; I have put them in brackets because I do not think they are particularly helpful to the reader. I decided that renumbering (or double numbering) would just add to the confusion. Section titles are mine. I have consulted the french translation of Michel van Parys and followed his lead on occasion.
[27] The 'veil' of Moses represents 'the old covenant', which in Christ is set aside: 'when one turns to the Lord, the veil is removed'.

Notes 317

[28] Ar: the things that dwell in you. Greek (Gk) kinountas, literally 'moving', but also in a negative sense; see W.G.H. Lampe, *A Patristic Greek Lexicon* (Oxford: Oxford University Press, 1961) 753–754. See #36. On the movements of the spirit, see Antony, Letter One 35–41; Samuel Rubenson, *The Letters of St. Antony: Monasticism and the Making of a Saint* (Minneapolis: Fortress, 1995) 199.

[29] Gk *aisthêtêria* (< *aisthanomai*, 'to sense, perceive'). *Aisthêtêrion* (sing.) denotes a sense organ, then an intellectual faculty, and finally the spiritual organ of the soul. See Lampe 52B–53A.

[30] On discernment (*diakrisis*), see *Life of Antony* 22.3 and 38.5.

[31] See #21, 49–51, 60, 61.

[32] Ar and G.

[33] See Mk 7:22, where it says that such evils come 'from within, from the human heart. . . . All these evil things come from within, and they defile a person', a theme that fits well with Stephen's discourse; see #78.

[34] Text: ἐννεώσει < *ἐννέωσις which, despite the existence of ἐννεός (Lampe, 476B), does not exist. Des Places emends to ἐννοήσει, 'aux pensées (?)'. We suggest ἐνθουσιώσει < ἐνθουσίωσις. See Lampe, 475A.

[35] Reading with des Places κενὴν instead of καινὴν, "new."

[36] Gk *akidiaseis* (read: ἀκηδιάσης) < *akêdia, accedia*, the 'noonday demon', spiritual apathy or listlessness.

[37] Reading with des Places εὐθὺς instead of ἐσθὴς; the latter is probably a misspelling of εὐθής, a late form of εὐθύς. See #67.

[38] Reading with des Places εὐθεῖς instead of ἐσθεῖς.

[39] Gk σχηματώδης, which is not attested; des Places translates 'Ne sois pas hypocrite'. See #19, μὴ σχημάτιζε, 'Do not put on a false front'. See Lampe, 1360A, where σχημάτισμα, 'pretense', is paired with κενοδοξία, 'vainglory'. See Mt 6:5, 16, and Paul of Tamma, 'An Untitled Work' 102.

[40] Gk *porneia*.

[41] Ar: Do not be troubled or agitated, but be confident, calm, fearing God.

[42] Gk *schêmatize* (see #12); Ar: do not be indifferent.

[43] See Eph 4:22, 'You were taught to put away your old self, corrupt and deluded by its lusts', and Col 3:9.

[44] See #4.

[45] From these scriptural allusions it is clear that the 'teacher' (*didaskolos*) is Christ; among numerous examples, see Mt 8:19, Jn 1:38, 3:2, 8:10 and 13:14. See #29.

[46] Throughout this translation we have translated *anthrôpos* as 'person' and *anêr* as 'man'.

[47] See also *Life of Antony* 2.3–3.1.

[48] For #34 and 36 see Lk 14:8-11, which concludes, 'For all who exalt themselves will be humbled, and those who humble themselves will be exalted'.

[49] Ar: the things that dwell in you. Gk kinountas; see #3.

[50] We have followed des Places in translating *hêgemonikon*, 'principal', as 'spirit'. The *hêgemonikon* was understood as 'the principal part of the soul, the intellect', and 'the seat of contemplative and mystical life' (Lampe 600AB).

[51] These seem to be the eleven Virtues, which are pictured in wall paintings at Bawit (though their names differ somewhat from those at Bawit); see Jean Clédat, *Le Monastère et la Nécropole de Baouît*, Mémoires publiés par les membres de L'Institut Français d'Archéologie Orientale du Caire 12 [one volume in two

parts] (Cairo: IFAO, 1904) 23, and Marguerite Rassart-Debergh, 'A propos de trois peintures de Saqqara', in Hjalamar Torp, et al., ed., *Acta ad Archaelogiam et Artium Historiam Pertinentia* (Rome: Bretschneider, 1981), 'B. Des murs et des Vertus: la cellule 709', 193–201, and Plates I and II following p. 206. Paul of Tamma, 'On Humility' 9 (chapter five above), speaks of twelve Virtues; at Bawit Ama Sibylla is pictured in the midst of the eleven, making twelve medallions. On Sibylla see the Appendix to this volume.

[52] See Paul of Tamma, 'An Untitled Work' 100.

[53] See Paul of Tamma, 'An Untitled Work' 101. Gregory of Nyssa, *Homilies on the Song of Songs* 10, comments on this verse of the Song of Solomon; see *Saint Gregory of Nyssa: Commentary on the Song of Songs*, trans. Casimir McCambley (Brookline, MA: Hellenic College Press, 1987) 188–190.

[54] See Paul of Tamma, 'An Untitled Work' 102, which seems to reflect this sentence.

[55] See Paul of Tamma, 'An Untitled Work' 103.

[56] See Paul of Tamma, 'An Untitled Work' 104.

[57] 'Can' translates *dunasai*, literally 'have power', *dunamis*; the two are etymological siblings.

[58] See Paul of Tamma, 'An Untitled Work' 105–107.

[59] See #36.

[60] See Paul of Tamma, 'An Untitled Work' 108–109.

[61] See Paul of Tamma, 'An Untitled Work' 109.

[62] In Ex 16:3 the Israelites grumble against Moses in the wilderness. See Paul of Tamma, 'An Untitled Work' 110–111. 'Egypt' may have referred to Lower Egypt, the area around Babylon (Cairo) and the delta, so Stephen is also telling his disciple not to be in the desert while his thoughts are elsewhere (home?). 'Egypt' may also represent here the body and its passions.

[63] See Paul of Tamma, 'An Untitled Work' 112.

[64] Literally 'have a practice [*meletên*] in your mouth'. *Meletan* meant to meditate by quietly reciting the psalms to oneself on the lips.

[65] 'Grace' translates *charisma*, 'grace, charism', while 'granted' renders *charisêtai*.

[66] *Hypophere* also suggests 'put up with, bear, endure'.

[67] Reading τὸ ὄρος instead of τὸ ὅρος, which des Places mistakenly has. In monastic literature, 'mountain' often designates a monastic community.

[68] Text: ἐὰν ἀπέλθῃς εἰς τὸ ὄρος, which is a bit awkward, yet became formulaic for 'if you leave for the mountain', that is, 'if you leave for a stricter monastic community'. Today, if a monk lives on Mount Athos, he is already στό ὄρος, 'on the mountain', yet such a monk may leave his cell ἵνα ἀπέλθῃ εἰς τὸ ὄρος, meaning to the solitary wilds.

[69] See #33.

[70] Or 'graces': *charismata*.

[71] Ar and G add here: For the fear of God delivers (us) from every sin.

[72] G: Do not be without knowledge, but fear (God) and keep his commandments; Ar: Do not be without knowledge and do not be destitute of God, but fear God and keep his commandments.

[73] See #33, 48.

[74] See #58.

[75] Isolation: *xeniteian*; 'stranger': *xenou*.

[76] See #4. Ar adds: and observes his commandments; G adds: and keeps his commandments.

[77] G: If you ask something of God and do not receive it right away, do not be faint-hearted, for God puts man to the test in order to test his patience, but ask with all your heart with patience, and you will receive what you ask.

[78] For the rest of the par. G has: When you are at table, remember the commandment of God, so that you do not dishonor your grace and may be at peace; and do not hate tribulation and suffering in order to have joy and peace, for man lives by means of great tribulation.

[79] The text, εἰς τέκνον, should read ὡς τέκνον.

[80] See #9.

[81] That is, David is the 'type' (prosôpon) of all those who love God. In 67a Stephen says to take David as a type. In a classic use of typology, Stephen says that David battled physically while the disciple battles spiritually with thoughts (#67b).

[82] See #95.

[83] Although Des Places translates τὸν Ἀμαλήκιτον φαινόμενον as 'qui semblait l'Amalécite', we believe that φαινόμενον is a marginal gloss that crept into the text.

[84] Text: διὰ τῆς πετάσεως τῶν χειρῶν Μωυσέως, which is a lexical gem. Πέτασις is unattested (the Septuagint uses ἐπῆρεν for Moses' holding out his hands in Ex 17:11); from Ps 142:6 (LXX), διεπέτασα τὰς ξεῖράς μου πρὸς σέ, 'I stretched out my hands to you', a monk coined διὰ τῆς πετάσεως. The first sentence of [67d] has διὰ τῆς διαπετάσεως.

[85] Does 'seven' here perhaps refers to the seven deadly sins, τὰ ἑπτὰ θανάσιμα ἁμαρτήματα? Seven, however, is a common number in the Bible; see, for example, Rev 15:7 and 16:1, which speaks of 'the seven bowls of the wrath of God'.

[86] Παγιδευτής, 'layer of traps', seems to be unattested; 1 Tim 3:7 and 2 Tim 2:26 use παγίδα.

[87] Text: σπηλογχνίας, which is unattested; des Places translates as 'cavernes'. It must be a corruption for either εἰς σπηλαιῶνας, 'into a series of caves', or εἰς σπήλαια καὶ λόχμας, 'caves and thickets'.

[88] Des Places supplies ὑμῶν. Ar: If you are sitting in your cell or if you are with people, concern yourself only with your own soul and blame yourself; do not pass judgement on anyone and do not blame anyone but let your blame fall on your own head, as it is written in Paul: 'Weep for one another's sins, and with regard to your faults, think that they are yours'.

[89] See Paul of Tamma, 'An Untitled Work' 200.

[90] See Paul of Tamma, 'An Untitled Work' 201.

[91] Literally 'straightness', euthutêta; see #9, 67. See Paul of Tamma, 'An Untitled Work' 202.

[92] See Paul of Tamma, 'An Untitled Work' 203–4.

[93] See Paul of Tamma, 'An Untitled Work' 205.

[94] See Paul of Tamma, 'An Untitled Work' 206–7.

[95] See Paul of Tamma, 'An Untitled Work' 208. In Greek, the accentual and vocalic rhythm of 'Do not allow your heart' is inspired by Ps 140 (LXX).

[96] See Paul of Tamma, 'An Untitled Work' 209.

[97] See Paul of Tamma, 'An Untitled Work' 210–211.

98 See Paul of Tamma, 'An Untitled Work' 212–217.
99 See Paul of Tamma, 'An Untitled Work' 218.
100 See Paul of Tamma, 'An Untitled Work' 219–220. 'An Untitled Work' breaks off at this point.
101 In the previous sentence 'cleanses' translates *katharizôn*; in this quotation from John, 'prunes' renders *kathairei*, which also means 'cleanse', while 'remove' translates *airei*.
102 'Narrow' translates *stenês* while 'simple' renders *stenoumenos*.
103 The arabic text for pars. 78–85 is completely different; see the Appendix to this chapter. For the ethiopic version of par. 78 see Arras, 63–64, chap. 13[10]b.
104 Des Places suggests changing 'you' (pl.) (ὑμῶν) to 'us' (ἡμῶν), presumably in order to agree with 'we enter', but Lk has 'you'.
105 Reading ὑμῶν with des Places instead of ἡμῶν.
106 Stephen has slightly altered Mt 6:10, which reads 'your will be done, in heaven as on earth'.
107 Mt 6:13, with the longer ending added by some New Testament mss. G: 'for yours is the kingdom forever and ever. Amen'. The Lord 'will give power and strength to his people' [Ps 68:35], and he says again, 'If you give me your hearts, I will give you my power'.
108 'Shows favor' and 'grants' both translate *charizetai*, from *charis*, 'grace'. See #46. This granting of the Spirit or grace to the person who perseveres is a common theme in early monastic literature; see Chapter Four above.
109 Reading ἐβραγχίασεν with des Places (Ps 68:4 LXX) instead of ἐβροχίασεν. The author thought ἐβροχίασεν was the etymologically correct derivation from βρόγχος, which shows sophistication and education.
110 Supplying a negative with van Parys.
111 The view of Mary as the type of the contemplative life goes back to Origen, for whom Martha's concerns are 'bodily' (σωματικῶς) and with 'work' (πρᾶξιν), while Mary's are 'spiritual' (πνευματικῶς) and with 'contemplation' (θεωρία). See 'Fragments on Luke', in M. Rauer, ed., *Origenes Werke, Die griechischen christlichen Schriftsteller* 9; Leipzig, 1930), ΛΘ, repr. in ΒΙΒΛΙΟΘΗΚΗ ΕΛΛΗΝΩΝ ΠΑΤΕΡΩΝ 15, ΩΡΙΓΕΝΗΣ (Athens: Ekdosis tês apostolikês diakonias, 1958) 77–78. An english translation may be found in Joseph T. Lienhard, *Origen: Homilies on Luke, Fragments on Luke*, The Fathers of the Church 94 (Washington, D.C.: The Catholic University of America Press, 1996) 192–193 (#171).
112 Text: μηδέν ἀδικάζειν, which should be μηδένα δικάζειν.
113 Ar: For the person who does not concern himself with others prays to God and glorifies him because his complete concern is for the Lord at all times.
114 Text: εὐχητής = εὐχέτης (assimilated to ὑμνητής).
115 Text: περιεζωσμένος ἐστὶν ἡ ὀσφῦς αὐτοῦ (which Des Places indicates with 'sic'), which should be either περιεζωσμένη ἐστὶν ἡ ὀσφῦς αὐτοῦ or περιεζωσμένος ἐστὶν τὴν ὀσφὺν αὐτοῦ.
116 According to Paul a godly grief leads to salvation while a worldly grief 'produces death'.
117 Is Stephen thinking of massive statues of lions? Text: ἐστηρισμένος for ἐστηριγμένος.
118 Ar and G add: so no one can take it away from you [see Lk 10:42].
119 Reading ἔκλεξαι (corrected by des Places from ἐλκέξεσαι, which the same scribe has written at the top of the page) instead of ἔργασαι, which has been assimilated from ἐργασία, 'work'.

[120] See #70.
[121] G: this precious stone, which is your soul.
[122] G: 'Those who love me have received the good part; I will fill their treasury with good things'.
[123] A lacks; G: My son, if you pursue evil thoughts, they will flee far from you.
[124] See #43.
[125] G: For the fruit a person bears is united with holiness.
[126] Literally 'with/in one soul *(psychê)*, whereas 'doubt' translates *dipsuchia*.
[127] 'Intentions' translates *dialogismoi* while 'thoughts' are *logismoi*.
[128] Lev 11:44, however, does not include the second part of the sentence.
[129] On pruning, see n. 102. Ar and G have more biblical citations in this paragraph.
[130] Literally 'beginning', *archê*. On such a return, see Antony, Letter One 28–31; Rubenson, 199.
[131] This is the concluding doxology in Ar.
[132] Translated by Maged S.A. Mikhail from Sauget, 391–394.
[133] This paragraph made its way into the ethiopic collection of apophthegms; see Arras, chap 13[10]b: Ethiopic: CSCO 238:85-86; Latin trans.: CSCO 239:63-64. It is, as far as is known, the only ancient written source to find its way into the Ethiopic collection; see Lucien Regnault, 'Aux origines des collections d'Apophtegmes', *Studia Patristica* 18 (1989) 61–64, at 64.

9

Holy Men and Businessmen:

Monks as Intercessors in Fourth-Century Egypt

Introduction

IN RECENT YEARS scholars have inserted many up-to-date windows into the ancient monastic dwelling of the holy man of late antiquity. With these constructions they have shed new light on the way we see the holy man: as patron,[2] thaumaturge,[3] mediator and teacher,[4] and intercessor.[5]

The most famous—or infamous—of these roles is undoubtedly that of the thaumaturge or miracle-worker. He inhabits the landscape of late antique monasticism as a larger than life figure, as an icon often depicts its central figure larger than subsidiary figures. When Saint Antony the Great is not fending off hordes of marauding demons, he is healing the crowds of ailing suppliants who come to see him: 'Through Antony the Lord healed many there who were suffering from bodily illnesses and purified others of their demons'.[6] Antony the Wonderworker became so sought after, the *Life of Antony* reports, that he had to flee the admiring throngs: 'When Antony saw that he was being bothered by crowds of people and not being allowed to withdraw as he wished and intended, he. . . . decided to go to the Upper Thebaid where they did not know him'.[7]

The monk as miracle-worker comes almost wholly from the early monastic Lives—the *Life of Antony*, the *Historia Monachorum*, Palladius' *Lausiac History*, the *Life of Pachomius*, among others—the literary texts by which most people are familiar with early monasticism. A woman suffering from a hemorrhage of some kind expresses her confidence that, if she can only see Pachomius, 'the Lord will grant me healing'. She goes to the holy man, touches him and his clothing, and is healed.[8] The thaumaturge is virtually absent, however, from other strata of early monastic sources, such as the

Apophthegmata or Sayings of the desert fathers and mothers. This discrepancy has not gone unnoticed by scholars, who argue that the Lives offer an anachronistic portrait 'where later theological, ecclesiastical, and instructional concerns have shaped the evidence'.[9] Historians prefer documentary evidence that 'comes without interpretation and serves as a valuable data base through which to test the interpretive reliability of the later literary sources'.[10]

What usually goes unnoticed, however, are the connections between the literary and documentary sources. Perhaps this is because these links—connective tissue, really—are spiritual and thus difficult to quantify and delimit. In the *Life of Antony*, a Count Archelaos finds Antony on the saint's outer mountain and 'he asked Antony simply to pray for Polycratia', whose excessive asceticism had weakened her whole body. 'So', the *Life* says with muted understatement, 'Antony prayed', and the young woman was healed some distance away in Laodicea. 'Everyone was astonished when they understood that the Lord had stopped her suffering at the time when Antony was praying and petitioning the goodness of the Lord on her behalf'.[11] The *Life of Antony* here corroborates what the papyri tell us. In Letter 1 of the Nepheros archive (translated below), a woman named Tapiam appeals to Nepheros: 'I, Tapiam, have been ill and am still confined to my bed. We entreat you, therefore, to pray for us to be made healthy and whole. Indeed, our children were ill earlier and through your prayers they got well. We believe that your Lord, because you are righteous, will listen to you'. Tapiam's faith is the same as the count's, their appeals are the same, and the results are the same. The documentary and literary sources here corroborate each other.

What is striking here is both the miracle and the conviction of both Count Archelaos and Tapiam that the holy man's prayers are more efficacious than their own (Tapiam to Nepheros: '*your* Lord'). They share this belief with others who sought out holy men in late antiquity, either in person or through letters, as we see preserved in documentary evidence or in literary sources. I suspect that we moderns note the miracle but often fail to notice the prayer, but to miss the connection, the life-giving flow of blood, between prayer and miracle, belief and result, misses the symbiosis that these pairs shared in early monasticism. As the apostle James reminded his jewish-christian community in the first century, 'The prayer of faith will heal the sick' (James 5:15). Many of the christian faithful, from the first century into the fourth and beyond, including the writers of the letters translated below, took James at his word. His brother had promised the same. When a woman with a hemorrhage touched the fringe of Jesus' cloak in the belief that doing so would cure her, Jesus responded, 'Take heart, daughter, your faith has made you well' (Mt 9:22). The woman who sought to touch Pachomius' clothing was living out her evangelical faith. The holy men of the fourth century, and those who sought them out, lived within the same belief structure as the New Testament writers.

In the early monastic account from Upper Egypt of Abba Aaron, the holy man raises the dead by sprinkling water which he has blessed; a vineyard worker falls from a tree and seems to be dead, but is restored when sprinkled with holy water supplied by Abba Aaron; a rich man has his sight restored when he washes his face with water blessed by Abba Aaron; a stillborn child is made alive when sprinkled with earth taken from the doorstep of Abba Aaron's house.[12] All of these miracles depend on the faith of the people who petition Abba Aaron. In the story of the vineyard worker, the man's co-workers understand this; they tell the injured man's son, 'Go to the holy man Abba Aaron and get a small bowl of water from him in faith and throw it on your father. Maybe he will wake up'.[13] The workers have faith, yet still have their doubts. These vineyard workers are the same people in the fourth century who wrote letters on papyrus and pottery to holy men seeking their prayers and intercessions. Undoubtedly the people who wrote the letters translated below also had their doubts, but there can be no doubt that they had faith, both in God and in the powers of the holy man, nor that they believed in the power of prayer wielded by the holy person. The faith, and faith in the holy man's prayers, closely connect these petitioners with their coreligionists found in the literary texts.

If the spirituality of faith and prayer connect documentary and literary sources, then business aspects of the papyri form not a disconnect but a counterconnection, as it were, with the literary accounts: they document pecuniary aspects of early monastic life about which the literary sources are largely silent. Thus they provide valuable corroborative and supplementary witness to early monasticism. The business requests in the papyri translated below, rather than detracting from the intercessory nature of faith—as if business somehow sullied prayer—make the letters doubly intercessory: many of the letters ask for intercessory prayer while many other letters ask the same holy man to intercede in some business dealing—to supply some product, to intervene in a troubled business dealing, or to send some business to the writer—and other letters ask for both at the same time. 'As so often', Roger S. Bagnall has observed, 'documentation follows trouble', whether secular or religious.[14] The writers of these letters matter of factly combine business and religion; they have faith in the holy man and in the holy man's intercession in both spiritual and worldly matters. The intercessor of late antiquity could be both holy man and businessman. This should not surprise us, really. We know from the literary sources that semi-anchoritic and anchoritic monks practised small cottage industries—plaiting rope, making mats or baskets, weaving burial shrouds—the profits from which they would use to buy food to feed themselves and the poor. Larger, cenobitic, communities practised commerce on a large scale,[15] perhaps not too unlike some of the large monasteries in Egypt today do with their varied agricultural and mercantile concerns. The papyri below detail the obvious: monastic communities had holy men among them, but they also had to have businessmen. The letters below show that holy men and businessmen could be one and the same.

Many of the monks portrayed in the monastic Lives—Antony, Pachomius, Macarius the Great—are well known, partly thanks to modern publications. The documentary evidence, papyri and ostraca written in Greek and Coptic, is little known, however, and some of it has not been published in English. This evidence supplements the literary texts in immediate and visceral ways. As Claudia Rapp has observed, the documentary evidence reminds us 'that the day-to-day interactions between the holy man and his followers were centred on prayer and not the more spectacular miracles that were so artfully depicted by later hagiographers'.[16] A letter, badly spelled, to an unknown addressee from Oxyrhynchus at the beginning of the fourth century combines greetings, a request for prayers, faith in the power of the holy intercessor, and the transacting of business—all elements found in the three archives translated below:

> *Address on verso:* . . . [from] Boêthos, son of Acheilleion
>
> . . . I had to come down to Panga so that, God willing, there may perhaps be something to sell. It will especially be necessary for you too to pray for me so that God may hear your prayers and a straight path may be prepared for us.[17]
>
> I send my greetings to my sweetest brethren[18] Dionysodora and her slave Acheillis. I send my greetings to my sister Macaria and Romana and to all our (brethren) by name, and, if you want, I will buy some old jars of olives at three (talents) per jar. If I [receive?] . . . write to me.
>
> [I pray] that you (pl.) are well.[19]

A letter written in Coptic on a pottery shard from Eudoxia to Psan or Pson, the disciple and successor of Epiphanius of Thebes, shows how appeals to a monastic holy man continued into the early seventh century.[20]

> Above all, I embrace the footstool for your feet. Have pity, then, I beg and entreat you, my holy father, by interceding for God on my behalf to have mercy on me and forgive me my sins. I have sinned against him and he will not relieve me of my infirmity,[21] for my transgressions and sins are very very numerous and weigh upon me. He has handed me over to my enemies. Have pity, then, and entreat God on my behalf that I be delivered from this scourge that afflicts me. My holy father, do not delay in entreating God for me, for you are the ones who make entreaty for the whole world.
>
> Be well in the Lord, my beloved, holy, and revered father, Apa Pson the anchorite. I am the sinner Eudoxia,

whose sins are very numerous. Have pity, therefore, and help me.[22]

Another letter written on pottery with the same provenance shows that in the early seventh century letters seeking intercession were still asking for both prayer and commerce. A writer named Peter first asks Elias and Isaac of the Monastery of Epiphanius for 'half a *solidus* worth of linen' and then declares, 'But most of all, my holy and revered sirs, entreat the Lord for us,[23] when you lift up your holy hands, for the sake of my numerous sins'.[24] But not all was commerce; often what leaves an indelible impression with the modern reader is the heartfelt cry. A certain Valeria petitions Paphnutius:

> I am afflicted with a severe illness, a terrible shortness of breath. Thus I have believed and still believe that if you pray on my behalf I shall obtain healing. I pray to God, I pray to you also: remember me in your holy prayer. Even though I have not come in person to embrace your feet, yet in spirit I have come to embrace your feet.[25]

Her distress echoes down the centuries. Her suffering, and her hope, make her our sister.

The documentary letters translated below are typical of their genre: they both enlighten and tantalize. They even frustrate. They briefly throw open the windows of late antique monasticism and let us see real human beings with their quotidian transactions and heartfelt concerns. But all too quickly these letters slam those windows shut again, and we are outside trying to look in, left with as many questions as we have answers. We may, in fact, have more questions than answers. These documentary letters also tell us that there are windows provided by early monastic documentary sources that are different from the windows put in by the monastic Lives: the construction is different, and the light let in by each type is different. In the past, scholars peered in at early monasticism almost wholly through literary texts. Scholars now want to use and incorporate documentary evidence, including archeology. For the fourth century in particular, the earliest period of monastic activity, the documentary windows are, so far, small and few in number. We need both kinds of windows to see in. Once inside, we need both in order to see out.

Claudia Rapp has recently drawn attention to early monastic intercessors from the fourth to the seventh century: Paphnutius, Nepheros, John of Hermopolis, Barsanuphius of Gaza (5th–6th c.), and Epiphanius of Thebes (6th–7th c.).[26] I wish to follow up on her article by translating the relevant documentary texts and offering a supplementary commentary. I will restrict the focus of this chapter to Paphnutius (Part I), John (II), and Nepheros (III), all of whom lived in fourth-century Egypt.[27] I offer here new translations of material related to Paphnutius and John and the first translation into English of material related to Nepheros.[28] I have also supplied a brief introduction to each intercessor.

I.

Eight Letters to Paphnutius[29]

Introduction

Modern letter (and e-mail) writers assume the ordinary. Ancient letter writers did the same, and the results can sometimes be frustrating for scholars trying to find the facts within and behind the letters. In the case of the Paphnutius archive, we do not know for certain who Paphnutius was, or where he lived.[30] With regard to a date for the letters, we are more fortunate: they can be placed in the middle of the fourth century, and thus are contemporary with Saint Antony in his old age (Antony died in 356).[31] The recipient of the letters was an ascetic named Paphnutius (Papnoute in Coptic), 'beloved and most pious and beloved of God'.[32] He was an anchorite who was probably connected with a monastery.[33]

Paphnutius' community, like that of Nepheros' (Part III below), may have been Melitian, members of what was originally a rigorist group opposed to the perceived laxity of the bishop of Alexandria and seen as schismatic by the alexandrian hierarchy.[34] But as James E. Goehring has observed, 'In all likelihood, their identity as Melitian had little impact on the local population. Their primary social identity was that of monk, and it was as monks that they related to their local community. While they surely understood themselves as Melitians and their allegiance as such was recognized, it appears to have made no difference to their lives as monks'.[35] With regard to monastic organization and lifestyle, Goehring adds, 'there is really very little that clearly distinguishes an "orthodox" from a "schismatic" monk'.[36] For the purposes of this chapter on the holy man as intercessor, it does not matter whether Paphnutius and his community were Melitian or not. Perhaps a monk is a monk is a monk.

The letters to Paphnutius, though varied in tone and content, often follow a four-fold pattern—though not each letter has all four parts:

1. Greetings, often fulsome.
2. The writer's statement of belief in the power of Paphnutius' prayers and a request for his prayers with regard to a specific matter, often an illness.
3. Either a statement or request concerning some business or other matter.
4. Greetings to members of the community and a concluding wish for the good health of the holy man.

The first letter, from a certain Ammonius, contains a statement that is both typical and ordinary:'I always know that through your holy prayers I shall be saved from every temptation of the Devil and from all human treachery, and now I beg you to remember me in your holy prayers, for after God you are my salvation'. The first response to Ammonius' declaration could well be '"After God you are my salvation"! What about Christ?' Coptic spirituality has been criticized as 'Christless',[37] but Christ is very present in these letters: in Letter 7, Athanasius declares that 'I put my faith in the Saviour of all'; in Letter 3, Pianius prays 'to Christ that I may be considered worthy also to embrace you with my own eyes'; in Letter 4 Paphnutius is called 'Christbearing' by Valeria, who 'sends greetings in Christ'. In that same letter, Valeria petitions Paphnutius, 'I beg and entreat you, most valued father, to ask that I may [receive help] from Christ and obtain healing'. It is clear from these letters that the writers see Paphnutius as a mediator between them and God, both God the Father and Christ.

What are they asking Paphnutius' intercessions for? Valeria is afflicted 'with a severe illness, a terrible shortness of breath'. In Letter 6, Heracleides tells the holy man of 'the illness that has attacked me and is such a burden to [me]', and asks him 'to [send] the oil', presumably holy oil for healing.[38] In Letter 7, Athanasius speaks of several members of his family who are ill. Although plea for intercessory prayer for illness is the most common request, in Letter 8 Justin asks Paphnutius 'to remember me in your holy prayers, master, that we may be able to participate in the cleansing of sins'. Justin makes it clear why he, and they, are petitioning Paphnutius in particular: 'for we believe that your citizenship is in heaven. There we perceive you to be our master and new patron.' Although on earth, Paphnutius has one foot, or both feet, in heaven. The writers of these letters believed that Paphnutius, because of his holiness, was closer to God than they and had God's full attention. Perhaps they were right.

Letter 1[40]

Ammonius to Paphnutius[41]

Address on verso:
To (my) honored (and) beloved father Papnouthios[42]

> To the beloved and most pious and God-pleasing and blessed father Papnouthios, greetings from Ammonios[43] in the Lord God.

I always know that through your holy prayers I shall be saved from every temptation of the Devil and from all human treachery, and now I beg you to remember me in your holy prayers, for after God you are my salvation.[44]

Our brother [Didymos] replied to my letter and, just as you told me to do, I wrote back to him concerning the matter.

I pray that you may be in good health for many years, most sweet father. May the God of peace preserve you for the longest time.

Letter 2[45]

Ausonius to Paphnutius

Address on verso:
Ausonios to the beloved father Apa Papnouthios[46]

> Ausonios[47] to the beloved father Apa Papnouthios.

Remembering Your Piety's instructions, I sent for Horos, who is from Philonikos,[48] and reminded him, and I asked Gallos to remind me about everything so that, as far as possible, I might demonstrate my strong interest. I earnestly beg you to direct my interests in this and all other matters. Remember me in your holy prayers.

May God keep you in good health, beloved father, as you pray on our behalf.

Letter 3[49]

Pianius to Paphnutius

Address on the verso:
To my beloved brother Papnoutios, anchorite of the monastery (?) of monks[50]

To the excellent Apa Papnoutios, who is most desirous of knowledge, Pianios[51] sends his greetings in the Lord God.

Availing myself of the person who is eagerly making his way to Your Piety, I considered it necessary to send greetings to Your Reverence by means of a letter, praying to Christ that I may be considered worthy also to embrace you with my own eyes. For [although I can see you now] in the Spirit, [I wish to] greet [you in person] each day.[52] I beseech [Your] Holiness to deign [to] pray [for my sins, that] God may deliver me from . . . [and from the] needs that weigh heavily on [me].

Greet the brothers from [us] . . . Send greetings from [me] on behalf of . . . the household slave of Athanasios,[53] Eu[. . .], for he too is numbered among those who love Your Piety.

I send my greetings to my honored master Athanasios and to Eusebios and Harêous (?) and to all the brothers [who are] with Your Holiness . . . and his brother, Dôrotheos, [greet] you.

I pray that you have many years of good health in the Lord, my most desired sir.

Letter 4[54]

Valeria to Paphnutius

Address on verso:
To the most honorable father Appa Paphnoutios from (his) daughter[55] Valeria

To the most valued and Christ-bearing[56] Appa Paphnouthis, who is adorned with every virtue, Valeria sends greetings in Christ.

I beg and entreat you, most valued father, to ask that I may [receive help] from Christ and obtain healing. I believe that through your prayers I may obtain healing, for revelations are manifested through ascetics and religious.[57]

Indeed, I am afflicted with a severe illness, a terrible shortness of breath. Thus I have believed and still believe that if you pray on my behalf I shall obtain healing. I entreat God, I entreat you also: remember me in your holy prayer. Even though I have not come in person to embrace your feet, yet in spirit I have come to embrace your feet.

I send greetings to my [daughters] Bassiana and Theoklia. Do remember them in your holy prayer. My husband also sends you his warmest greetings; do pray on his behalf also. My whole household also sends their greetings. I pray for your health, most honorable father.

Letter 5[58]

Dôrotheus to Paphnutius

To the most honorable and God-pleasing brother. Dôrotheos of Oxyrhynchus, the worthless servant, greets you in the Spirit and in the love of Christ.

Above all, I entreat the God and Father of our Saviour Jesus Christ to grant me to find favor in his sight that you may receive my letter. I too shall have cause to rejoice when the good servant welcomes me in a letter and eagerly offers up prayers on my behalf with a sincere intention to the Master. For I trust that. . . .

. . . but on account of your most glorious and most revered way of life, since you have renounced worldly pretensions and abhorred the boastfulness of the vainglorious. Therefore we also strongly approve of the report about you wisely demonstrating your most noble contest, and we desire to emulate by means of the same way of life your love of what is good. God has, it seems, generously allowed you to meet the enemy at the appropriate time and to have an effective remedy, for 'they are redeeming the time', proclaims the thrice-blessed Apostle, 'because the days are evil'.[59]

I was also hoping, if the Lord permits, to behold your countenance, since we are on the way, but I fear to come lest [you] ever [rebuke] us and we be put to shame. [Certainly] we believe that if it is [God's will] that we should meet you, you will first [inform] us through the person bringing you this brief letter.

Therefore, give [him] the message whether you wish us to come or not, lest [we do] . . . we fulfil our own . . . love for you . . . [concerning] you, most honored in the Spirit, [and the] brothers who are with you. . . .

Letter 6[60]

Heraclides to Paphnutius

Address on verso:
Hêrakleidês to Apa Papnoutios, the father beloved by God

> Hêrakleidês to Apa Papnoutios, the father beloved by God.

You always find time to pray for us, and through your prayers we ask for help from the Most High. But now I entreat you even more to do [this] both in my name and with regard to the illness that has attacked me and is such a burden to [me], and to [send] the oil . . .[61] [for] I do [not] believe I can be helped in any other way. . . . Christ-bearing[62] as long as you have health.

I pray that you long have good health in our Lord Christ, as you pray continuously for me, most pious father. The prophet also cries out, 'In affliction I called on him and he heard me'.[63] I tell you, I am now the one who is afflicted, where neither from a brother nor from anyone else can help come to help me—except I do have hope through our Lord Christ through your prayers.

Letter 7[64]

Athanasius to Paphnutius[65]

Address on verso:
Athanasios in the Lord God to the most honored and beloved father Papnoutios

> To the most honored and beloved father Papnoutios, greetings in the Lord God from Athanasios.

May Almighty God and his Christ grant that Your Piety long remain among us and remember us in your prayers, for if Your Holiness continues to do so, we will everywhere be in good health. Therefore, I entreat you to remember us even more frequently. For the prayers that you offer are accepted for the sake of your holy love, and [we will be well] to the extent that you request it in [your] holy prayers.

I shall do you the justice [of believing] that [you] everywhere [make] mention of us, for indeed I know that [you love] us. My concern is especially for [Didymê] and for my [mother], for Didymê [is ill] and my mother is ill. . . . As a result, my [greatest] struggle [is] that suffering [these things] as I do . . . in addition to [being] extremely exhausted. Yet I put my faith in the Saviour of all.

Living in the midst of [these] illnesses as we do, we are pleased that you also cared enough to send to us our good son Hôriôn. Theodosios . . . Antiochos,[66] Didymê, our mother, everyone in our household—we very much revere you and greet you, most honored, beloved father. May divine Providence keep you strong for the longest time, beloved, most honored, as you ever remember us.

Letter 8[67]

Justin to Paphnutius

Address on verso:
To my [honored] and beloved brother,
Papnouthios the Christ-bearer,[68] from Justin

[To my honored and beloved brother, Papnouthios the Christbearer, greetings from Justin.]

. . . which [letter] [it was necessary] for me to write to Your Goodness, beloved sir, for we believe that your citizenship is in heaven.[69] There we perceive you to be our master and new patron.[70] Therefore, in order not to write a great deal and babble— for 'in speaking a great deal they will not escape sin'—[71] I beseech you, therefore, to remember me in your holy prayers, master, that we may be able to participate in the cleansing of sins. For I am one of the sinners. Deign to accept, I beseech you, this small amount of oil through our brother Magarios.[72]

I send my warmest greetings to all our brothers in the Lord.

May divine Providence preserve you in good health, beloved sir, for a very long time in the Lord Christ.

II.

Three Letters to
Apa John of Hermopolis[73]

Introduction

We know even less about John than we do about Paphnutius. He lived in the fourth century in the region of Hermopolis (modern el-Ashmunein), a city on the west side of the Nile and the boundary between Middle and Upper Egypt. The three surviving letters follow the form of the letters to Paphnutius, although the tone of the first two is much more urgent: Abraham, in the second letter, is in 'trouble', while in the first letter Psoïs is being dunned for money. He gave money to John to get him released (from prison?) and, he says, John has not followed through; as a result, Psoïs is frantic because he has put up his children as collateral for the debt. Psoïs and Abraham call on John because, as Psoïs tells him, 'all souls live through you on account of your godliness [towards] the Almighty'. As Abraham declares, 'you . . . are truly a man of God'. Because of this, 'I trust that through your most holy prayers I may also be freed from this trouble I am in and return to all of you'.

Letter 1[74]

From Psoïs to John

Address on verso: Give to my master, the anchorite [John]

To my master, beloved Apa John.

I give thanks to God and to whomever will help me with you, through you and through God, for all souls live through you on account of your godliness [towards] the Almighty. So now help me: write a letter to Psoïs from Taetos, the tribune, to release me—if I have not already been released. I ask this because Psoïs' son has already demanded seven gold *solidi*[75] from me and his assistant another gold *solidus*. You received money from me so I might be released, but they have not released me.[76] I ask God that you either get me released or return to me the eight gold *solidi*. I am Psoïs, son of Kyllos, from the village of Pôchis in the Antaeopolite nome.[77] Now, then, for God's sake do not neglect to do this, master, for <I>[78] have already put up my children as collateral to the money lender for the gold and never serve in the army, being unfit for service. Because of my finger, I have a good reason for this: it has not festered, but it hasn't healed, either.

Letter 2[79]

From Abraham (?) to John

Address on verso:
To my most honored and devout master, [Apa John]

To my most honored and devout master,
Apa John, from Abraham,[80] greetings in the
Lord God.

Just as I have faith in your concern for me and for my house and[81] offer thanks to Your Worship, so too be assured that I keep your holy person in mind. Therefore I send greetings to Your Reverence with this letter of mine, entreating you to remember both me who respectfully greets you and all my house in the prayers that you [always] offer up each and every day to the Lord our Saviour.

I trust that through your most holy prayers I may also be freed from this trouble I[82] am in and return to all of you. So, master, you who are truly a man of God,[83] be so good as to keep me[84] in your thoughts. Greet from me all the brothers who labor with you. May God Almighty preserve you for a long time for us, sinners that we are, that through your most holy prayers we may be kept safe from harm[85] our whole lives.

Letter 3

Chaeremon to John[86]

Address on verso: To my honored brother John, Chairêmôn

To my master, Father John, hermit,[87] (from) Chairêmôn.

First of all, I salute your inimitable disposition, master, and entreat you to remember me, Chairêmôn, in your prayer. If you do this, you will be doing me the greatest favor. Bless me, too, and pray to my Lord God night and day for me.

I greet the beloved and those who love the word of my Lord God. Keep in the faith (?). . . .

But after God on High I rely on Your Piety and am persuaded that through your prayers I cannot [fail].

III.

Sixteen Letters to Nepheros & His Community[89]

Introduction

The sixteen letters translated below from Greek and Coptic date to the 350s.[90] They are addressed to a holy man named Nepheros, who was a priest at the Hathor Monastery and for the nearby town of Nêsoi; he was also, perhaps, superior of the monastery.[91] Nepheros seems to have been in charge of the community's business dealings with those outside the monastery.[92] The Hathor Monastery was apparently located in the Heracleopolite nome[93] and the community may have been Melitian, which may also have been the case with Paphnutius' community (Part I above).[94]

The first letter, from Paul and Tapiam to Nepheros and Ophellios, follows the pattern of many of the letters to Paphnutius and John: (1) they greet the monks and offer their best wishes; (2) they request the monks' prayers for them in their illness and exile from home; (3) they ask that 'a few loaves of bread', perhaps blessed bread, be sent to them; (4) finally, they greet others in the monastery and pray for the addressees' good health. Paul and Tapiam evince the same faith in the holy man's sanctity and in the power of his prayers as those who write to Paphnutius and John: in Letter 1 they declare, 'We believe that your Lord, because you are righteous, will listen to you', while in Letter 4, Paul says that he knows 'that it is gain for my soul to be remembered in your prayers since you place your hope in God'.

While Paul and Tapiam want Nepheros to know about their familial concerns of illness, concern for their children, and exile (Letters 1, 4, and, from Horion, 10), most of their letters, written by Paul, focus on matters of business. A certain Papnouthis, a monk (from the Hathor monastery?), has not delivered some promised grain, and Paul writes repeatedly about this nagging concern, begging Nepheros to do something (Letters 2, 4, 5, 6, & 7); at one point, Paul exasperatedly calls Papnouthis 'that ingrate' (Letter 6) and later bitterly complains, 'I utterly marvel at how he neither feels any shame for the monastic habit he wears when he lies nor shows any respect for you, who are worthy of all respect; nor does he plan to return the funds that he has had for so long' (Letter 7). In addition to Paul's dealings with the scoundrel Papnouthis, he regularly buys and sells commodities for the monastery (Letters 4, 5, 6, 8, & 9).[95] The other letter writers (Letters 10–16) mostly follow the usual practice of asking the holy man to intercede in spiritual and/or commercial matters: Horion (Letter 10), like Paul and Tapiam, laments his 'exile from home'; Kapiton (Letter 11) reports that his children's clothing has been stolen; Serapion (Letter 12), after greeting seemingly everyone in the monastery, importunes Nepheros to get some clothing for him, deal with (possibly) the sale of some land, and procure some grain. He is, apparently, impatient, because he twice exhorts Nepheros, 'Do not neglect to do this, most reverend father, do not neglect to do this!' One can imagine Nepheros, with this letter in hand, like Saint Augustine bewailing the 'worldly' matters overwhelming him in his position of authority.

Letter 1[96]

Paul and Tapiam to Nepheros and Ophellios

Address on verso:
Paul to my beloved sirs (and) brothers
Nepheros and Ophellios, and to the other (brothers)

To Ophellios [and the other] beloved brothers, Paul and Tapiam send greetings in the Lord.

Above all, we pray night and day that our letter finds all of you well in soul and body; then we also pray to remind you now of your loving kindness[97] so that in your prayers you may remember us by name on account of our exile from home[98] and on account of our children.

I, Tapiam, have been ill and am still confined to my bed.[99] We entreat you, therefore, to pray for us to be made healthy and whole.[100] Indeed, our children were ill earlier and through your prayers they got well. We believe that your Lord, because you are righteous, will listen to you. We also pray to finish our lives in our own home and want those closest to us to be freed from the tribulation of the world—provided that our Lord and Master considers us worthy to be preserved in our exile from home.

For your part, Brother Nepheros, sir, make us a few loaves of bread from the grain that Papnouthis owes us and send them to us so I may share them with my children.[101] I want, if God wishes, to come see you and bring them in the boat.

We greet by name all our beloved brothers and the virgins of God and our father Horiôn and our mother Tienhor and Pina and all our other brothers by name.

May divine Providence keep you healthy at all times in soul and body.

Letter 2[102]

Paul to Nepheros

Address on verso: Paul to beloved brother Nepheros

. . . Re]member, honored brother, to get the sixteen *artabas*[103] which are ours, which Papnoutis the son of Hôrion has, so that, God willing, our children may have them. And, I entreat you, remember us in your prayers. You will do this, I believe, even without being reminded.

I send my greetings to (my) honored brother Ophellios and to my beloved brothers. I pray, beloved sir, for your health in soul and body.[104]

Letter 3[105]

Paul to Nepheros

Address on verso:
[Paul] to our most honorable father [Nepheros]

Paul to our most honorable (and) beloved father Nepheros.

I make mention of the gift[106] which we have, honored father, from Your Reverence. But, in fact, we have not yet received any oil.[107] When, God willing, I do get it—for these days I am anxious about providing for my children—as soon as I get it, with great joy I will send word to you. These provisions are nourishment for our souls and for our hope in the future. I have sent through our brother Hôrion, a monk from the monastery of Ankyron . . . Taêse,[108] a [female monk?] from. . . .

Letter 4[109]

Paul to Nepheros

Address on verso: Paul, to my beloved master Nepheros

> Paul sends greetings in God to the most honorable, beloved Nepheros.

Above all, I pray night and day to be considered worthy of Your Piety and to be summoned whenever Your Clemency[110] wishes when you are in Alexandria, knowing that it is gain for my soul to be remembered in your prayers since you place your hope in God. Therefore I ask you to remember me and my children in your prayers on account of our exile from home so God may grant us to finish our lives among our own people.[111]

You have considered me worthy to appoint me to take the three small bundles[112] and supervise their sale and to send you olive oil for your use.[113] They were sold for fourteen *myriades*.[114] The jar of olive oil was bought for sixty *myriades*. God willing, when it is brought to me, I will send it on to you. I am honored when you deign to receive anything from me.

I ask, if it is not a burden, that if you receive the sixteen *artabas*[115] of wheat from Papnoutios, son of Hôrion, make [bread from it]. . . .[116]

Written in the margin: God willing, when the bread is ready, send us a wickerbasket full.

I [pray] for [your] good health, man [of God].

P.S. When someone among you who has sheep can supply sheepskins, I need three or four.

Letter 5[117]

Paul to Nepheros

Address on verso:
[Paul] to the most honorable, beloved Nepheros

Paul to the most honorable, beloved Nepheros.

By means of our brothers Aspidas and Paul <I have written> to Your Piety so that, if it seems good to you, you will take the wheat that Papnouthis, son of Hôrion, owes us and with it distribute three *artabas*[118] of bread to the needy and, keeping the remaining thirteen artabas for yourself, send us three as bread. As quickly as possible, if you can, send us a wickerbasket full.

When it pleases you to write us back, remember to let us know whether you received the olive oil that we sent through our sister Taêse, whom we put at your service.[119] And do not hesitate to write us about what you need in Alexandria. Inform Protos about the iron that he wrote to me about: the commodity is not available in Alexandria at this time.

We send greetings to all the brothers with you. We ask you, along with them, also to remember us in your prayers.

May the [Lord] of the [Universe preserve] you in soul and body.

Letter 6[120]

Paul to Nepheros

Address on verso:
Paul to my beloved sir, the [incomparable] father Nepheros[121]

Through my honored brother Theodosios I planned to send ten *sextarii*[122] of olive oil to Your incomparable[123] Piety but, since it is very difficult to find a suitable jar, we have not sent them yet.

When, with God's approval, a suitable one comes to hand, we will proclaim our delight as we recall your love[124] for your fellow man.

I entreat you, honored father, to persuade that ingrate Paphnoutis, son of Hôrion, to give us three *artabas*[125] of wheat now and our father Prôtos will make for us fifteen *metra* of fine wheat flour and fifteen loaves of bread and send them to us.[126] Summon my enemies Ailourion and Paphnutis, who are always mishandling my business, and convince them to settle accounts with me. . . .

Greet. . . .

Written in the margin: (Let me know) when you receive two *solidi*[127] from Hôr, who is a monk in Ankyron and a relative of Eudaimonos, the son of Abaskantos, . . . share in . . . from Kollouthos.

Letter 7[128]

Paul to Nepheros

Address on verso: Paul to . . . Nepheros

[I asked] you to importune [Papnuthis], son of Hôrion, and get the sixteen *artabas*[129] of wheat from him.[130] I utterly marvel at how he neither feels any shame for the monastic habit he wears when he lies nor shows any respect for you, who are worthy of all respect; nor does he plan to return the funds that he has had for so long.[131]

(Greetings) to my honored Ophellios and to our most revered mother Tienôr and Pina and Hôriôn.[132] I send my greetings [to all of our other brothers, too]

(written in the margin) by name. May the Lord keep you well in soul and body.

Letter 8[133]

Paul to Nepheros

Address on verso:
[Paul] to my honored (and) beloved father [Nepheros]

Paul to Nepheros, my honored (and) beloved
father and brother.

I am now grateful that you have deigned to write to us.[134] I want to inform you now that Gennadios has sold the six bundles[135] for ninety-four *myriades*, with which he has bought five *sextarii* of olive oil for twelve *myriades* each, an *[A]nemourion*[136] of melted pitch for ten *myriades*, and a bar of iron weighing three *mnas* for twenty *myriades*, for a total of ninety *myriades*, leaving four *myriades*.[137]

I thought it necessary, then, to write to you first of all so you might remember us in your prayers and, second, to notify you about these things.

Since you notified us about Hôriôn by means of a letter, I want you to know that [Hôriôn himself has said that _____ has summoned him][138] to the military camp[139] to [hand over] the money for me, but so far she has given me nothing. If it seems right to you, write her about this, since she has ordered him to give her the money, so that when she receives a letter from . . . , she will be ashamed and will produce the money and (Hôriôn) [will be discharged (from his obligation)]. We will let [you] know by letter what happens.

We send our greetings to [all] our beloved brothers, [Ophellios and] Prôt[os] [and] Ammônios [and] our [father] Hôriôn and [our mother Tienôr] and. . . .

Written in the margin: If Papnouthis neglects [to deliver] the wheat,[140] let him know that [he will be forced to comply] with the oath he took[141] or you will no longer welcome him at the *synaxis*.[142]

Letter 9[143]

Paul to Nepheros, Kolobos, and Prôtos

Address on verso:
Paul to my masters and fathers
Nepheros and Kolobos and Prôtos

[To my beloved fathers Nepheros and Kolobos and Prôtos], the [masters][144] of my soul, Paul sends greetings in the Lord.

I confess my gratitude for God's providence that you have considered me, the lowest of the low, worthy to assist you. I have, accordingly, bought the olive oil and at the same time have filled a jar with twenty *sextarii*, each *sextarius* worth one hundred three and a half pieces of silver.[145]

I ask, therefore, that you remember me and my children in your prayers and that you give me your instructions. I confess my gratitude for God's providence that you have considered me worthy to receive instructions from Your Pious Persons.

I pray that you are well for many years and prosper in God, beloved brothers.

Letter 10[146]

Horion to Nepheros

Address on verso: Hô[riôn] to my master, father Neph[eros]

Hôrion sends greetings in the Lord God to
my master, father Nepheros.

I pray first of all to Almighty God for your perfect good health so that this my letter may find you healthy and in good spirits. I know, my master (and) father, that after the Lord God your prayers have brought me good health and, because of your (pl.)

prayers, I once again have confidence, in the Lord God, that in the end we will be restored to our homes,[147] for I know that as long as you remember me in your prayers the Lord God will not forsake me.[148]

While we are here, do not hesitate to write to me about the things you need. I am happy to have you call on me for whatever you want, for after God I have you as helper and father.

I send my greetings to my honored brother Ophellios and to my mother Tinor and to our sister Pina. . . .

Letter 11[149]

Kapiton to the two Nepherotes

Address on verso:
Kapitôn, to the two Nepherotes,
beloved brothers (and) priests of the Hathyr Monastery

> Brother Kapitôn sends his warmest greetings in God to the two Nepherotes, beloved and Christbearing[151] brothers of the Hathyr Monastery.

I hold it as 'sure and worthy of full acceptance'[152] first of all to acknowledge your relationship[153] with God so that through your prayers I may return to you safe and sound. I especially send my greetings to father Pesans and to all the 'soldiers of Christ'[154] who are with you and to all the others by name.

Hurry, then, fathers—since I have heard that my clothes have been stolen in Pselemachis,[155] [which someone] from Tampeti[156] wrote to me about [so I would come] to Pselemachis and Tampati—[157]so that you may leave with them for Tampeti to see our father Pamoun, the priest. . . .

Letter 12[158]

Serapion to Petechon and Nepheros

Address on verso:
Give (this letter) to the priest Nepheros. From Serapiôn, a monk of Mouê Komê[159]

To my beloved father, Apa Petechôn, father of the monastery,[160] greetings from Serapiôn, your [son] in the Lord.

First of all, I send hearty greetings to you, most esteemed [father]. I send greetings to my father Nepherôs the priest, that you may pray [for] me in your holy prayers, and to the other Nepherôs, a priest, I send hearty greetings to you.[161] I greet Euphelis, I greet Jacob, I greet Bêsas the monk. I send greetings to K[u]lol and to Kasis, his brother. I greet Pouti and his son. I greet Aeiôn, I greet Ariôn, I greet Hêraklas, I greet Amêr, I greet P...choleukis. I greet Hôr, Amêr's brother; I greet Apa Nilos (?); I greet Apoutis, along with his brother, Syros. I greet Hêreu, I greet Keime and his brother Paris; I greet Papeis; I greet Papnoutis, Anoubion's brother; I greet Hêraklês; I greet Herminos, the lector; I greet Hôr, from (?) Tahmourô,[162] I greet Lôtos; I send greetings to Aleitis; I greet Apa Hôriôn.
 I am writing to you, Apa Nepherôs. When I left you, I came—thanks be to God—to Omboi. I send hearty greetings to you (pl.). Find Paul, a sailor from Toetô,[163] in order to get the clothing from him and two tunics and three scythes, and get them from him. He has two sons, Hatrês and Pkylis. Do not neglect to do this.
 I greet Apa Ôtas and Kasis. I greet Paêsis and I greet Petros and Hôriôn. I greet everyone at the monastery, humble and great. I greet Serapiôn [from] Tahmouro; I greet Kapiton; I greet all of you, my brothers, that you may pray for me.
 I am writing to you, Nepherôs: take care of the small [piece (?)] of land, since I am coming. Do not neglect to do this, most reverend father, do not neglect to do this! . . . Get the grain, since I am coming; put it in the cemetery,[164] since I am coming. . . . Nepherôs, since I am coming, most reverend father.
 I pray that you have good health for many years. . . .

Letter 13[165]

Lykarion to Nepheros

Address on verso:
Give (this letter) to Nepherôs, the priest of Nêsos,
in (the monastery of) Phathôr

To (my) beloved f[ather Nepherôs], the priest,
[greetings] from Lykariôn [in the Lord].

First of all, it is necessary to [send greetings] to [Your] Inimitable [Disposition[166] and] then [also to the] brothers with [you]. The person whose [way of life] is to renounce [being a meddler] has been sent as a light to [those sitting in darkness].[167] Do not [neglect to] dem[onstrate your gentleness].[168]

I send my greetings by [name] to all [the beloved] brothers [who are] with you who love [God]. . . .

[I pray] that [you] have good health in the Lord for many [years], beloved [father].

Letter 14[169]

_____ to Nepheros

. . . brother Nepherôs . . . on account of
which . . . [tri]mêsion. . . .[170]

May Divine Providence preserve you in your way of life in good health and high esteem, beloved, most reverend. . . .
. . . and we . . . our Pina.[171] . . .

Letter 15[172]

(Coptic)
Apa Papnoute to Nepheros and Paieou

Address on verso (in Greek):
Apa [Papnout]e. Give (this letter) to Nepherôs the priest.

It is Apa Papnoute who writes (this letter) [to Nepherôs the] priest and to Paiêou the deacon, the beloved of the Fifth . . . who love the brothers and foreigners.
Truly your zeal . . . your fragrant aroma[173] has roused a multitude. Hurry, my beloved [brothers, and come with the steward][174] south to Pmeshôut.[175] Pinoute has his pillow . . . tomb.

Reverse: I greet Panêf the deacon and . . . and all the brothers by name. As for you, [beloved brother] Paiêou, I am well aware of your zeal. Do not be negligent [but] come yourself to Pmeshôut.

Letter 16[176]

(Coptic)
Papnoute (?) to Nepheros (?)

Address on verso:
Give (this letter) to Nepherô[s] from Papn(oute?) the priest[177]

. . . in . . . gave . . .[178] with her. He brought [forty talents][179] for her and . . . he gave (her) these documents[180] dealing with the other hundred. He swore[181] that Tshenêt would bring it to him. She [said that] the forty talents would be [coming] [but?] the other two hundred sixty. . . .[182] He said[183] that . . .[184] Êlei, the monk Pme, John, Barôn, the priest Satorneilos, Siôn, and many others in the city were coming for his assurances,[185] saying, "We found the other hundred and fought with Wôônsh[186] until we collected the other two hundred sixty talents.
We greet all the brothers by name.

NOTES

[1] I wish to thank Augustine Casiday for his bibliographical help and suggestions and Maged S. Mikhail for advice about Coptic. Apostolos N. Athanassakis assisted with the translation of the Paphnutius archive (Part I).

[2] Peter Brown, 'The Rise and Function of the Holy Man in late Antiquity', *Journal of Roman Studies* 61 (1971) 80–101, rpt. in Brown, *Society and the Holy in Late Antiquity* (London: Faber, 1982); idem., 'The Saint as Exemplar in Late Antiquity', *Representations* 2 (1983) 1–25; idem., 'The Rise and Function of the Holy Man in Late Antquity, 1971–1997', *Journal of Early Christian Studies* 6:3 (1998) 353–376.

[3] See Benedicta Ward, 'A Sense of Wonder: Miracles of the Desert', in *The Lives of the Desert Fathers*, trans. Norman Russell, CS 34 (Kalamazoo: Cistercian Publications, 1980) 39–46.

[4] Philip Rousseau, 'Ascetics as mediators and as teachers', in *The Cult of Saints in Late Antiquity and the Middle Ages: Essays on the Contribution of Peter Brown*, ed. James Howard-Johnston and Paul Antony Hayward (Oxford: Oxford University Press, 1999) 45–59.

[5] Claudia Rapp, '"For next to God, you are my salvation": reflections on the rise of the holy man in late antiquity', in Howard-Johnston and Hayward, edd., *The Cult of Saints* 63–81.

[6] *Life of Antony* 14.5; trans. Tim Vivian and Apostolos N. Athanassakis, *The Life of Antony: The Coptic Life and the Greek Life*, CS 202 (Kalamazoo: Cistercian Publications, 2003) 93.

[7] *Life of Antony* 49.1; Vivian and Athanassakis, CS 202: 163.

[8] *Vita Pachomii* 41; trans. Armand Veilleux, *Pachomian Koinonia*, 1: *The Life of Saint Pachomius and His Disciples*, CS 45 (Kalamazoo: Cistercian Publications, 1980) 64–65. For a series of miracles by Pachomius, see *Vita Pachomii* 41–45, Veilleux, CS 45:64-69.

[9] James E. Goehring, 'Egyptian Monasticism', in Vincent L. Wimbush, ed., *Ascetic Behavior in Greco-Roman Antiquity: A Sourcebook* (Minneapolis: Fortress Press, 1990) 456.

[10] Goehring, 456. The documentary evidence, however, requires a great deal of sifting, weighing, and interpretation; see Roger S. Bagnall's introduction to his *Egypt in Late Antiquity* (Princeton: Princeton University Press, 1993) 3–14, and the volume as a whole.

[11] *Life of Antony* 61.1-3; Vivian and Athanassakis, trans., 189.

[12] Tim Vivian, trans., *Paphnutius: Histories of the Monks of Upper Egypt and the Life of Onnophrius*, CS 140, rev. ed. (Kalamazoo: Cistercian Publications, 2000) 123, 128–129, 125, 133–134.

[13] Vivian, CS 140:123.

[14] Bagnall, 174.

[15] For a general overview, see Jean Gascou, 'Monasteries, Economic Activities of', *The Coptic Encyclopedia*, ed. Aziz S. Atiya (New York: Macmillan, 1991) 5:1639-1645. On the development of the pachomian 'villages', see James E. Goehring, *Ascetics, Society, and the Desert: Studies in Early Egyptian Monasticism* (Harrisburg, Pennsylvania, 1999) 89–109.

[16] Rapp, 67.

[17] This 'us' may be an epistolary way of saying 'me'.

[18] Gk: ἀδελφούς, literally 'brothers'.

[19] Bernard P. Grenfell and Arthur S. Hunt, edd., *The Oxyrhynchus Papyri* (London: Egypt Exploration Fund, 1898) 12.1494 (pp. 251–252). The editors say that 'The handwriting suggests a date not much later than A.D. 300, while the high price of olives . . . indicates a reign not earlier than Diocletian's'.

[20] On Psan, see H. E. Winlock and W. E. Crum, *The Monastery of Epiphanius at Thebes* (New York: Metropolitan Museum of Art, 1926; rpt. Arno Press, 1973) 222.

[21] Literally: bring out the enemy. It is possible that 'enemy' refers to 'the Enemy', that is, Satan; such a designation is common in early coptic Christianity.

[22] W. E. Crum and H. G. Evelyn White, *The Monastery of Epiphanius at Thebes* (New York: Metropolitan Museum of Art, 1926; repr. Arno Press, 1973), Part II, #199 (text, 55; translation, 206–207).

[23] Or: for me. The reading is uncertain.

[24] Crum and Evelyn White, #279 (text, 73; translation, 227).

[25] Letter 4 of the Paphnutius archive, translated in full below.

[26] Claudia Rapp (see n. 5 above), '"For next to God, you are my salvation"'.

[27] For a partial translation of the letters of Barsanuphius and John, see *Letters from the Desert: Barsanuphius and John*, translation and introduction by John Chryssavgis, Popular Patristics Series (Crestwood, New York: St Vladimir's Seminary Press, 2003); a complete translation is forthcoming. For the Epiphanius archive, see Crum and Evelyn White, *The Monastery of Epiphanius at Thebes*, Part II.

[28] Earlier translations of Paphnutius and Nepheros are given below. All translations here are my own.

[29] Letters 1–7 are translated, with the assistance of Apostolos N. Athanassakis, from the text edited by H. Idris Bell, *Jews and Christians in Egypt* (London: The British Museum, 1914) 100–120; Letter 8 is translated from the text edited by Adolf Deissmann, *Light from the Ancient East* (Grand Rapids, Michigan: Baker, 1978 [rpt of the 4th German edition of 1922]) 215–216 (#23). Both Bell and Deissmann supply english translations. A recent english translation of the letters by Robert F. Boughner with an introduction by James E. Goehring may be found in Wimbush, ed., *Ascetic Behavior in Greco-Roman Antiquity* 456–463. See Wimbush, 456 n. 1 for other 'sparse' documentary evidence concerning egyptian monasticism before the fifth century.

[30] For a full discussion, see Bell, *Jews and Christians in Egypt*, 100–103. The *Coptic Encyclopedia* does not have an article on this Paphnutius.

[31] Bell, 100; Deissmann, 215.

[32] The spelling of his name varies. On the various Paphnutii known in Egypt in late antiquity, see Bell, 101–102, and Vivian, *Paphnutius*, 42–50.

[33] For a discussion of Paphnutius' monastic community, see James E. Goehring, 'Monastic Diversity and Ideological Boundaries in Fourth-Century Christian Egypt', *Journal of Early Christian Studies* 5:1 (Spring 1997) 61–84, esp. 68–73; repr. in Goehring, *Ascetics, Society, and the Desert* 196–218.

[34] On the Melitians, see Janet Timbie, 'Melitian Schism', *The Coptic Encyclopedia*, ed. Aziz S. Atiya (New York: Macmillan, 1991) 5.1884-1885; Bagnall, 305–308; and Tim Vivian, *Saint Peter of Alexandria: Bishop and Martyr* (Philadelphia: Fortress Press, 1988) 15–40.

[35] Goehring, *Ascetics, Society, and the Desert*, 203–204. Bell, 102, believes that Paphnutius' community was not Melitian: 'We may then dismiss any Meletian connexion as improbable'. He adds, 102 n. 3, 'Doctrinally there is nothing to indicate

Meletian or Catholic sympathies'. Goehring, *Ascetics, Society, and the Desert*, says that Bell's arguments 'are hardly convincing' but does not offer counter arguments. For clearly melitian monastic texts, see Bell, 38–99 (*P. Lond.* 1913–1922); these texts, as Goehring reminds us, 188–189, 'remain our most certain evidence of a significant monastic movement among the Melitians in the fourth century'.

[36] James E. Goehring, *Ascetics, Society, and the Desert*, 188. For a discussion of Paphnutius' monastic community, see Goehring, *Ascetics, Society, and the Desert*, 196–218.

[37] For a rebuttal to this criticism, see Tim Vivian, '"Christ in the Desert"—A Response', *American Benedictine Review* 52:4 (December 2001) 393–420.

[38] See below Letter 6 of the Paphnutius archive and letter 3 of the Nepheros archive.

[39] In one story about Daniel of Scetis (6th c.), monks arguing over the corpse of a saint declare about Abba Daniel, 'The old man already belongs to heaven'. (Daniel, the monks are saying, has no fear of combat with the Enemy—Satan—while they do, so they need the body of the dead saint as a holy relic to protect them from evil.) See Tim Vivian, 'Witness to Holiness: Abba Daniel of Scetis', *Coptic Church Review* 24: 1 & 2 (Spring/Summer 2003) 2–52, at 42.

[40] *P. Lond.[London papyrus]* 1923. Bell, 103–104; translation, 104. I have not indicated the bracketing and sublinear dots of the published texts, indicating with brackets only those words that are very uncertain. Following Emerson's warning about obeying a 'foolish consistency', I have spelled most names as they appear in the text, including orthography, except for common english names like 'John' and 'Paul'.

[41] Papnouthios, a hellenized form of Coptic Pa-pnoute ('he of God'), was a common name in late antique Egypt, with a wide variety of spellings; see Tim Vivian, *Paphnutius*, 42–50.

[42] The address is preceded by a sign, either of a cross with a Greek 'rho' ('r') at the top or a Chi-rho, the symbol for Christ. Address in Greek: Τῷ κυρίῳ ἀγαπητῷ πατρὶ Παπνουθιῷ. The use of *kurios*, 'lord, master', even 'sir' ('mister' in Modern Greek) and *despotês*, 'lord, master', in these letters is difficult to translate into English. The usage was also common in coptic letters: ⲡⲁϫⲟⲉⲓⲥ ⲛⲉⲓⲱⲧ, which is the equivalent of Greek κύριός μου πατήρ. For one example, see Crum and Evelyn White, #271 (text, 71; translation, 224). I have chosen throughout to use 'honored' instead of 'lord' or 'master' to capture the sense of *kurios* when it is used adjectively with other words such as 'brother' or 'father', with additional words necessary in English placed in parentheses. I have used 'honored sir', for *kurios* and 'master' for *despotês* when they stand alone, though the two terms are symantically close; see G. W. H. Lampe, *A Patristic Greek Lexicon* (Oxford: Clarendon, 1961) 339A. I wish to thank Prof. A. N. Athanassakis for his advice on this matter. Although 'lord' and 'master' sound outdated in modern English, we need to remember that the people of late antiquity, including Christians, lived in a hierarchical society and owned slaves.

[43] Bell notes, 103, that Ammonios 'was far too common' a name 'for any identification to be even probable'. He lists a known anchorite, presbyter, and bishop, but concludes that this Ammonios 'is quite as likely to have been a man unknown to fame as any of the persons called Ammonius who occur in the records of the fourth century'.

Notes 369

[44] In the Epiphanius archive, a certain Andreas says to a deacon that he has confided or trusted in 'your fatherhood next after God': ⲁⲓⲅⲱ ⲅⲧⲁⲓ ⲉⲧⲉⲕⲏⲛⲧⲉⲓⲱⲧ ⲭⲓⲛⲡⲛⲟⲩⲧⲉ. Crum and Evelyn White, #192 (p. 54, text; 205, translation). A certain Lazarus tells Epiphanius, 'I have no one to help me except God and you': ⲏ[ⲛ]ⲧⲁⲓ ⲕⲉⲃⲟⲏⲑⲟⲥ ⲛⲥⲁⲡⲛⲟⲩⲧ[ⲉ] ⲛ̅ⲡ̅ⲏ̅ⲁⲕ. Crum and Evelyn White, #271 (text, 71; translation, 224–225).

[45] P. Lond. 1924. Bell, text and translation, 105.

[46] 'Apa' or 'Abba' was an honorific title given to esteemed, usually senior, monks. The word, Aramaic in origin (see Mk 14:36, Rom 8:15, Gal 4:6), means 'Father'. Modern egyptian Arabic uses 'Abouna', 'our Father'.

[47] This Ausonios may have been prefect of Augustamnica from 341–342; see Bell, 100.

[48] Bell, 106 n. 5, suggests that this is a village in the Heracleopolite nome, 'but the fact does not greatly help to determine the provenance of the Papnuthius correspondence'.

[49] P. Lond. 1925. Bell, 106–107; translation, 107.

[50] Bell notes, 108 n. 25, that the reading for 'monastery', μ]ονῖς (= μονῆς), is uncertain (all letters are partial). The name 'Pi]anis' (the author of the letter) is possible, but 'monk', μοναχός, after it 'is impossible'.

[51] The name is not attested elsewhere, and the first three letters are uncertain.

[52] See 1 Cor 5:3.

[53] On Athanasios, see Letter 7.

[54] P. Lond. 1926. Bell, 108–109; translation, 109.

[55] That is, spiritual daughter.

[56] χρηστοφόρῳ = χριστοφόρῳ; see Lampe, 1528B s.v. χρηστόφορος, and 1533A s.v. χριστόφορος. See below Letters 6 and 8 of the Paphnutius archive and Letter 11 of the Nepheros archive. See Ignatius, Epistle to the Ephesians 9.2. In coptic letters, Christophoros is used adjectively. In one letter, the writer calls the monk Isaac ⲡⲣⲱⲙⲉ ⲉⲧⲫⲟⲣⲉⲓ ⲙ̅ⲡⲉⲭⲣ̅ⲥ̅ ⲛ̅ⲟⲩⲱⲱ̅ⲙⲉ, 'the man who truly bears Christ'; Crum and Evelyn White, #306 (text, 79). For other examples, see #133 (text, 38), #142 (text, 41), #180 (text, 52), #315 (text, 80), #474 (text, 106), and #515 (no text given; translation, 282).

[57] Gk: θρησκευόντων, literally 'worshippers', 'practitioners of religious rites or rituals', but clearly some kind of monastic or ascetic group is indicated. Lampe suggests, 654B, that θρησκευτής may mean 'monk'. θρησκεύω sounds like a late form formed by analogy to λατρεύω, etc. Τῶν θρησκευόντων should be τῶν θρησκευομένων. Yet Lampe cites many instances of the active form. I wish to thank Prof. Athanassakis for these comments.

[58] P. Lond. 1927. Bell, 110–112; translation, 112–113.

[59] Eph 5:16. There is an untranslatable play on words here: 'the time' renders Greek *ton kairon*, whereas 'the appropriate time' above it translates *kata ton kairon*. So Dôrotheos is affirming that Paphnutius is indeed 'redeeming' the time *(kairon)* because God has granted him the opportunity *(kairon)* to do so.

[60] P. Lond. 1928. Bell, 114; translation, 114–115.

[61] Presumably oil for healing; see Letter 3 of the Nepheros archive below.

[62] See notes 56 and 67.

[63] See Ps 117:5 (118:5) and Jon 2:3.

⁶⁴ *P. Lond.* 1929. Bell, 118; translation, 119.

⁶⁵ As Bell notes, 115, 'This letter, the most imperfect of the whole series, is also from one point of view the most interesting'. See Bell, 115–118 for his intriguing suggestion that this letter may be from Saint Athanasius, Bishop of Alexandria: 'It seems clear that the writer is a man of education and with some literary sense. He writes too with respect indeed but in a tone of perfect equality; one could imagine him to be a person of authority, and he speaks of his household as if it were of some size' (116). Bell concludes, 118, 'The most we can say is that there is at least a reasonable possibility that we have in the present document a specimen of the hand of the great champion of orthodoxy'. If Paphnutius' community was Melitian, however (see n. 34 and 94), it is inconceivable that this Athanasius is the famous bishop of Alexandria: he was the sworn enemy of the Melitians and Arians.

⁶⁶ As Bell notes, 116, among Athanasius' extant letters is one to an Antiochos. The name was apparently not common in christian Egypt.

⁶⁷ *P. Heid.* [Heidelberg papyrus] i.6. This letter comes from the Heidelberg papyri, not from the London papyri, but may belong to the Paphnutius archive. Deissmann, *Light from the Ancient East* 215–216 (#23). Deissmann published an earlier version of the text in *Die Septuaginta-Papyri und andere altchristliche Texte der Heidelberger Papyrus-Sammlung*, Veröffentlichungen aus der Heidelberger Papyrus-Sammlung I (Heidelberg: Carl Winter, 1905) 94–104 (#6). The published texts are identical except that in lines 2–3 Deissmann originally conjectured χρηστοφόρου, 'the son of Chrêstophoros', which he later changed to χρηστοφόρῳ, 'Christbearer', the reading adopted here (see notes 56 and 62 above). The text of this letter has also been edited by Mario Naldini, *Il Cristianismo in Egitto: Lettere private nei papiri dei secoli II–IV* (Firenze: Le Monnier, 1968) 191–194 (#41), with essentially the same text (he also reads χρηστοφόρῳ).

⁶⁸ See notes 56, 62, and 67 above.

⁶⁹ See Phil 3:20.

⁷⁰ Rapp, 69, translates 'common patron'. Deissmann and Naldini believe κενόν equals καινόν ('ai' was pronounced as short 'e' at this time, as in Modern Greek), 'new', whereas Rapp believes it should be κοινόν, 'common', 'highlighting Paphnutius' role within his group of monastics'.

⁷¹ Prv 10:19 (LXX).

⁷² I.e. Makarios (Macarius).

⁷³ Translated from B. R. Rees, ed., *Papyri from Hermopolis and Other Documents of the Byzantine Period*, Graeco-Roman Memoirs 42 (London: Egypt Exploration Society, 1964) 12–18. There is also a fragmentary letter from John and others, 19–20, possibly to a high-ranking Church official, asking him to intervene on their behalf with a judge because they are facing trial on a false charge.

⁷⁴ Rees, ed., #7. Text, 13–14; translation, 14.

⁷⁵ Nomisma (pl. nomismata) could indicate a coin or, more specifically, the gold *aureus* or *solidus*.

⁷⁶ Gk: καὶ ουκ ἀπόλυσόν μαι [sic]. Rees translates it thus: 'and they (?) have not released me', taking ἀπόλυσον as an aorist past tense (see p. 14, line 11: ἀπέλυσαν?). As Rees comments, 13, 'the letter itself is clearly the work of a man whose knowledge of Greek was inadequate to the occasion: the grammar and syntax are both highly irregular, and yet the writer is often ambitious in his use of words and phrases'.

Notes   371

⁷⁷ Text: Ἀνταιουπολείτου. Antinoopolite? Antinoopolis (modern Sheikh Abâdeh) in Middle Egypt, on the east side of the Nile and across from Hermopolis, was the administrative center of the Thebaid.

⁷⁸ Gk: ἔδωκας. Rees translates the verb as a second-person singular, which is correct, but wonders, 13, whether it should be first person. It seems to make more sense to regard the final sigma as a mistake; if one removes it, the verb is first-person singular. Otherwise, John has put up Psoïs' children as collateral.

⁷⁹ Rees, ed., #8. Text, 15–16; translation, 16.

⁸⁰ Rees translates, 16, as 'Apa John, . . . son of Abraham', but notes, 16 n. 2, 'The trace read as eta may well have been the result of an erasure, and there is certainly very little room for another proper name before Ἀ]βραάμ: it is possible, therefore, that Abraham was the name of the writer'.

⁸¹ Adopting Rees' suggestion, 16, line 4.

⁸² Gk ἐσμέν, which I take as an epistolary 'we', meaning 'I'. Rees translates as 'we'.

⁸³ See 1 Tim 6:11 (Dt 33:1; Ps 90 [title]).

⁸⁴ Gk ἡμᾶς, which I take as an epistolary 'us' meaning 'me'. Rees translates as 'us'.

⁸⁵ Or: saved; Gk διασωσθῶμεν.

⁸⁶ Rees, #9. Text, 17–18; translation, 18.

⁸⁷ Gk: ἀποτακτικῷ; Rees, 18, line 2, cites other papyri where the term means 'hermit' or 'anchorite'. On this term, see James E. Goehring, 'The Origins of Monasticism', in Harold W. Attridge and Gohei Hata, eds., *Eusebius, Judaism and Christianity* (Detroit: Wayne State University Press, 1992) 235–255, repr. in Goehring, *Ascetics, Society, and the Desert*, 13–35; and Goehring, *Ascetcs*, 53–72.

⁸⁸ This last sentence, three lines in Greek, was written vertically in the left margin.

⁸⁹ Translated from Bärbal Kramer and John C. Shelton, eds., *Das Archiv des Nepheros und verwandte Texte, Teil I, Das Archiv des Nepheros: Papyri aus der Trierer und der Heidelberger Papyrussammlung* (Mainz am Rhein: Philipp von Zabern, 1987). The editors supply german translations of the letters, which I have consulted. The collection contains forty-two letters; I have translated only the sixteen to Nepheros.

⁹⁰ Goehring, *Ascetics, Society, and the Desert*, 189, says that the Nepheros archive 'appears to come from the same Melitian community [as *P. Lond* 1913–1922, the Melitian archive; see n. 33 above] at a slightly later date in the same century, in the 350s'. See Kramer and Shelton, 3–5.

⁹¹ See Kramer and Shelton, 9–10.

⁹² Kramer and Shelton, 9.

⁹³ On the monastery, see Kramer and Shelton, 11–20. They identify the Hathor Monastery of these letters—also called Phathor and Hathyr or Hathyrti—with one of the same name in the melitian London papyri edited by Bell (see n. 35 above) and say the identification is 'conclusive' (13, 20).

⁹⁴ Goehring argues, *Ascetics, Society, and the Desert*, 203, that the archives of Paphnutius (c. 340s) and Nepheros (350s) come from the same community as *P. Lond.* 1913–1922 (see above, n. 34), which was definitely Melitian. He says, 189–190, that the monastery of Hathor in the Upper Kynopolite nome is 'the apparent source' of the London papyri (*P. Lond.* 1913.3 and 1920.2). The Nepheros archive also comes from a monastery of Hathor, said to be located in the

Herakleopolite nome (*P. Neph.* 48). Kramer and Shelton, 20–21, connect the Hathor community with the one in *P. Lond.* 1913–1922, edited by Bell, and place its letters at a slightly later date. Goehring concludes, 203 n. 22: 'Neither archive contains the certain evidence of Melitian origin offered by the P. Lond. VI 1913–1922 collection'. Kramer and Shelton give sixteen points that suggest that Nepheros' community was Melitian and conclude, 21, 'None of the abovementioned peculiarities of this archive is by itself proof that we are dealing here with a "Melitian" archive. Nevertheless, taken all together they seem to justify the conclusion that the Christians of our texts were indeed rather unusual Christians. But if this is true, then we practically cannot avoid the further conclusion that they were "Melitians"'. Bagnall, 308, believes that both communities were Melitian.

[95] A letter from the Nag Hammadi finds is similar; Sasnos, a monk or priest, or both, is asked to intercede in a matter and to supply something: 'Make Peter, who is harassing our brother Appianos through Papnoutios' people in the matter of the rents, hold off for a few more days until they find an opportunity to come to you and settle their problem'. The writer then appeals to Sasnos' love in Christ and asks him, if it is not a burden, to get ten loads of chaff for him and let him know the cost. *P. Nag. Hamm.* [Nag Hammadi papyrus] 68; quoted from Bagnall, 224.

[96] Kramer and Shelton, eds., 36; translation, 40. The numbering of the letters corresponds to the numbering in Kramer and Shelton's edition.

[97] Gk: φιλανθρωπίαν *(philanthrôpia)*. See n. 110 below.

[98] 'Exile from home': Gk ξενειτίαν (= ξενιτείαν). Although *xeniteia* became a technical term in monastic vocabulary to indicate desirable 'solitude' or 'isolation from the world', it also retained its meaning of 'travel in a foreign land', 'exile', which appears to be the meaning here. The editors agree, 40, that it means 'exile': "uns und unsere Kinder wegen unseres Weilens in der Fremde'. As one Egyptian letter writer in late antiquity put it, 'it is better for you to be in your homes, whatever they may be, than abroad' (Bagnall, 40). For a full discussion, see Kramer and Shelton, eds., 27–29. See Letters 4 and 10 below.

[99] For letters from the archive of Epiphanius asking for relief from illness, see Crum and Evelyn White, #246 (text, 64; translation, 217), #250 (text, 65; translation, 218), #329 (text, 82; translation, 240), #359 (text, 88; translation, 249).

[100] The first person plural pronouns in this sentence may be epistolary plurals that equal first person singular pronouns; the pronouns in the preceding and following sentences make it difficult to determine.

[101] This may very well be blessed bread intended for sacramental purposes. Kramer and Shelton, 20–21, connect such bread to the desires of the Melitians to have bread blessed by their own priests.

[102] Kramer and Shelton, eds., 41; translation, 42.

[103] The *artaba* was an egyptian measure varying from 24 to 42 *choinikes;* the *choinix* was about a quart, one person's daily allowance of grain. Bagnall, 332, notes that various artabas 'were in use, but the common one was equal to 4.5 *modii Italici,* or 38.78 liters. An artaba of wheat weighed a bit over 30 kg. . . . The nonstandard forty-choinix artaba sometimes referred to would thus have held about 25.2 kg'.

[104] There is apparently a line of illegible marginal writing.

Notes 373

[105] Kramer and Shelton, eds., 43; translation, 44.

[106] Gk: εὐλογείας (= εὐλογίας). *Eulogia* had a wide variety of meanings (see Lampe, 569A–570A): blessing, gift, benefit, consecrated eucharistic elements, gift of blessed bread, alms. The editors, 43 line 2, say it is not at all clear what Paul means here, but they do not believe he means blessed bread.

[107] Given the *eulogia*, blessed bread, mentioned immediately above, it seems likely that this oil is blessed oil sent by the priest Nepheros for sacramental purposes (see James 5:14). This was a common practice of holy men: John of Lycopolis often 'gave oil to the afflicted and healed them in that way'; Russell, trans., *The Lives of the Desert Fathers*, 53.

[108] In Letter 5 Paul refers to Taêse as 'our sister Taêse'.

[109] Kramer and Shelton, eds., 45; translation, 48.

[110] Gk.: *philanthrôpia* (see n. 97 above). The editors point out, 46, lines 5–6, that *philanthrôpia* was a form of address reserved for the highest-ranking laity and for the emperor. See H. I. Bell, 'Philanthropia in the Papyri of the Roman Period', in *Hommages à Joseph Bidez et Franz Cumont* (Brussells: Latomus, 1949) 31–37.

[111] See n. 98 above.

[112] As the editors note, 47 line 16, 'Unfortunately, we do not learn what kind of product Paul received and sold in bundles. . . . The product must have been produced in the Hathor Monastery and marketed in Alexandria'.

[113] Bagnall, 30, notes that 'oil' without further modifiers refers to a vegetable oil.

[114] See Kramer and Shelton, eds., 4–5, on quantities and prices. 'Eighty *talents* equal twelve *myriades*, which is the price of a single *sextarius* (for all practical purposes, half a liter) of oil in Letter 8.7'. See also Naphtali Lewis, *Life in Egypt under Roman Rule* (Oxford: Clarendon, 1983), 'Appendix: The Prices of Good and Services', 208–209.

[115] See n. 103 above.

[116] If the conjecture of 'bread' is correct, this may be blessed bread. See Letter 1 and n. 101 above.

[117] Kramer and Shelton, eds., 49; translation, 50.

[118] See n. 103 above.

[119] Paul mentions her in Letter 3.

[120] Kramer and Shelton, eds., 51–52; translation, 54.

[121] For the word translated as 'incomparable', only ασ ('as') is visible, with a trace of a third letter. The editors suggest either ἀσκ[ητῇ], 'ascetic/monk', or ἀσυ[νκρίτῳ], 'incomparable', a word used early in the letter (see n. 123 below).

[122] A *sextarius* was almost a pint.

[123] Gk ἀσυνκρίτῳ = ἀσυγκρίτῳ; see n. 121 above.

[124] Gk: *philanthrôpia*; see n. 110 above.

[125] See n. 103 above.

[126] Kramer and Shelton, eds., 53 lines 16–17: 'Fifteen *metra* of wheat flour and fifteen loaves of bread are produced here. With the hypothesis that one *psômion* [loaf of bread] contained one *metron* of wheat flour, we would arrive at the equivalents: 30 metra = 3 artabas, 1 metron = 1/10 artaba.'

[127] Gk: ὁλοκόττινους (*holokottinous*), which probably means a *solidus*, a gold coin; see n. 75 above.

[128] Kramer and Shelton, eds., 55, translation, 56.

[129] See n. 103 above.

130 See Letter 5.

131 As the editors note, 55, 'What Paphnutius' lie consists of, Paul does not say. We can only conjecture that Paphnutius maintains that he is not indebted to Paul. Perhaps he even later swore falsely (see Letter 8). That could very well be possible, for the monks were wont to swear by their schêma [habit]'. See Letter 8 below.

132 For these people, see Letters 1, 2, and 10 (Ophellios), 1, 8, and 10 (Tienôr), 1 and 10 (Pina), and 1 and 8 (Hôriôn).

133 Kramer and Shelton, eds., 58, translation 60.

134 The plural here could be an epistolary plural meaning 'me'.

135 On 'bundles', see Letter 4 and n. 112 there.

136 See Kramer and Shelton, eds., 58–59, line 8. Since the dictionary meaning of *anemourion*, 'windmill', is impossible here, the editors suggest that the word indicates some kind of receptacle that takes its name from the city of Anemourion in Cilicia, just as Knidion is a measure of wine that takes its name from Knidos in southwest Asia Minor.

137 The *mna*, Latin *mina*, was a measurement of weight equaling 100 *drachmae*, about 15.2 oz. troy. See notes 114 and 122 above for *myriad* and *sextarius*, respectively.

138 Two lines of writing are badly damaged; this is the editors' conjecture. A name, apparently feminine, is mostly gone.

139 Gk: παρεμβολῇ. See Kramer and Shelton, eds., 60, lines 18–19, for a full discussion and references. The term occurs also in the *Life of Antony* 12.3. Kramer and Shelton note that the military camp in Alexandria played an important role in the melitian crisis; it was there in 335 that a melitian bishop and his supporters attacked Athanasius.

140 See Letters 2, 6, and 7.

141 See Letter 7 and n. 131 there.

142 Any assembly, but among monastics the weekend gathering for fellowship, scripture reading, talks, a meal, and, often, the Eucharist. Paphnutius was apparently a monk at the Hathor Monastery, or at least a frequent visitor.

143 Kramer and Shelton, eds., 63–64; translation, 64–65.

144 Gk: *[ku]r[iois]*.

145 On the *sextarius*, see n. 122 above.

146 Kramer and Shelton, eds., 67, translation 69.

147 See Letter 1 and n. 98 there.

148 In this sentence both 'master' and 'Lord' translate *despotês*.

149 Kramer and Shelton, eds., 72, translation 73.

150 'Nepherotes' is the greek plural of 'Nepheros'.

151 See n. 56 above.

152 See 1 Tim 1:15 and 4:9.

153 Gk: *diathesin*; see n. 166 below.

154 See 2 Tim 2:3.

155 Pselemachis lay in the twelfth Heracleopolite *pagus* (district).

156 Tampeti was a town in the Oxyrhynchus nome.

157 Two lines of writing have lacunae. I have followed the editors' first suggestion. Another possibility is: my clothes have been stolen in Pselemachis [by some people] from Tampeti [who are traveling] in Pselemachis and Tampeti. See their suggestions, 75, lines 16–25.

[158] Kramer and Shelton, eds., 74–75, translation 77.
[159] The editors believe, 77 line 23, that Μονὴ Κώμη(ν) represents the Coptic name Neson Kome.
[160] Kramer and Shelton, eds., 75: 'The πατὴρ τῆς μονῆς is the abbot of the monastery, probably also the founder of the monastery'.
[161] On the two Nepherotes, see Letter 11.
[162] A town in the Heracleopolite nome.
[163] There were two towns with this name, one in the Great Oasis and the other in the Lower Thebaid; probably the latter is intended here.
[164] The editors note, 77: 'Not until the 4th c. in Egypt does the word apparently come into general usage to designate a cemetery. . . . it follows that the grain from the monastery, or, as the case may be, from the parish of Nesoi, was stored in the cemetery. In the present passage it should probably thus be understood that Nepheros was to have the wheat of Serapion harvested and put in the storage room in the cemetery'.
[165] Kramer and Shelton, eds., 78, translation 79.
[166] Gk: *diathesis*; see n. 153 above.
[167] The editors term this sentence a 'Gnome', an apophthegm; see Mt 4:16.
[168] Six lines are very fragmentary; I have translated the conjectures given by the editors.
[169] Kramer and Shelton, eds., 79 (no translation).
[170] The *trimêsion*, Latin *tremissis*, was a coin worth 1/3 *solidus* or *aureus* and equaling 8 *keratia*.
[171] For Pina, see Letter 10.
[172] Edited by Gerald M. Browne in Kramer and Shelton, edd., 81; translation 81.
[173] Or: incense. This is a common phrase in early coptic monasticism.
[174] Browne's conjecture, 81 line 4.
[175] ⲡⲛⲉⲯⲱⲟⲩⲧ; probably a personal name (Browne).
[176] Edited by Gerald M. Browne in Kramer and Shelton, edd., 82, translation 83.
[177] The editors comment, 83 line 31, that neither name is absolutely certain and that the writer cannot be positively identified with the Apa Papnoute of Letter 15.
[178] The first six lines of the letter are mostly missing.
[179] On the talent, see n. 114 above.
[180] Or: letters.
[181] See Letter 7 and note 131 above.
[182] One line is mostly missing and the beginning of another.
[183] Or: she said; or: I said.
[184] The end of one line and all of the next are missing.
[185] Coptic *ourj (ôrj)* could also mean here a 'deed of security'.
[186] This is Shelton's suggestion; Browne translates it 'fought with a wolf'. Coptic *ouônsh*, which means 'wolf', also occurs as a name; see W. E. Crum, *A Coptic Dictionary* (Oxford: Clarendon, 1939) 485b.

Appendix

Ama Sibylla of Saqqara:
Prioress or Prophet? Monastic, or Mythological Being?

ONE OF THE MOST INTRIGUING FIGURES to rise from the ruins of ancient coptic monasticism is Ama Sibylla, whom we know through word and portrait. Her name, appearing in numerous inscriptions, still has some of the allure that Henri Munier described more than seventy-five years ago: 'Among the celebrated figures cited on the epitaphs, our attention lingers over a single name, strange and disconcerting; and that name belongs to a woman whom the Copts call Ama Sibylla'.[1] At the turn of the twentieth century, archeologists unearthed hundreds of names during the excavations at the monastery of Apa Jeremias at Saqqara, from the mighty (the archangels Michael and Gabriel) to the lowly (carpenters, watchmen, and gravediggers), as well as numerous portraits, ranging from splendid icons of Christ and Mary to grafitto-like scratchings.[2] But amid this population, other than the Virgin Mary, there are few women. Ama Sibylla is the striking exception: her name is invoked over eighty times at Saqqara, her name appears on two stelae from Hermonthis,[3] and her portrait was painted at Bawit (see below). Who was Sibylla? Does she tell us anything about monastic women in late antique Egypt?

There seem to have been large numbers of female monastics in Egypt in the fourth and fifth centuries, but few of their names, and none of their writings, have survived.[4] The *Historia Monachorum in Aegypto* reports that in Oxyrhynchus female monastics outnumbered males two to one, while the arabic version of Besa's *Life of Shenoute* relates that the White Monastery had 2,200 male and 1,800 female monks.[5] Whether or not these numbers are exact, there must have been hundreds, or even thousands, of female monastics in late antique Egypt. Unfortunately, of the lives and histories of these women almost nothing remains.[6] For example, women are occasionally mentioned on grave inscriptions at Saqqara, but the epitaphs are fragmentary and who the women were, and whether they were lay or monastic, is uncertain.[7] One tantalizing inscription asks the saints for prayers for *Ama* (Mother) Susanna, 'the mother of the great monastery', but since there is no other reference at Saqqara to a 'great monastery', its provenance is unknown and Susanna remains a cipher.[8]

The Monastery of Apa Jeremias

The monastery of Apa Jeremias, just south of modern Cairo, was probably founded at the end of the fifth century and functioned until the middle of the ninth century.[9] Very little is known about Jeremias (Jeremiah), and it is not certain whether he founded the monastery that bears his name or whether he was the eminent successor of the founder. A limestone slab demonstrates his importance: 'This is the seat of Apa Jeremias'. Sir Herbert Thompson, the editor of the inscriptions at Saqqara, concluded that 'from the careful and ornamental nature of the work, this probably does record the place where the Founder of the monastery used to sit'.[10] Jeremias was venerated not only at Saqqara but also at Bawit and its dependencies.[11] According to John of Nikiou, writing late in the seventh century, the future emperor Anastasius (491–518) visited Jeremias at his monastery during the nobleman's exile in Egypt (474–491).[12] Since John says that 'shortly after' this visit Anastasius was recalled from banishment (89.14), this must have taken place around 490. John, however, is not very precise about either Jeremias or his monastery, saying only (89.4) that Anastasius and his party ascended 'the mountain to the convent [monastery] of the God-clothed S. Abba Jeremiah of Alexandria'. By 'Alexandria', John may mean that Jeremiah was from that city, or it may mean that his monastery was in or near Alexandria (which might be reasonably inferred from context); if the latter, then this Jeremiah cannot be Jeremias of Saqqara, since Saqqara lay south of modern Cairo. At any rate, we cannot be certain that the Jeremiah of whom John speaks is the Apa Jeremias of Saqqara. Can there be any more certainty about one of the monastery's best-attested personages, Ama Sibylla?

Ama Sibylla

Sibylla is known to us, as we mentioned above, through both word and portraiture. At Saqqara are several surviving representations

Ama Sibylla of Saqqara   381

of a woman. These figures, unfortunately, can no longer be identified, but it seems reasonable to suggest that they represent Sibylla. 'Clothed like the monks in a long tunic and cloak, her head covered with a *maphorion* (a shawl edged with fringe) and carrying a codex', she 'is pictured among the saints in the eastern niche of Cell F, and upon a column of the Main Church as well as in two other cells. However, there is no inscription to identify her'.[13] Marguerite Rassart-Debergh, who has carefully studied the paintings at Saqqara, provides the following description of the woman on the column:

> The other is a woman whose clothing and posture evoke those of holy men. She is standing, dressed in a light tunic covered by a dark cloak; on her head she wears, like Mary, the 'maphorium,' which is surrounded by a halo; she clasps to her left breast a codex with a richly worked binding; to her right is a bearded person whose left side and clothing are equally conspicuous in the photo.[14]

Although these depictions can not conclusively be identified as Sibylla, at Bawit two rooms (apparently) contained paintings of Ama Sibylla with the Virtues: Chapelle III with eleven medallions—ten Virtues with Sibylla at the center; and Chapelle VI with twelve Virtues surrounding her.[15] Here the identification is certain. Jean Clédat, who excavated the site, provides a description of the painting in Chapelle III:

> In the left side of the east wall is a small niche or *apse* 1.20 m. high and .65 m. long at the span. On the outside is a large molding encircling the arch of the niche and supported by two heavy and uneven small columns whose bases rest on the ground. . . . The border of the molding is decorated with small, similar heads. . . . Each of these figures bears a name written beside it and outside the circle.[16]

The eleven medallions, from right to left, are: Pistis (Faith), Elpis (Hope), 3 and 4 have been destroyed [perhaps Agapê (Love) and Parthenia (Virginity), Thbbio (Humility), Tbbo (Chastity), Our

Mother Ama Sibylla,[17] Mntrmrash (Gentleness), Gratia (Grace), Hypomonê (Patience), the last figure is lost [perhaps Sophia (Wisdom].[18]

It is not mere coincidence, I believe, that the monks had a female figure in the midst of the virtues (or: Virtues; inscriptions commonly refer to them as 'the Virtues of the Holy Spirit').[19] Of the seven virtues listed above, five are grammatically feminine, as were many of the greco-roman virtues that made their way into monastic spirituality.[20] Saint Gregory of Nyssa spoke of monks giving birth to the virtues: 'In reality it is possible for everyone to become a mother in this regard'.[21] The monks at Bawit may have seen Sibylla as the 'Mother of the Virtues', and possibly as their spiritual mother and patron in the cultivation of the virtues.[22] As R.-G. Coquin observed, the Virtues were not for the monks 'simple personifications like those of the hellenistic world or, more ancient, those of pharaonic Egypt, but rather constituted a particular order among the angelic hierarchies'.[23] These Virtues were, quite literally, gifts of the Holy Spirit, and they continued to be important in the Coptic Church.[24]

The vagaries of archeology (which continually remind us how much we have lost and how much more we have to learn) have provided a curious juxtaposition between Bawit and Saqqara. At Bawit, Sibylla is clearly pictured with the Virtues, but I have not been able to find any inscriptions concerning her at that monastery. At Saqqara, by contrast, there are no (extant) representations of Sibylla with the Virtues, but inscriptional references concerning her abound.[25] More than eighty inscriptions at Saqqara invoke the name of Ama Sibylla, usually with the Father, Son, and Holy Spirit, the Virgin, Apa Jeremias, and Apa Enoch preceding her and other saints following after.[26] With Enoch and Jeremias, she makes up 'the triad of Saqqara'.[27] Most of these inscriptions are petitions for prayer or intercession, some for the living, but most for the dead. Some invoke Jeremias and Enoch, but not Sibylla (on Enoch and Sibylla, see below). Many of these texts are damaged, and it can not be determined whether she was originally listed; however, enough inscriptions survive without Sibylla to show that she was intentionally left off some lists of saints being invoked.[28] Inscription 53 is unusual in that it lists Sibylla ahead of Jeremias; 76 is unique in giving all the fathers listed the title 'Apa', while Sibylla has no title.

Inscription #169 (4.50) is representative: 'O Father and Son and Holy Spirit, Apa Jeremias, Apa Enoch, Ama Sibylla,[29] our mother Mary, remember me, brother John, the father of the *diakonia*'.[30] Inscription #206, 'The List of Wine for the Festivals and the Seasons and Sundays', provides a fragmentary calendar of festivals, unfortunately without dates.[31] It lists Sibylla third, after New Year's Day (Thoth 1) and Eve (Zoê): 'The Day of Ama Sibylla, 1 cup, 1 large vessel'.

Two particularly important inscriptions for understanding who Sibylla was are striking in that they give Sibylla an appellation; unfortunately, both are fragmentary, and fragmentary in precisely the same way: they break off after the first five letters of her appellation:

#290 (4.90): [Am]a Si[byll]a the pro[ ]

#304 (4.94): [A]ma Sibylla the pro[ ].

Thompson suggests, 4.90, that the appellation should be completed 'the prophet' (he uses 'prophetess'), *tepro[phêtês]*; the 't', the feminine article, is certain, he says. If Sibylla was the founder or leader of a women's monastery, it would be reasonable to suggest that the appellation should instead read *tepro[estês]*, 'the superior' or 'the prior' of the monastery. But it seems that Thompson was indeed correct: Sibylla was revered as a prophet at Saqqara. And her role in the prophetic pantheon was due to her relationship with the biblical and extra-biblical figure of Enoch.[32]

ENOCH, JEREMIAS, AND SIBYLLA

The biblical Enoch, in one genealogy (Gn 5:17-24, Lk 3:37), was the father of Methuselah (who was also venerated at Saqqara);[33] in another (Gn 4:17a, 18a) he was the son of Cain and the father of Irad.[34] Enoch walked so closely with God that 'then he was no more, because God took him' (Gn 5:24, NRSV). Enoch's 'translation' to heaven gave rise to legends about him and his knowledge of heavenly mysteries *(1 Enoch)*. At Saqqara occurs the striking association of Jeremias and Enoch, who are almost always together, both in inscriptions and in paintings.[35] Enoch and Jeremias are pictured in eight rooms at Saqqara.[36] In one room the Virgin is flanked by Enoch and Jeremias;[37] in another in a niche on the east wall is 'the Virgin and Child with Jeremias and Michael on the left, Enoch and Gabriel on the right.[38] All the names are marked. Enoch holds a pen which he is dipping into a basin on a little stand'. This comports with the painting in one cell on which Enoch unrolls the Book of Life.[39] The east wall of another cell probably shows Enoch next to Jeremias.[40] Quibell believed that the two cells in the 'tomb church' at Saqqara were built for Jeremias and Enoch, and suggested that Enoch was 'a colleague or successor of Jeremias', as well as being named after the biblical patriarch.[41] But his conclusion that Enoch was a historical person (that is, a monk of late antique Egypt) must be carefully scrutinized.

In both the jewish and christian apocryphal tradition, Enoch is a 'heavenly scribe' or the 'scribe of righteousness'.[42] Because of his righteousness, God raised him to heaven (as one coptic text puts it) 'and did not let him see death, through the supplication of Michael and his army'.[43] With his own hand Enoch writes 'in the register' the sins, wickedness, and good deeds of 'the whole world'; Michael then takes them and presents them to God.[44] In the Coptic *Apocalypse of Paul*, the apostle describes his encounter with Enoch, as he was being snatched to the seventh heaven.[45] As 'the scribe of righteousness', Enoch tells Paul 'Many are the promises of God and His good gifts, but not very many men shall partake of them'.[46] In one coptic apocryphon, Enoch even seems to have the crucial role of scribe in the ongoing Judgement of the dead, 'charged with writing down the sins and good deeds' of humankind: '[Enoch], scribe of [righteousness], do not hasten to write [the sins of the sons] of men'.[47] His title on grave stelae found at Saqqara is also that of scribe.[48] These probably reflect a knowledge of Enoch as scribe during the Judgement (an ongoing Judgement, apparently, rather than a Last Judgement).[49] Since Enoch is identified as a scribe at Saqqara and holds the Book of Life, there seems to be little doubt that he was not a monk but was, rather, the biblical and extra-biblical patriarch known so vividly from *1 Enoch* and other pseudepigraphal works.

Analogously, Adam and Eve are also widely pictured at Saqqara, and the feast day of Eve (Zoê) is near the top of a liturgical calendar.[50] The presence of these biblical personages quite naturally leads to the question of what literature was being read at Saqqara and Bawit. Do the representations of Adam, Eve, and Enoch demonstrate a knowledge of only the canonical Old Testament, or are they based on such extra-canonical works as the *Apocalypse of Adam, Testament of Adam, Life of Adam and Eve,* and *1 Enoch*?[51] The *Apocalypse of Adam* was found at Nag Hammadi, and thus clearly has a coptic connection and may also have a monastic link,[52] but there is no surviving evidence for any of these other works at Bawit or Saqqara.[53] The 'wall of the prophets' at Bawit pictures and quotes from sixteen Old Testament prophets, all of them canonical.[54] Nevertheless, the depiction of Enoch as scribe and holder of the Book of Life shows monastic familiarity with extra-canonical tradition and points to a knowledge of *1 Enoch* at Saqqara. It also provides clear evidence for understanding the role of Ama Sibylla (who, as we have seen, was also pictured with a codex).

SIBYLLA / SIBYL

A fragment of an Enoch apocryphon has Enoch receiving prophecies from his virgin sister. According to Birger A. Pearson, the fragment's most recent editor, 'it is clear from what follows that Enoch's sister is no ordinary virgin! She is a prophetess, and there can be little doubt but that she is none other than the Sibyl'.[55] Jewish literature does provide names for other sisters of Enoch, but none names Sibyl or Sibylla as a sister.[56] It is precisely the coptic tradition that identifies her as both prophet and sister of Enoch. In 'The Book of the Installation of the Archangel Gabriel', Gabriel says, 'Moreover I am, O Lord, the one who came to Sibyl [Sybla], the virgin sister of Enoch the scribe of righteousness. I protected her, and rescued her from the hand of the wicked Devil who desired to do evil to her'.[57] In a coptic text telling the story of the discovery of Christ's tomb by Eudoxia, Constantine's sister, an old man says to Eudoxia, 'Blessed is the chosen race of which Sibyl [Sibylla], the sister of Enoch the scribe, prophesied'.[58] This tradition, as far as I can determine, was unknown at Saqqara.[59]

The Sibyl who uttered prophecies dates at least to the fifth century BC and was widely known in numerous, perhaps a dozen, manifestations in antiquity.[60] There was an egyptian Sibyl. Eventually, both Jews and Christians claimed her to support their own traditions: in jewish tradition she was the daughter or daughter-in-law of Noah;[61] in some versions of the *Romance of Alexander the Great*, she appears as the sister of Solomon;[62] she was also identified with the Queen of Sheba.[63] She finally became 'an independent witness to the truth of the Christian faith and was quoted hundreds of times by the Church Fathers'.[64] Half of the collection attributed to the Sibyl, the *Sibylline Oracles*, comes from Egypt and seems to be jewish in origin; in Book 5 the Sibyl is syncretistically a friend of Isis.[65] Some of the *Oracles* is clearly christian, especially Book 8. Were the *Sibylline Oracles* known at Bawit and Saqqara? No evidence shows that the oracles were translated into Coptic. Fragmentary as it is, however, the surviving evidence can not be conclusive.[66]

So how did Sibylla find her way into coptic monasticism? Probably through her 'brother' Enoch. The discoveries at Nag Hammadi and elsewhere have made us aware of the widespread popularity of apocryphal and 'non-canonical' books in late antique Egypt. Among these texts, the *Book of Enoch* was among the most popular; a greek version of it was found at Akhmim.[67] Among the coptic fragments of the *Book of Enoch* are some whose allusions to the Trinity along with Enoch betray their christian origins, or at least their christian redaction. In these fragments Enoch speaks of his sister, Sibyl.[68] Sibyl's transformation seems to have worked its way from the *Sibylline Oracles* through the *Book of Enoch*, where she becomes a 'prophet', and from there, because of her sisterly association with the biblical patriarch, into the monastic devotional practice that we have seen at Bawit and Saqqara.[69]

Because of Sibylla's close literary (at Akhmim) and inscriptional (at Saqqara) association with Enoch and her painted association with the Virtues (at Bawit), and because of her probable identification as a prophet, there seems no doubt now that Ama Sibylla was indeed the Sibyl of Greek legend.[70] Coptic piety and christian imagination transformed her into a christian saint.[71] As such, she entered coptic-arabic tradition: 'The Wisdom of Sabila' was a very popular apocalyptic text in the arabic christian tradition, attested at Mount Sinai in a ninth- or tenth-century manuscript, and became well known in Egypt by the thirteenth century and perhaps earlier.[72] An archeologist early in the twentieth century 'strenuously repudiated' such a conclusion, believing that Sibylla was 'a female saint, a religious or founder of a monastery'.[73] Today, in our historical and personal searches for an identifiable female monastic in the egyptian desert, many of us would like to agree. As much as we might like to see Sibylla as a desert prioress, however, it must be concluded that she was (in modern terms) a mythological being.[74]

The ancients, we might add, even the more recent ancients, were not as bothered as we by the melding of the mythological and the historical. The hymn *'Dies Irae'*, or 'Day of Wrath', probably written by a Franciscan in the thirteenth century, begins by calling equally on both David and the Sibyl as witnesses: *'Dies irae, dies illa / solvet saeclum in favilla, / teste David cum Sibylla'* ('Day of wrath, that dreadful day / will dissolve this world into ashes, / as David testified with the Sibyl').[75] A seventeenth-century russian iconostasis depicts Enoch, along with other Old Testament worthies, in the far right corner of the upper register.[76] It is also interesting to note that the portrayal of the pagan Sibyl with the christian virtues has a parallel in the Sistine Chapel, where Michelangelo 'juxtaposed five Sibyls . . . with the Old Testament prophets'.[77]

APA JEREMIAS AGAIN

Returning now to antiquity, our placing Sibylla/Sibyl into a biblical and christian, yet mythological, pantheon raises a further question about the historicity of Apa Jeremias, the eponymous monk of Saqqara. As we saw above, the only outside evidence that Jeremias was a historical person comes from John of Nikiou, and it is shaky, at best. Jeremias' close association with Enoch could easily make one doubt his historicity. Two pieces of evidence suggest, however, that he was indeed a monk and was probably the founder of the monastery that bears his name. The first witness is the limestone slab saying 'This is the seat of Apa Jeremias'. The second witness is another inscription (and it is ironic that Jeremias is linked here with Ama Sibylla); in identifying the place where a liturgical act of prostration, widespread among the monks of Middle Egypt, took place,[78] this inscription says,

O Father, O Son, O Holy Spirit, Apa Jeremias, Apa Enoch, Ama Sibylla, our father Peter, our father Paul, our father John: this is the place where our lord and father Apa Jeremias prostrated himself until he removed the sins of the people of the whole world. May [his] holy blessing descend upon us. Amen, Amen, so be it, Amen.[79]

This act of prostration was clearly an historical event. Mythological personages like Enoch may unscroll the Book of Life, like Sibylla they may join company with the Virtues, but probably only a flesh and blood person, like Jesus, like Jeremias, can prostrate himself for the sins of the world.

NOTES

[1] Henri Munier, 'La Sibylla alexandrine chez les Coptes', Bulletin de la Société archéologique d'Alexandrie 20 (1924) 196–201, 196.
[2] See J. E. Quibell, Excavations at Saqqara, vol. 3, Excavations at Saqqara (1907–1908) (Cairo: IFAO, 1909), and vol. 4, The Monastery of Apa Jeremias (Cairo: IFAO, 1912). For the inscriptions, see Sir Herbert Thompson, 'The Coptic Inscriptions', in Quibell, 3.27-75, 4.47-125. For one example of commoners, see Plate XI,3, and Quibell's touching description (3.100): 'Close to the door of the chamber "where Jeremies used to sit" was a small room (706) which served for the guards, and on the wall of this the watchmen had found leisure to daub in red paint figures intended for their portraits. Over each one is a name such as "Father Hor, the watchman"; above their heads is a drawing of a ship'. For an interesting list of occupations found in the inscriptions, see Quibell, 3.77.
[3] Munier, 196.
[4] A few apophthegmata—Theodora, Syncletica, and Sarah—are attributed to women. The best study on female monastics is Susanna Elm, 'Virgins of God': The Making of Asceticism in Late Antiquity (Oxford: Clarendon, 1994); see especially 'Part II: Egypt'. For a bibliography, see Tim Vivian 'Reading the Saints: Early Monastic Texts and Resources Available in English', Cistercian Studies Quarterly 28.1 (1993) 17–58, esp. 56–58; and Vivian, 'Reading the Saints II', Cistercian Studies Quarterly 33.3 (1998) 329–344.
[5] Historia 5; trans. Norman Russell, The Lives of the Desert Fathers, CS 34:67. J. Leipoldt, Schenute von Atripe, Texte und Untersuchungen 25:1, N.F. 10:1 (Leipzig, 1903) 93–94.
[6] For two tantalizing papyrus fragments from the early fourth century from a female (monastic?) community, see James E. Goehring and Robert F. Bougner, 'Egyptian Monasticism (Selected Papyri)', in Vincent L. Wimbush, ed., Ascetic Behavior in Greco-Roman Antiquity: A Sourcebook (Minneapolis: Fortress, 1990) 462–463. See Alanna M. Emmett, 'An Early Fourth-century Female Monastic

Community in Egypt?', in Ann Moffatt, ed., *Maistor: Classical, Byzantine and Renaissance Studies for Robert Browning*, Byzantiana Australiensia 5 (Canberra: Australian Association for Byzantine Studies, 1984) 77-83; Averil Cameron, 'Desert Mothers: Women Ascetics in Early Christian Egypt', in E. Puttick, ed., *Women as Teachers and Disciples in Traditional and New Religions* (Lewiston, PA: Mellen, 1993).

[7] See #37, 41. They were probably laywomen.

[8] #27 (Plate XLVI,2); 3.36-37. For a discussion of the 'mother of the great monastery', see Thompson, 37 n. 7. The texts surrounding Abba Daniel of Scetis associate a monastery of Abba Jeremias with a women's monastery, but this is undoubtedly a different monastery dedicated to Jeremiah (or Jeremias): In one story, Daniel and his disciple travel south from Scetis into the Upper Thebaid for the feast day of Abba Apollo. They then go on to Hermopolis, where Daniel says to his disciple, "'Go and knock at that monastery for women,'" for there was a monastery there called the Monastery of Abba Jeremiah, and about three hundred female monks were living there'. See Léon Clugnet, *Revue de Orient Chrétien* 5 (1900) 49-73, 254-271, 370-391, at 67.

[9] Quibell (above, n. 2), 4.ii; Paul van Moorsel and Mathilde Huijbers, 'Repertory of the preserved wallpaintings of Apa Jeremiah at Saqqara', in *Acta ad Archaeologiam et Artium Historiam Pertinentia*, ed. Hjalmar Torp, et al. (Rome: Bretschneider, 1981) 125.

[10] Quibell, 3.33, inscription 14 (Plate XLIV,4).

[11] René-Georges Coquin and Maurice Martin, 'History', p. 773 in the article 'Dayr Apa Jeremiah (Saqqara)', *The Coptic Encyclopedia*, ed. Aziz S. Atiya (New York: Macmillan, 1990) 3.772-779.

[12] John of Nikiou, *Chronicle* 89.4-14; Robert Henry Charles, trans., *The Chronicle of John, Coptic Bishop of Nikiou* (London: Text and Translation Society, 1916; rpt. Amsterdam: APA-Philo Press, n.d.) 121-122.

[13] Marguerite Rassart-Debergh, 'Paintings', p. 778, in 'Dayr Apa Jeremiah (Saqqara)', *The Coptic Encyclopedia* 3.772-79; see also Rassart-Debergh, 'L'image de la femme au couvent Saint-Jérémie à Saqqara', *Le Monde Copte* 16:48-59; and Rassart-Debergh, 'La decoration picturale du monastère de Saqqara. Essai de reconstitution', in Torp (above, n. 9) 50. A photograph of the column may be seen in *ibid.*, following p. 124, Planche IIa, 'Main Church, colonne ornée d'une figure féminine'.

[14] Rassart-Debergh, 'La décoration'(above, n. 13) 23. Plate IIa = Quibell 3, Plate XI, 2.

[15] Jean Clédat, *Le Monastère et la Nécropole de Baouît* (Mémoires publiés par les membres de L'Institut Français d'Archéologie Orientale du Caire 12; [one volume in two parts] Cairo: IFAO, 1904) 23, discusses only one room, but see Rassart-Debergh, 'Trois Peintures', in Torp (above, n. 9) 193-201.

[16] Clédat, 23. For a drawing of the plan of Chapelle III, see Fig. 12, p. 13; for a drawing of one of the medallions, see Fig 18, p. 23. Unfortunately, Clédat did not supply a photograph or drawing of the niche.

[17] 'Mother' is often applied to Mary at Saqqara, but it is always *maau* and not *ama*; in #26 (and possibly #83) both Mary and Sibylla are *tnmaau*, 'our mother'.

[18] See Paul of Tamma, 'On Humility' 9 in Chapter Five above. See also Stephen of Thebes, *Ascetic Discourse* 37 in Chapter Eight above; Édouard des Places, 'Le 'Discours Ascétique' d'Étienne de Thèbes: Texte grec inédit et traduction',

Le Muséon 82 (1969) 35–59, 40. For a general discussion, see R.-G. Coquin, 'Les Vertus ('Aretaí) de l'Esprit en Egypte', in *Mélanges d'histoire des religions offerts à Henri-Charles Puech* (Paris: Presse universitaires de France, 1974) 447–457, esp. 449–455 for lists of Virtues.

[19] Coquin, 'Les Vertus', 447–448.

[20] See Verna E.F. Harrison, 'A Gender Reversal in Gregory of Nyssa's First Homily on the Song of Songs', *Studia Patristica* 27 (1993) 38. In *The Shepherd of Hermas*, Vision 3.8, Hermas has a vision of seven women who seem to correspond to the Virtues; in Similitudes 9.15, Hermas gives a catalogue of twelve Virtues. See Coquin, 'Les Vertus', 4450, for New Testament and early christian references.

[21] Gregory of Nyssa, *On Virginity* 14.3; Michel Aubineau, ed., *Grégoire de Nysse: Traité de la virginité*, Sources chrétiennes 110 (Paris: Cerf, 1966) 438/40.

[22] It may also have been precisely because Sibylla was a woman that she was omitted from some of the inscriptions at Bawit invoking the monastic pantheon.

[23] Coquin, 'Les Vertus', 456–457.

[24] See Coquin, 'Les Vertus', 457, for examples from the fourteenth and fifteenth centuries that correspond closely to this list above. A homily attributed to Theodosius of Alexandria (MS. Vat. 61 bohairic), in explicating the text 'Virgins will be brought in to the king after her; also all her friends will be brought to him' (Ps 44:15 LXX), provides a considerably expanded list of 'the virgins and the friends of the Virgin, that is, her good deeds': virginity, chastity, continence, anachoresis, gentleness, kindness, perseverance, piety, hospitality, goodness, zeal, knowledge, hope, love, continuous prayer, a holy fasting, brotherly love, generosity, patience, spiritual joy, compassion, pity, wisdom, prudence, orthodox faith, unspeakable power, good character, a perfect nobility, kindness, compassion towards all, good zeal, desire for the truth, gratitude in the midst of every affliction, a heartfelt love of God at all times, peace, knowledge of the truth, humility of heart, correct thinking, a good manner of living, well perfected virtue, a pure vigilance, purity of soul and body, renunciation, that is, the detachment from material things that leads the soul to every good' (fol. 117v–118r). I wish to thank Rev. Prof. Mark Sheridan for a copy of his transcription and translation of this text. He notes 'that the conception of the virtues found in the Theodosius homily belongs to a different tradition where they are only personified. The date of the homily, in its present form, is not earlier than the ninth century. If there was a Sahidic version, that could be sixth century, but I am dubious about the authorship of Theodosius'.

[25] See Rassart-Debergh, 'Trois Peintures', 199: 'at Bawit ten or twelve Virtues surrounding Ama Sibylla; at Saqqara, only five Virtues, and nothing allows us to identify Ama Sibylla [among them]'.

[26] Sir Herbert Thompson, 'The Coptic Inscriptions', in Quibell, 3.27-75, 4.47-125. Since Thompson does not provide a list of all the references to Ama Sibylla, I will give one here. Vol. 4, p. 49, #1–3; vols. 3–4 (numbers now refer to inscription numbers and not page numbers): 1, 5, 12, 23, 26, 29-32, 43-44, 48, 50, 53-54, 59, 62, 65, 76, 82, 120, 150, 169, 170, 173, 174, 188, 190, 199, 202-4, 206, 208-9, 219, 222, 224, 232-33, 240, 247, 249-52, 260, 266, 268, 282, 288, 290, 302, 304, 312, 318-19, 329, 334. For a complete list, see now Cäcilia Wietheger, *Das Jeremias-Kloster zu Saqqara unter besonderer Berücksichtigung der Inschriften*, Arbeiten zum spätantiken und koptischen Ägypten 1 (Altenberge: Oros Verlag, 1992) 238. She provides a comparative table, 497–509, and a descriptive catalogue, 301–474.

Notes

[27] Wietheger, 238.

[28] See, for example, #3, 22, and 27 (Quibell (above, n. 2), 3).

[29] The spelling of 'Sibylla' ranges widely: Sible, Sibila, Sibylla, Sibla, Sïbylla, Sibêlla, and Sibyla. On coptic and greek orthography of her name, see Munier, 197–198, n. 4.

[30] On *diakonia*, see Quibell, vol. 3, #48 n. 1; in #207 (vol. 4, p. 63), Brother Phib is called 'the father of the *diakonia*'.

[31] For ou<oei>sh, 'season', the text has ouôsh, 'wish, will, desire'. For a comparable, but very fragmentary, list, see Clédat, 5.

[32] In a paper given at the third Saint Shenouda Society Coptic Conference at UCLA on 28 July 2001, Gawdat Gabra discussed the partial excavations of a hitherto unknown monastery at al-Mansuriya, 25 km. north of the Giza pyramids. One room of this monastery has wall paintings that depict numerous figures, among them Sibylla, who once again is represented with Jeremias and Enoch. At al-Mansuriya, Sibylla is also termed a 'prophet'. Gabra tentatively dates the wall paintings to the 6th or 7th centuries.

[33] See #15, 27.

[34] In a coptic Enoch fragment, Enoch is addressed as 'Enoch, son of Iared' *[sic]*; see W. E. Crum, *Theological Texts from Coptic Papyri*, Anecdota Oxoniensia (Oxford: Clarendon, 1913) 6.

[35] Inscriptions at Saqqara with Enoch's name (almost always with Jeremias) are too numerous to list. See Thompson, 'The Coptic Inscriptions', in Quibell, 3.27-75, 4.47-125.

[36] Rooms F, D, 1807, 1719, 1724, 1725, 1733, 1727. See van Moorsel and Huijbers, in Torp (above, n. 9), following p. 186, Plate C and Plate XXV; see also *ibid.*, Plates XVI–XVII (1719), Plate XXId and e (1725), and Plate XXIIIc (1727).

[37] Room 172; see Quibell, 4.23 (plates XXII, XXIIIa).

[38] Room 1733.

[39] Cell F, the east wall; see Rassart-Debergh, 'La décoration', 50 (Plate IXb); Quibell, 3.55 (#93; Plate LV).

[40] Cell D; Rassart-Debergh, 'La décoration', 52–54.

[41] Quibell, 4.11.

[42] Birger A. Pearson, 'The Pierpont Morgan Fragments of a Coptic Enoch Apocryphon', in *Studies on the Testament of Abraham*, ed. George W.E. Nickelsburg (Missoula: Scholars Press, 1976) 238. See also E.A. Wallis Budge, *Coptic Martyrdoms Etc. in the Dialect of Upper Egypt. Coptic Texts*, vol.4 (New York 1977 (London 1914) 41.

[43] Budge, *Miscellaneous Coptic Texts*, vol. 5, parts 1 & 2 (New York: AMS, 1977 [London, 1915]), Coptic: 407–408, English (corrected): 940.

[44] Budge, *Miscellaneous Coptic Texts*, Coptic: 345, English: 909. See also Crum (above, n. 34), 9.

[45] 'Then we went up to the seventh heaven, and I saw an old man [. . .] light and whose garment was white. His throne, which is in the seventh heaven, was brighter than the sun by seven times': *The Apocalypse of Paul*, in James M. Robinson, ed., *The Nag Hammadi Library*, revised edition. (HarperCollins, San Francisco, 1990).

[46] Budge, *Miscellaneous Coptic Texts*, Coptic: 561, English: 1048.

[47] Pearson, 'The Pierpont Morgan Fragments', 238 and 244.

[48] Quibell (above, n. 2), vol. 4, #233, 295, 304, 329, 340.

49 Pearson, 'The Pierpont Morgan Fragments', 238.
50 Inscription #206.
51 For these works, see James H. Charlesworth, ed., *The Old Testament Pseudepigrapha* (2 vols.; Garden City, NY: Doubleday, 1983). *First Enoch*, one should note, was (and is) canonical in the Ethiopian Church.
52 For a recent discussion of the Nag Hammadi corpus and bibliography, see Birger A. Pearson, 'Nag Hammadi Codices', in *The Anchor Bible Dictionary*, ed. David Noel Freedman (New York: Doubleday, 1992) 4:984-993, esp. 989: 'the ascetic lifestyle' of many of the documents 'could be appreciated in a monastic setting'. Scholars are still divided on the connection between the Nag Hammadi texts and Pachomian monasticism; for example, Gary Lease believes, 'Nag Hammadi: Archaeology', *ibid.*, 983, that the archeological evidence 'says little or nothing about the supposed link between the Pachomian community at Pbow and the Nag Hammadi gnostic literature'.
53 For a discussion of the 'primary Adam book' (the so-called *Apocalypse of Moses*) in Egypt, see Michael E. Stone, *A History of the Literature of Adam and Eve* (Atlanta: Scholars Press, 1992) 39–41; on its possible egyptian origins, see *ibid.*, 60.
54 Room 9, east wall; see Clédat 54–61, Plates XXXI–XXXIV. The prophets are Isaiah, Jeremiah, Ezekiel, Daniel, Hosea, Joel, Amos, Micah, Abdias (Obadiah), Jonah, Nahum, Habbakuk, Sophonias (Zephaniah), Haggai, Zechariah, and Malachi.
55 Birger A. Pearson, 'The Pierpont Morgan Fragments', 235. Her name is not given in the fragment but according to Pearson, 239, 'there can be no doubt about her identity'. In the fragment published by Crum, 8, Sibylla's name is lost but the unidentified woman hears 'the voice of Enoch, her brother'.
56 Pearson, 'The Pierpont Morgan Fragments', 239.
57 Coptic text from C.D.G. Müller, ed., *Die Bücher der Einsetzung der Erzengel Michael and Gabriel*, Scriptores Coptici 31 [Coptic texts] and 32 [translations] (Louvain: CSCO, 1962) 73; cited by Pearson, 'The Pierpont Morgan Fragments', 239 (Pearson's translation). One notes here Sibyl's close connection with Michael and Gabriel in several inscriptions.
58 Cited by Pearson, 'The Pierpont Morgan Fragments', 240. *Sibylla* is, in fact, the ancient spelling; see Arthur Stanley Pease and David S. Potter, 'Sibyl', in *The Oxford Classical Dictionary*, third Edition, ed. Simon Hornblower and Antony Spawforth (Oxford: Oxford University Press, 1996) 1400–1401.
59 Wietheger (above, n. 26), 238, agrees.
60 See Ursula Treu, 'Die Oracula Sibyllina und Ägypten', in Peter Nagel, ed., *Graeco-Coptica: Griechen und Kopten im byzantischen Ägypten* (Halle-Wittenberg: Martin-Luther Universität, 1984) 55. Treu notes, 55, that the name is not Greek.
61 J. J. Collins, 'Sibylline Oracles', in Charlesworth, ed., *The Old Testament Pseudepigrapha* (above, n. 48), 1:317. On the Jewish Sibyl, see Collins, 'The Sibylline Oracles of Egyptian Judaism', Ph.D. Dissertation: Harvard, 1972.
62 W. E. Crum, *Theological Texts from Coptic Papyri* (1913) 4 n. 2.
63 See Jeanne Lucien Herr, 'La Reine de Saba et le Bois de la Croix', *Revue archéologique*, 4th series, 23 (1914) 1–31, 18–19.
64 Collins, 1.322, 324.
65 Collins, 1.322. Books 3, 5, 8.131-38, 11-14. Books 3 and 5 were known to Clement of Alexandria. On the *Oracles* see also Treu (above, n. 57) 56–59.

⁶⁶ Gesine Schenke Robinson has stated that 'the Sibylline Oracles are quoted as if they were canonical texts' in Codex Berolinensis P 20915, a fourth/fifth-century papyrus codex. See Robinson, 'Codex Berolinensis P 20915: A Progress Report', in *Ägypten und Nubien in spätantiker und christlicher Zeit*, vol. 2, *Schriftum, Sprache, und Gedankenwelt*, ed. Stephen Emmel, et al. (Wiesbaden: Reichert, 1999) 174.

⁶⁷ Munier, 200.

⁶⁸ W. E. Crum, *Anecdota Oxoniensia* (1913) 4.

⁶⁹ See Munier, 201. Munier, 197, believed that 'the cultus of Sibylla remained confined to monasteries that acknowledge Saint Apollo as founder', but this can not be conclusively demonstrated. Sibylla, it seems, even survived on into arabic coptic tradition. Hany Takla informs me that there is an arabic text in the Patriarchal Library in Cairo entitled 'The Dream that the One Hundred Wise Men Saw and which was Explained by Sibyla the Wise' (Simaika Catalogue of the Patriarchal Library #781 [Lib No. Lit. 212]). This is the first part of an eight-part undated arabic manuscript and apparently is unavailable for inspection at present.

⁷⁰ Wietheger concludes, 238, that Sibylla is 'eine fiktive Figur', who became known through the apocryphal literature.

⁷¹ See Collins, 1.324.

⁷² The oldest recensions of the arabic 'Wisdom of Sabila' are Melkite, but the story was later picked up and expanded by the non-Chalcedonian Copts. I wish to thank Mark N. Swanson for communicating this information; for the arabic sources, see Swanson's dissertation, 'Folly to the Hunafa': The Cross of Christ in Arabic Christian-Muslim Controversy in the Eighth and Ninth Centuries A.D.' (Rome: Pontificio Istituto di Studi Arabi e d'Islamistica, 1992) 20–22, 35–39.

⁷³ A. Mallon, sited by Munier, 197. Rassart-Debergh, 'L'image de la femme', 56, poses the question whether Ama Sibylla was the founder of a monastery for women near the monastery of Abba Jeremias and concludes that 'The sources are mute with regard to this question'.

⁷⁴ I do not use the term 'mythological' pejoratively in the sense of a falsehood; rather, I understand the term as connoting a sustaining religious story. It is obvious that for the monks of Bawit and Saqqara, Ama Sibylla, to whom the monks directed their prayers, was very real.

⁷⁵ The poem is traditionally attributed to Thomas of Celano; for the text, see F.J.E. Raby, ed., *The Oxford Book of Medieval Latin Verse* (Oxford: Clarendon, 1981) #259, 392–394.

⁷⁶ Konrad Onasch and Annemarie Schnieper, *Icons: The Fascination and the Reality* (New York: Riverside, 1997) 222.

⁷⁷ *Ibid.*

⁷⁸ For a discussion of the archeological and literary evidence for this rite, see Chapter Six in this volume.

⁷⁹ Quibell, 4.55 (#188).

Bibliography

ABBREVIATIONS

CSCO   Corpus Scriptorum Christianorum Orientalium
LCL   Loeb Classical Library
SCh   Sources chrétiennes
SOC Collectanea   Studia Orientalia Christiana Collectanea

Agpia: The Prayer Book of the Seven Canonical Hours. Sydney: C.O.P.T., rev. ed., 1997.

Alcock, Anthony, ed. and trans. *The Life of Samuel of Kalamun by Isaac the Presbyter*. Warminster: Aris & Phillips, 1983.

Amélineau, E., ed. *The Life of Maximus and Domitius, Histoire des monastères de la Basse Égypte*. Annales de Musée Guimet 25. Paris, 1894.

———. 'Vie de Paul de Tamoueh'. *Monuments pour servir à l'histoire de l'Égypte chrétienne: Mémoires publiés par les membres de la mission archéologique française au Caire*. Paris, 1888.

el-Anthony, Maximous. 'Windows into Heaven: Icons in the Monastic Life Today', in Elizabeth S. Bolman, ed., *Monastic Visions: Wall Paintings from the Monastery of St. Antony at the Red Sea*. New Haven: Yale University Press, 2002.

'Apocalypse of Paul', trans. H. Duensing, in Wilhelm Schneemelcher, ed., *New Testament Apocrypha*, 2.726-727. Rev. ed., Louisville: Westminster/John Knox, 1992.

Arras, Victor. *Collectio Monastica*, CSCO 238–239, Scriptores Aethiopici 45–46. Louvain: Peeters, 1963.

Atalla, Nabil Selim. *Coptic Art*, Vol. 1, *Wall-Paintings*. Cairo: Lehnert & Landrock, n.d.

Athanassakis, Apostolos N., and Tim Vivian, trans. *The Life of Saint George of Choziba and the Miracles of the Most Holy Mother of God at Choziba*. San Francisco: Catholic Scholars Press, 1994.

Bacht, H. 'La loi du 'retour aux sources' (De quelques aspects de l'idéal monastique pachômien)'. *Revue Mabillon* 51 (1961) 6–25.

Bagnall, Roger S. *Egypt in Late Antiquity*. Princeton: Princeton University Press, 1993.

Bartelink, G. J. M. *Vie D'Antoine*. Sources Chrétiennes 400; Paris: Cerf, 1994.

Basil of Caesarea. *On the Holy Spirit*, David Anderson, trans., *St. Basil the Great: On the Holy Spirit*. Crestwood, New York: St. Vladimir's Seminary Press, 1980.

Basset, René, ed. and trans. *Le Synaxaire arabe jacobite (redaction copte)*. Patrologia Orientalis 1.3. Turnhout: Brepols, 1980.

Battle, Michael. 'The Problem of the Aethiop: Identity and Black Identity in the Desert Tradition'. *Sewanee Theological Review* 42:4 (Michaelmas 1999) 414–428.

'Bawit'. *The Coptic Encyclopedia*, ed. Aziz S. Atiya, 2.362-372. New York: Macmillan, 1991.

Bell, David N., trans. *Besa: The Life of Shenoute*. Kalamazoo: Cistercian, 1983.

———. 'Christ in the Desert'. *The American Benedictine Review* 50:4 (December 1999) 381–396.

Bell, H. Idris. *Jews and Christians in Egypt*. London: The British Museum, 1914.

———. 'Philanthropia in the Papyri of the Roman Period', in *Hommages à Joseph Bidez et Franz Cumont*, 31–37. Brussells: Latomus, 1949.

Betts, Robert Brenton. *Christians in the Arab East: A Political Study*. London: SPCK, 1979.

Bolman, Elizabeth S., ed. *Monastic Visions: The Wall Paintings at the Monastery of Saint Antony by the Red Sea*. New Haven: Yale University Press, 2001.

Bondi, Roberta. *To Love as God Loves: Conversations on Prayer with the Early Church*. Philadelphia: Fortress, 1987.

Boniface (Luykx), Archimandrite. *Eastern Monasticism and the Future of the Church*. Redwood Valley, California: Holy Transfiguration Monastery; Stamford, Connecticut: Basileos Press, 1993.

Brakke, David. *Athanasius and the Politics of Asceticism.* Oxford: Clarendon Press, 1995.

Bratton, Susan Power. 'The Original Desert Solitaire: Early Christian Monasticism and Wilderness'. *Environmental Ethics* 10.1 (Spring 1988) 31–53.

de Broc, H., trans. *Isaie de Scété: Recueil ascétique,* 2nd ed. Spiritualité orientale no.7 bis. Begrolles en Mauges: Abbaye de Bellefontaine, 1985.

Brown, Peter. 'The Rise and Function of the Holy Man in late Antiquity'. *Journal of Roman Studies* 61 (1971) 80–101.

———. 'The Rise and Function of the Holy Man in Late Antiquity, 1971-1997'. *Journal of Early Christian Studies* 6:3 (1998) 353-376.

———. 'The Saint as Exemplar in Late Antiquity'. *Representations* 2 (1983) 1–25.

———. *Society and the Holy in Late Antiquity.* London: Faber, 1982.

———. *The Making of Late Antiquity.* Cambridge, MA: Harvard University Press, 1978.

Budge, E.A. Wallis, ed. and trans. *Coptic Martyrdoms Etc. in the Dialect of Upper Egypt. Coptic Texts,* vol. IV. New York 1977 (London 1914).

———. *Miscellaneous Coptic Texts in the Dialect of Upper Egypt.* 2 vols., rpt, New York: AMS, 1977.

Bunge, Gabriel. *Akêdia: Die geistliche Lehre des Evagrios Pontikos von Überdruss.* Cologne: Luthe-Verlag, 1983.

———, and Adalbert de Vogüé, trans. *Quatre ermites égyptiens d'après les fragments coptes de l'Histoire Lausiaque.* Spiritualité Orientale 60. Begrolles-en-Mauges: Bellefontaine, 1994.

Burgess, Stanley M. *The Spirit and the Church: Antiquity.* Peabody, Massachusetts: Hendrickson, 1984.

Burmester, O. H. E. *A Guide to the Monasteries of the Wadi 'N-Natrun.* Cairo: Société d'archéologie Copte, 1954.

Burton-Christie, Douglas. *The Word in the Desert: Scripture and the Quest for Holiness in Early Christian Monasticism.* New York–Oxford: Oxford University Press, 1993.

Butler, Cuthbert, ed. *The Historia Lausiaca of Palladius.* Cambridge: The University Press, 1898–1904; rpt Hildesheim: Olms, 1967.

Cameron, Averil. 'Desert Mothers: Women Ascetics in Early Christian Egypt', in *Women as Teachers and Disciples in Traditional and New Religions*, ed. E. Puttick. Lewiston, PA: Mellen, 1993.

Camplani, Alberto, ed. *L'Egitto Cristiano: Aspetti e Problemi in Età Tardo-Antica*. Rome: Institutum Patristicum Augustinianum, 1997.

Caseau, B. *Euodia: The Use and Meaning of Fragrances in the Ancient World and their Christianization (100–900)*. Ann Arbor: University of Michigan Press, 1994.

Cassian, John. *Conferences*, trans. Colm Luibheid. New York: Paulist Press, 1985.

———. *The Conferences*, trans. Boniface Ramsey, *John Cassian: The Conferences*. Ancient Christian Writers, 57. Mahwah, New Jersey: Paulist, 1997.

———. *Institutes*. Jean-Claude Guy, ed., *Institutions cénobitiques*. SCh 109. Paris: Cerf, 1965.

Chadwick, Owen, trans. *Western Asceticism*. The Library of Christian Classics. Philadelphia: The Westminster Press, 1958.

Charlesworth, James H., ed. *The Old Testament Pseudepigrapha*. Garden City, New York: Doubleday, 1983.

Chevillat, Alain and Evelyne. *Moines du désert d'Égypte*. Lyon: Terre du Ciel, 1990.

Chittister, Joan. *Wisdom Distilled from the Daily: Living the Rule of Saint Benedict Today*. San Francisco: Harper-San Francisco, 1990.

Chitty, Derwas J. *The Desert a City*. Crestwood, New York: St. Vladimir's Seminary Press, n.d.

———, rev. by Sebastian Brock. *The Letters of Ammonas*. Oxford: SLG Press, 1979.

Chryssavgis, John, trans. *Letters from the Desert: Barsanuphius and John*, Popular Patristics Series. Crestwood, New York: St. Vladimir's Seminary Press, 2003.

Clackson, S.J. *Coptic and Greek Texts relating to the Hermopolite Monastery of Apa Apollo*. Oxford: Griffith Institute/Ashmolean Museum, 2000.

Clark, Elizabeth A. *The Origenist Controversy: The Cultural Construction of an Early Christian Debate*. Princeton: Princeton University Press, 1992.

———. *Reading Renunciation: Asceticism and Scripture in Early Christianity*. Princeton: Princeton University Press, 1999.

Clédat, Jean. *Le Monastère et la necropole de Baouît*. Cairo, IFAO, 1904–1906.

Clement of Alexandria. *The Instructor* 1.2, trans. A. Cleveland Coxe, *Fathers of the Second Century*, The Ante-Nicene Fathers, vol. 2. Rpt Grand Rapids: Eerdman, 1979.

Cocchini, Francesca. 'Il Progresso Spirituale in Origene', in *Spiritual Progress: Studies in the Spirituality of Late Antiquity and Early Monasticism*, ed. Jeremy Driscoll and Mark Sheridan, 29–46. Rome: Pontificio Ateneo S. Anselmo, 1994.

Collins, J. J. 'Sibylline Oracles', in James H. Charlesworth, ed., *The Old Testament Pseudepigrapha*. Garden City, New York: Doubleday, 1983.

———. 'The Sibylline Oracles of Egyptian Judaism'. Ph.D. Dissertation: Harvard University, 1972.

The Coptic Liturgy (of St. Basil). Cairo: J.B.P.H., 1993.

Coquin, René-Georges. 'Apollon de Titkooḥ ou/et Apollon de Bawit?' *Orientalia* 46 (1977) 435–446.

———. 'Les Vertus ('Aretaí) de l'Esprit en Egypte', in *Mélanges d'histoire des religions offerts à Henri-Charles Puech*, 447–457. Paris: Presse universitaires de France, 1974.

———. 'Pamin, Saint'. *The Coptic Encyclopedia*, ed. Aziz S. Atiya, 6.1878. New York: Macmillan, 1991.

———. 'Paul of Tamma, Saint'. *The Coptic Encyclopedia*, ed. Aziz S. Atiya, 6.1923-1925. New York: Macmillan, 1991.

———, and Maurice Martin, 'History', p. 773, in 'Dayr Apa Jeremiah (Saqqara)'. *The Coptic Encyclopedia*, ed. Aziz S. Atiya, 3. 772-79. New York: Macmillan, 1991.

———, and Pierre-Henry Laferriere. 'Les inscriptions pariétales de l'ancienne église du monastère de S. Antoine, dans le désert oriental'. *Bulletin de l'Institut Français d'Archéologie Orientale de Caire* 78 (1978) 267–321 + Plates XXXXVII–XCII.

Cragg, Kenneth. *The Arab Christian: A History in the Middle East*. Louisville, Kentucky: Westminster/John Knox, 1991.

Cremaschi, L. *Parole dal deserto: Detti inediti di Iperechio, Stefano di Tebe e Zosima*. Magnano: Edizioni Qiqajon (Bose), 1992.

Crum, W. E. *A Coptic Dictionary*. Oxford: Clarendon, 1939.

———. *Theological Texts from Coptic Papyri*. Anecdota Oxoniensia. Oxford: Clarendon, 1913.

———, and H. G. Evelyn White. *The Monastery of Epiphanius at Thebes*. New York: Metropolitan Museum of Art, 1926; rpt Arno Press, 1973.

Daniszewski, John. 'Mideast Enmities Outlast Muslims' Month to Purify'. *Los Angeles Times*, February 22, 1996, A9.

Darrouzès, Jean. 'Étienne le Thébain', in *Dictionnaire de Spiritualité*, 4.1525-26. Paris, 1961.

'Dayr Anba Antuniyus', *The Coptic Encyclopedia*, ed. Aziz S. Atiya. New York: Macmillan, 1991.

'Dayr Apa Jeremiah (Saqqara)', *The Coptic Encyclopedia*, ed. Aziz S. Atiya, 3.772-79. New York: Macmillan, 1991.

Dechow, Jon. *Dogma and Mysticism in Early Christianity: Epiphanius of Cyprus and the Legacy of Origen*. Macon, Georgia: Mercer University Press, 1988.

Deferrari, Roy J., ed. and trans. *Saint Basil: The Letters*. 4 vols., Loeb Classical Library. Cambridge: Harvard University Press, 1926.

Deissmann, Adolf. *Die Septuaginta-Papyri und andere altchristliche Texte der Heidelberger Papyrus-Sammlung*, Veröffentlichungen aus der Heidelberger Papyrus-Sammlung I. Heidelberg: Carl Winter, 1905.

———. *Light from the Ancient East*. Grand Rapids: Baker, 1978 [rpt of the fourth edition of the German edition of 1922].

den Heijer, Johannes. 'The Composition of the *History of the Churches and Monasteries of Egypt*: Some Preliminary Remarks', in David W. Johnson, ed., *Acts of the Fifth International Congress of Coptic Studies*, 2: 209-219. Rome: C.I.M., 1993.

Desprez, Vincent. 'Saint Antony and the Beginnings of Anchoritism', *American Benedictine Review* 43 (1992) 61–81 and 141–172.

———. *Le monachisme primitif: Des origines jusqu'au concile d'Éphèse*. Spiritualité orientale 72. Bégrolles-en-Mauge: Bellefontaine, 1998.

Dillard, Annie. 'Schedules', in Geoffrey Wolff, ed., *The Best American Essays 1989*. New York: Ticknor & Fields, 1989.

Di Sarzana, Chiara Faraggiana. '*Apophthegmata Patrum*: Some Crucial Points of their Textual Transmission and the Problem of a Critical Edition'. *Studia Patristica* 29 (1997).

Donahue, Cecil. 'The ΑΓΑΠΗ of the Hermits of Scete'. *Studia Monastica* 1 (1959) 37–49.

Doresse, Jean. 'Deux monastères coptes oubliés'. *La Revue des Arts* 2 (1952) 3–14.

Dörries, Hermann. 'The Place of Confession in Ancient Monasticism'. F. L. Cross, ed., *Studia Patristica* 5.3. Texte und Untersuchungen 80 (1962) 284–311.

Doutreleau, Louis, ed. *Didyme l'Aveugle: Traité du Saint-Esprit*. Paris: Cerf, 1992.

Draguët, René, ed. *Les cinq recensions de l'ascéticon syriaque d'Abba Isaie: Introduction au problème isaien. Version des logoi I-XIII avec des parallèls grecs et latins*. CSCO 289-290 (Syriac text), 293–294 (Greek and Latin texts and French translation), Scriptores Syri 120–121, 122–123; Louvain: CSCO, 196.

Drake, H. A. *Constantine and the Bishops: The Politics of Intolerance*. Baltimore and London: Johns Hopkins University Press, 2000.

Driscoll, Jeremy. 'Exegetical Procedures in the Desert Monk Poemen'. *Mysterium Christi: Symbolgegenwart und theologische Bedeutung. Festschrift für Basil Studer*, ed. Magnus Löhrer and Elmar Salmann, 155–178. Rome: Pontificio Ateneo S. Anselmo, 1995.

―――. 'Spiritual Progress in the Works of Evagrius Ponticus', in *Spiritual Progress: Studies in the Spirituality of Late Antiquity and Early Monasticism*, ed. Jeremy Driscoll and Mark Sheridan, 47–84. Rome: Pontificio Ateneo S. Anselmo, 1994.

Dyobouniotis, K.I. 'Étienne le Sabbaïte', in *Hieros Syndesmos* 8 (16), no. 193 (May 15, 1913) 9–12, and no. 194 (June 1, 1913) 10–13.

Dysinger, Luke, OSB. 'The Significance of Psalmody in the Mystical Theology of Evagrius of Pontus'. In Elizabeth A. Livingstone, ed. *Studia Patristica* 30: 176-182. Louvain: Peeters, 1997.

Elm, Susanna. *'Virgins of God': The Making of Asceticism in Late Antiquity*. Oxford: Clarendon Press, 1994.

Emmett, Alanna M. 'An Early Fourth-century Female Monastic Community in Egypt?', in *Maistor: Classical, Byzantine and Renaissance Studies for Robert Browning*, ed. Ann Moffatt, 77–83. Byzantiana Australiensia 5. Canberra: The Australian Association for Byzantine Studies, 1984.

Evagrius Ponticus. *The Praktikos: Chapters on Prayer*, trans. John Eudes Bamberger. Cistercian Studies Series, 4. Kalamazoo: Cistercian Publications, 1981.

Evagrius Scholasticus. *Ecclesiastical History; The Ecclesiastical History of Evagrius*, ed. J. Bidez and L. Parmentier. Amsterdam: Hakkert, 1964.

———. *A History of the Church by Evagrius*. London: Samuel Bagster, 1846.

Evelyn White, H.G. *The Monasteries of the Wâdi 'N Natrûn*. Three vols.; reprint, New York: Arno, 1973.

Evetts, B. T. A., ed. and trans. *The Churches and Monasteries of Egypt and Some Neighbouring Countries, Attributed to Abû Sâlih, the Armenian*. Oxford: Clarendon Press, 1895.

Fedden, H. Romilly. 'A Study of the Monastery of Saint Antony in the Eastern Desert'. *Bulletin of the Faculty of Arts of the University of Egypt* 5.1 (1937) 1–60.

Feiss, Hugh OSB. *Essential Monastic Wisdom: Writings on the Contemplative Life*. San Francisco: HarperSanFrancisco, 1999.

Forget, Iacobus, trans. *Synaxarium Alexandrinum*. Rpt Louvain: Imprimerie Orientaliste L. Durbecq, 1953 [1922].

Frend, W. H. C. *The Rise of the Monophysite Movement*. Cambridge: Cambridge University Press, 1972.

———. *The Rise of Christianity*. Philadelphia: Fortress, 1984.

Frost, Peter. 'Attitudes toward Blacks in the Early Christian Era'. *The Second Century* 8 (1991) 1–11.

Garitte, Gérard. 'Le 'Discours Ascétique' d'Étienne le Thébain en Géorgien'. *Le Muséon* 83 (1970) 73–93.

———. 'Panégyrique de saint Antoine par Jean, évêque d'Hermopolis'. *Orientalia Christiana Periodica* 9:3 (1943) 100–134, 330–365.

Gascou, Jean. 'Enaton, The'. *The Coptic Encyclopedia*, ed. Aziz S. Atiya, 3.954-58. New York: Macmillan, 1991.

———. 'Monasteries, Economic Activities of'. *The Coptic Encyclopedia*, ed. Aziz S. Atiya, 5: 1639-1645. New York: Macmillan, 1991.

Goehring, James E. *Ascetics, Society, and the Desert: Studies in Early Egyptian Monasticism*. Harrisburg, Pennsylvania, 1999.

———, and Robert F. Bougner. 'Egyptian Monasticism (Selected Papyri)', in Vincent L. Wimbush, ed., *Ascetic Behavior in Greco-Roman Antiquity: A Sourcebook*, 462–463. Minneapolis: Fortress, 1990.

Gould, Graham. 'An Ancient Monastic Writing Giving Advice to Spiritual Directors (Evagrius of Pontus, *On Teachers and Disciples*)'. *Hallel* 22 (1997) 96–103.

———. 'The Influence of Origen on Fourth-Century Monasticism: Some Further Remarks', in Gilles Dorival and Alain Le Boulluec, eds., *Origeniana Sexta: Origène et la Bible/Origen and the Bible*, 591–598. Leuven: University Press, 1995.

———. 'Recent Work on Monastic Origins: a Consideration of the Questions Raised by Samuel Rubenson's *The Letters of St. Antony*'. *Studia Patristica* 25 (1993) 405–416.

Grébaut, Sylvain. 'La Prière de Langinos'. *Revue de l'Orient Chrétien* 15 (1910) 42–52.

Gregory of Nyssa. *Commentary on the Song of Songs*, trans. Casimir McCambley OCSO. Brookline, Mass.: Hellenic College Press, 1987.

———. Gregory of Nyssa. *On Virginity*, ed. Michel Aubineau, *Grégoire de Nysse: Traité de la virginité*. Sources chrétiennes 110; Paris: Cerf, 1966.

Grenfell, Bernard P., and Arthur S. Hunt, eds. *The Oxyrhynchus Papyri*. London: Egypt Exploration Fund, 1898.

Grillmeier, Aloys, in collaboration with Theresia Hainthaler. *Christ in Christian Tradition*. Second, revised edition. London: Mowbray–Atlanta: John Knox Press, 1975.

Grossi, V. 'Cross, Crucifix'. *Encyclopedia of the Early Church*, ed. Angelo Di Berardino, 1.210. New York: Oxford, 1992.

Grossmann, Peter. *Abu Mina: A Guide to the Ancient Pilgrimage Center*. Cairo: Fotiadis & Co. Press-Cairo, 1986.

Gruber, Mark Francis. 'Coping with God: Coptic Monasticism in Egyptian Culture' in Nelly van Doorn-Harder and Kari Vogt, eds., *Between Desert and City: The Coptic Orthodox Church Today*. Oslo: Novus forlag, 1997.

———. *Journey Back to Eden: My Life and Times among the Desert Fathers*. Maryknoll, New York: Orbis Books, 2002.

———. 'The Monastery as the Nexus of Coptic Cosmology', in Nelly van Doorn-Harder and Kari Vogt, eds., *Between Desert and City: The Coptic Orthodox Church Today*. Oslo: Novus forlag, 1997.

Guillaumont, Antoine. 'Anachorèse et vie eucharistique dans le monachisme ancien', rpt in Guillaumont, *Études sur la spiritualité de l'orient chrétien*. Spiritualité orientale 66. Bégrolles-en-Mauges: Abbaye de Bellefontaine, 1996, 113–123.

———. 'Histoire des moines aux Kellia'. *Orientalia Lovaniensia Periodica* 8 (1977) 187–203.

———. 'Macarius the Egyptian, Saint'. *The Coptic Encyclopedia*, ed. Aziz S. Atiya. 5:1491a-1492a. New York: Macmillan, 1991.

———. 'Les moines des Kellia', in Myriam Orban, ed., *Déserts chrétiens d'Égypte*. Nice: Culture Sud, 1993.

———. 'Les moines des Kellia aux 4ᵉ et 5ᵉ siècles', in 'Saint Antoine et les moines du désert'. *Dossiers Histoire et Archéologie* 133 (December 1988).

———. 'Le Problème des deux Macaire dans les Apophthegmata Patrum'. *Irénikon* 48 (1975) 41–59.

Guy, Jean-Claude, ed., *Les Apophtegmes des pères: Collection systématique. Chapitres I–IX*. Sources chrétiennes 387. Paris: Cerf, 1993.

———. 'Le centre monastique de Scété dans la litterature du Ve siécle'. *Orientalia Christiana Periodica* 30 (1964) 129–147.

———. 'Un Dialogue monastique inédit: ΠΕΡΙ ΛΟΓΙΣΜΩΝ. *Revue d'ascetique et mystique* 33 (1957) 171–188.

———. *Recherches sur la tradition grecque des Apophthegmata Patrum*. Brussells: Société des Bollandistes, 1962.

Haas, Christopher. *Alexandria in Late Antiquity: Topography and Social Conflict*. Baltimore: Johns Hopkins, 1997.

Hammond, N. G. L., and H. H. Scullard. *The Oxford Classical Dictionary*, 2nd ed. Oxford: Clarendon Press, 1970.

Harvey, Susan Ashbrook. 'On Holy Stench: When the Odor of Sanctity Sickens'. *Studia Patristica* 35: 90-101, ed. M.F. Wiles and E. J. Yarnold. Leuven: Peeters, 2001.

Herr, Jeanne Lucien. 'La Reine de Saba et le Bois de la Croix'. *Revue archéologique*, 4th series, 23 (1914) 1–31.

John of Nikiou. *Chronicle*, trans. Robert Henry Charles, *The Chronicle of John, Coptic Bishop of Nikiou*. London: Text and Translation Society, 1916; repr. Amsterdam: APA-Philo Press, n.d.

Jones, Alan. *Soul Making: The Desert Way of Spirituality.* San Francisco: Harper & Row, 1985.

Judge, E. A. 'The Earliest Use of Monachos for "Monk" (P. Coll. Youtie 77) and the Origins of Monasticism'. *Jahrbuch für Antike und Christentum* 20 (1977) 72–89.

Jullien, Michel. 'Voyage dans le désert de la Basse-Thébaïde aux couvents de Saint-Antoine et de Saint-Paul'. *Les Missions Catholiques* 16 (1884) 188–273.

Kardong, Terrence G. 'John Cassian's Teaching on Perfect Chastity'. *American Benedictine Review* 30 (1979) 249–263.

Les Kellia: Ermitages coptes en Basse-Égypte. Geneva: Musée d'art et histoire, 1989.

Kelly, J. N. D. *Early Christian Creeds.* London: Longmans, 1950.

———. *Golden Mouth: The Story of John Chrysostom.* Ithaca, New York: Cornell University Press, 1995.

King, Margot H. *The Desert Mothers.* Toronto: Peregrina Publishing, 2nd ed., 1989.

Kosack, Wolfgang. *Historisches Kartenwerk Ägyptens.* Bonn, 1971.

Kramer, Bärbal, and John C. Shelton, eds., *Das Archiv des Nepheros und verwandte Texte, Teil I, Das Archiv des Nepheros: Papyri aus der Trierer und der Heidelberger Papyrussammlung.* Mainz am Rhein: Philipp von Zabern, 1987.

Krause, Martin. 'Menas the Miracle Worker, Saint'. *The Coptic Encyclopedia,* ed. Aziz S. Atiya, 5:1589-90. New York: Macmillan, 1991.

Lampe, G. W. H. *A Patristic Greek Lexicon.* Oxford: Clarendon Press, 1961.

Layton, Bentley. *Catalogue of Coptic Literary Manuscripts in the British Library Acquired Since the Year 1906.* London, 1987.

Lease, Gary. 'Nag Hammadi: Archaeology', in *The Anchor Bible Dictionary,* ed. David Noel Freedman. New York: Doubleday, 1992.

Leclercq, Henri. 'Alexandrie, Archéologie', in Fernand Cabrol and Henri Leclercq, edd., *Dictionnaire d'archéologie chrétienne,* I:1118-1142. Paris: Letouzet et Ané, 1907–53.

Leech, Kenneth. *Experiencing God: Theology as Spirituality.* San Francisco: Harper and Row, 1985.

Leipoldt, J. *Schenute von Atripe*. Texte und Untersuchungen 25:1, N.F. 10:1; Leipzig, 1903.

Lewis, Agnes Smith. 'Hidden Egypt: The First Visit by Women to the Coptic Monasteries of Egypt and Nitria with an Account of the Condition and Reasons for the Decadence of an Ancient Church'. *The Century Illustrated Monthly Magazine* 68 (1904) 745–758.

Lewis, Naphtali. *Life in Egypt under Roman Rule*. Oxford: Clarendon, 1983.

Lienhard, Joseph T., trans. *Origen: Homilies on Luke, Fragments on Luke*. Fathers of the Church 94. Washington, D.C.: The Catholic University of America Press, 1996.

Louth, Andrew. *The Wilderness of God*. Nashville, Tennessee: Abingdon, 1991.

Lucchesi, Enzo. 'À propos d'une édition récente des oeuvres de Paul de Tamma'. *SOC Collectanea* 28 (1995) 161–166.

———. 'Une version copte du Sermo Asceticus d'Étienne le Thébain'. *Analecta Bollandiana* 115.3-4 (1997) 252.

Lyster, William. *The Monastery of Saint Paul*. Cairo: The American Research Center in Egypt Press, 2000.

MacDonald, D.R., ed. *The Acts of Andrew and Matthias in the City of the Cannibals*. Atlanta: Scholars Press, 1990.

Mahfouz, Naguib. *Palace Walk*. New York: Doubleday, 1990.

Malherbe, Abraham J. *Paul and the Popular Philosophers*. Minneapolis: Fortress, 1989.

Mandilaras, Basil G. *The Byzantine Papyri of the Greek Papyrological Society*. Vol. 1. Athens: The Greek Papyrological Society, 1993.

Marriott, G. L. 'Macarius of Egypt: His Epistle *Ad Filios Dei* in Syriac'. *The Journal of Theological Studies* 86 (1968) 42–44.

Martin, Maurice. 'The Renewal in Context', in Nelly van Doorn-Harder and Kari Vogt, edd., *Between Desert and City: The Coptic Orthodox Church Today*. Oslo: Novus forlag, 1997.

Matthew the Poor. *Community of Love*. Crestwood, New York: St. Vladimir's Seminary Press, 1984.

McGuckin, John. *Saint Gregory of Nazianzus: An Intellectual Biography*. Crestwood, New York: St. Vladimir's, 2001.

McNary-Zak, Bernadette. 'Pachomian Remission'. *Coptic Church Review* 23:4 (Winter 2002) 107–110.

Meinardus, Otto F.A. *The Copts in Jerusalem*. Cairo: Commission on Oecumenical Affairs of the See of Alexandria, 1960.

———. *Monks and Monasteries of the Egyptian Desert*. 1st ed., Cairo: The American University at Cairo Press, 1961.

———. *Monks and Monasteries of the Egyptian Desert*. Cairo: American University in Cairo Press, rev. ed., 1992.

———. 'Recent Developments in Egyptian Monasticism'. *Oriens Christianus* 49 (1965) 79–89.

———. *Two Thousand Years of Coptic Christianity*. Cairo: The American University in Cairo Press, 1999.

———. 'Zur monastischen Erneuerung in der koptischen Kirche'. *Oriens Christianus* 61 (1977) 59–70.

Meredith, Anthony. *The Cappadocians*. Crestwood, New York: St. Vladimir's Seminary Press, 1995.

Merton, Thomas. 'Prayer and Self-Growth', side two. Credence Cassettes; Kansas City: The National Catholic Reporter Publishing Co., n.d.

———. *The Wisdom of the Desert: Sayings from the Desert Fathers of the Fourth Century*. New York: New Directions, 1960.

———. *Zen and the Birds of Appetite*. New York: New Directions, 1968.

el-Meskeen, Father Matta. *Coptic Monasticism and the Monastery of St. Macarius: A Short History*. Cairo: St Macarius, 1984.

Meyendorff, John. *Imperial Unity and Christian Divisions: The Church 450–680 A.D.* Crestwood, New York: St. Vladimir's Seminary Press, 1989.

Mikhail, Maged S., and Tim Vivian, trans. 'Life of Saint John the Little'. *Coptic Church Review* 18:1 & 2 (Spring/Summer 1997) 1–64.

Munier, Henri. 'La Sibylla alexandrine chez les Coptes'. *Bulletin de la Société archéologique d'Alexandrie* 20 (1924) 196–201.

Naldini, Mario. *Il Cristianismo in Egitto: Lettere private nei papiri dei secoli II-IV*. Firenze [Florence]: Le Monnier, 1968.

Norris, Kathleen. *The Cloister Walk*. New York: Riverhead Books, 1996.

Olivera, Bernardo. *How Far to Follow? The Martyrs of Atlas*. Petersham, Massachusetts: Saint Bede's Press, 1997; Kalamazoo: Cistercian Publications, 2003.

Onasch, Konrad, and Annemarie Schnieper. *Icons: The Fascination and the Reality*. New York: Riverside, 1997.

O'Neill, J.C. 'The Origins of Monasticism', in Rowan Williams, ed., *The Making of Orthodoxy: Essays in Honour of Henry Chadwick*, 270–287. Cambridge: Cambridge University Press, 1989.

Origen. *De principiis* 1.3.5, Frederick Crombie, trans., *The Ante-Nicene Fathers*. Rpt. Grand Rapids: Eerdmans, 1979.

———. 'Fragments on Luke', LQ, in M. Rauer, ed., *Origenes Werke*. Die griechischen christlichen Schriftsteller 9. Leipzig, 1930. Rpt in ΒΙΒΛΙΟΘΗΚΗ ΕΛΛΗΝΩΝ ΠΑΤΕΡΩΝ 15, ΩΡΙΓΕΝΗΣ. Athens: Ekdosis tês apostolikês diakonias, 1958.

Orlandi, Tito. *Paolo di Tamma: Opere*. Rome: C.I.M., 1988.

———. 'Le opere di Paolo di Tamma', in Alberto Camplani, ed., *L'Egitto Cristiano: Aspetti e Problemi in Età Tardo-Antica*. Rome: Institutum Patristicum Augustinianum, 1997.

———. 'La vita di Paolo di Tamma e i monaci del Medio Egitto', in Camplani, ed., *L'Egitto Cristiano: Aspetti e Problemi in Età Tardo-Antica*, 68–70. Rome: Institutum Patristicum Augustinianum, 1997.

———. *Vite dei Monachi Phif e Longino*. Testi e documenti per lo Studio dell'antichità 51. Milan: Cisalpino-Goliardica, 1975.

Palladius. *Palladius: The Lausiac History*, trans. Robert T. Meyer. New York: Newman Press, 1964.

Palmer, G. E. H., et al., trans. *The Philokalia: The Complete Text*. Volume 1 [of 4]. London: Faber and Faber, 1979 [–1982].

Parmentier, Martin. 'Evagrius of Pontus' "Letter to Melania"'. *Bijdragen, tijdschrift voor filosofie en theologie* 46 (1985) 2–38.

Partrick, Theodore Hall. *Traditional Egyptian Christianity: A History of the Coptic Orthodox Church*. Greensboro, North Carolina: Fisher Hall Press, 1996.

Pearson, Birger A. 'Nag Hammadi Codices', in *The Anchor Bible Dictionary*, ed. David Noel Freedman, 4.984-993. New York: Doubleday, 1992.

———. 'The Pierpont Morgan Fragments of a Coptic Enoch Apocryphon', in *Studies on the Testament of Abraham*, ed. George W.E. Nickelsburg. Missoula, Montana: Scholars Press, 1976.

Pearson, Birger A., and Tim Vivian. *Two Coptic Homilies Attributed to Saint Peter of Alexandria*. Rome: C.I.M., 1993.

Pease, Arthur Stanley, and David S. Potter. 'Sibyl'. *The Oxford Classical Dictionary*. Third Edition, edd. Simon Hornblower and Antony Spawforth, 1400–1401. Oxford: Oxford University Press, 1996.

Peel, Malcolm, trans. *The Teachings of Silvanus*, in *Nag Hammadi Codex VII*, ed. Birger A. Pearson, 249–369. Leiden: Brill, 1996.

Petersen, Joan M. *Handmaids of the Lord: Holy Women in Late Antiquity and the Early Middle Ages*. Kalamazoo: Cistercian Publications, 1996.

Pezin, Michel. 'Nouveau fragment copte concernant Paul de Tamma (P. Sorbonne inv. 2632)', in Jean-Marc Rosenstiehl, ed., *Christianisme d'Égypte: Hommages à René-Georges Coquin*, 15–20. Cahiers de la Bibliothèque Copte. Paris-Louvain: Peeters, 1995.

Places, Édouard des. 'Le 'Discours Ascétique' d'Étienne de Thèbes: Texte grec inédit et traduction'. *Le Muséon* 82 (1969) 35–59.

Pollok, Jan. 'The Present State of Studies on *The Apophthegmata Patrum*: An Outline of Samuel Rubenson's and Graham Gould's Perspectives', in Marek Starowieyski, ed., *The Spirituality of Ancient Monasticism*, 79–89. Cracow: Tyniec, 1995.

Pseudo-Macarius. *The Fifty Spiritual Homilies and The Great Letter*, trans. George A. Maloney. New York: Paulist, 1992.

Price, R. M., trans. *Cyril of Scythopolis: The Lives of the Monks of Palestine*. Kalamazoo: Cistercian Publications, 1991.

Quibell, J.E. *Excavations at Saqqara (1908–9, 1909–10)*, vol 3, *Excavations at Saqqara (1907–1908)*. Cairo: IFAO, 1909; vol. 4, *The Monastery of Apa Jeremias*. Cairo: IFAO, 1912.

Raby, F.J. E., ed. *The Oxford Book of Medieval Latin Verse*. Oxford: Clarendon, 1981.

Rapp, Claudia. '"For next to God, you are my salvation": reflections on the rise of the holy man in late antiquity', in James Howard-Johnston and Paul Antony Hayward, eds., *The Cult of Saints in Late Antiquity and the Middle Ages*, 63–81. Oxford: Oxford University Press, 1999.

Rassart-Debergh, Marguerite. 'L'art des "fils des pharaons"', in P. Miquel, et al., edd. *Déserts chrétiens d'Égypte*. Nice: Culture Sud, 1993.

———. 'La décoration picturale du monastére de Saqqara. Essai de reconstitution', in Hjalmar Torp, et al., eds., *Acta ad Archaeologium et Artium Historiam Pertinentia*. Rome: Giorgio Bretschneider, 1981.

———. L'image de la femme au couvent Saint-Jérémie à Saqqara'. *Le Monde Copte* 16: 48-59.

———. 'Paintings', p. 778, in 'Dayr Apa Jeremiah (Saqqara)'. *The Coptic Encyclopedia*, ed. Aziz S. Atiya, 3:772-779. New York: Macmillan, 1991.

———, and Jacques Debergh. 'A propos de trois peintures de Saqqara', in Hjalmar Torp, et al., edd., *Acta ad Archaeologium et Artium Historiam Pertinentia*, 11.187-203. Rome: Giorgio Bretschneider, 1981.

Rees, B. R. ed. *Papyri from Hermopolis and Other Documents of the Byzantine Period*. Graeco-Roman Memoirs 42 (London: Egypt Exploration Society: 1964.

Regnault, Lucien. 'Aux origines des collections d'Apophtegmes'. *Studia Patristica* 18 (1989) 61–64.

———. *The Day-to-Day Life of the Desert Fathers in Fourth-Century Egypt*. Petersham, Massachusetts: St. Bede's Press, 1999.

———. 'John Colobos, Saint'. *The Coptic Encyclopedia*, ed. Aziz S. Atiya, 5: 1359-1361. New York: Macmillan, 1991.

———. 'Isaiah of Scetis, Saint'. *The Coptic Encyclopedia*, ed. Aziz S. Atiya, 4:1305-1306. New York: Macmillan, 1991.

———. *Les Sentences des pères du Désert*. Sablé-sur-Sarthe: Solesmes: Abbaye Saint-Pierre, 1976.

———. *Les Sentences des pères du desert: serie des anonymes*. Solesmes: Abbaye Saint-Pierre, 1985.

———. *La vie quotidienne des pères du désert en Égypte au IVe siècle*. Paris: Hachette, 1990.

———. 'Le vrai visage d'un père du désert ou abba Jean Colobos a travers ses apophtegmes', in E. Lucchesi and H. D. Saffrey, eds., *Mémorial André-Jean Festugière: Antiquité païenne et. chrétienne*, 225–234. Geneva: Patrick Cramer, 1984.

Roberts, Colin H. *Manuscript, Society, and Belief in Early Christian Egypt*. Schweich Lectures, 1977. London: Oxford University Press, 1979.

Robinson, Gesine Schenke. 'Codex Berolinensis P 20915: A Progress Report', in *Ägypten und Nubien in spätantiker und christlicher Zeit*, vol. 2, *Schriftum, Sprache, und Gedankenwelt*, ed. Stephen Emmel, et al. Wiesbaden: Reichert, 1999.

Robinson, James M. 'The First Christian Monastic Library', in Wlodzimierz Godlewski, ed., *Coptic Studies: Acts of the Third International Congress of Coptic Studies*, 372–378. Warsaw: PWN, 1990.

———. 'The Pachomian Monastic Library at the Chester Beatty Library and the Bibliothèque Bodmer'. The Institute of Antiquity and Christianity, The Claremont Graduate School, *Occasional Papers* #19.

Rousseau, Philip. 'Ascetics as mediators and as teachers', in *The Cult of Saints in Late Antiquity and the Middle Ages: Essays on the Contribution of Peter Brown*, ed. James Howard-Johnston and Paul Antony Hayward, 45–59. Oxford: Oxford University Press, 1999.

Rubenson, Samuel. 'Christian Asceticism and the Emergence of the Monastic Tradition', in Vincent L. Wimbush and Richard Valantasis, edd., *Asceticism*, 49–57. New York–Oxford: Oxford University Press, 1995.

———. *The Letters of St. Antony: Monasticism and the Making of a Saint*. Minneapolis: Fortress, 1995.

Rufus, John. *Peter the Iberian*, ed. R. Raabe, *Petrus der Iberer: Ein Charakterbild zur Kirchen- und Sittengeschichte des fünften Jahrhunderts*. Leipzig, 1895.

———. *Plerophoriae* 7. F. Nau, ed., *Jean Rufus, Évéque de Maïouma, Plérophories*. Patrologia Orientalis 8.1. Paris: Firmin-Didot, 1912.

Russell, Kenneth C. 'Cassian on a Delicate Subject'. *Cistercian Studies Quarterly* 27 (1992) 1–12.

———. 'John Cassian on Asceticism'. *Review for Religious* 56 (1997) 156–168.

———. 'Reaching Saint Antony Across the Scholarly Barriers'. *Logos* 38:1-4 (1997) 93–127.

Russell, Norman, trans. *The Lives of the Desert Fathers: The Historia Monachorum in Aegypto*. Kalamazoo: Cistercian Publications, 1980.

Samir, Khalil. 'Stephen the Theban'. *The Coptic Encyclopedia*, ed. Aziz S. Atiya, 7.2154-1255. New York: Macmillan, 1991.

Sauget, Joseph-Marie. 'Onofrio'. *Bibliotheca sanctorum* 9 (1967) 1187–1197.

———. 'Une version arabe du "Sermon Ascétique" d'Étienne le Thébain'. *Le Muséon* 77 (1964) 367–406.

Severus, Sulpicius. *Dialogue* 1.17, trans. Bernard M. Peebles, in Gerald G. Walsh, et al., *Niceta of Remesiana: Writings, Sulpicius Severus: Writings . . .* Fathers of the Church, 7. Washington, D.C.: Catholic University of America Press, 1970.

Sextus, Pythagoras. *The Sentences of Sextus*, ed. Henry Chadwick. Cambridge: Cambridge University Press, 1959.

———. 'The Sentences of Sextus', trans. Frederik Wisse, in *The Nag Hammadi Library in English*, ed. James M. Robinson, 454–459. San Francisco: Harper & Row, 1977.

Shapland, C. R. B. *The Letters of Saint Athanasius Concerning the Holy Spirit.* New York: Philosophical Library, 1951.

Sheridan, Mark. 'The Development of the Interior Life in Certain Early Monastic Writings in Egypt', in Marek Starowicyski, ed., *The Spirituality of Ancient Monasticism. Acts of the International Colloquium held in Cracow-Tyniec, 16–19th November 1994*, 91–104. Cracow: Tyniec, 1995.

———. '"Steersman of the mind": The Virgin Mary as Ideal Nun (an interpretation of Luke 1:29 by Rufus of Shotep)'. *Studia Patristica* 30, ed. Elizabeth A Livingstone. Leuven: Peeters, 1997.

———. 'Il mondo spirituale e intellettuale del primo monachesimo egiziano', in Camplani, ed., *L'Egitto Cristiano* (see above) 177–216.

Shoucri, Mounir. 'Dayr Abu Mina'. *The Coptic Encyclopedia*, ed. Aziz S. Atiya, 3.706-707. New York: Macmillan, 1991.

Spidlik, Thomas. *The Spirituality of the Christian East: A Systematic Handbook*. Kalamazoo: Cistercian Publications, 1986.

Starowicyski, Marek, ed., *The Spirituality of Ancient Monasticism. Acts of the International Colloquium held in Cracow-Tyniec, 16–19th November 1994*. Cracow: Tyniec, 1995.

Stevenson, J., ed., *A New Eusebius*. London: SPCK, 1957.

Stewart, Columba. 'Radical Honesty about the Self: The Practice of the Desert Fathers'. *Sobornost* 12 (1990) 25–39.

———. '*Working the Earth of the Heart*': *The Messalian Controversy in History, Texts, and Language*. Oxford: Clarendon Press, 1991.

———. 'Writing About John Cassian in the 1990s'. *American Benedictine Review* 48:4 (December 1997) 341–346.

Stone, Michael E. *A History of the Literature of Adam and Eve*. Atlanta: Scholars Press, 1992.

Strothmann, Werner, ed. *Die syrische Überlieferung der Schriften des Makarios*. 2 vols. Wiesbaden: Harrossowitz, 1981.

Swanson, Mark N. 'Folly to the Hunafa': The Cross of Christ in Arabic Christian-Muslim Controversy in the Eighth and Ninth Centuries A.D.' Rome: Pontificio Istituto di Studi Arabi e d'Islamistica, 1992.

Swete, Henry Barclay. *The Holy Spirit in the Ancient Church: A Study of Christian Teaching in the Age of the Fathers*. London: Macmillan, 1912.

Taft, Robert. 'Praise in the Desert: The Coptic Monastic Office Yesterday and Today'. *Worship* 56 (1982) 513–529.

Takla, Hany N. 'The Library of the Monastery of St. John the Little: A Colophon from a Vatican-preserved Coptic Manuscript'. *Saint Shenouda the Archimandrite Society Newsletter* 3.1. <http://www.stshenouda.com/newsltr/nl3_1.htm>.

———. 'Martyrs and Martyrdom in the Coptic Church'. *Bulletin of Saint Shenouda the Archimandrite Coptic Society* 1 (1983–84) 1–229.

Timbie, Janet. 'Melitian Schism', *The Coptic Encyclopedia*, ed. Aziz S. Atiya, 5:1884-1885. New York: Macmillan, 1991.

Timm, Stefan. *Das christlich-koptische Ägypten in arabischer Zeit*. 6 vols. Wiesbaden: L. Reichert 1984–1992.

Treu, Ursula. 'Die Oracula Sibyllina und Ägypten', in Peter Nagel, ed., *Graeco-Coptica: Griechen und Kopten im byzantischen Ägypten*. Halle-Wittenberg: Martin-Luther Universität, 1984.

Tromp, Johannes. 'Two References to a Levi Document in an Epistle of Ammonas'. *Novum Testamentum* 39:3 (1997) 235–247.

van Cauwenbergh, P. *Étude sur les moins d'Égypte depuis le Concile de Chalcédoine (451) jusqu'à l'invasion arabe (640)*. Paris, 1914.

van Doorn-Harder, Nelly, and Kari Vogt, edd. *Between Desert and City: The Coptic Orthodox Church Today*. Oslo: Novus forlag, 1997.

van Doorn-Harder, Pieternella. *Contemporary Coptic Nuns*. Columbia, South Carolina: University of South Carolina Press, 1995.

van Moorsel, Paul. *Les Peintures du Monastère de Saint-Antoine près de la Mer Rouge. La peinture murale chez les Coptes*. Mémoires publiés par les membres de l'institut français d'archéologie orientale du Caire CXII. Cairo: IFAO, 1998.

———, and Mathilde Huijbers. 'Repertory of the preserved wallpaintings from the monastery of Apa Jeremiah at Saqqara'. *Acta ad archaeologiam et artium historiam pertinentia*, ed. Hjalmar Torp, et al., 9:131-135 and Plates IV–V. Rome: Bretschneider, 1981.

van Parys, Michel, trans. 'Étienne de Thèbes: Enseignement sur la vie monastique', in Paul Tirot, et al., *Enseignement des pères du désert: Hyperéchios, Étienne de Thèbes, Zosime*. Spiritualité Orientale 51; Begrolles-en-Mauges: Bellefontaine, 1991.

Veilleux, Armand. 'Monasticism and Gnosis in Egypt', in Birger A. Pearson and James E. Goehring, eds., *The Roots of Egyptian Christianity*, 271–306. Studies in Antiquity and Christianity. Philadelphia: Fortress, 1986.

Veilleux, Armand, trans. *Pachomian Koinonia*. Three volumes. Kalamazoo: Cistercian Publications, 1980–1982.

Vivian, Tim. '"Christ in the Desert"—A Response', *American Benedictine Review* 52:4 (December 2001) 393–420.

———. 'Coptic Palladiana II: The Life of Evagrius (*Lausiac History* 38)'. *Coptic Church Review* 21.1 (Spring 2000) 8–23.

———. '"Everything Made by God is Good": A Letter concerning Sexuality from Saint Athanasius to the Monk Amoun'. *Église et Théologie* 24 (1993) 75–108.

———. *Four Desert Fathers*, Popular Patristic Series. Crestwood, New York: St. Vladimir's Seminary Press, 2004.

———. '*Life of Antony* by St. Athanasius of Alexandria'. *Coptic Church Review* 15.1 & 2 (Spring and Summer 1994) 3–58.

———. *Journeying into God: Seven Early Monastic Lives*. Minneapolis: Fortress, 1996.

———. *Paphnutius: Histories of the Monks of Upper Egypt and the Life of Onnophrius*. Cistercian Studies Series 140. Rev. ed. Kalamazoo: Cistercian Publications, 2000.

———. 'Reading the Saints: Early Monastic Texts and Resources Available in English'. *Cistercian Studies Quarterly* 28.1 (1993) 17–58.

———. 'Reading the Saints II'. *Cistercian Studies Quarterly* 33.3 (1998) 329–344.

———. 'Saint Antony and the Monastery of Saint Antony', in Elizabeth S. Bolman, ed., *Monastic Visions: The Wall Paintings at the Monastery of Saint Antony at the Red Sea*. New Haven: Yale University Press, 2002.

———. *Saint Macarius the Spiritbearer*, Popular Patristic Series. Crestwood, New York: St. Vladimir's Seminary Press, 2004.

———. *Saint Peter of Alexandria: Bishop and Martyr*. Philadelphia: Fortress, 1988.

———. 'Witness to Holiness: Abba Daniel of Scetis', *Coptic Church Review* 24: 1 & 2 (Spring/Summer 2003) 2–52.

———, and Apostolos N. Athanassakis, trans. 'The Ascetic Discourse of Stephen of Thebes'. *Cistercian Studies Quarterly* 34.4 (1999) 425–454.

———, and Apostolos N. Athanassakis, trans. *The Life of Antony: The Coptic Life and The Greek Life*. Cistercian Studies Series 202. Kalamazoo: Cistercian Publications, 2003.

———, and Apostolos N. Athanassakis. 'Spiritual Direction from the Early Monastic Mothers and Fathers on Observing a Holy Lent: Chapter III of the Greek *Systematic Apophthegmata*, "On Compunction"'. *Sewanee Theological Review* 44:1 (Christmas 2000) 60–78.

Vogt, Kari. 'The Coptic Practice of the Jesus Prayer: A Tradition Revived', in Nelly van Doorn-Harder and Kari Vogt, edd., *Between Desert and City: The Coptic Orthodox Church Today*. Oslo: Novus forlag, 1997.

Vogüé, Adalbert de. *To Love Fasting: The Monastic Experience*. Petersham, Massachusetts, Saint Bede's Press, 1989.

Waddell, Helen. *Beasts and Saints*. London: Darton, Longman and Todd, 1995 [1934].

Walters, C. C. *Monastic Archaeology in Egypt*. Warminster: Aris & Phillips, 1974.

Ward, Benedicta, trans. *The Sayings of the Desert Fathers: The Alphabetical Collection*. Cistercian Studies Series 59. Kalamazoo: Cistercian Publications, 1975, rev. ed. 1984.

———. *The Wisdom of the Desert Fathers: Apophthegmata Patrum from the Anonymous Series*. Oxford: SLG Press, 1975.

Watson, John. 'Abba Kyrillos: Patriarch and Solitary'. *Coptic Church Review* 17: 1 & 2 (Spring & Summer 1996) 7–48.

———. *Among the Copts*. Portland, Oregon: Sussex Academic Press, 2000.

Wietheger, Cäcilia. *Das Jeremias-Kloster zu Saqqara unter besonderer Berücksichtigung der Inschriften*. Arbeiten zum spätantiken und koptischen Ägypten 1. Altenberge: Oros Verlag, 1992.

Williams, C. A. *Oriental Affinities of the Legend of the Hairy Anchorite*. 2 volumes. Urbana: University of Illinois Press, 1925–1926.

Wimbush, Vincent L., and Richard Valantasis, edd. *Asceticism*. New York & Oxford: Oxford University Press, 1995.

Winlock, H. E., and W. E. Crum. *The Monasteries of Epiphanius at Thebes*. New York: The Metropolitan Museum of Art, 1926.

Yanney, Rodolph. 'A New Martyr: Father Ruais Fakher'. *Coptic Church Review* 14.4 (Winter 1993) 109–112.

———. 'Preface'. *Coptic Church Review* 17: 1 & 2 (Spring & Summer 1996) 4.

Zacharius of Mytilene. *Syriac Chronicle* 4.1; F. J. Hamilton and E. W. Brooks, trans., *The Syriac Chronicle Known as that of Zachariah of Mytilene*. London: Methuen, 1899; rpt. New York: AMS, 1979.

Zacharius of Sakhâ. 'Vie de Jean Colobos', ed. E. Amélineau, *Annales du Musée Guimet* 25 (Paris, 1894) 316–410.

Index

A

Aaron 184
Aaron, Abba 327
Abba(s) 5, 8, 9, 41, 149, 211
Abimelech 184
Abraham 347, 348
Abraham (OT) xxx, xxxi, 75, 76, 150, 184, 290, 295
Abyss 176
Acacia(s) 176, 288
Acacius 245, 246, 268, 272
Acherousia, Lake 178
Adam 13, 16, 61, 384, 385
Ad filios Dei 101–137
Affliction(s) 301, 306, 309, 329, 342
Agape 210, 227
Akhmim 142, 212, 386
Al-Ashmunein See Shmoun
Alexandria 26, 28, 31, 34, 37, 242, 243, 244, 245, 246, 254, 257, 261, 262, 267, 274, 335, 357, 380
Almighty, the 240, 268, 269, 348
Al-Minya 207
Almsgiving 14
Amalekite 303
Ammonas 111, 118, 119, 120, 121, 123, 287
Ammonius 336, 338
Amoun 26, 27, 30, 103, 205
Anachôrêsis 150
Anastasius 380
Anchorite 329, 335, 348
Anchoritic Monasticism 41, 181, 207, 328
Andrew 189
Angel(s) 163, 166, 183, 219, 225, 247, 265, 313
Animal(s) 175
Anoub (Anoup) 143, 208, 212
Antaeopolite nome 348
Antelope 156
Anthropomorphism 30
Anti-Christ 243
Antinoë 142, 156, 163, 164
Antiquities Development Project 61
Antony of Scetis, Apa 156
Antony, Saint 5, 6, 26, 27, 28, 38, 42, 43, 60, 62, 63, 85, 89, 91, 111, 113, 114, 115, 116, 117, 118, 121, 123, 205, 211, 213, 256, 286, 287, 325, 326, 328, 335
Antony, Saint, Monastery of xxxii, 59–98, 205
Cave of Saint Antony 83, 88–92
Old Church 74

Origins 65–67
Past and Present 65–70
Travel to 62–65
Wall paintings 61, 68, 74–76
An(o)up See Anoub
Aph(o)u 143, 156, 157
Apocalypse of Adam 385
Apocalypse of Paul 384
Apollo, Abba 142, 143, 155, 205, 206, 207, 208, 209, 210, 212, 213, 214, 215, 216, 217, 218, 219, 221, 223, 225
  Monastery of 208
Apollonopolis Magna See Edfu
Apophthegmata 5, 6, 26, 30, 46, 103, 105, 110, 118, 141, 143, 144, 149, 151, 211, 242, 243, 288, 289, 291, 326
Apostle 274, 303, 341, 384
Arcadius 264
Archelaos 326
Arians 108
Army 269, 270, 271, 272, 348
Arrogance 175, 294
Arsenius 13, 287
Ascetic 220, 242, 244, 247, 340
Ascetic discipline 110, 144, 285
Ascetic Discourse of Stephen of Thebes 294–314
Ascetic practice(s) 218, 219, 222, 247, 251
Al-'Asal, al-Safi ibn 286
Asyut 207
Athanasius 336, 342
Athanasius, Abba 142
Athanasius, Saint 28, 32, 75, 106, 107, 108, 109, 118, 146
Athlete 8, 15, 221
Athos, Mount 84
Augustine, Saint 354
Ausonius 338
Azotus 185

B
Babylon See Cairo
Balaam 182
Baptism 162
Baramus, Monastery of 31, 32, 34, 41
Barbarians 142
Barsanuphius 331
Basil the Great, Saint 106, 107, 109
Bawit 142, 205, 207, 208, 212, 213, 379, 380, 381, 382, 385
Bear(s) 180
Bedouins 42
Belly 168, 294
Belt (monastic) 255
Beni Suef 62, 63
Beor 182
Besa 379
Bible 8, 72, 118, 289
Bishoi, Saint 40, 43, 142, 164
Bishoi, Saint, monastery of 28, 31, 32, 33, 34, 37, 42, 45, 67, 80
Blasphemy 272
Blessing 256, 290
Boêthos 329
Bolman, Elizabeth S. (Betsy) 61, 65, 68, 75, 76, 77, 79, 83, 84, 85, 86, 89, 90, 91
Book, the (Bible) 314
Book of the Installation of the Archangel Gabriel, the 385
Book of Life 384, 388
Bread 256, 262, 306, 353, 355, 357, 358, 359
Brother(s) 222, 223, 226, 257, 258, 271, 298, 355, 356, 364, 365
Business 327–328, 353, 359

C
Cain 383
Cairo 28, 32, 34, 62, 63, 69, 71, 72, 213, 215, 380

Cancer 262
Cappadocian(s) 106
Cares 294
Cassian, John 30, 32, 114, 141
Cave of Saint Antony 83, 88–92
Cell(s) 7, 11, 37, 43, 44, 144, 146, 148, 149, 150, 174–177, 178–190, 212, 242, 259, 263, 264, 297, 298, 299, 301, 304, 310, 311
Cells, the See Kellia
Cemetery 363
Cenobitic monasticism 66, 148, 285, 328
Cenobium 254
Chaeremon 349
Chalcedon, Council of 239, 243, 244, 246
Chapel of the Holy Virgin Mary 42
Chastity 16, 126, 297
Cherubim 74, 167
Children 348, 353, 355, 356, 357, 361
Chorath (Wadi Cherith) 184, 185
Christ xxx, xxxi, 40, 49, 60, 73, 74, 90, 93, 94, 107, 108, 112, 120, 122, 148, 149, 150, 154, 159, 161, 162, 164, 168, 170, 173, 187, 190, 207, 208, 209, 214, 215, 217, 221, 224, 225, 227, 241, 243, 245, 248, 250, 253, 260, 262, 272, 274, 290, 291, 310, 336, 339, 340, 341, 342, 344, 362, 379
  Divinity of 272
Christ-bearing/bearer 340, 342, 343
Christian(s) 111, 239, 243
Church of Saint Antony and Saint Paul 67

Church(es) 13, 38, 39, 207, 210, 215, 226, 227, 240, 250, 252
Church of the Virgin 39
Citeaux 104
Clothing 354, 362, 363
Cluny 34, 104
Colzim, Mount 60, 61, 66
Commandment(s) 128, 147, 158, 170, 171, 176, 178, 179, 219, 299, 301, 305, 306, 308, 313
Compassion 162, 183, 223, 252, 253
Communion 155
Conservators 76–78
Constantine 26, 103, 385
Constantinople 31
Contrition 127
Conversation Concerning Thoughts 5–21
Coptic Orthodox Church 28, 29, 32, 33, 34, 48, 103, 104, 143, 382
Copts 30, 36, 43, 286, 379
Corinth 254
Cornelius 185
Council of Constantinople 107
Covenant 181, 184
Cowardice 303
Cowl 255, 258, 263
Creator 240, 262
Crocodiles 163
Cross 223
Cross-bearer 307
Crown 188
Cure(s) 261
Cyril IV, Pope 64

D
David 126, 189, 218, 273, 301, 307, 387
Deacon 365
Dead, raising of 258, 327

Death 128, 271
Deer 260
Deir Abu Maqar See Macarius the Great, Saint, Monastery of
Deir al-Baramus See Baramus, Monastery of
Deir Anba Bishoi See Bishoi, Saint, Monastery of
Deir Anba Bula See Paul, Saint, Monastery of
Deir el-Maimoun See Pispir
Deir el-Souriani See Syrian Monastery
Demon(s) 7, 11, 14, 43, 114, 115, 145, 153, 183, 186, 188, 251, 262, 263, 264, 325
Desert 14, 25, 44, 46, 63, 179, 183, 189, 260, 387
Desires 305
Devil 7, 8, 9, 11, 12, 13, 14, 15, 16, 38, 60, 93, 109, 110, 120, 126, 145, 159, 160, 181, 295, 303, 307, 313, 336, 338, 385
Didymus the Blind 106, 107, 109, 146
Dies Irae 387
Dionysius 244
Dionysodora 329
Dioscorus 243
Disciple(s) 259, 260, 264, 290
Distraction(s) 7, 9, 13
Documentary sources 326
Donkey 311
Dorotheus 341
Dove(s) 11, 293
Dreams 187

E

Easter 92, 244
Ecclesiastes 147
Edfu 213
Eggs, ostrich 39, 40

Egypt xxx, xxxi, xxxii, 14, 26, 27, 28, 30, 32, 33, 35, 39, 45, 48, 49, 59, 60, 61, 67, 68, 104, 110, 111, 114, 116, 117, 118, 143, 146, 168, 214, 224, 239, 240, 243, 245, 268, 298, 328, 379, 384
Elder 143
Elias 330
Elijah 119, 150, 152, 184, 185
Elisha 119
Emperor 268, 269
Enaton 242, 243, 245, 246, 254, 266, 267, 268, 269
Enemy/ies 125, 126, 128, 188
Enemy, the (Satan) 126, 303
Enoch 216, 382, 383–385, 387, 388
  1 Enoch 384, 385, 386
Ephraem, Saint 29, 40
Epiphanius of Thebes 331
Epiphanius, Monastery of 330
Eremitism 148
Esna (Latopolis) 207
Ethiopian 159
Eucharist 47, 49, 207, 213, 273
Eunomius 109
Euchites 242
Eudoxia 329
Eudoxia (sister of Constantine) 385
Eusebius 146
Evagrius of Pontus 7, 30, 147, 205, 288
Evagrius Scholasticus 243, 244, 245
Eve 61, 383, 384, 385
Evil/s 12, 14, 114, 124, 182, 273, 294, 295, 299, 305, 307, 341, 385
Exegesis 146
Exile 353, 354, 355

Ezekiel 142, 154, 158, 159, 163
Ezekiel (prophet) 169

F
Faith 223, 255, 271, 273, 327, 343, 348
Fanous, Abouna 85–88
'Far, Abouna' 82–83
Fasting 16, 124, 125, 146, 175
Father, the 111, 122, 206, 216, 219, 223, 224, 225, 228, 275, 306, 341, 382, 383, 388
Fifty Spiritual Homilies 109, 111–113, 118, 120
Fish 310
Flavia 252
Flour 359
Food 294
Forgive/ness 13, 16, 209, 211, 212, 217, 220, 221, 223, 227, 228, 270, 306, 307, 329
Fornication 7, 11, 12, 13, 126
Friend 167
Fruit 308, 309, 311, 312

G
Gabriel 74, 208, 379, 384, 385
Gaius 254, 257
Galala (Gebel al-Galala) 62, 88
Gatekeeper 255, 256
Gentleness 168, 250
Gnôsis 113, 148
God xxx, xxxi, 7, 8, 9, 12, 13, 14, 16, 17, 29, 40, 43, 44, 48, 60, 82, 106, 109, 110, 111, 113, 114, 115, 117, 119, 120, 121, 122, 124, 125, 127, 128, 142, 143, 145, 148, 149, 150, 151, 152, 153, 157, 158, 160, 161, 163, 166, 169, 171, 172, 173, 174, 175, 176, 177, 178, 179, 180, 181, 182, 183, 184, 185, 186, 187, 188, 206, 209, 210, 211, 213, 214, 217, 219, 220, 221, 222, 224, 225, 226, 227, 228, 239, 241, 244, 245, 246, 251, 252, 254, 259, 260, 261, 262, 263, 264, 267, 271, 272, 273, 290, 291, 293, 294, 295, 296, 297, 298, 299, 300, 301, 302, 303, 304, 305, 307, 308, 309, 310, 312, 313, 314, 327, 329, 330, 336, 337, 338, 339, 340, 341, 342, 347, 348, 355, 356, 357, 359, 361, 362, 383, 384
God of Jacob 259
Godly/Godliness 291, 304
Gold 266, 297, 309
Golgotha 90
Good 124, 294, 310
Good God, the 112, 120, 121, 124, 126, 127
Good God, the Holy Power, and the Paraclete, The 101–137
Good works 148
Gospel 7, 220, 296, 311
Grace 119, 150, 160, 181, 182, 183, 189, 298, 313
Graffitti 75
Grain 353, 354, 355, 357, 363
Great Letter, The 111–113
Great Persecution 103

H
Habit, monastic 258, 354, 359
Hagiography 142, 239, 328
Haman 169
Handiwork 13, 14, 16, 259, 273
Hathor (Hathyr) Monastery 353, 362
Healing 183, 226, 251, 325, 330
Health 338, 340, 343, 353, 355, 356, 361, 363, 364

Heart, the 120, 125, 126, 127, 146, 175, 176, 178, 179, 187, 224, 228, 258, 288, 289, 290, 294, 296, 299, 301, 302, 304, 305, 310, 311, 312, 313, 314
Heaven (see Kingdom of Heaven) 13, 178, 182, 188, 247, 306, 343
Hêgoumenos 242, 256, 267
Hellên, Apa 154
Hemorrhage 325, 327
Heracleopolite nome 353
Heraclides 342
Hermit 38
Hermonthis 379
Hermopolis 347
Hermopolis Magna 207
Hermopolite nome 208
Hesychia 8
Hilaria, Saint 41
Hilarion 41
Hippodrome 245
Historia Monachorum 29, 141, 205, 207, 325, 379
History 239, 247, 248
Holy/Holiness 8, 9, 240, 311, 312
Holy man 325–365
   as Intercessor 325, 328–330, 335, 336, 338–344, 347–349, 353–365
   as Mediator 325
   as Patron 325
   as Teacher 325
   as Thaumaturge 325
Holy power 110, 112, 114, 117, 118, 120, 122
Holy Week 94
Holy Spirit 8, 13, 106–109, 110, 111, 112, 114, 115, 116, 117, 118, 119, 120, 122, 123, 128, 144, 167, 184, 206, 209, 216, 219, 220, 221, 227, 228, 253, 256, 263, 264, 273, 275, 307, 313, 339, 341, 382, 383, 388
Horion 354, 361–362
Humility 16, 17, 127, 128, 145, 148, 151, 166–169, 179, 180, 209, 239–241, 243, 248, 250, 255, 258, 295, 296
Hunger/Hungry 305, 313
Hypocrite 169, 174

I
Icon(s) 39, 325
Idolatry 240, 241
Illness 254, 262, 325, 330, 336, 340, 353, 355
Incense 174, 182, 183, 188
Inscription(s) 379, 380, 382, 383, 386
Intercession 217, 336
Irad 383
Iron 360
Isaac 330
Isaac (OT) 75
Isaac, Abba 211
Isaac, Abouna 63, 70–73, 78
Isaiah 213, 224, 290, 295
Isaiah of Scetis 286
   Logoi 286
Israel 143

J
Jacob 75, 273, 291, 309
James 327
Jeremias (Jeremiah), Apa 208, 216, 217, 380, 383–385, 387–388
Jeremias, Apa, Monastery of 208, 213, 215, 216, 217, 379, 380, 382, 383
Jerusalem 180, 182, 183
Jesus 8, 93, 106, 111, 118, 120, 143, 151, 290, 291, 292, 327, 341, 388

Jesus Christ 162
Jesus Prayer 84
Jijber 103
John 216, 248
John of Hermopolis 331, 347–349, 353
John the Little, Saint 75, 142, 211
John the Little, Saint, Monastery of 25, 32, 34, 35, 41
John of Niki(o)u 380, 387
John Rufus 243, 245
John the Virgin 154
Joseph 154, 273
Joshua 189, 303
Judah 168, 169
Judgement 248, 250, 299, 384
Judging 304
Julian (the Apostate) 66
Jullien, Michel 62, 63, 64, 65, 69, 89, 90, 91
Justin 336, 343–344

K
Kapiton 354, 362
Keep (*qasr*) 38, 41, 42, 67, 86
Kellia 26, 30, 31, 66, 85, 104, 143, 213
Kind/ness 176, 304, 355
Kingdom 168, 307
Kingdom of God 13, 112, 150, 290, 306, 313
Kingdom of Heaven 151, 290, 293, 294, 312
Kiss 264
Klysma 142
Knowledge 16, 125, 148, 273, 298, 301, 307
Koeis 159
Kolobion 255
Kôs 156

L
Labor 178, 187
Laughter 294
Laura 66, 267, 268, 271, 273
Lausiac History 325
Law 297, 301, 302
Lazarus 75–76, 89
Lazarus, Father 78–85, 91, 92
Leo, Pope 268, 269
Leo I 246
Leodicea 326
Letters of Ammonas 118–122
Letters of Saint Antony 113–117, 146
Lewis, Agnes Smith 64
Liar 187
Life of Apa Phib 205–236
Lion 178, 180
Life of Adam and Eve 385
Life of Antony 27, 32, 59, 114, 118, 120, 121, 146, 151, 289, 325, 326
Life of Apollo 205, 206, 207
Life of Longinus 242, 247–275
  History 242–246
  Theology and spirituality of 239–241
Life of Macarius of Scetis 211
Life of Pachomius 325
Life of Shenoute 379
Lithazomenon 269
Lives of the Desert Fathers 46
Logismoi (thoughts) 6, 7, 214
Logoi 288
Longinus 239–275
Lord 13, 16, 26, 106, 114, 115, 128, 143, 148, 150, 151, 153, 154, 160, 162, 163, 166, 168, 169, 179, 180, 182, 183, 184, 187, 189, 206, 210, 219, 220, 221, 222, 223, 224, 225, 227, 247, 255, 259, 261, 263, 264,

267, 270, 273, 274, 291, 296,
300, 301, 307, 309, 310, 314,
325, 326, 329, 339, 341, 342,
344, 348, 353, 355, 359, 364,
385
Lord's Prayer 306–307
Lot 12, 183
Love 145, 175, 176, 253, 297, 299,
303, 307, 308, 341, 359
Lucius, Apa 240, 242, 248, 250,
252, 253, 254, 258, 260, 269
Lust 9
Lycia 251, 253, 255, 257, 258
Lycopolis 207
Lykarion 364

M

Macarius of Alexandria 77, 103
Macarius the Great, Saint 26, 27,
30, 31, 77, 92, 103–106, 107,
108, 109, 110, 111, 114, 116,
117, 118, 122, 123, 205, 211,
215, 328
Macarius the Great, Saint, Monastery of 29, 31, 32, 34, 35, 36,
37, 42, 43, 47, 67, 103, 104, 164
Mamre 184
Manna 184
Manoah 183
Maphorion (maphorium) 381
Marcian, Emperor 243, 267
Mark the Ascetic, Saint 88
Mark, Saint 244
Martha 308
Martyr(s) 43, 251
Martyrium 252
Mary, Saint 74, 83, 91, 223, 379,
381, 382, 384
Mary 307, 308
Matoës 213
Matthew the Poor
  See el-Meskeen, Matta

Maximous, Abouna 68, 69, 70, 77,
85, 86, 87
Meditation 144, 147, 150, 167,
259
Melitian 335, 353
Memphis 143, 207
Menas, Saint, monastery of 257
Merchant 257, 258
Mercy 162, 186, 329
Meroit 158
Merton, Thomas 6, 7, 45, 70
el-Meskeen, Matta, Fr. 35, 36, 47
Metanoia See Repentance
Methuselah 383
Michael, Saint 42, 74, 160, 208,
210, 226, 379, 384
Michelangelo 387
Middle Egypt 142, 143, 205, 212,
214, 217, 387
Midrash 143
Military camp 360
Miracle(s) 240, 253, 262, 264,
326, 327
Miracle-worker 325
Monasteria 66
Monasticism xxx, xxxi, 37, 47, 48,
68
Monastic dwelling(s) 227
Money 266, 295, 347, 348, 360
Moneylenders 266
Monk(s) 6, 7, 8, 9, 11, 15, 17, 28,
30, 32, 36, 43, 44, 46, 207, 208,
211, 212, 213, 214, 215, 217,
219, 242, 255, 257, 259, 267,
268, 269, 270, 272, 273, 285,
289, 290, 292, 325, 335, 353,
356, 363, 384, 387
  Female 379
  As Intercessors 325–365
Moses 168, 290, 295, 303
Moses, Abba 141
Moses, Abouna 81, 82, 220

Most High 168
Mother of God 40, 63
Mouê Komê 363
Mystery 209, 267
Myth 40, 41

N
Nag Hammadi 385
Needy 358
Neighbor 9, 13, 17
Nepheros 326, 331, 353–365
Nepheros archive 326
Nêsoi 353
New Seeds of Contemplation 45
New Testament 118, 327
Nicaean Creed 107
Nile 28, 29, 59, 61, 103, 163, 208, 347
Nineve 76
Night 260
Nishčrôou 155, 156
Nitria 26, 28, 29, 30, 31, 77, 103, 104, 143
Noah 386
Nocturnal fantasies 15
Nofer, Abouna 48
Nofer, Abu See Onnophrius

O
Oath 360
Obedience 291
Oil 342, 356, 357, 358, 360, 361
Old Testament 143
Onnophrius, Saint 60, 62, 152, 210, 215
Onofrio, San See Onnophrius
Ophellios 353, 355, 356, 359
Or, Abba 242
Oratory 251
Origen 30, 106, 107, 109, 119, 146

Origenism 30, 31
Ox 298
Oxyrhynchus 212, 213, 328, 341, 379

P
Pachomius, Saint 28, 66, 113, 143, 205, 325, 327, 328
Paëse, Apa 155, 156
Pagans 162
Pain 255
Palamon, Abba 113
Palestine 31
Palladius 27, 141
Pallium 255
Palm branches 269
Palm Sunday 93
Pambo, Abba 45, 60, 62
Pamin, Apa, monastery of 222
Pamoun 143, 154
Panga 329
Paphnutius (Papnoute), Apa 330, 331, 335–344, 347, 353
Papnoute, Apa 365
Papohe 155, 206, 208, 209, 218, 222, 226
Paraclete 111, 114, 116, 118, 119, 120, 122, 123, 127, 128
Passions 128, 273, 298
Patience 240, 256
Patient endurance 151, 178, 190
Patriarchs 274
Paul 216
Paul (and Tapiam) 353–361
Paul, Apostle 114, 118, 126, 143, 162, 167, 185, 221, 248, 259
Paul the Great 256
Paul the Hermit, Saint xxx, 42, 66
Paul the Simple 83, 90
Paul, Saint, Monastery of xxxii, 62, 74, 85–88

Paul of Tamma 141–190, 286,
   287–288, 289
  'An Untitled Work' ('Sitting in
   Your Cell') 141, 174–177,
   286, 287, 288
  Letter 141, 172–173
  Life of 142–143, 206
  Life of Paul of Tamma 141, 142,
   143, 154–164, 216
  'On Humility' 141, 149, 150,
   166–169
  'On Poverty' 141, 170–171
  On the Cell 141, 147–153,
   178–190
Peace 146, 153, 162, 167, 170,
  175, 226, 241, 247, 259, 260,
  263, 264, 296, 297, 298, 301,
  310, 311, 338
Perčoush 157
Peshčepohe 157
Peter 330
Peter, Saint 118, 126, 162, 216,
  248, 306
Peter of Alexandria 75, 76
Peter's, Saint 266
Petra, Apa 218
Phanuel 183
Phib (Abib) 143, 157, 158,
  205–236
Philemmon, Fr. 34, 43
Philip 185
Philo 146
Pianius 336, 339
Pilgrims 68, 89, 91
Pisentius 75
Pispir, Mount 60, 61, 66
Pita, Apa 155, 156
Pity 330
Pkôou 161
Plow 309
Pneumatomachoi 108
Poemen, Abba 44, 122, 211, 213

Polycratia 326
Poor 150, 178, 179, 180, 184, 186,
  190, 241, 300
Possessions 290
Poverty 145, 150, 170–171, 172,
  186
Power 110, 111, 118, 121, 122,
  123, 126, 127, 168, 189, 190,
  240, 248, 295, 297, 303, 313,
  314, 327
Pray/Prayer(s) 7, 13, 16, 17, 124,
  128, 146, 150, 166, 167, 174,
  175, 213, 215, 241, 242, 252,
  254, 257, 263, 289, 307, 314,
  326, 327, 328, 330, 336, 337,
  338, 339, 340, 341, 342, 343,
  348, 353, 355, 356, 357, 358,
  361, 362, 363
Pride 127, 294
Priest 362, 363, 365
Prophet(s) 169, 244, 260, 274,
  303, 342, 383, 385, 386
Prostration 209, 211, 212, 213,
  214, 215, 216, 217, 220, 227,
  253, 258, 270, 388
Proterius 243, 244, 245, 246
Proverbs 143, 147
Providence 343, 344, 361, 364
Psalms 143, 146, 147, 151, 227,
  298
Psan (Pson) 329
Pseudo-Macarius 109, 117
Pshai-nte-Jeremias 161, 162
Psoïs 348
Poverty 313
Providence 355
Purity of Heart 146

Q
Queen of Sheba 386
Quiet 241

R

Ras Gharib 85
Redemption 291
Red Sea 28, 62, 68
Reed 176
Religious (monks) 255
Religious frenzy 294
Reliquary 39
Renunciation 250, 290, 294
Repentance (*metanoia*) 145, 210, 211, 212, 213, 214, 215, 217, 224, 228, 270
Resurrection 223
Righteous 225
Righteousness 128, 304, 384, 385
Romance of Alexander the Great, the 386
Romans, the, Monastery of 31, 32
Rope 241, 259, 263, 264
Rufinus 66
Rule, monastic 67
Ruler 240

S

Sabas, Saint, Monastery of 286, 287
Sacrifice 206, 219
Sadat, Anwar 43, 88
Sailor(s) 174
Saint(s) 170, 180, 186, 188, 189, 190, 216, 217, 218, 220, 224, 239, 248, 253, 254, 260, 261, 272, 274, 290, 297, 305, 308, 313, 314, 382, 387
Salih, Abu 66
Salvation 147, 172, 214, 219, 223, 241, 250, 262, 336, 338
Samuel, Bishop 43, 78
Saqqara 205, 207, 213, 215, 216, 379, 380, 382, 383, 384, 385, 386

Satan 14, 16, 114, 310
Saul 302
Saviour 162, 170, 210, 215, 221, 223, 224, 226, 227, 247, 250, 254, 296, 306, 341, 343, 348
Sayings of the Desert Fathers and Mothers *See Apophthegmata*
Sayings of Saint Macarius 122
Scapular 255, 258
Scetis 27, 28, 30, 31, 32, 66, 77, 103, 104, 122, 141, 142, 143, 164, 286
Scorpions 303
Scripture(s) 5, 8, 14, 144, 250, 260, 287, 289, 290, 302, 304
Sea 259
Semi-anchoritic monasticism 41, 66–67, 104–105, 207, 328
Sentences of Sextus 147
Seraphim 167
Serapion 354, 363
Septuagint 144
Serenus, Saint 212
Serpent(s) 293
Severus, Sulpicius 66
Sexual fantasies 7
Sexual sin 295
Sheep 357
Sheepskins 357
Shenouda III, Pope 28, 33, 43, 80
Shenoute the Great, Saint 28, 66, 141, 205, 212
Ship(s) 174
Shmin 142, 143
Shmoun (al-Ashmunein) 206, 207, 208, 218
Sibyl 385, 386
Sibylla, Ama 216, 379–388
    as mythological being 387–388
Sibylline Oracles 386

Sicard, Father 64
Sick, the 226, 251, 327
Sign 252
Silence 14, 27, 167, 240
Silvanus 149
Silver 361
Sin(s) 8, 14, 16, 125, 162, 166, 167, 175, 176, 177, 209, 211, 214, 215, 216, 217, 220, 221, 223, 224, 227, 228, 299, 304, 307, 329, 330, 337, 343, 344, 384, 388
Sinai, Mount 286, 287, 386
Sinemoun 218
Sinners 349
Sioout 156, 161
Sirach 143, 147
Sisoës, Abba 104, 122
Sistene Chapel 387
Slander 7, 13, 294, 300
Slave(s) 252, 299, 307
Sleep 260
Snake(s) 260, 303
Snares 303
Socrates 31
Sodom 12
Sohag 212, 213
Soldiers 270, 271, 272
Solitary 37
Solitude 8, 15, 27, 148, 149, 151, 152
Solomon 184
Son, the 108, 206, 216, 219, 223, 228, 382, 383, 388
Song of Songs 147
Sophia 382
Soul, the 109, 120, 125, 127, 167, 185, 220, 225, 248, 250, 251, 254, 264, 267, 269, 274, 292, 298, 304, 313, 348, 355, 356, 359
Soures, Apa 155

Spirit 253, 303, 330, 340
  Disturbing spirit 180
  Evil spirit 187, 252, 260
  Lying spirit 180
  of God 185, 309
  of Truth 307
  Unclean 251, 265
Spirit *See* Holy Spirit
Spiritbearer 123
Spirituality, monastic 105–106, 113, 115, 118–122, 146, 148–153, 239–241, 288–293
Stephen of Thebes 285–314
  Ascetic Discourse of (*Logos Askêtikos*) 285–293, 294–314
    Arabic version of #77–85 313–314
    Structure and Spirituality of 288–293
  And Paul of Tamma 287–288
  Precepts (*Entolai*) 286
  Regulations (*Diataxis*) 286
Steward 365
Suffering(s) 127, 160, 166, 168, 181, 223, 255, 256, 325, 330
Superior 250, 256, 258
Susanna, Ama 379, 380
Symbol 40
Synaxis 154, 160, 210, 213, 227, 360
Syria 111, 117
Syrian Monastery 29, 31, 32, 34, 35, 37, 39, 40, 41, 43
Swastika 40

T
Tabennisi 28
Tahrouj 222
Tall Brothers 31, 205
Talmud 144

Tamma(h) 142
Taparooue 225
Tapiam 326, 353
Teacher 285
Teachings of Silvanus 147
Tears 211
Temptation 16
Tent 184
Terôt-Ashans 156
Thaumaturge 325
Thebaid 207, 213
Thebes (Luxor) 207, 285
Theoctistus 251
Theodore, Apa 242
Theodore Lector 244
Theodosius 107
Theophilus of Alexandria 30, 31
Thirst/y 306, 313
Thoughts *(logismoi)* 6, 7, 8, 11, 12, 13, 15, 214, 242, 301, 302, 304, 310
Timothy 167
Timothy Aelurus 243, 244, 245, 246
Timothy, Pope 245
Titkooh (Titkois) 206, 207, 208, 209, 212, 218, 222, 223, 225
Tobias 183
Tobit 183
Toil 301
Tomb(s) 271, 272, 365
Tome of Leo 239, 242, 245, 267, 268, 271, 272
Tongue 296
Touhô 142, 157
Transfiguration 248
Transgression(s) 299, 313, 329
Tribulations 313
Trinity 107, 208, 228
Troops 269
Tropici 108

Turtledove 172
Truth 14, 270

U
Unicorn 172
Union
    With Christ 148

V
Vainglory 187, 189, 240, 241, 243, 273, 285, 300, 341
Valeria 330, 336, 340
Vanity 240
Victory 151, 178, 187, 189
Vigils 124, 125, 128
Virgin, the See Mary
Virgin(s) 167, 355
Virtue(s) 14, 16, 145, 151, 167, 184, 250, 340, 381–382, 388
Virtues of Saint Macarius 111, 122–123, 212

W
Wadi al-Natrun xxxii, 25–57, 61, 64, 67, 77, 103
Wadi Arabah 62
War 269
Warfare, spiritual xxix, xxx, 126, 127, 145, 149, 151, 153, 169, 172, 174, 181, 183, 189, 290, 292, 293, 294, 297, 301, 303
Watchman 294
Wayne, John 240
Weakness 149, 183, 186
Weeping 124
Wheat 358, 359, 360
White Monastery 212, 213, 379
Wickedness 294
Widow 186
Will 306, 341
Wisdom 148, 166, 174, 180, 291, 298, 309–310

'Wisdom of Sybilla' 386
Wisdom of Solomon 147
Wisdom tradition 143, 147
Wise man 143, 148, 149, 182, 184, 185, 310
Withdrawal 180
Woman/Women 11, 12, 15, 251, 261, 263, 300, 325, 327, 379, 381, 387
Wonder(s) 251, 254
Work 241, 242, 300
Works 295, 300, 304, 305
World, the 290, 294, 300, 314
Wretch/ed 168, 184

Y
Yousab el Abah, Bishop 88
Yustus el-Antony, Father 88
Yustus, Bishop 65, 80, 81

Z
Zacharias 183
Zacharius of Mytilene 244, 245
Zachary 210, 227
Zafarana 62, 85
Zeal 260
Zeno, Abba 211
Zeno, Emperor 41
Zenon 265
Zion 168

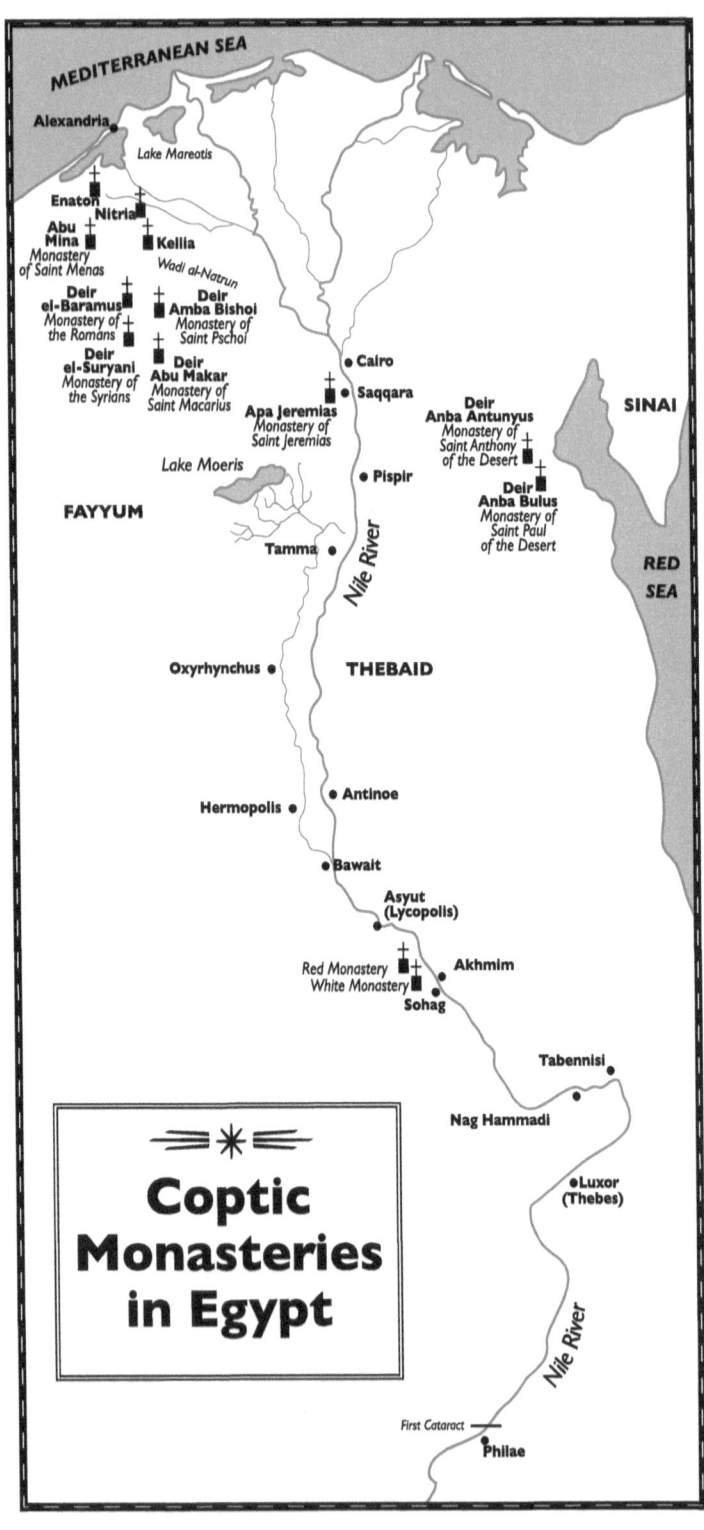

www.ingramcontent.com/pod-product-compliance
Lightning Source LLC
Chambersburg PA
CBHW031227290426
44109CB00012B/196